Boris Pasternak

The Poet and His Politics

Boris Pasternak

The Poet and His Politics

Lazar Fleishman

Harvard University Press
Cambridge, Massachusetts
London, England
1990

This book is printed on acid-free paper, and its binding materials
have been chosen for strength and durability.

Library of Congress Cataloging-in-Publication Data
Fleishman, Lazar
  Boris Pasternak : the poet and his politics / Lazar Fleishman.
    p.   cm.
  Includes bibliographical references.
  ISBN 0-674-07905-1 (alk. paper)
  1. Pasternak, Boris Leonidovich, 1890–1960—Political and social
views. 2. Authors, Russian—20th century—Biography.   I. Title.
PG3476.P27Z6788   1990
891.71'42—dc20   89-39442
  [B]   CIP

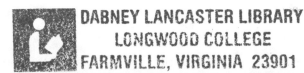

To the memory of my mother and father,
Pesia and Solomon Fleishman

Preface

This book grew out of my studies of Boris Pasternak that began in the Soviet Union in the early 1960s, when I was a beginning university student. Only a year or two had passed since the poet's death. Despite the obvious signs of de-Stalinization, which promised (as many then wanted to believe) the intellectual liberation of Soviet society from old dogmas, in those years the choice of such a theme for scholarly research was somewhat risky. There was a strange ambiguity in almost all of the infrequent references to Pasternak in the Soviet press. No one denied that he was a remarkable poet, perhaps even one of the greatest of the twentieth century. But this evaluation usually referred to only a few of his works and to only some of the stages in his literary career. Most important, an indelible mark of shame hung over Pasternak: *Doctor Zhivago* had only recently been branded an anti-Soviet political lampoon, fabricated with the special goal of damaging the Soviet state and having nothing at all to do with art. Not only was it unthinkable to disagree with this judgment; even to mention the name of the work was frowned upon.

Doctor Zhivago was only part of the problem, however. Even more damaging was the fact that in all the different periods of Pasternak's life, literally in every text and perhaps in every phrase he wrote, there existed an essential evasiveness, relativism, and ambivalence. These qualities stood in sharp contrast to the directness, straightforwardness, and adherence to unquestionable truths which had been considered the supreme virtues of Soviet literature and thinking since the early thirties. Thus the very ambivalence in statements about Pasternak in the official Soviet press only reproduced, on a more primitive level of course, the fundamental qualities of Pasternak's work.

Despite the fact that few printed materials were then available to me (and, perhaps, precisely because they were not), I immersed myself in archival research. Pasternak's manuscripts, which could be found at the beginning of the 1960s in the state archives, by no means constituted a monolithic whole. There were incidental and isolated documents, scattered in various places and in various collections, relating to different aspects of Soviet and prerevolutionary Russian culture. Pasternak's oeuvre had not yet become a fashionable area of scholarly research, and as far as I could tell from the lists of registered readers, I was in many instances the first person to examine these documents. Among the unexpected discoveries were the theses of his 1913 talk "Symbolism and Immortality," early drafts of the novella *Liuvers' Childhood,* the first version of the article "The Quintessence," and some of the poet's letters. No matter how insignificant these finds may look from today's perspective, they did contradict contemporary conceptions of Pasternak and offered me a glimpse of that side of his creative work and literary contacts which lay behind the scenes, concealed from outsiders. On the basis of this unpublished and unknown archival material it became possible to determine what role the literary milieu had played during the earliest stage of Pasternak's career, as well as the place he occupied in the bitter struggles of the various camps constituting the Russian avant-garde.

The unauthorized nature of my Pasternak studies was the main reason that, as long as I remained in Russia, they did not go beyond the preparatory phase. This was not the result of a direct ban or official pressure. But the goal I had set—to understand the poet's works and literary position in the context of his times—seemed unrealizable because not only Pasternak himself but the whole Russian literary scene of the twentieth century were forbidden topics in the Soviet Union. Many names were taboo, and countless facts had been expunged from the official annals. In addition, the works of western and émigré scholars had remained, for all intents and purposes, unavailable to most of their Soviet colleagues. In 1974 I emigrated to Israel and joined the department of Russian and Slavic philology at the Hebrew University of Jerusalem. There I found myself at a crossroads between east and west, a place where opposites met and where the cultural traditions of prerevolutionary Russia and Europe were still cherished. There I was able to understand more fully that unique and mysterious phenomenon of twentieth-century culture known as Pasternak.

By that time Pasternak scholarship could already claim remarkable successes. The work of Roman Jakobson and Gleb Struve, Victor Erlich and Michel Aucouturier, Henry Gifford and Jacqueline de Proyart, Olga Hughes and Robert Conquest, Dale Plank and Guy de Mallac, Andrei Siniavsky and Yury Lotman—to mention only a few—had set out the basic features of Pasternak's poetics and laid the foundation for a careful study of his life and work. Toward the end of the 1970s, however, a crisis could be noted in Pasternak studies. It became increasingly clear that further progress would be impossible without an effort to place the poet in his historical and cultural context. Then, as now, this might sound like a truism: it is all too well known that literary life and works are linked to the other arts, philosophical trends, and scientific discoveries, as well as to political, economic, and social conditions. Yet, in the case of Pasternak, what seems to us a commonplace gained acceptance with considerable, even painful, difficulty.

Back in the seventies, any study of Pasternak in the context of his times was regarded as somehow inappropriate. More than any other writer, Pasternak seemed remote from the literary and political controversies of his era—it was thought that he distanced himself deliberately. Both the poet's contemporaries and later critics were convinced that Pasternak was turned toward the timeless universals of art, "eternity" or at least "the future," and quite indifferent to his own times. The poet himself was largely responsible for the prevalence of this view. The frequently quoted lines from a poem in *My Sister, Life*—"Dear ones, what millennium is it outside?"—seemed to capture his position. Even the question of Pasternak's literary genealogy puzzled the scholars. The fact is that his pronouncements often seem to agree with diametrically opposed literary currents and to separate him from the very programs to which he allegedly adhered. This special kind of poetic self-definition is strikingly illustrated in *Safe-Conduct*, where Pasternak recounts how, after discovering his closeness to or "congruence" with Mayakovsky, he felt it necessary to alter radically his own poetic diction and manner, if not his entire world view. When evaluating his literary position or assessing a literary phenomenon, Pasternak always adhered to "noncongruence." Yet the negative formula, noncongruence, cannot express all aspects of Pasternak's behavior or thinking.

I was astonished to learn how closely this lyrical poet, one of the most esoteric of all twentieth-century Russian writers, was bound up with the historical realities and, in a narrower sense, the political tumult of his times. Many of his enigmatic statements and perplexing actions remain inexplicable otherwise. The revolutionary epoch is reflected in a more profound and complex way in Pasternak's writings than in the work of many poets of his generation, including Mayakovsky and Akhmatova, Esenin and Tsvetaeva, Mandelshtam and Khlebnikov.

As a central figure in the Russian literary avant-garde, and one of the boldest reformers of Russian verse, Pasternak along with Akhmatova came to be regarded by some as a venerable embodiment of the so-called Silver Age. Throughout the unbelievably cruel experiences of his life, he retained the moral values and artistic conceptions characteristic of the prerevolutionary era. No matter how significant Pasternak was as a poet and a writer, no matter how great his contribution was to the literature of our century, the story of his life is not less important, on the historical plane, than any of his literary texts. Pasternak the thinker, the witness of an epoch, stands as high as Pasternak the poet. This is clear not only to the literary historian who can benefit from retrospectively evaluating the poet's era; his contemporaries saw it as well. Whether Pasternak was condemned to silence, or whether he was allowed to publish translations or sporadic selections of poetry, his very existence served as decisive proof of the tenacity of art, despite the stifling situation in the country and the demands imposed on artists by the regime.

This is why my book is devoted more to the writer than to his works. Although I touch on many of his writings, either published or only planned, analysis as such is not my main goal. I mention the works here only to the extent that they represent important milestones in the poet's artistic or ideological evolution.

The results of my previous study of Pasternak appear in three books published in Russian: *Stat'i o Pasternake* (Essays on Pasternak; Bremen, K-Presse, 1977), *Boris Pasternak v dvadtsatye gody* (Boris Pasternak in the Twenties; Munich, Wilhelm Fink, 1981), and *Boris Pasternak v tridtsatye gody* (Boris Pasternak in the Thirties; Jerusalem, Magnes Press, 1984). Needless to say, the present volume, which is directed at a broader, English-speaking readership, cannot help drawing on the material in my earlier Russian-language works. But this is my first attempt to present Pasternak's life as a whole from the standpoint of what I feel is decisive: his close ties to his epoch.

This book could not have been written without the generous support of various organizations and individuals. A Pew Foundation grant enabled me to start my work in summer 1986, and a Guggenheim Memorial Foundation fellowship in 1987 allowed me to take a leave of absence to finish the first draft. The Center for Russian and East European Studies and the Slavic Department of Stanford University (with its administrative assistant, Catalina Ilea) were always responsive in providing research assistance. My special thanks go to Frederick Choate for his indispensable editorial help. My son Raphael contributed greatly with his knowledge of computers in overcoming the challenges of modern-day word processing. I am also grateful to my Stanford students Rachel Susan May, Julie Cassiday, and Carol Ingrid Yesk for their expert help at various stages of the work. I benefited enormously from intellectual exchanges with my colleagues as well as from the challenging comments of graduate and undergraduate students, participants in my seminars at the Hebrew University of Jerusalem, Berkeley, the University of Texas at Austin, Yale, and Harvard, where I taught before joining Stanford's Slavic Department. My debt to Wojciech Zalewski (Stanford University Libraries), Ronald Bulatoff, Elena Danielson, Olga Dunlop, Marilyn Kann, and Hilja Kukk (Hoover Institution Libraries and Archives), and Tatyana and the late Alexis Rannit (Yale University Libraries) is immense. I wish to acknowledge my deep gratitude to Lindsay Waters and Joyce Backman of Harvard University Press for their unfailing help. My meetings and correspondence with members of the Pasternak family in Moscow and Oxford were very important.

It is impossible to name here all the people to whom acknowledgments are due. But I shall express my warmest thanks to those who encouraged me to undertake the task of putting into a single volume a portrait of the days of the poet and whose critical comments were invaluable: Edward Brown, Alexander Dallin, John Dunlop, Victor Erlich, Donald Fanger, Joseph Frank, Gregory Freidin, Irwin Toby Holtzman, Olga and Robert Hughes, Simon Karlinsky, Herbert Lindenberger, John Malmstad, Richard Schupbach, Florence and Edward Standiewicz, William Mills Todd III, Andrew Wachtel, Anna and Boris Wassermann. Finally I must thank my wife, Irene, and our children, Ella and Raphael, who displayed unparalleled patience and understanding throughout my work on the book.

Contents

Illustrations

(following page 176)

Boris Pasternak

The Poet and His Politics

Note on Transliteration

In transliterating Russian words and proper names I have used the Library of Congress system in the notes and a slightly modified form of that system in the text (for reasons of recognizability and readability).

1

Origins

The theme of origination plays an exceptionally important role in Pasternak's poetic mythology. One of the central sentences in his *Safe Conduct* reads: "The clearest, most memorable and important thing in art is its actual emergence, and while recounting a great variety of things, the world's finest works of art in fact tell of their own birth." [1] When we search for the essence of Pasternak's own life and work, we find that it represents a transposition of this creed onto the history of his childhood and family.

The world of the European avant-garde exerted an enormous influence on the young Boris Pasternak. But strongly and consistently he asserted the decisive role of the family in artistic formation. In fact, his often-declared fidelity to a familial past and to cultural traditions would seem to be an unprecedented phenomenon in twentieth-century art. Even in his first autobiographical statement (a brief note of fifteen lines published in 1924), Pasternak found it necessary to declare: "I owe much, if not all, to my father, the academician Leonid Osipovich Pasternak, and my mother, a superb pianist." [2] Of course, like many of his other statements, this one was aimed polemically against the dominant attitudes of the time—against the disparagement of prerevolutionary culture so characteristic both of Pasternak's literary circle and of Soviet ideological doctrine in general. But the statement also contains, as is always the case with Pasternak, a deeply personal meaning.

Boris Pasternak was born on January 29, 1890 (Old Style), and spent almost his entire life in Moscow, a city that more than any other in the Russian Empire was subject to radical change at the beginning of the twentieth century. During the last years of his life Pasternak was considered by his contemporaries to be a relic, one of the last living embodiments of the Muscovite nineteenth-century cultural tradition.[3] But if we investigate his family origins, it becomes clear that the poet's familial ties to Moscow were less strong than was imagined half a century later.

Pasternak's parents moved to Moscow only in 1889, not long before Boris, their first child, was born. They came from the provinces to the south, from Odessa—a city within the Jewish Pale of Settlement founded a scant one hundred years earlier. During the first quarter of the nineteenth century (when Pushkin lived there for a while), Odessa was the most cosmopolitan city in the empire, with its colorful mixture of cultures, languages, and mentalities.[4] Here in 1862, to a poor Jewish family headed by the owner of a small inn, the poet's father, Leonid Osipovich Pasternak, was born. During his childhood, an ever greater role in the city life of Odessa was played by "foreigners"—Greeks, Italians, and Frenchmen. The Jews who had settled in Odessa at the end of the eighteenth century were predominantly engaged in commerce, banking, various trades (tailors, cobblers, watchmakers) or in the management of roadside inns. Leonid Pasternak loved to reminisce about his native city and to visit it. Several times in his youth Boris stayed in Odessa with his younger siblings at his grandparent's home. There is no direct reflection of these trips in his works, but traces of his family connections with Odessa can be found in his epic poem "1905." One of his lyrics written during World War II was prompted by news of the liberation of Odessa from German occupation.[5]

As far as education and culture were concerned, the Odessa Jews stood higher than the Jews in other parts of Russia. It was here that journals were published which reflected the rise of national consciousness of the Russian Jews: *Rassvet* (Dawn; 1860–61, 1879–1881), *Sion* (Zion; 1861–62), and *Den* (Day; 1869–1871).[6] The names of Jewish doctors, lawyers and scholars were famous throughout Russia. The cult of university education brought about by the Haskalah (Enlightenment) movement swept up the parents of Leonid Pasternak as well. In their eyes, the attraction of their son toward drawing was an inexcusable distraction, and it was treated severely as mischievous behavior. Lacking an education themselves, they saw no other means for their children to move up in the world except through the pursuit of a solid profession. Leonid Osipovich entered the university as a medical student, but completed a degree in law, despite the fact that neither career interested him in the slightest. His course of study was simply a concession to the pressure of his parents.

Later, when comparing himself with his close friend, the prominent artist Valentin Serov (who was born into a family of musicians and was raised in the house of the artist Ilya Repin), Leonid Pasternak emphasized the profound differences in the nature of their creative paths: "Circumstances favored Serov from the very beginning of his career as an artist; this contributed to the development of his spirit of independence . . . All this reinforced his self-confidence and facilitated his entry into the world of art. Once he had become a professional artist, he continued to move in the same circles which he had known since early childhood and to which he belonged not only by birth and by upbringing, but by his closeness to Repin. The difficulties which I had to overcome were unknown to Serov."[7]

Although Pasternak had to force his way with great difficulty into the artistic elite of the capital, he never regretted the effort. On the contrary, he felt that the hardships of life had an ennobling function. Together with the ethical norms assimilated from his parents, these difficulties convinced him of the need to earn his own bread through relentless labor, to depend on himself and to be in debt to no one. Strict internal discipline, self-control bordering on self-abnegation, the understanding that art demands extreme devotion and endless sacrifice—all this was inherited from Leonid Osipovich by his children, and especially by his eldest son.

Leonid Pasternak's life program collided with harsh experience at the very beginning of his career, when he fell in love with a young pianist, Rozalia Isidorovna Kaufman, and faced a difficult decision about marriage. The crisis connected with this decision led him to the brink of a nervous breakdown.[8] It was provoked by an internal conflict between love for a girl of great charm, refined intellect, and outstanding artistic talent—and fidelity to his art. The answer to his tormenting doubts came in the form of a creative outburst that resulted in his painting *Letter from Home*. This canvas moved the young provincial artist into the ranks of the best-known representatives of the young generation in Russian art. Even before it was exhibited, the painting earned the highest praise possible for a Russian artist at that time: it was acquired by Pavel Tretiakov for his renowned gallery in Moscow. The painting was displayed with great success at the annual exhibit of the Peredvizhniki (Wanderers) in Petersburg. This unexpected triumph resolved Leonid Pasternak's personal doubts. In February, the young couple celebrated their wedding in Moscow.

Just as the marriage coincided with an upturn in Leonid Pasternak's artistic career, so it marked a transition for his wife, but in the opposite direction. From earliest childhood Rozalia Kaufman had displayed exceptional musical ability. Her first concert as a pianist took place when she was eight years old, and there was no doubt among her contemporaries that she would have a decisive impact on the European music scene. But marriage and the birth of her first child put an end to her concertizing. Rosalia Pasternak devoted all her energies to home, family, and children; she limited herself to playing *Hausmusik* and giving private lessons.[9]

It seemed to everyone that the Pasternak's life was an example of what Leonid Osipovich himself called "a harmonious marriage." Husband and wife lived together for fifty years. Their four children were Boris, Alexander (1893–1982), Josephine (1900), and Lydia (1902–1989). Not only Boris but each of the other children displayed genuine artistic gifts, and each contributed to Russian cultural life either in the Soviet Union or outside its borders. Despite the fact that the catastrophic events of the twentieth century led everywhere to the unraveling of traditional family relations, and despite the fact that after the departure of the parents and daughters abroad in 1921 the Pasternak family found itself divided by national and political boundaries, the somewhat patriarchal cult of the "family" was preserved by all the Pasternaks. Leonid Osipovich's last words to his daughters before his death were: "Live in peace and harmony." Nevertheless, not long before he died, having lost his beloved wife and reviewing his past life, Pasternak repeated his favorite thought: "Artists shouldn't settle down with a wife and children." [10]

It was during the 1890s, the first decade of his life in Moscow, that Leonid Pasternak managed to win a place of distinction in the cultural life of Russia. The young man from the provinces brought with him a quality that was rare among Russian artists of the time: a familiarity with the latest phenomena in western culture and, in particular, with advanced principles of artistic training. In 1882–1885 he had lived and studied in Munich, then the second most important (after Paris) international art center. The private lessons Pasternak began to give after he had settled in Moscow attracted students by virtue of his innovative training methods.[11] At the same time, he began to take part in regular exhibitions of the artistic society, the Wanderers. The most characteristic traits of this group were their social and ideologically charged themes and their realistic style. When modernist currents emerged on the scene at the end of the 1890s, the Wanderers quickly became a symbol of the most backward, provincial, and stagnant tendencies in art. But at the beginning of the 1890s, when Leonid Pasternak made his debut, this group was associated with the renewal of Russian culture. Within this trend Pasternak played a special role, along with Valentin Serov, Mikhail Nesterov, Isaak Levitan, and Konstantin Korovin: these young artists emphasized not the thematic content of the canvas but the formal side of artistic technique.

In 1894 Pasternak was invited to teach at the Moscow School of Painting, Sculpture, and Architecture. He was to instruct the portrait class. This invitation coincided with the school's profound reorganization, in the course of which other younger artists (Serov, Arkhipov) joined its teaching staff. It was a personal triumph for Pasternak, both as a teacher and as an artist: a few years earlier he had twice tried to enroll in the school as a student but was not accepted. The achievement was all the more noteworthy because of Pasternak's origins, which placed him, a Jew, at a disadvantage in Russian society. The school's trustee was the governor of Moscow, Grand Duke Sergei Alexandrovich (uncle of Tsar Nicholas II), whose antisemitic policies had been revealed by his decision in 1891 to expel Jewish artisans from Moscow. He was the supreme authority who confirmed all new appointments to the school. Pasternak's success, as well as his later official recognition when he was awarded the highly prestigious title "Academician of Painting," made him an outstanding representative of the Jewish people in Russian art, along with the landscape painter Isaak Levitan and the sculptor Mark Antokolsky. Like them, Leonid Pasternak felt himself to be more of an artist than a Jew; he was more powerfully attracted to modern Russian and European culture than to the religious, social, and political problems of Russian Jewry. But for precisely this reason he never took the step, mistakenly ascribed to him by later writers, of converting to Orthodoxy for the sake of a successful professional career in Russia. Such a step would not have been in keeping with his conception of moral decency or his mission as an artist.

Pasternak taught at the school for a quarter century, until 1918. During his tenure the school not only became the best center of art instruction in Russia (surpassing the Academy of Art in Petersburg), but its graduates included leading representatives of the avant-garde that transformed Russian painting before the 1917 Revolution and for the first time placed it on a level with modern art in Europe. It is sufficient to mention that among the school's students were Kazimir Malevich and Vladimir Tatlin, Mikhail Larionov and Natalia Goncharova, Vladimir Mayakovsky and David Burliuk. Their professors by no means fostered these radical artistic tendencies. On the contrary, the actions of the young rebels led to confrontations and caused not a few bitter experiences both for Pasternak and his colleagues. In hindsight it is clear, however, that the capital of avant-garde painting became Moscow and not Petersburg precisely because of the invigorating atmosphere at the Moscow School of Painting—its teachers paved the way for modern Russian culture to emerge.

Leonid Pasternak took a skeptical attitude toward the avant-garde currents that dominated Russian and European culture from around 1910. In his paintings of the 1890s he drew close to impressionism, and the sharp transition from the old naturalistic technique, characteristic of the Wanderers, to the new style stands out very clearly.[12] Although he recognized the great accomplishments of French impressionism and Cézanne in landscape and still life, however, Leonid Pasternak denied its significance in the very genre that attracted him the most: portrait painting. Here Pasternak was the creator of an impressionism of a special type, the distinctive feature of which was the combination of rapidity (the instantaneous recording of the situation being sketched) with "Rembrandtish" psychological depth. These qualities are evident both in the portraits he painted and in his innumerable pencil sketches. So that nothing would interfere with his quick sketches, he learned to draw people by hiding the paper under a hat in his lap, thereby neither giving himself away as he was working nor disturbing the model. Pasternak achieved both mastery and fame by portraying his own children. Aside from the technical problems that attracted him in rendering a special children's world (as fundamentally different from the adult world) and aside from the possibility of concentrating on this theme in a natural home setting free from all the tensions present elsewhere, these drawings gave the artist the chance to always return to his favorite theme—family and home. It is difficult to name another Russian artist more strongly inspired by this theme.

The transition in Leonid Pasternak's style—from the realism of the Wanderers to impressionistic swiftness—took place during the 1890s and the beginning of the 1900s and his son Boris was able to follow these changes closely. He saw how from the depths of one artistic style another could be born. These shifts were not characterized by a succession of easy, ready-made forms, but they occurred, gradually, the result of a long and arduous process. This sheds light on some features of his future poetry and his literary style, as well as his place in the literary milieu. One of the chief characteristics of Boris Pasternak's early poetics—the blending of specific impressionistic[13] and futurist traits in his verse—echoed the same syncretic unity that had existed in the fusion between realism and impressionism in his father's paintings. It is no accident that in an early article, "The Black Goblet" (written in 1914 and published in 1916 in a futurist almanac), Boris traces the genealogy of futurism—despite all the latter's attempts to dissociate itself from its predecessors—to the "reality of the Wanderers" and to the home lessons of "its teachers, the symbolists and impressionists."

His father's direct influence is evident in Boris' adolescent drawings.[14] Leonid Pasternak thought seriously about these sketches by his son, emphasized his potential talent as an artist, and said that, if he wanted, Boris would become a good artist. Although in 1903 Boris decided to switch to music composition, his childhood interest in drawing shows itself clearly throughout his later poetry, in the special attention to visual detail and in the predominance of scenic descriptions.

The possibility of observing from childhood and in a family setting the work of his father had an impact on the future poet in another way as well: it led him to see paintings not only as museum exhibits hanging motionless on walls, but as unfolding entities; it taught him to see an inner dynamic within the canvas. The idea of a picture as a process, of course, lay at the heart of cubist conceptions. Not long before his death, the poet acknowledged that acquaintance with cubist paintings after 1910 had a great influence on him. To the extent that the ideas of cubism developed organically out of the very problematics of painting, Boris was prepared for the reception of cubism by his entire childhood experience. He knew that a painting moves and changes unceasingly, so that the artist himself never knows for sure when his picture is finished. Quoting Valentin Serov, Leonid Pasternak used to say that a client simply takes away from the painter what he believes to be a finished artifact; as far as the artist is concerned, his canvas remains forever unfinished.[15]

The similarities between the attitudes of the two Pasternaks, father and son, cannot be reduced simply to coincidences in their aesthetic views. If we compare Leonid's writings with Boris' statements on art, we are struck by their nearly identical attitudes and tastes. But what is even more striking is the similarity of verbal styles, the character of their thought, and even the way they construct their sentences. The sharply idiosyncratic stylistic traits of the poet's expression seem, at first glance, unique. Upon more careful examination, they prove to be similar to the literary peculiarities of his father—and, to a certain extent, to the style of his brother Alexander's memoirs, and the literary works of his sisters Josephine and Lydia. There is, in other words, a sharply individualized "family style." This phenomenon is especially striking because it occurs during the twentieth century, when political storms were sweeping away the long-established forms of family life.

On October 11, 1927, Marina Tsvetaeva wrote to Leonid Pasternak:

> Let me say to you that you are undoubtedly the happiest of fathers, for your son is rendering you great honor.
>
> Not long ago in a collection of the works of modern poets I read his autobiographical note, which begins with the words: "I owe much, if not all, to my father, the academician Leonid Osipovich Pasternak, and my mother . . ." If you recall (as your son clearly did when he wrote these lines), this is the way that Marcus Aurelius began his book, *Meditations*.
>
> During our times (which I hate), when every little bird who falls from the nest thinks that he has descended from the heavens, such a confession is completely unheard of and only confirms the noble origin of its author. True greatness never ascribes to itself the greatness to which it is entitled. It is a question of continuity and of generations.[16]

To the very end of his days, Boris Pasternak never stopped measuring his own work and deeds against those of his father, who left Russia for good in 1921. His father's example gave the poet a benchmark of artistic honesty; it provided a standard of fidelity to principles during a time of continuous social and cultural change. In 1941 he wrote to his cousin:

> Recently I went through a trunk full of Papa's sketches, first drafts, all his workaday junk. Apart from the joy and pride this sight always fills me with, I found it devastating. Such things cannot be

assessed without an appreciation of the difference between now and the nonscholastic era when the natural development of a person's activities filled his life as vegetation fills space, when everything was in motion and each individual existed to distinguish himself from all the others.[17]

Leonid Pasternak's gallery of portraits included many famous artists, musicians, writers, politicians, historians, philosophers, and scholars: Gerhardt Hauptmann and Maxim Gorky, Albert Einstein and Verhaeren, Lenin and Prince Peter Kropotkin, the pianist Busoni and the violinist Mischa Elman, the philosopher Lev Shestov and the singer Fyodor Chaliapin, the pianist Joseph Hoffman and Sergei Rachmaninov, the conductor Arthur Nikisch and the poet Chaim Nachman Bialik. But he had the closest relations with the writer who, along with Pushkin, had always been for him the most cherished: Leo Tolstoy. Leonid Pasternak's acquaintance with Tolstoy began in the spring of 1893 with the annual exhibition of the Wanderers in Moscow. Tolstoy liked Pasternak's painting, *The Débutante,* and he asked to meet the young artist. Pasternak told Tolstoy about his illustrations for *War and Peace,* and Tolstoy invited him to visit. Leonid Osipovich began to see the Tolstoys both in Moscow and at Yasnaia Poliana, and he painted a number of portraits of the writer and his family. Of all the portraits painted of him, Tolstoy considered Pasternak's to be the most successful. In 1898, Tolstoy proposed that Pasternak illustrate his unfinished novel *Resurrection.* Since the author was writing the novel in serial form for the journal *Niva* (Cornfield), Pasternak was therefore drawn into the very process of creation. In his memoirs, written in 1928 for the German journal *Das literarische Echo,* the artist described the feverish and intensive course of the work; during the proofreading, the author made many changes in the text, and the artist had to alter his drawings accordingly. This work left its mark in the consciousness of the artist's children: in 1956, in his autobiography, Boris devoted several passages to this episode, and Alexander related in his memoirs how the games he played at that time with his brother included imitating his father's work in illustrating the novel for the journal.[18] The artist's close relations with the Tolstoy family continued until the writer's death; Pasternak was a guest at Yasnaia Poliana in 1901, 1903, and 1909.

According to the poet's reports, he himself saw Tolstoy twice. Once was just after Tolstoy's death, in November 1910 at the Astapovo railway station. Boris traveled there with his father, who hastened to record the features of the great writer from nature for the last time.

As for the earlier encounter, it is said to have taken place in Boris' early childhood, when he was four, and the poet was later inclined to invest it with providential meaning. On November 22, 1894, Tolstoy and his daughters visited the Pasternaks and stayed for a chamber concert prepared especially for him by Rozalia, the violinist Grzhimali, and the cellist Brandukov. They played Tchaikovsky's Trio for Piano and Strings, op. 50, *In Memory of the Great Musician* (written in 1882 upon the death of Nikolai Rubinstein). This event is recorded in Leonid Pasternak's watercolor located at the Tolstoy Museum in Moscow. Boris graphically recalls the evening in his 1956 autobiography:

> During the night I was awakened by sweet and melancholy music which I had never experienced before that time. I cried out and began to weep from anguish and fear. But the music drowned out my tears, and only when the part of the trio which had awakened me had been played to the end did they hear me. The curtain, behind which I had been lying and which divided the room in half, separated. My mother appeared, bent over me and quickly calmed me. They probably took me out to meet the guest, or perhaps I saw the living room through the frame of the open door. The room was filled with tobacco smoke ... The grey heads of two or three old men merged with the rings of smoke. One I later knew well and saw often. This was the artist N. N. Gué. The image of the other, as with most of them, accompanied throughout my life, especially because my father illustrated his books, traveled to see him, respected him and because our entire home was filled with his spirit. This was Lev Nikolaevich.

Later the poet adds: "That evening marked the boundary between the forgetfulness of infancy and my later childhood. From that night, my memory began its activity and my consciousness began to work, henceforth without great gaps and mistakes, like an adult's." [19]

Veiled references to this episode are contained in Boris Pasternak's earlier autobiography *Safe Conduct* (1929–1931) and his 1921 poem "Tak nachinaiut. Goda v dva" (So They Begin), but the poet began to speak directly and in detail about it only in the 1950s, in *An Essay in Autobiography* and in his verbal reminiscences. His story does not seem absolutely reliable. Lydia Chukovskaia writes in her diary about Anna Akhmatova's humorous and skeptical reaction to it. [20] Akhmatova's distrustfulness, of course, is justified. A modern scholar has shown, for example, that Gué could not have attended the concert, since he had died five months before.[21] But even the whole depiction of how Boris cried and how he was introduced to Tolstoy may be placed in doubt: in describing the evening in his memoirs Leonid Pasternak said not one word about it. He did, however, tell of one embarrassing event that took place when, during the piano trio, the children's nanny "slowly and with an air of importance" walked with an empty teacup from the nursery through the room filled with guests into the kitchen.[22] It is hardly likely that if Rozalia Isidorovna had been forced to quiet the crying Boris during the concert, or if she had brought him out to meet the guests, Leonid would have omitted this more interesting detail from his account.

So it is possible to conclude that the meeting between the future poet and Tolstoy in 1894 is simply a legend. Why does Pasternak return to it so persistently in his autobiographical writings—at first vaguely and then openly? In talking about art in *Safe Conduct,* he states that "lies" are inherent in art and adds that such lies or, to put it another way, such "lyrical truths" are a much more accurate recording of facts than any factual statement. The meeting with Tolstoy, which introduces the reader to the theme of Boris' early initiation into literary tradition, serves precisely as an example of this kind of lyrical truth.

Even more fanciful is the interweaving of *Dichtung* and *Wahrheit* in Boris Pasternak's reminiscences about events of the summer of 1903. This was the first time that, owing to the birth of their youngest daughter, Lydia, his parents decided to forgo their usual summer trip to their house on the Black Sea. Starting in this year, the Pasternaks began to spend their summers at various dachas near Moscow.[23] The first summer was spent at Obolenskoe, near Maloyaroslavets, and it turned out to be a turning point for Boris and his parents as well. It is hardly unusual, therefore, that he touches upon these events in both *Safe Conduct* and *An Essay in Autobiography.* But the two accounts differ substantially in content. By comparing them to the memoirs of the poet's father and brother, the following picture emerges.

The Pasternak children had grown up in the city, and this was their first acquaintance with the countryside outside Moscow. When he arrived at the dacha, the thirteen-year-old Boris busied himself with a school assignment, the gathering of plants for a herbarium. (The poet would later say that botany was his "first passion.") His brother, aged ten, was both his constant companion during these forays and his partner when they played "Indians." During their walks the brothers experienced sensations they had never known before: they heard piano music being played at a neighboring dacha in a way that was quite new, with strange and inexplicable pauses. Such music bore no resemblance to the pieces they had grown accustomed to play at home under their mother's guidance. As it turned out, it was Alexander Scriabin composing his Third Symphony (the *Divine*). This became clear after Leonid Osipovich accidentally made the acquaintance of his neighbor during a stroll. Thus, in the summer of 1903, through thickets of shrub and a child's game of "Indians," Boris discovered the composer who would have a profound influence on his creative impulses, on the scope of his interests, on his search for a profession, and on his life in general. The idea of the indivisible link between the world of nature and the world of culture became one of the motifs of Pasternak's poetics.

The encounter with Scriabin's music inspired the boy to begin his own study of musical composition. But first, during the same summer, another event occurred that was of equal significance. Pasternak tells about it in his autobiography of 1956:

> That autumn, our return to the city was delayed by an unfortunate accident which I had. My father had begun his painting "To the Night Pastures." It portrayed girls from the village of Bocharovo at sunset, riding at full speed and driving a herd of horses toward the marshy meadows at the base of our hill. Once when I had joined them, I tried to jump a wide stream and fell off my galloping horse. I broke my leg, which was somewhat shorter when it mended; this later freed me from military service during every call-up.[24]

This story is recounted by the poet as if the border between real life and its depiction on his father's canvas had been eliminated ("Once when I had joined them"). In this sense there exists a striking parallel between this "artistic" episode and the "musical" experience of the summer: just as his infatuation with Scriabin's music and the beginning of his studies of composition grew out of his botanical interests, his accident and physical trauma seemingly resulted from the painting begun by his father.

No less remarkable is the way Leonid Pasternak himself reported the episode in his memoirs. Even after several decades, he could barely conceal his sorrow that his conception of a "monumental" painting was to remain unrealized. The artist loved to repeat that every work of a painter remains unfinished, but the failure to complete this work was particularly painful for him. It was to have been one of his largest and most important canvases (with the horses and riders life-size). In this new work the artist, who was chiefly known for his intimate portraits, set himself new and challenging technical tasks ("precise and strong brushstrokes," the achievement of "laconic expression," the depiction of moving figures).[25] The painting, which was to have represented a wildly galloping group of village girls riding bareback ("Russian peasant Valkyries") was "a most difficult assignment in every respect: composition, drawing, color and whirlwind of movement! . . . But an unfortunate accident (my older son broke his leg while he was also galloping on a bareback horse; he fell when he reached an unexpected obstacle—a ditch) did not allow me to complete the work I had begun."[26]

In summarizing what is known about this episode, one can say that the fate of the son and the fate of the father's art were strangely interwoven. As he later looked back upon his life, the poet emphasized the "salutary" and "curative" aspect of the fall. The death of the artistic conception that was so important for the father turns into the salvation, even the rebirth, of the son. The poet comprehends this rebirth in terms of spiritual, not physical, life: bound up with the episode from the summer of 1903 was his decision to abandon painting and to "adopt a new faith," musical composition. In addition, if we are to believe Boris' letter sent to his schoolmate Alexander Shtikh about ten years later, the fact that he had to lie motionless in a cast for a long time after the accident produced the particularly keen "sense of rhythm" that led him to write music.[27] The same letter to Shtikh contains one more significant detail: the accident occurred on August 6. This day, imbued with special meaning in the Russian Orthodox Church, is called the day of the Second Salvation or the Transfiguration.[28] Pasternak returns to the date in his poem "August," which appears in *Doctor Zhivago*. The hero has a premonition about his own death on the 6th, and we cannot help seeing in this poem a reflection of the poet's experience of the summer of 1903.[29] The poem is evidence of the deep psychological and mythological context in which he saw the sudden change experienced at this point in his life.

The same theme of father and son emerges in a much different way in one of Boris Pasternak's earliest stories "Suboctave Story."[30] The central element of the plot is the killing by an organist, during an inspired improvisation, of his only son by crushing him in the instrument's coupler mechanism. It is difficult to say why in this case Boris Pasternak's theme of fatherly influence acquires demonic overtones, while in all other instances it is treated in a positive manner. It is usually impossible to give an unequivocal interpretation of the artistic ideas of great poets—by their very nature they are ambivalent and elusive. But it seems that a partial explanation of the paternal theme in this story can be found in the fact that Leonid Pasternak had profound misgivings about Boris' "decadent" predilections in poetry and art; noticeable differences in tastes begin to emerge around 1910, and the father disapproved of his son's creative tendencies. In September 1959, Boris recalled in a conversation with Z. A. Maslenikova:

> There is an attitude toward literature, that all the great writers have lived in the past, and there can be nothing good in the present. I like that . . . My father felt that way. He revered Tolstoy, but all that came after—symbolism, futurism and so forth—he didn't acknowledge. My own writings got a lukewarm response in my family. My father would have been happy only with what I have written in the recent period. It's a pity that he has never read it.[31]

Yet these differences, revealed in the period of Boris' literary debut soon after 1910, did not shake the general family unity. A wonderful monument to the family philosophy was Leonid Pasternak's painting *Congratulations,* which depicts all four of his children, with Boris in front. The painting was made in connection with the Pasternak's silver wedding anniversary and was originally intended to include the parents along with the children. In the final version, however, the figures of the parents were left out. Technically, this monumental canvas echoed the tasks the artist had set for himself in the unfinished work *To the Night Pastures,* and it was seen by his contemporaries as a work crucial to Leonid Pasternak's development as an artist. People who viewed it at the time were struck by the fact that, in his treatment of colors and planes, the painter was approaching postimpressionism.[32]

The painter considered *Congratulations* to be part of a future triptych with which he intended to decorate his retirement home near Odessa. The conception of these paintings marked the transition to a new means of artistic expression, the mastery of technical innovations, as well as competition with the paintings of the masters of the Italian Renaissance. He studied these master works in 1904, during his first trip to Italy. Above all he was struck by Venice and it similarity to Odessa.[33] Leonid Pasternak made his next trip to Italy with his family in 1912, and Boris' impressions of Venice are vividly described in *Safe Conduct* in 1931. "Competition" with the Renaissance masters in his work on the family portrait was not merely confined to formal experiments; it was tied up with the personal reflections of the artist. The triptych was to have been a kind of "double" return to Leonid's roots: to Renaissance painting, which the artist (and Boris as well) felt was an eternal source of modern culture, and to his native city, which reminded him of Venice. World war, the revolution, and his subsequent move to Germany in 1921 did not permit the fulfillment of these plans. But his intentions found a distinctive expression during the last decades of the artist's life.

After 1910, Leonid Pasternak drew close to a number of Jewish cultural and political figures in Russia. As a result, with the outbreak of the February Revolution in 1917, he was recognized as the leading artist of Jewish origin, representative of the Jews in Russian art.[34] Leonid Pasternak never sought this reputation. It is even possible that he regarded it with skepticism: he never considered ethnicity relevant in evaluating works of art. But Leonid's more frequent contacts with influential Jewish circles indicate his sympathy toward the awakening of national Jewish sentiment. That there were almost no such contacts before 1910 is explained not by Pasternak's indifference to the future of Jewish culture in Russia, but by the circumstance that the idea of self-determination and revival among Russian Jews did not come to the fore until after the 1905 Revolution. And it was just around 1905 that the "Jewish question" became one of the most important issues for the Russian liberal intelligentsia in general.[35]

Pasternak's attraction to Jewish circles was undoubtedly prompted by his personal acquaintance with Chaim Nachman Bialik, which began in the summer of 1911.[36] Before this meeting Leonid Pasternak had never read a single line of the great Jewish poet and did not even know his name. He first read Bialik's poetry in the Russian translation of Vladimir Jabotinsky (later a leader of the Zionist movement, but then a journalist well known throughout Russia). Bialik's book became extremely popular among the Russian intelligentsia, and prominent Russian symbolist poets began translating his verse. Of course, even before 1911 the Pasternaks' friends and acquaintances in Moscow always included a number of Jews. But only after 1910 did Leonid Pasternak engage in organized activity aimed at the social and cultural emancipation of the Jews. This actually characterizes not so much his own position as that of his generation as a whole. From 1918 to 1921 in Moscow, and then in Berlin, Pasternak painted a series of portraits of representatives of the Jewish intelligentsia (particularly Yiddish and Hebrew writers). In 1918 he turned to writing for the first time, with the book *Rembrandt and the Jews in His Works*. This was published in Russian by the Berlin publisher S. D. Saltzmann in 1923, and then in Hebrew by Bialik's publishing house. In the same year Bialik, who considered Leonid Pasternak to be the best modern Jewish artist and his work a harbinger of the renaissance of Jewish art, published an ecstatic article about him in the Berlin Hebrew weekly *Ha-Olam* (The World).[37] According to the memoirs of the Jewish journalist Gershon Svet, Pasternak attended Zionist meetings in Berlin.[38] In the spring of 1924 he made a trip to Egypt and Palestine, joining an art expedition sponsored by the Russian publisher Alexander Kogan. In his memoirs the artist tells about the creative enthusiasm that seized him during visits to Jerusalem and the Judean desert. On the return trip to Europe, his companion on the steamship was Bialik, who subsequently visited the Pasternaks in Berlin.[39]

It would be wrong to overemphasize the degree of Leonid Pasternak's "return" (as Bialik called it) to Jewish culture. It would also be wrong to speak about the artist's Zionist convictions, although his friends in Palestine in the 1930s discussed the possibility of moving him there from Nazi Germany. But it is obvious that the rise of Zionism evoked his sympathy, just as he had profound sympathy for the various revolutionary movements and revolutionary leaders of the new Russia. Still he never adopted any particular political platform: as an artist, Pasternak felt obliged to avoid taking part in political strife or even directly expressing his opinion on political matters. Both before and after the revolution, however, he held certain political views, sympathies, and antipathies that were basically in consonance with those of the liberal Russian intelligentsia. He passionately hailed the February Revolution, the downfall of the monarchy, and the emergence of democracy in Russia in 1917.

He also welcomed the October Revolution in the belief that the Bolshevik order would be able to cure the ills caused by the tsars. During these years he painted a number of portraits of Lenin and other Bolshevik leaders. His departure from Soviet Russia for Germany in 1921 was not an act of protest or a form of political emigration. It was due to the hardships of everyday life in Moscow during the period of War Communism and the need to seek medical treatment for his wife and for himself. In addition, after the revolution Leonid Pasternak was no longer comfortable at the reformed School of Painting, Sculpture, and Architecture, which began to be dominated by radical representatives of the left in art with party mandates in their pockets. These radical artists believed that Pasternak and his generation were completely out of tune with the ideological needs of the revolution. Nevertheless, while living abroad, Leonid Pasternak maintained his Soviet passport and each year paid a visit to the Soviet Embassy on the anniversary of the October Revolution. His ties with the sizable Russian émigré community in Berlin were weak. In the second half of the 1930s, when the artist received official notification from the authorities that, as a non-Aryan, he was not allowed to paint, [40] he seriously considered going back to Soviet Russia. With a certain amount of naiveté, he overestimated the warmth of the reception that would await him there.[41] The seventy-five-year-old artist thought that the sharp about-face in Soviet cultural policy, which had led to the dismissal of avant-garde artists from all leading positions, would have a beneficial effect on his position in the Soviet Union. In fact, however, in the sinister atmosphere of the Stalinist purges of 1936–1939, Leonid Pasternak's art would have been considered even more of an anachronism than before. As recently published documents from the family correspondence show, Boris Pasternak sent his parents signals that were intended to dispel their illusions and prevent their return. Although Leonid Osipovich's paintings were already packed for shipment to the USSR, the artist did not return to Moscow. As soon as he was allowed to join his younger daughter in England, he moved there and died in Oxford on May 31, 1945.

As he was dying, he asked his daughters either to place a Christian cross on his grave or to invite a rabbi to give a burial service. The very possibility of such a deathbed request from an artist who had always remained indifferent to all religious ritual cannot but surprise us. The request was certainly a form of protest against the monstrous inhumanity that emerged during World War II and that shook the artist during the last years of his life.[42] But it was also rooted in yet another aspect of the artist's family past.

The Pasternaks were Sephardic Jews. From generation to generation they recounted stories of their origin from Don Isaac ben-Yehuda Abravanel (1437–1508), the great Jewish philosopher and political leader, who was in turn said to be descended from the royal house of

David. The family stories told of the resettlement of their ancestors from Palestine to the Pyrenees at the time of the fall of the First Temple. One can also find in the annals of Jewish and European culture numerous references to the contributions of Don Isaac's eldest son, Yehuda Abravanel (known by the pen name Leone Ebreo). He was a remarkable philosopher of the Italian Renaissance and a poet who wrote the famous treatise, *Dialoghi d'amore*. In extant documents, perhaps the earliest expression of this version of the Pasternak's descent from Abravanel is contained in a letter from Leonid in Berlin to Boris in Moscow in December 1924. With regard to his sister and her family he exclaims: "Ah, the proud, priestly scions of Abrabanel! . . . An exceptional breed of people (so unmodern!)."[43] Soon the same version, but in this case with regard to Boris Pasternak, was repeated in print by Valentin Parnac, a Russian poet well versed in the history of the Jews in Spain who translated medieval Jewish poetry into Russian.[44]

Leonid Pasternak was obviously proud of his ancestry. He spoke about it in a letter to David Shor, written on October 30, 1929, in conjunction with the pogrom in Hebron.[45] This genealogical fact was mentioned also in the monograph-album devoted to him in 1932. It is interesting that before the revolution Leonid Pasternak made no public statements to this effect. So one can assume that the emphasis on family roots was connected, first of all, with the artist's increased contacts with Jewish circles in Moscow and Berlin and, additionally, was a reaction to the family separation that occurred in 1921. After Boris traveled to Berlin in 1922–23, and Alexander in 1924–25, the sons were never to see their parents again.

In this sense, the history of the Abravanel family might be perceived as a kind of historical parallel to the fate of the Pasternak family. Every work about Don Isaac tells how 1492 (the year the Jews were driven from Spain) forced this influential physician, philosopher, and politician into exile, and how the events of the time became a personal tragedy for his eldest son, Yehuda, who was saved by fleeing from Seville to Naples but was forced to abandon his infant son (later forcibly baptized in Portugal). This story was made known by Leone Ebreo's elegy "Lament on the Times," a poem written in Hebrew in 1503, first published in 1857, and translated during the 1920s into several European languages (including French by Valentin Parnac).

The history of the Abravanels finds a reflection in the biographical myth advanced by Boris Pasternak not long before his death. The

Christian themes and symbolism in *Doctor Zhivago* published in the
west in 1957, seemed so inconsistent with the entire character of his
work, and with everything known about his family, that questions
rained down upon the author concerning his religious convictions. In
a letter to Jacqueline de Proyart on May 2, 1959, Pasternak said that
he had been baptized by his nanny in Moscow during his early infancy and that the social position of his parents forced them all to
keep it a secret.[46] The publication of the letter provoked rumors that
Leonid Pasternak was baptized before he was invited to teach at the
Moscow School of Painting (in 1894). These rumors were immediately and categorically denied by the artist's daughter Lydia Pasternak
Slater,[47] but the question whether Boris Pasternak was baptized, and
if so when, went unresolved.

I will return later to a characterization of Pasternak's views on
Christianity when I discuss *Doctor Zhivago*. For now suffice it to say
that, by insisting he had been baptized in early infancy, the poet indicated that this did not happen at a time when such a step would have
seemed more natural: toward the end of the 1940s, when he was
writing verses on Gospel themes for his novel. Pasternak's baptism
during the 1930s would be wholly improbable; both his official status
in Soviet literature and, even more so, the position of the Orthodox
Church in the Soviet Union must exclude such a hypothesis. Nor
could he have embraced Orthodox Christianity in the period from
1910 through the 1920s. Filling out an enrollment questionnaire at
Marburg University in 1912, in response to a question regarding religious faith, Pasternak wrote: "mosaisch" (Jewish).[48] When he married Eugenia Lurie in 1922, although he flatly rejected his future
mother-in-law's insistence on a hoopa (wedding canopy), he agreed
to register the marriage with a rabbi (despite the fact that, in the first
years after the revolution, a marriage registration was not at all man-
datory).

Thus the version of his baptism in the 1890s seems to be as much
a myth as his story about the personal encounter with Tolstoy at the
same time. But, like every myth, it contains a grain of truth. It is quite
possible that it was an allusion to the tragic history of Leone Ebreo
and his infant son, as reflected in "Lament on the Times." This poem,
and the details of its author's family history, could have been related
to Pasternak by Parnac. Just as the family past of the Abravanels
could be seen as a historical parallel to the decline of the family during the twentieth century, so too was the motif of "illicit" infant bap-

tism transformed into the biographical legend created by Boris Pasternak. The present was inextricably intertwined with the past.

This play with historical parallels has an important meaning in a more general respect. The Abravanel theme, like the theme of the Italian Renaissance, also contained, both for Leonid Pasternak and for Boris, the idea of the organic unity of culture. This must be set against the theme of the disintegration of family bonds, a central motif in Boris Pasternak's works. The novella *Aerial Ways*, written soon after the poet's return from Berlin where he had seen his parents for the last time, and which dealt with the Russian revolution and civil war, centers on the tragic instability of the concept of fatherhood. In the verse novel *Spektorsky* the poet stresses the destruction of the traditional way of life and the family. It is impossible to explain this stubbornly recurrent theme without understanding the crucial importance of his father and his family for Boris Pasternak.

2

University Years

"Like a ravine between two mountain peaks, Pasternak was squeezed between his father's painting and his own adolescent (and very powerful) music. Where was there room here for the third, the poet, to emerge?" Marina Tsvetaeva wrote this in 1932.[1] As we have seen, Pasternak switched to music after his accident on August 6, 1903. He later said that music swept over him like an elemental force. Of course the turn to composition would have been unthinkable without his earlier piano lessons, concertgoing, and the special atmosphere created by his mother's household performances. But the significance of the 1903 accident consisted primarily in the ensuing transformation of the future poet from (to use the words of *Safe Conduct*) a passive "model"—as part of the unrealized conception of his father's painting *To the Night Pastures*—into an artistically active and independent individual. One can only guess whether there would have been such a sharp change under normal conditions, that is, if he had not fallen from the horse and been laid up for weeks in a state of complete immobility.[2] In the aforementioned letter to Shtikh, written in 1913 when he had started writing poetry regularly, Boris recounted that it was then that he first sensed rhythm as a pure movement, at the core of both poetry and music.

The other stimulus for this transformation was the music he overheard at the dacha in Obolenskoe. Pasternak's first chance to observe the process of musical composition was in connection with Scriabin's Third Symphony.[3] In works about Pasternak one sometimes finds claims that he was Scriabin's pupil. This has no factual foundation. It was precisely in 1903 (when Pasternak was Scriabin's neighbor) that

the composer discontinued the pedagogical activity that he had always disliked. And the only face-to-face meeting with Scriabin, in the
course of which Boris showed the composer his musical works, occurred in 1909. This meeting took place at a time when the youth
was already abandoning his dreams of becoming a professional musician.

In a brief autobiographical note in 1924, Pasternak said that he had
taken a full course of composition. He pursued these studies under
the guidance of extremely demanding teachers who were well known
in the musical world of the time. The first was Yuly Engel (1868–
1927), one of the most sophisticated and broadly educated of Russian
musicians, a music critic and composer, and a friend of the Pasternak
family.[4] He was succeeded by Reingold Glière (1874–1956). Glière,
who achieved some fame as a composer in the postrevolutionary
years, was also a highly acclaimed music teacher: among his first pupils, preceding Pasternak, were Sergei Prokofiev and Nikolai Mias-
kovsky.

The memoirs of Alexander Pasternak bear witness to the deliberate
and systematic nature of Boris' efforts from the beginning of his studies with Engel. His accomplishments were quite impressive. This is
evident from two works for piano: The Prelude in G-sharp Minor
(dated December 8, 1906)[5] and the Sonata in B Minor,[6] which have
been performed a few times since the early 1970s and have been recorded. Although rather short, these compositions provide enough
material to judge the extent of Scriabin's influence on him, as well as
to characterize the development of Pasternak's own musical style.

While living abroad from 1904 to 1909, Scriabin experienced a
radical transformation in the nature of his musical creativity. He
achieved fame only after his return to Russia, when his new works
(the Third Symphony, *Poème de l'extase,* and *Prometheus*) were performed in Moscow and Petersburg in 1909–10. During the period of
his regular musical studies, Pasternak was familiar with the Third
Symphony only in the rough form in which he had overheard it in
1903 at Obolenskoe. The artistic qualities of the new Scriabin were
not fully revealed him before 1909. The composer's stay in Moscow
during that year was brief—two months in all—but it was then that
he began to see the Pasternak family often,[7] and then that he had the
fateful meeting with Boris described in great detail in *Safe Conduct*
and briefly mentioned in the *Essay in Autobiography.* During this encounter Boris showed his musical compositions to his idol, probably

including the Prelude. According to the poet, Scriabin's response exceeded all expectations: "Scriabin heard me out, approved, encouraged me, and gave me his blessing."

Such approval might have prompted anyone else to continue with redoubled energy. But, as Pasternak recounts in both autobiographies, the meeting led to his decisive break with music. He offers various explanations. If, in *Safe Conduct,* the rupture is motivated by the composer's lack of complete candor in a conversation with the novice regarding the absence of perfect pitch, then in 1956 a different cause is cited: the youth's lack of solid technical skills, and his contempt for tedious exercises. In both instances attention is directed to insufficient expertise, but it is explained differently in each version, and we cannot tell which is closer to the truth. Despite the account in *Safe Conduct,* however, the transition did not take place instantaneously; it stretched out over several years. Until his late twenties, Pasternak's new interests—philosophy and literature—coexisted with continued musical studies (although the latter became more amateurish). The reasons for his abandonment of music were probably more complex than those suggested by the poet himself.

Although Pasternak the musician remained under the powerful sway of Scriabin, he was influenced by the works of the composer's earlier period. In this sense, the closer Pasternak came to his idol, the more anachronistic his musical forays must have appeared both in his own eyes and in Scriabin's, especially when contrasted with the new features of Scriabin's musical style after *Poème de l'extase.* For the rest of Pasternak's life, the *Poème* remained the boundary beyond which his love and understanding of Scriabin did not go. What is involved here are not only the peculiarities of musical language. Beginning in 1904 Scriabin became ever more absorbed by philosophical and mystical ideas that were consonant with the theories of the Russian symbolists. The artist was seen as a theurgist whose mission would be to achieve a synthesis of all the arts. Yuly Engel recalls his meetings with Scriabin during the summer of 1904, on Lake Geneva:

> He spoke about the Third Symphony, which he had then written ("there has never been such music"), about "divine play" as the basis of the creation of the world and of artistic creativity, about the essence of art, about socialism, about religion, in short, about everything.
> All the arts must come together, he said, but not into drama as with Wagner; art must combine with religion and philosophy into

an indivisible unity in such a way as to create a new Gospel which may replace the old and outmoded one. I dream of creating such a Mysterium. All this means that we have to build a special temple, perhaps here (and without looking he made a vague gesture in the direction of the mountain panorama), or perhaps far from here, in India.

But mankind is still not ready for this. We have to begin preaching and point the way along new paths. I myself will preach, perhaps even from a boat, just as Christ did.[8]

This was what attracted the Russian symbolist poets to Scriabin's music. In 1907 he met Dmitry Merezhkovsky in Paris, in 1908 Yurgis Baltrushaitis, and in 1912–13 Viacheslav Ivanov and Konstantin Balmont. He established particularly close relations with Ivanov and Baltrushaitis. What the symbolists saw in Scriabin was not simply a striking musical genius, but the harbinger of an artistic revolution.

Music was of central importance in the philosophical and aesthetic program of symbolism. Conceiving music as a synthesizing form of art, the symbolists believed that it would accomplish a fundamental transformation in the universe and in the history of mankind. Their cult of music was combined with the notion of Mystery—the religious rite in which the disparate arts would converge and carry artistic creativity beyond the bounds of "icon creation" into the realm of "life creation." Ivanov considered Beethoven's symphonies and Wagner's music dramas to be stages along the way to this goal. In the future mystery, as he put it, the boundaries dividing the listeners and spectators from the active participants would disappear.

The year 1910 marked a crisis in the history of Russian symbolism. It became clear that the movement was breaking up into two hostile camps. One, headed by Viacheslav Ivanov, constituted the theurgist line (going back to Vladimir Solovyov). The opposite camp, with Valery Briusov as its major spokesman, rejected all of symbolism's claims to transcend the limits of art, to fuse art and life, and to subordinate art to religious or mystical goals. Scriabin's close relations with the symbolist poets strengthened the theurgist wing of this literary school. From the winter of 1907–08 he was obsessed with plans for his magnum opus, "The Mysterium." All his other works, including the Third Symphony, *Poème de l'extase,* and *Prometheus,* he considered to be mere preparation for this supreme goal. The project echoed the symbolists' theories about the rapidly approaching end of the universe and its imminent rebirth: Scriabin's grandiose conception aimed at the radical transformation of the world and of all humanity; it was intended to save mankind from destruction. When the composer realized that the composition of "The Mysterium" would take more time and energy than he had imagined, he decided to concentrate on an "Acte préalable" (Prefatory Act). Here sound was supposed to be conjoined with light, the word with dance. The musical text of the composition was ready at the time of the composer's death, but it was never written down by him and was preserved only in the form of scattered drafts; the poetic text was completed in the fall of 1914.[9] Scriabin experienced a great deal of uncertainty about the quality of the verses, but his friends Baltrushaitis and Ivanov allayed his fears.

Scriabin's verses strike us today as epigonic, flaccid, and hopelessly lacking in content. In the realm of music Scriabin was an audacious innovator who opened up new horizons; the radicalism of his musical discoveries place him on a par with Schönberg and Stravinsky.[10] But in the realm of poetry he was mesmerized by symbolism, which soon after 1910 was dealt a crushing blow by the new literary currents of acmeism and futurism. While he was working on "Prefatory Act" Scriabin became acquainted with a miscellany of the Russian futurists, *A Slap in the Face of Public Taste,* which caused a great sensation when it was published in December 1912. He was intrigued by the futurists' formal experiments with "words at liberty" and was particularly attracted by the poems of Velimir Khlebnikov.[11] But Scriabin's own poems for "Prefatory Act" are imitative, rhetorical, and filled with decrepit clichés. Of all the symbolist poets to emulate, Scriabin chose the most anachronistic figure even for those years: Konstantin Balmont. This was because Scriabin perceived poetry "musically", focusing on the magic of sound and assigning only an auxiliary role to meaning.

Pasternak's 1956 autobiography leaves not a shadow of doubt that his contact with Scriabin, in regard to perception and influence, stopped with the *Poème de l'extase.* He reacted negatively both to the formal innovations of Scriabin's later works and to the mystical verbiage that accompanied them. His break with music and the turn to philosophy were prompted by the need to overcome Scriabin's influence.

There is no Russian composer so deeply imbued with philosophical interests as Scriabin. From his earliest years, his musical works were accompanied by abstract self-commentaries. This philosophical tendency became even more pronounced toward the end of his life. Not only his major programmatic compositions, but also his last piano sonatas and even his miniatures were conceived as musical renditions of elusive philosophical concepts. As Yurgis Baltrushaitis put it, "Scriabin is not only a musician, but a philosopher, and perhaps more of a philosopher than a musician." [12] Scriabin and his symbolist friends were fond of repeating the Platonic idea of the organic relationship between musical language and philosophical thought. Among Scriabin's acquaintances prior to his friendship with the symbolists was the professor at Moscow University, Sergei Trubetskoy (1862–1905), who was, after the death of Vladimir Solovyov, Russia's greatest living philosopher. Upon Trubetskoy's recommendation, Scriabin joined the Moscow Psychological Society and for a short while took an active part in its discussions. The scope of Scriabin's interests was wide, but he was unused to any kind of systematic philosophical work or even a program of intense reading. He found it difficult to read any book through to the end,[13] and, according to Boris Schloetzer, his knowledge of philosophy was perfunctory. His philosophical views were eclectic, just as his attempts to write verse were blatantly amateurish. Scriabin's knowledge of recent currents in European thought was just as murky as his training in the history of philosophy. Such important forces in early twentieth-century philosophy as Bergson or German neo-Kantianism apparently were unknown to him.

In *Safe Conduct* Pasternak notes that it was on Scriabin's suggestion that he, a freshman at the law school of Moscow University, suddenly decided to transfer to the history and philology department. The poet says nothing about his personal reasons for this step, but they become clear as we study the facts of his biography during these years.

In comparison with Scriabin, Pasternak's philosophical studies strike us with their concentrated professionalism and systematic approach. History and philology were perhaps the strongest disciplines taught at Moscow University during the prerevolutionary years. Around the turn of the century, many well-known historians lectured there—V. O. Kliuchevsky, P. G. Vinogradov (who later moved to Oxford), and Robert Vipper—and specialists in Greek history, N. I. Novosadsky and Sergei Sobolevsky. The philosophy department was less impressive but, thanks to Sergei Trubetskoy and his brother Evgeny, the teaching of philosophy at Moscow was the best in Russia. The beginning of the century was marked by a sharply increased public interest in philosophical problems; this was aided by the activity of religious and philosophical societies that sprang up at the time, as well as by the intense discussion of philosophical questions in symbolist circles.

Pasternak's university studies after he left the law school were by no means purely philosophical. Apparently his enthusiasm was more or less equally divided between the philosophical, historical, and philological disciplines. Moreover, even within the realm of philosophy, he seemed to be more strongly attracted by its historical aspect. Among the subjects Pasternak took were courses taught by two fine historians, Alexander Savin and Robert Vipper, who were complete opposites from a professional standpoint. Vipper gravitated toward broad generalizations and theoretical conceptions (to a large extent colored by Marxism). Savin's scholarly methods were based on the meticulous study of a wealth of concrete details (he spent several years in England working in archives) and were characterized by the rejection of speculative theoretical constructions. His courses demonstrated a striking encyclopedic erudition and yet were an example of strict self-discipline. Pasternak's later comments in his memoirs show that he preferred Savin over all the other historians at the university. And most important, Pasternak preserved his love for history throughout his life, striving to view the shifting currents of modern times from a historical perspective and often reproving his contemporaries during the Soviet period for their "indifference to history."

Another teacher Pasternak liked was a specialist in classical philology, Apollon Grushka, whose commentaries on Lucretius made a particularly strong impression on him.[14] But courses in philosophy taught by the prominent professors G. I. Chelpanov and L. M. Lopatin earned Pasternak's criticism. He had them in mind when he ironically noted in *Safe Conduct:*

> The range of subjects that were lectured on to our group was as far from ideal as the actual method of instruction. It was a strange mixture of superannuated metaphysics and unfledged enlightenmentism. And in order to reconcile them, both these trends had been stripped of the last remnants of meaning which they might still have possessed taken separately. The history of philosophy thus turned into belletristic dogmatism, while psychology degenerated into a mass of frivolous, journalistic inanity.[15]

Both Lopatin and Chelpanov remained aloof from recent currents in European philosophy, news of which had penetrated widely into Russia in the early 1900s and had seized the minds of young people.

The interests of Pasternak's contemporaries were divided between three philosophical tendencies: Henri Bergson, Edmund Husserl, and the Marburg School. The most popular in Russia was Bergson. But as far as we can judge from existing documents, Pasternak as a student showed no interest in him. Much closer to the poet were the ideas of Husserl, whose militant follower Gustav Shpet began to teach in those years at the university, becoming one of the major figures in Moscow's philosophical circles. (Among the papers preserved from Pasternak's student years are notes relating to Shpet's seminar on Hume.) An affinity for Husserl can be felt in Pasternak's early works.[16] But, at the same time, he undertook a systematic study of works by the Marburg neo-Kantians. Here Pasternak the student was left pretty much on his own, since Marburg had no representatives on the faculty. At the same time, the Marburg School was well known in Russia and was widely covered in the philosophical press. Toward the end of the first decade of the century in Russia, particularly in Moscow, there appeared many adherents of German neo-Kantianism who had been trained at its two main centers, Freiburg and Marburg, and who popularized the newest tendencies of German thought. Among the Russian students and admirers of Hermann Cohen were Dimitry Gawronsky, V. E. Sezeman, A. Koralnik, A. Gurliand, D. Koigen, B. Savalsky (who published a large dissertation on the Marburg School in 1908), G. Gordon, B. Fokht (to whom Andrei Biely's poem "The Philosopher" is dedicated), G. E. Lanz,[17] B. V. Vysheslavtsev, and somewhat later Matvei Kagan, a close friend of Mikhail Bakhtin. According to Biely, "Without even coming to Moscow, Cohen and Rickert reigned within the walls of the university, for their 'disciples' from Moscow sent them young people for the full treatment: they organized a genuine export of young people to Marburg and Freiburg, where the venerable minotaurs devoured them completely and had full command over them."[18]

Biely himself went through a period of strong attraction to neo-Kantianism around 1910. He began to use its concepts and terminology in combative polemical articles that were intended to lay the foundations for a theory of Russian symbolism. This wide use of neo-Kantian terminology in literary battles, in the purely literary press, contributed to further dissemination of the ideas of the Marburg School among the Moscow artistic elite. But Biely employed these sources, and many others, in an extremely desultory and indiscriminate manner, heaping together various tendencies of contemporary German thought without displaying the slightest bit of professional competence. It is no accident that Gustav Shpet mocked this side of Biely's literary activity, calling his philosophical jargon simply outer "apparel," a "philosophical tail coat."

All this leads us to the question of what led Pasternak in his student years toward Marburg. Unlike other contemporary philosophical tendencies, the Marburg School made no claims about advancing a new world view, but it did offer a strict theory of science and a system of scientific methodology. It was meant to serve as the theoretical foundation for all scientific disciplines and for philosophy in general. It thereby satisfied the "yearning for theory" of Pasternak's generation. Just as his transfer to the university's philosophy department was provoked by Pasternak's efforts to surpass Scriabin in this sphere, his zealous study of the Marburg philosophers originated in his desire to understand more fully the aesthetics of those who were the mentors of his generation in literature, Andrei Biely and the other symbolists. We see in this a trait of Pasternak's that he himself would address forty years later in his poem "Vo vsem mne khochetsia doiti do samoi suti" (I always want to go to the essence).

All of Pasternak's studies during his university years proceeded under the banner of "self-consciousness." This term appears everywhere, not only in his philosophical notes but in his early literary drafts and correspondence. It was precisely this quest for self-consciousness that attracted him to the Marburg School, whose activity was interpreted by contemporaries to be the culmination of a logical evolution—from Kant through Hegel to Cohen—of philosophy as a scientific discipline. This is why, in talking about the Marburg School in *Safe Conduct*, Boris Pasternak stressed its systemic character. Another quality that appealed to him was its historicity. The teaching of the history of philosophy at Moscow University disappointed him because of its superficial attention to the past. In the Marburg School, history was not a haphazard admixture of names, facts, and trends; it described the internal necessity of the movement of European thought and saw in this development a consistent succession of philosophical problems. The history of European philosophy was seen as an integrated whole.[19] Pasternak's historical interests, as well as his readings in philosophy and his study of mathematics and natural science,[20] therefore received a solid theoretical grounding. The ideas of the Marburg School led him to the important conclusion that a basic unity permeates all human culture.

Such were the reasons that edged Pasternak toward a study of Plato, Kant, Leibniz, and Hume through the prism of Natorp and Cohen, even before he made a trip to Marburg in the summer of 1912. It would be a mistake to portray him during these student years as an orthodox follower of Hermann Cohen. The Marburg School and Husserl undoubtedly seemed to be the latest word in European philosophy, but during his university years he had to study the textbooks and monographs of a number of other representatives of German and Russian academic philosophy (Eduard von Hartmann, Lipps, and so forth). It is against this rather dreary background that we must consider his decision to look for a change and to visit Marburg during the summer semester of 1912.

In *Safe Conduct* the circumstances surrounding this decision are presented as routine and insignificant: the idea of traveling to Marburg came to Pasternak impulsively, as a result of a chance meeting in a café with one of his friends at Moscow University, Dmitry Samarin (who was a year younger than Pasternak). In a certain sense, this episode was no less strange than Pasternak's turn to the systematic study of philosophy after his meeting with Scriabin. In order to understand just how strange it was, we need to look more closely at Samarin and his milieu.

Samarin and two of his closest friends, Sergei Mansurov and Nikolai Trubetskoy, were talented and remarkable young men. They belonged to cultured families in Moscow society, and each in his own way made a contribution to Russian intellectual life. Nikolai Trubetskoy (1890–1939) was the son of the philosopher Sergei Trubetskoy, rector of Moscow University. After the October Revolution, in 1920 in Sofia, Nikolai published the pamphlet *Europe and Mankind*, which inaugurated the Eurasian movement in the Russian emigration. His linguistic works brought him renown and, along with Roman Jakobson, he created the modern discipline of phonology. Sergei Mansurov's father was the director of the Moscow archive of the Ministry of Foreign Affairs and an authority on ancient Eastern Christianity.[21] In the spring of 1913 Sergei helped Pasternak to prepare for the difficult graduation exams (in history with Vipper and in the history of philosophy with Lopatin). The main sphere of his interests lay in the history of the Christian church, and he intended to pursue a career as a college professor. But in 1926 he became a priest, dying three years later from tuberculosis. Dmitry Samarin came from a well-known Slavophile family. He died of typhus in his early thirties, at the end of the Civil War. Despite his phenomenal erudition (particularly in the history of philosophy), he left no real trace in scholarly literature; as far as we can judge from the scraps of information that have survived, his main interest was in the history of Christianity and Russian folk beliefs. The force of his ideas was apparently conveyed most effectively in conversation and discussion. Together with his friends Trubetskoy and Mansurov, he joined (around 1909) the adolescents' religious and philosophical circle that met at the home of Moscow University Professor L. A. Komarovsky.[22]

In the first version of *Safe Conduct* Pasternak draws a parallel between Samarin and two clearly incompatible figures: the revolutionary Lenin and the hero of Tolstoy's *Resurrection,* Nekhliudov. We have in this a typical example of the penchant for paradoxical and strange comparisons so striking in Pasternak's poetry. But, as always with Pasternak, the comparison has a certain basis in fact. Samarin's sole published article was written on a theme outwardly very distant from Lenin and the Bolshevik revolution and having nothing in common with Hegel or Cohen (with whom Samarin was more thoroughly acquainted than his university teachers were). It is called "The Virgin Mary in the Orthodoxy of the Russian People" and was published soon after the revolution in the best Russian journal of the time, *Russkaia mysl* (Russian Thought).[23] This article will delight the modern reader with its extraordinary command of the material being discussed, its decisive analysis, and its bold conclusions. Samarin notes that the old Slavophiles claimed that the religious outlook of the Russian people is Christian. But they overlooked the specifically non-Christian, pagan aspects of these religious beliefs, despite the fact that precisely those traits should have been stressed insofar as the main idea of the Slavophiles was the uniqueness of the Russian national character. By analyzing ancient icons, Samarin tries to show where this uniqueness actually lies: the cult of the Virgin Mary among the Russian people by far overshadows the significance of Christ. In this way Christian monotheism is replaced by a dualistic conception. Popular orthodoxy, continues Samarin, is not a Christian religion and by its very nature is somewhat heretical.[24]

Pasternak was undoubtedly familiar with Samarin's article (at that time he too was preparing an article for *Russian Thought*), and it must have made a deep impression. It was precisely the decisiveness of Samarin's conclusions, his freedom from established dogma and prejudices, and his feeling of an organic, unbreakable bond with the

people's outlook that made Pasternak draw a parallel between the
heir to "the best of the Russian past" (quoting *Safe Conduct*) and the
leader of October Revolution.

Throughout the rest of his life, Boris Pasternak reminisced about
Dmitry Samarin. When in 1936 he moved to the writers' colony at
Peredelkino, he found himself near an old estate of the Samarin family. One of their descendants appears in Pasternak's poem from World
War II ("Staryi park" [The Old Park]). But most striking is the fact
that, in the fate of Yury Zhivago and the circumstances of the last
years of his life, there are features that resemble the fate of Samarin.
This parallel was first noted by the Russian émigré critic Mikhail Koriakov in 1959, after the publication in the west of the *Essay in Autobiography* (which mentions not only Samarin but his friends Mansurov and Trubetskoy).[25] In a letter of April 9, 1959, to one of his
foreign correspondents, Pasternak indirectly confirmed the validity of
the parallel between Zhivago and Samarin.[26] Memories of his old university classmate were evoked by his reflections in *Doctor Zhivago*
on the distinctive characteristics of the Russian people and their
course in history. It is no accident that these memories acquired a
"religious and philosophical" coloration that corresponds to the
main intellectual interests of Samarin and his milieu.

But it is just this context of religious philosophy that makes it so
paradoxical that Pasternak attributed his decision to go to Marburg
to the meeting with Samarin. Indeed, it is difficult to imagine two
more mutually exclusive opposites than the scientific philosophy of
Cohen's school and the religious philosophers in Russia at the beginning of the century. All available documents leave no doubt that Russian religious philosophy failed to affect Pasternak in his youth. It
attracted his attention only much later, when he started writing *Doctor Zhivago*.

The trip to Marburg was a relatively brief episode in the poet's life.
He was enrolled in the university's philosophy department on May 9,
1912 (three weeks after the beginning of the summer semester), and
he left Marburg after receiving his certificate (*Abgangszeugnis*) on
August 3.[27] This summer semester was Hermann Cohen's last term at
the university before his retirement—the last chance for Pasternak to
hear the founder of the Marburg School in his citadel. The philosophy department was busy with preparations for the celebration of
Cohen's seventieth birthday at the beginning of July. The professor's
colleagues and former students were expected to flock in from all over

Germany and Europe, and the publication of an international fest-schrift was planned to coincide with the jubilee.

In the summer of 1912 four faculty members worked in the philosophy department: Professors Hermann Cohen and his closest disciple and associate, Paul Natorp, University Lecturer Nicolai Hartmann, and Associate Professor Georg Misch, a recent arrival. Among the students there was a sizable Russian colony: twenty-seven Russian nationals were enrolled (mainly Baltic Germans and Jewish youths from the Pale), among whom ten (including Pasternak) studied in the philosophy department and eight in the medical school.[28] Among the students of philosophy was Pasternak's contemporary from Odessa, Sergei Rubinstein, later a prominent Soviet philosopher and psychologist. The department also included two emigrants from Russia who were working on their dissertations, Henry Lanz and Dimitry Gawronsky (who later taught philosophy in Switzerland and the United States). Its ties to Russia were enhanced by the presence of the junior representative of the Marburg School, Nicolai Hartmann. A Baltic German, he was born in Riga and studied in Russian- and German-language schools there and in Petersburg. In 1907 he defended his dissertation in Marburg and began his teaching career there.[29] Later the "critical ontology" he developed under the influence of Husserl and Scheler became one of the most significant schools in European thought. At about the time Pasternak arrived in Marburg, one could already detect in Hartmann's philosophical orientation a movement away from Cohen and in the direction of Husserl's phenomenology.

From the seven courses (not counting "exercises") offered by the philosophy department during the summer semester, Pasternak chose two seminars, Cohen's on ethics (scheduled for Monday, Tuesday, and Friday at five in the afternoon) and Hartmann's on logic.[30] He did not sign up for Natorp's course in logic (evidently because he was already familiar with this subject[31]), nor did he take Hartmann's course in the history of modern philosophy or any of Misch's three courses.[32] In both seminars Pasternak gave a report. His work in Hartmann's course led him, upon his return to Russia, to a degree thesis on Leibniz. Boris' paper on Kant's *Critique of Practical Reason* was praised by Cohen, who began to speak with Pasternak about the possibility of remaining to continue his studies at Marburg and even invited him to his home one Sunday for lunch. He also indicated that possible financial problems should not interfere with Pasternak's graduate studies at Marburg.[33]

A few decades later, speaking of the artist, Pasternak declared: "One need not distinguish / Victory from defeats." [34] The trip to Marburg became for Pasternak one of those victories indistinguishable from defeat. Pasternak refused Cohen's flattering proposal and decided to return to Moscow, where he still had one year left before graduation. In order to appreciate fully the refusal of Cohen's alluring offer, we must note that a year earlier, at the beginning of 1911, a scandal erupted at Moscow University from the crude meddling of the minister of education in matters of the university's autonomy, which resulted in the resignation of nearly one third of the faculty ("an incident unprecedented in the history of higher education," as Vladimir Vernadsky described the event[35]). Although the majority of those resigning were not from the humanities and were specialists in natural science, the intellectual climate in the university deteriorated sharply.

Pasternak turned down Cohen's proposal not because of indifference to scholarly pursuits as such. In *Safe Conduct* he recounts that he experienced a more powerful excitement from scholarship than most other students. And in her memoirs, his cousin Olga stresses that the twenty-year-old Boris seemed born for a scholarly career. But the artistic milieu in which the poet was raised fostered skepticism and a certain disdain toward academicians. Pasternak was put off by the idea of a respectable and secure academic career, particularly in the philistine form it could take at a German university. In a letter from that period to Shtikh, Boris describes the faculty members at Marburg as "beasts of intellectualism." [36]

Pasternak's decision was also affected by his tumultuous romantic experiences in June 1912. In *Safe Conduct* he mentions only one of them, relating to Ida Vysotskaia, who was daughter and granddaughter of millionaire tea merchants known throughout Russia. Boris was well received in their household as a private tutor, having become friends with Ida during the gymnasium period. Ida made a brief trip to Marburg with her younger sister, evidently because their cousin Dimitry Gawronsky was there working on his dissertation. In addition to the account in *Safe Conduct,* the circumstances of his unsuccessful declaration of love to Ida are reflected in Pasternak's poems "Marburg" (1915) and "Ia tozhe liubil" (I also loved; 1928). But the very same June days also saw the development of complex romantic relations between Boris and his cousin Olga Freidenberg, which had begun back in 1910. Pasternak never wrote a word about this love affair in any of his works, and in *Safe Conduct* he mentions Olga's trip to Germany in the summer of 1912 and their meeting in Frankfurt-am-Main only in passing.

These emotionally devastating events led to a burst of poetic inspiration. For it was in Marburg that Pasternak once again felt the irresistible attraction to the "twilight" (his word) of art, and it was now that he immersed himself in writing. The break from philosophy and the turn to literature proved to be related steps, and it is no accident that one of the poems he wrote at the time, "Gliadi—on doktor filosofii" (Look—he is a doctor of philosophy), is a sharp invective against German university philosophers. The eagerness to embark on a course of professional literary activity is shown by his plans to begin prose translations from German. But just as his break from music was more prolonged in real life than he retrospectively described it in *Safe Conduct,* his actual farewell to philosophy took place not in Marburg but after his return to Moscow and graduation from the university. All we know about Pasternak's last year at Moscow University underscores the astonishing way in which he combined philosophical and literary interests after he had decided against a professional career as an academic philosopher.

What I have in mind primarily is his paper "On the Nature and Method of Psychology."[37] From this, as well as from notes of this period preserved in the family archives, we can see that Pasternak had fundamentally assimilated the scientific methodology, problems, and ideas associated with the Marburg School. He chose as his topic a theme that was at the center of a sharp polemic among philosophers of the day: the relationship between psychology and logic, or psychology and epistemology, the possibility of constructing a "philosophical psychology" in opposition to the empirical psychological science reigning at that time.

The exact date of the paper is unknown, but it is likely that Pasternak worked on it at the beginning of 1913, not long before graduation. It was basically an exposition of the first eight chapters of Paul Natorp's *General Psychology,*[38] which had just been published. Pasternak's attention could have been directed to the book by one of his Moscow professors, Gustav Shpet, who was deeply interested in Natorp and followed his debates with Husserl.[39] But it is possible that Pasternak needed no such prompting, and at Marburg he would have heard about the forthcoming publication of the book. He chose the topic because its central ideas had something in common with his own contemplations. Closest to him was the idea that the "miracle" (Pasternak's word) of consciousness consists in its subjectivity and its complex, contradictory nature; this subjectivity is inherent not only to the thinking subject (the "I") but to the very contents (*Inhalte*) of his experience of the world. Related to this idea was another, particularly important for the poet: the denial of the active nature of consciousness (or human psychology as a whole) and the emphasis on its passive character. Consciousness is not so much activity as the interaction of content and subject.

Does this student essay have any value for us now? Without a doubt. First of all, it convincingly shows Pasternak's high professional level as a student of philosophy, and compels us to agree with Hermann Cohen in his evaluation of the student's philosophical and scientific abilities. Second, despite the modest goals of the report (evidently written to fulfil a curriculum requirement), it reveals a striking degree of independence and maturity in philosophical thinking. In the choice of theme and the method of presentation, we can feel the topics that personally occupied Pasternak as a poet. Some of Natorp's ideas are transformed beyond recognition. The problematics of Natorp's work clearly interested him because they were relevant to his own literary and poetic reflections (see my discussion of Pasternak's early prose fragments in Chapter 3), and between those concerns and Natorp's ideas there is a relationship of coincidence and similarity, not borrowing and imitation.

The same relationship between Pasternak's philosophical and literary thought is evident in unpublished notes preserved among his university notebooks. Here as well the main theme is subjectivity. Pasternak counterposes art and psychology and claims that, within a specific realm (the consciousness of culture), they are two separate and irreconcilable opposites. But, again as always in Pasternak, these opposed extremes share common elements: both psychology and art address the same "material," the subjectivity of human consciousness. They have a common goal: to derive this subjectivity, in all its vivid concreteness, from "everyday consciousness," to reconstruct it from objective content. Here Pasternak follows Natorp, who declared that the method of psychology is "reconstruction" and who set this method against the method of all objective sciences (which, according to the Marburg School, construct, rather than reconstruct, their own object). Art and psychology are therefore related methodologically. But art, according to Pasternak, is "more psychological than psychology." It is broader than psychology and therefore must be placed more in the sphere of objective (rather than subjective) knowledge. Unlike psychology, artistic creativity is not limited by the reduction of ideas to impressions but, on the contrary, leads to general philosophical conclusions, so that it is possible to say that the "movement of the idea" originates in the complexity of artistic language.[40] The entire vocabulary of Pasternak's conceptions belongs completely to the philosophical literature of the period. But once again we see here how he strives to draw his own conclusions from what he has read, and how persistently he directs his philosophical thinking to the problematics of art.

Since his senior essay on Leibniz, written in the spring of 1913, is lost, it is difficult to judge whether it was so strongly permeated with reflections on art. But it is obvious that the complex of reasons dictating Pasternak's turn to the life and writings of Leibniz was tied to his developing poetic world view and to broader historical and cultural parallels. Leibniz had exerted a particularly strong influence on Russian science; the Russian Academy of Sciences was formed in the eighteenth century at his initiative. Lomonosov in the eighteenth century, and a number of leading Russian philosophers and scientists at the turn of the twentieth, felt Leibniz' enormous impact. Suffice it to name here the mathematician Nikolai Bugaev (father of the poet Andrei Biely) and his pupil, the great scholar-encyclopedist Pavel Florensky, the philosophers Nikolai Lossky and Vladimir Ilin, and particularly Lev Lopatin, one of Pasternak's university teachers. The attraction to Leibniz was reflected as well in modernist poetry, in the works of the decadents Valery Briusov and Alexander Dobroliubov. The trip to Marburg only strengthened Pasternak's interest in Leibniz. In *Safe Conduct* he mentions him several times in passing, but each of these brief references is significant. Along with mathematical infinity, Leibniz is named as one of the themes touched upon in conversation with Dmitry Samarin before the trip to Germany. Christian Wolff, "Leibniz' pupil," is evoked in a story about the first day Mikhail Lomonosov spent in Marburg. Later Pasternak speaks about the "French volumes" of Leibniz and Descartes and about his report in Hartmann's seminar on Leibniz. Other statements by Pasternak contain veiled references to the German philosopher. For instance, the discussion of "force" in modern physics in the second part of *Safe Conduct* is undoubtedly inspired by Leibniz. Another Leibnizian concept, *materia prima* (related to the concept of force), is reflected in the 1914 poem of the same name. The concept of the animate monad merges in Pasternak's writings with his thoughts on subjectivity, and Leibniz' analysis of infinitely small quantities certainly influenced the formation of Pasternak's early poetic style. It is also no accident that Sergei Bobrov, Pasternak's closest friend and literary cohort of that time, discusses the concept of the monad in a theoretical treatise of 1913. In addition, allusions to the study of Leibniz can be found in the reference to "infinitely small elements" in Pasternak's 1936 poem, "Khudozhnik" (The Artist).

Despite the fact that Pasternak's philosophical studies in 1909–1913 are documented only in fragmented form by the material now available, it is possible to say with certainty that the established view of him as a faithful disciple of the Marburg School is untenable. A deep interest in philosophical literature led Pasternak to Marburg, one of the recognized contemporary centers of philosophy. But his studies there reinforced his conviction of the relativity of every philosophical system. Despite his obvious fascination with Hermann Cohen, Pasternak was nevertheless more attracted to the younger generation of the Marburg School, to Natorp and Hartmann. Much in the same way that his musical experience drew him into the realm of philosophy and to a systematic study of the philosophical classics, so too Pasternak's philosophical studies helped to form the distinctive qualities of his poetic language.

3

Literary Debut

The beginning of Pasternak's literary activity can be dated to 1909. At that time he was associated with a student literary and artistic circle called Serdarda. We know very little about it. The memoirists who have written about Pasternak's early period—his brother Alexander and Konstantin Loks—never belonged to the circle, and were it not for Pasternak's *Essay in Autobiography*, the existence of Serdarda would probably have escaped the attention of scholars (in *Safe Conduct* it is mentioned fleetingly). But Pasternak's testimony in the 1956 autobiography should be approached with great caution, not only because it contains mistakes in memory, unavoidable over such a length of time, but also because it was written when the author was completely reevaluating his past. In 1956 he was inclined to reject what had previously been dear to him and to exaggerate the importance of things that actually played a much less decisive role in his life.

We can assume that Pasternak assigned just such a disproportionately significant role to Serdarda. But it is precisely because of this exaggeration that we are now able to recreate, more or less concretely, the poet's milieu in his early university years. Some of the circle's participants later left a mark on Russian culture; others were saved from oblivion only by their mention in the *Essay in Autobiography*.

The poet Sergei Durylin belonged to the first of these two groups. He came from a Moscow merchant family and was almost ten years older than Pasternak. When they met he already had behind him a life of restless intellectual and moral aspirations. During early adoles-

cence, he had experienced a conversion to Tolstoyism and Nietzsche-
ism, which was followed by involvement in the revolutionary unrest
of 1905, imprisonment, and then a passionate discovery of the teachings of Saint Francis of Assisi. Later he returned to the Russian Orthodox Church and was even ordained as a priest in the spring of
1918. During the 1920s he was arrested several times and sent into
internal exile. Under the pressure of Soviet officials he was forced to
renounce the cloth. He eventually became one of the foremost authorities on the history of literature and the Russian theater. Although
Pasternak throughout his life warmly recalled Durylin, their regular
meetings are limited only to the earliest period, 1909–1913. Durylin
had already established his literary reputation and knew Briusov, Ellis, and Biely. His publications also appeared in the influential journal
of the Moscow symbolists, *Vesy* (Libra). He was the first person to
whom Pasternak showed his early literary efforts, and Durylin's response was very encouraging.

Other members of Serdarda were the brothers Feinberg—Samuil
(later a Soviet composer) and Evgeny (later an artist)—and the composer Boris Krasin (the younger brother of one of the founders of
Russian Social Democracy, Leonid Krasin), who after the revolution
headed the musical department of the People's Commissariat of Education in Moscow. To all appearances Boris Sadovskoy was a member
of the circle. Sadovskoy was the same age as Durylin and by this time
had already published his first book of verse (*Late Morning*), a collection of articles (*Russian Muse*), and a few works of fiction. His sharp
critical articles in *Libra* won him a wide reputation. Despite his close
ties with Briusov, Sadovskoy, to judge from the style of his poetry and
his aesthetic tastes, had little sympathy for literary modernism. Like
another poet of his generation, Vladislav Khodasevich, he personified
a distinctively traditionalist, "passéist" reaction against modernism.
"At times it seems that for him Russian poetry ends not even with
Briusov, but with Fet," Khodasevich wrote about Sadovskoy.[1] He was
closest of all to the poetry of the first quarter of the nineteenth century: the age of Pushkin. Of all the poets of the "pleiad," he was
particularly fond of Nikolai Yazykov, and the sudden upsurge in interest in Yazykov at the beginning of the twentieth century was due
in a large measure to Sadovskoy.

Among the participants of Serdarda who left practically no trace in
the annals of Russian literature, Arkady Guriev deserves special mention. The strange name of the group belonged to him: he had heard

the word somewhere on the Volga during his wanderings. Guriev was a poet; his small collection *Bezotvetnoe* (Unanswered) was published in the winter of 1912–13. He also had a wonderful bass voice and loved to sing, but lost his voice after a nervous breakdown. In the eyes of Pasternak, Guriev was the personification of what Russians call a "samorodok": a person talented by nature who has no education or training. Pasternak later compared Guriev with the great poets of the day, Esenin and Mayakovsky. Although Guriev's published poems by no means justify this wild parallel, other witnesses confirm his originality and talent.[2]

The host at the Serdarda gatherings, Yulian Anisimov, was a poet and an artist. Because of frail health, he spent his winters in western Europe, returning to Moscow in the spring. In Paris he attended classes at the Sorbonne and took private painting lessons from Henri Matisse. In 1913 he published two books of verse (*Cloister*) and a translation of twenty-four poems from the first part of *Das Stundenbuch* (Book of Hours) by Rainer Maria Rilke. (Later he published two more poetry collections.) In the fall of 1911 he married Vera Stanevich, a twenty-one-year-old philosophy student in Moscow, who was also a writer of verse and prose. During the Soviet period she became a well-known translator of Goethe, Feuchtwanger, Thomas Mann, Balzac, Kafka, Jack London, and others. The Anisimov household remained a haven for young artists even after Serdarda disbanded. In the group Pasternak was evidently seen as a musician, since his literary activities were still unknown. After 1911, in the Anisimov salon as opposed to Serdarda, the literary interests of the participants clearly outweighed the musical or artistic.[3] In addition to Durylin and Sadovskoy, there were the neophyte poets Nikolai Aseev and Sergei Bobrov, and Pasternak's classmate at the university, Konstantin Loks (none of whom had belonged to Serdarda). Among others who frequented the Anisimov salon were the head of the Halcyon publishing house, Alexander Kozhebatkin, and the editor of the Petersburg journal *Apollon* (Apollo), the poet Sergei Makovsky.

With the exception of Sergei Durylin, who immediately recognized Pasternak's literary gifts and welcomed his first poetic attempts, and the newcomers Aseev and Loks, most of those at the Anisimov salon greeted Pasternak's first poems[4] with bewilderment, skepticism, and even ridicule. Anisimov and the poets of his artistic orientation (Guriev and Nikolai Meshkov) followed Sadovskoy in cultivating Russian national themes and the village idyll. They deliberately used an epigonic poetic style in striving to achieve musicality and clarity of expression. In contrast, Pasternak's poems were awkward and diffi-cult in language. Their unpredictable combinations of words and im-ages, which produced a first impression of chaos and cacophony, could divulge an inner harmony and odd but compelling logic only to the attentive reader. Landscape descriptions dominate this early po-etry, but landscape treated as a kind of musical composition, "an as-signment in harmony," executed by verbal means. In contrast to the verse of Anisimov, Guriev, Sadovskoy, and Durylin, Pasternak's cre-ated a blatantly non-Russian, cosmopolitan impression. There was no trace here of hymns to village Rus'. The dominant theme was the city, the new big city. However, unlike the urbanist works of Briusov or Verhaeren, Pasternak's city poems were devoid of contemporaneity; they were demonstratively timeless in character. Thus Pasternak's lyr-ics were out of tune equally with the passéist and with the modernist line in Russian poetry. They differed not only from the works of his predecessors and from the imitative verse of his contemporaries, but also from the poetry of the acknowledged leaders of symbolism, Briu-sov, Biely, and Blok, who were idolized by the younger poets. It was so difficult to find an analogue to Pasternak that Yulian Anisimov later (in the fall of 1913 at the height of the Beilis trial) even ascribed what he saw as all these "strange" characteristics of the poetry to Pasternak's non-Russian, Jewish origin. Incidentally, Boris' father was no less skeptical of his poems. The result of this daunting reception was that, in the years before his break with philosophy, Pasternak, as he himself later acknowledged, was ashamed of his poetic experi-ments and avoided showing them to people.

His work in prose, which began in the winter of 1909–10, was even more secretive. These prose experiments remained absolutely un-known until the 1970s, when some of Pasternak's rough drafts were published in various scholarly editions.[5] All the published, and the still unpublished, prose texts of this period are fragmentary and un-finished. And they are often highly resistant to interpretation. How-ever, taken together, they provide an idea of the specific features and tendencies of the young author's work.

Most striking are the symptoms of what Roman Jakobson later called a "poet's prose." This is shown, first of all, in the extreme at-tenuation and amorphousness of plot and of the eventful side of nar-ration in general. Clearly plot did not interest Pasternak at this time. But it is not only the absence of events that is striking. There are also no distinct and clearly defined, individualized portraits of characters, although embryonic personalities surface now and then and the prose sometimes seems to be gesturing toward novelistic intrigue. One character bears a name that is exotic to the Russian ear, Relikvimini, formed from the Latin verb *relinquere* (to leave behind or cause to remain). This figure serves to unite the greater part of these early drafts. But Relikvimini appears in different functions: sometimes as a character and sometimes as a narrator—an alter ego of the author. The distinction between these contrasting functions is deliberately blurred.[6] He is obviously an autobiographical figure: like Boris Pasternak, he is the son of an artist and the pupil of a composer.

No less odd, given the Russian setting of these prose works, are the names of other characters. Among them are namesakes of great historical and cultural figures of the past—Schleiermacher or Alexander the Great—and their names are used for etymological play. This is obviously done to lay bare the conventional and artificial nature of the reality depicted by the author. A friend of Relikvimini is called Mozart, and the narrator of the segment in which he appears, who is initially called Koinonievich, is suddenly renamed before the reader's eyes as Salieri (this of course is a reference to Pushkin's short tragedy, *Mozart and Salieri*). The name Dmitry Shestokrylov (Six-winged) alludes to the description of the seraphim in Pushkin's poem "The Prophet." The name Pyotr Bertoletsky plays on chemical and geological semantics: it is formed through association with the chemical term "Berthollet's salt," which in its turn came from the name of the French chemist C. L. Berthollet, whereas Peter of course is from the Greek for "stone." The Muscovite Kanadovich is declared to be a grand-nephew of the "Königsberg philosopher," Immanuel Kant. As for the name Koinonievich, it is derived from the Greek verb *koino-nein,* which means, among other things, "to have or do in common with; share; form a community."

Thus most of the names used by Pasternak in these prose works are persistently foreign-sounding, with transparent etymological meaning and macaronic makeup. As a result, the attention of the reader is continuously directed to the linguistic aspects of the text. From the very start of his literary work, then, Pasternak's interest is concentrated on the symbolic—and not the mimetic—features of narration. In his later prose fiction, he stresses the conditional nature of the verbal sign and the incongruous relationship between the name and what it denotes.

We find a similar play on names in the works of Pasternak's predecessors in Russian literature—in Pushkin's "The Coffinmaker," Gogol's "Nevsky Prospect," and Biely's "Symphonies" and *The Silver Dove*. But whereas this device is traditionally used to create a comic or satirical effect, in Pasternak it occurs not in a grotesque but in an absolutely serious, and even lyrical, context. The lyrical orientation of his prose is emphasized even in these youthful experiments by the preponderance of scenic descriptions at the expense of action. Some of the drafts are devoted entirely to extended landscape depiction, which may seem superannuated. They are, however, quite common in realistic prose of the nineteenth century, although Pasternak's prose differs from that as well. First of all, the sharp dynamism of the landscapes being described reveals links to contemporary Russian and French painting, primarily to the *rayonnisme* of Mikhail Larionov: several of Pasternak's descriptions appear to be verbal translations of Larionov's canvases. Second, the profusion of lyrical tropes in Pasternak's landscape prose stands in stark contrast to the conventions of realism. Finally, there is the unprecedented length of the sentences. In poetry sentences of such length would not be so conspicuous, since they are somewhat neutralized by recurring metrical borders. But in prose they add a note of lyrical extravagance.

In Pasternak's later prose, these idiosyncratic traits appear in a much more attenuated and muted form. The earliest fragments are therefore important because they allow us to see what are probably basic features of his artistic logic. In contrast to Jakobson, I understand "poet's prose" not as a lyric poet's attempt to assimilate a linguistic code that is foreign to him, but as an *inherently* hybrid, syncretic medium that preceded the separation of prose and poetry. It becomes clear why he would say later: "Poetry and prose are two polarities, indivisible one from another." [7]

The lyrical prose of the early Pasternak is a phenomenon quite different from the attempts of Andrei Biely, for instance, to synthesize prose and verse. Whereas Biely tried to impose certain metrical patterns on prose narration to make it rhythmical, Pasternak tries to use specifically poetic means to construct the *semantics* of the text. Precisely because attention is focused on the meaning of words, such components of normal prose works as plot, dialogue, or character have no relevance for the author. In this sense Pasternak's prose fragments written around 1910 are just as much an experimental field for his poetry as a laboratory for his subsequent prose. There is no doubt about the spontaneous and improvised nature of the sketches. They are verbal improvisations, just as improvisations on the piano, which still occupied him at this time, are exercises in musical logic.

Another important characteristic of these experiments is that fiction is indivisibly bound up with nonfictional self-expression: landscape sketches and embryonic elements of plot are interspersed with philosophical and aesthetic ruminations. The unfolding of the literary text is complicated here by unceasing "metatextual" self-commentary. Most of these prose fragments are as much theoretical reflections on the nature of art and its relation to life as they are works of literature. For that reason their central protagonist, Relikvimini, turns out to be an artist in the widest sense of the word—he is a "lyricist." Overflowing with impressions of life and unable to withstand their pressure, he starts to engrave them everywhere, on the street, on the pavement.[8] At the same time, all things are seen as longing to be depicted; the particular medium is a matter of indifference. The aesthetic conception behind these fragments highlights three components in the process of artistic creativity. First there is "reality without motion," inanimate things all around (which, much later, in *Safe Conduct* Pasternak calls "still-life models"). Then, rushing to meet them, there is pure lyricism, "motion without reality," which yearns for embodiment; this could be called the "lyrics of things." The third stage is "the movement of reality," a synthesis of both poles. Pasternak defines it as the drive of music after itself. In order to sew together the inanimate, motionless world and pure lyrics (understood as motion), the "life of the artist" is required. But Pasternak conceives of the life of the artist not as something autonomous and external; the artist for him is not an agent but a component part of the elemental process of transforming reality into art, a means of uniting them.[9] It thus becomes clear why for one of his characters the author chose the name Koinonievich.

Significantly, this triad forms a striking parallel to the structure of the process of cognition as portrayed by Paul Natorp in his work on psychology. The contents of consciousness in Natorp turn out to be, in Pasternak, the "still-life models," inanimate things, subjects for realization. The "I" of the subject in Natorp is, in Pasternak, "pure lyricism." Finally, the "cognizability" of objects in Natorp is, in Pasternak, "the movement of reality," the life of the artist, Koinonievich.

We do not know exactly when these prose fragments were written. But it would still be incorrect to evaluate this parallel with Natorp as proof of Pasternak's slavish dependence. Pasternak's works are marked by similarities and coincidences rather than by imitation or by the mechanical application of extraneous theoretical postulates. In general, both on the theoretical and the purely artistic plane, the fragments of 1910–1913 clearly display an author's idiosyncrasies. Whose pupil this particular author is it is impossible to say with certainty. Their language and style create the impression that the sketches might be of some unknown foreign origin, translations from a nonexistent western language. These works do point in the direction of Scandinavian literature, so popular in Russia at the beginning of the twentieth century.[10] But even this association does little to explain the distinguishing characteristics of this prose. With regard to literary technique, Pasternak here must be called an autodidact. In both the prose sketches and the poems of this period, we observe the slow and arduous process of differentiating literature from syncretic intellectual creativity.

From the fall of 1910, Pasternak, as well as a number of other Moscow poets of his generation, were associated with the newly established symbolist publishing house Musagetes. In 1946 he wrote: "The poetic culture of our age in any country of the world, including Russia and Georgia, is a natural outgrowth of symbolism and all the schools, both friendly and hostile, which have derived from it."[11] In view of this statement, the relationship between Pasternak and the poets of his circle to the symbolism is a key question. The founding of Musagetes was connected with the general crisis in Russian symbolism. At the end of 1909, *Libra,* the militant organ of the symbolist poets, ceased publication. Its editor Valery Briusov joined the well-established, academic "thick" journal *Russian Thought,* a move perceived as a betrayal of the modernist camp. In Petersburg the young poets who had attacked symbolist poetics and metaphysical themes, and espoused clarity, certainty, and exactitude of poetic language, rallied around the new journal *Apollon* (Apollo). But the clearest manifestation of the decline of the symbolist movement was the debate that involved its most prominent leaders in 1910. Briusov declared that symbolism was a literary school that had set purely literary goals. Now that it had achieved them, it had exhausted itself. In contrast, Ivanov and Blok in Petersburg, and Biely and Ellis in Moscow, asserted that the nature of symbolism had never been limited to narrowly aesthetic tasks, that its aim was the transformation of life and that herein lay its essential kinship with religion and mysticism.

The publishing house Musagetes was conceived as an attempt to unite the symbolist forces and to avert the school's erosion. It was to revive the movement by advancing symbolist theory on the firm basis of the latest philosophical currents. Andrei Biely emerged as the central figure at Musagetes. In 1909–11 all his activity was directed toward formulating the fundamental concepts of symbolist theory with the aid of German neo-Kantian philosophy. Having drawn close to the circles of Moscow philosophers in 1907–08 and having energetically taken part in their debates, Biely was the only one among the Russian symbolists who undertook such a vast assignment. His work answered the demands of young poets that the aesthetic theory of symbolism represent not a mere repetition of slogans inherited from decadence or early symbolism, but a reexamination of European culture in the light of new philosophical doctrines.

In this regard, the Musagetes program grappled with the same questions that led Pasternak to the philosophy department at Moscow University and in 1912 prompted him to go to Marburg. In addition, one of the distinctive features of the publishing house was its work with beginning writers. The "agitation for symbolism" by Andrei Biely and Ellis among the youth was expressed in the spring of 1911 by the Musagetes publication of *Anthology,* a poetry almanac that included not only such celebrities as Blok, Biely, Ivanov, Gorodetsky, and Ellis, but also novice poets such as Marina Tsvetaeva, Sergei Bobrov, Sergei Durylin, Alexei Sidorov, and Vladislav Khodasevich. Aside from the publishing opportunity, something else attracted young writers to Musagetes. These were three seminars organized at the publishing house in the fall of 1910. One of them, under the direction of Fyodor Stepun, a young neo-Kantian philosopher who had just graduated from Heidelberg University, was devoted to Kant's aesthetics. The second seminar explored Russian prosody in light of Biely's pioneering article, "Lyric Poetry and Experiment" (1909), which laid the foundations for the scientific study of versification in Russia and paved the way for the Russian formalists. Biely led this seminar and about fifteen people took part, including Durylin, Sidorov, and Bobrov, all frequenters of the Anisimov salon. The third group, which Ellis conducted, was devoted to the history of symbolism in Europe and focused on French poetry.

On November 1, 1910, Pasternak attended a lecture by Biely at M. K. Morozova's home, on "Tragedy in Dostoevsky's Works." [12] This lecture, which had been arranged by the Moscow Religious-Philosophical Society, proved to be a particularly significant event for the symbolists, since it was the occasion for the reconciliation of Biely and Blok, with the result that the latter subsequently joined Musagetes.

Of the three seminars sponsored by Musagetes in the fall of 1910, Pasternak attended only the one on Kant. This meeting offered him the possibility of looking at Kant not from the standpoint of academic philosophy but in light of new artistic currents. Neither the history of French symbolism (the reading of Baudelaire in Ellis' seminar) nor Biely's rhythmic studies interested him. In 1910 philosophical studies, it seems, were still more important than his attempts to write poetry and prose. Thus, while clearly sympathizing with the goals of the new publisher, Pasternak was somewhat removed from its purely literary concerns, attracted primarily by philosophical and aesthetic problems.

What was Pasternak's attitude toward Russian symbolism at this time? For him, symbolist poetry was the latest word in art, and its new horizons fascinated him. Its stylistic techniques offered an unprecedented fusion of poetry and music, something of particular importance to a person with his musical attachments. As for content, symbolism developed new methods of treating psychological, philosophical, and religious-mystical themes. But when we compare Pasternak's early literary efforts with the symbolists' poetry, it is impossible to detect any direct symbolist influence either in content or in technique. No matter how enthusiastically the young poet responded to new artistic phenomena, he always maintained a distance, even in his first steps as a writer. Like the symbolists, he sought points of contact between music and verse, but the very concept of poetic musicality lay on another plane for him. If for Balmont, Briusov, Biely, or Sologub, sound repetition played the main role and word meaning a subordinate one, for Pasternak the "musical" principle of unfolding the text was applied first of all to the semantics of the poem; sound repetitions had only an auxiliary function.[13] As for content, the sole theme Pasternak inherited directly from the symbolist poets was that theme of the modern city. But even his urbanism lacks specifically symbolist characteristics. All "metaphysical" or philosophical problems connected with modern civilization and its terrifying social ills are simply absent. In his depiction of the city Pasternak limits himself to the activity of a landscape artist, avoiding all ideological generalizations or mythologizing.

With the exception of Valery Briusov (with whom he met on various occasions from 1914 to 1924), Pasternak never mentions the representatives of the first generation of Russian symbolists—Merezhkovsky, Zinaida Hippius, Alexander Dobroliubov, and Konstantin Balmont—the poets who made their literary debut in the 1890s. Apparently their behavior and the decadence and épatage that characterized their work were unappealing.[14] Sergei Bobrov and his friends would later often mention another poet of this generation, Ivan Konevskoy, as one of their mentors. This was clearly done in opposition to the symbolist establishment. But there is no firm basis for determining Konevskoy's influence on Pasternak. As far as Briusov is concerned, despite the complimentary poem written by Pasternak in honor of his fiftieth birthday in 1923, and despite the obvious reverence he felt toward this legendary figure, Briusov's poetry never excited him very much.

As for the second generation of symbolists, the only poet Pasternak praised without reservation during these years (and for the rest of his life) was Alexander Blok. Pasternak's literary circle in Moscow was under the spell of the Blok cult (the young poets in Petersburg were less affected). Echoes of Blok's poems appear in Pasternak's first collection, *A Twin in the Clouds*. Nevertheless, it would be an exaggeration to state that Blok influenced Pasternak's poetics at the time of the latter's literary debut; the abyss between their poetic systems is too great. This lack of influence is all the more significant since some works of his friends (such as Anisimov) do show a very strong dependence on Blok's diction.

Such an indisputable mentor of the young poets as Viacheslav Ivanov left no discernible trace in Pasternak's development. Pasternak had a rather indifferent attitude toward Ivanov's poetry, and his deliberately archaic verse style had no impact as it did have, for example, on Aseev or Bobrov. But Ivanov's essays on literature and his philological studies undoubtedly seemed challenging to Pasternak. His personal encounters with Ivanov occurred in the summer of 1914, when Pasternak had already developed as a poet and, even more important, had gained his reputation as a futurist.[15]

Next to Blok, Andrei Biely was the second most important poet for Pasternak among his older contemporaries. He was always personally closer to Biely than to any of the other symbolist poets. Yet his attitude toward Biely's work was far more ambivalent than it was toward Blok's. On the one hand, like everyone else he was impressed by Biely's erudition and insatiable interest in every new discovery in science, philosophy, and culture. Biely seemed to feel equally at home in modern German philosophy, mathematics, physics, zoology, the history of religion, medieval mysticism, or psychology. There is no doubt that it was precisely Biely's encyclopedic range of interests and his fervent conviction that symbolism had absorbed all the achievements of modern civilization that attracted the young to Musagetes just at the time when the turmoil in Russian symbolism had become so palpable. That is why Pasternak later was not at all hypocritical when he described himself as Biely's pupil. When his contemporaries in Moscow came to be divided into the two camps around Briusov and Biely, Pasternak leaned toward the latter. Yet his praise of Biely was always tempered by critical reservations, which were occasionally very sharp. Even as a student, he recognized the dilettantism of Biely's philosophical views, the insufficient grounding of his theoretical speculations (which, nevertheless, was accompanied by remarkable insight), and his chaotic eclecticism. In the 1920s he grew extremely critical of Biely's later prose. This attitude was in strong contrast to the majority of young Soviet prose writers.

The period of initial unity in Musagetes continued for only a short time. In November 1910 Biely embarked on a long trip abroad, and after his return to Moscow in the fall of 1911 he no longer devoted so much energy to Musagetes and its seminars. In his later memoirs he said: "For me, 'Musagetes' expired in the fall of 1910."[16] Ellis, meanwhile, distanced himself from Biely and Metner, and relocated his seminar on symbolism to the studio of his friend, the sculptor Konstantin Krakht. The young people there, who continued to meet even after Ellis' departure abroad in the spring of 1911, soon acquired the name of Young Musagetes. But it was these gatherings that fostered, according to Biely, opposition to Musagetes among the younger generation. We have no evidence that Pasternak met with the Young Musagetes before his trip to Marburg or after his return in the fall of 1912. But on February 10, 1913, in Krakht's studio, Pasternak gave his first public talk. He delivered a paper on "Symbolism and Immortality" at a session of the Circle for the Study of the Problems of Aesthetic Culture and Symbolism in Art. Little is known about this circle,[17] but it evidently grew out of Ellis' old seminar.

The contents of Pasternak's paper first became known through its drastically revised summary in the *Essay in Autobiography*. The original theses (which Pasternak circulated before his talk) were discovered later and provide a more exact accounting of the report.[18] It turns out that, in comparison with the retrospective summary by the author, the paper was much less concerned with purely literary themes; it was semiliterary and semiphilosophical in nature. Thus it was reminiscent of the paper on Natorp that Pasternak had just written. In both, Pasternak started with the idea of autonomous, suprapersonal subjectivity, inherent in all things, "subjectivity without the subject." Since subjectivity, according to Pasternak, is not a property of the individual subject but a characteristic of the phenomenological world, then consciousness, and therefore immortality, is inherent in the very qualities of inanimate objects. This is revealed within the "aesthetic phase" or, in other words, when (to use the terminology from Pasternak's prose fragments) the life of the artist creates the movement of reality: when it sews together the inanimate world and pure lyricism. By stating in his paper of February 1913 that symbolism is concerned with this aesthetic phase, Pasternak indirectly refers to articles by Biely, "Critical Philosophy and Symbolism," [19] and by Ivanov, "Thoughts on Symbolism," [20] in which the main principle of symbolism is called "unification" and allusion is made to the etymology of the Greek word *symballein* (to join together, unite).

The paper's correspondence with the theories of Biely and Ivanov goes beyond this, however. To begin with, symbolism is understood by Pasternak not as a particular literary school but as a characterization of art in general.[21] Second, he rejects the opposition of symbolism and realism, which had become a burning issue in the literary polemics of the day. Such an opposition was destined to lose all meaning as soon as symbolism was declared to be an eternal property of culture and not a specific, historically conditioned movement. It was for this reason, to give an example, that Biely, in his essay of 1908, "Symbolism and Modern Russian Art," concentrated on artistic phenomena that blurred the distinction between realism and symbolism. He claimed that such examples as Chekhov or Briusov in his novel *Fiery Angel* proved that realism and symbolism are organically interconnected.[22] In his essay "Thoughts on Symbolism" Ivanov approached the problem of realism differently, but even his famous formulation of symbolism's artistic method (*a realibus ad realiora,* from reality to the more real) implied a rejection of the dichotomy between symbolism and realism. In this context it seems natural that, in February 1913, while reflecting on the process of artistic creativity, Pasternak also attributes a realistic character to symbolism and adds: "Symbolism achieves realism in religion," once again echoing Biely and Ivanov, who had advanced the theurgist nature of art.

Despite the fact that there are no direct references to Ivanov, Biely,

or Ellis in the theses, it can be said that all of Pasternak's pronouncements on symbolism are thoroughly permeated by their terminology.
This section of the report is literally written in their "language." But,
strange to say, Pasternak imbues their concepts with a new content,
one that challenges the very foundations of symbolist theory. Whereas
Biely and Ivanov stressed symbolism's intent to surpass the limits of
mere art, and whereas they understood the role of the artist as a "religious demiurge of life," Pasternak resolved the problem of the relationship of art to reality in a different way. Returning to an idea discussed in his early prose fragments, that the poet is not an "agens,"
but a "patiens," he claims that symbolic properties are revealed not
in the artist's works but in things themselves, which "demand artistic
embodiment." (It is for this reason that later, in *Safe Conduct,* he
offers the syncretic definition: "Art is realistic as a process and symbolic as a fact." [23]) With this, Pasternak overturns the entire system of
concepts on which the theory of the symbolist school was based.

It is therefore impossible to state unequivocally whether Pasternak
solidarizes himself in this report with the theory of symbolism, or
whether he distances himself from it. It would be most correct to say
that he does both. We subsequently discover such a profoundly ambivalent attitude to the events and phenomena of literary life (and not
only literary life) in almost all of the poet's statements. But, whatever
the case may be, it is important that the chief protagonist of Pasternak's first public literary or theoretical talk was "symbolism." The
poet, who had yet to appear in print, begins with an outline of his
position vis-à-vis symbolism, a movement already in decline. In this
sense, it is all the more paradoxical that he linked the concept of
symbolism to immortality.[24]

The weeks preceding Pasternak's report witnessed the stormy emergence of two new modernist movements, acmeism and futurism, both
of which were hostile to symbolism (and to each other). Why, then,
did Pasternak connect his talk about poetry and immortality with
symbolism, as if to immortalize it, rather than discussing these two
more recent schools? Symbolism was for Pasternak not simply a literary phenomenon, like the new schools, but a synonym for a whole
epoch in art, an expression of innovative thinking and aesthetics. Special importance was attached to the idea of syncretism in art; both
the symbolists and Scriabin were equally obsessed with it. Pasternak
experienced this idea biographically, so to speak, insofar as he had
experimented with drawing, music, and philosophy, before finally

turning to poetry. These phases did not simply mark a changing succession of external masks, but a process of internal evolution and spiritual growth. Each new stage did not cancel the previous ones, but absorbed them.

Thus the paper on "Symbolism and Immortality" epitomized Pasternak's thoughts over a number of years about the inner relationship of music, philosophy, and poetry. In light of the report, his extravagant and unexpected actions, such as his breaks with music and philosophy, appear to be mature decisions, the fruits of unceasing intellectual quest. The turn to literature forced him to discard the symbolist idea of the primacy of music among the arts. In one of the fragments from this time, he calls this idea a prejudice.[25] Music has its own "inferiority complex": musicians have always, Pasternak says, "been inclined toward philosophy." Although Pasternak names only Beethoven in this context (and suggests Scriabin), this sentence provides a key to understanding his own early years. From the theses of "Symbolism and Immortality," it becomes clear that this inclination is caused by music's desire to discover the "meaning" of its rhythm. Nowhere can this meaning be found except in the word. But in order to achieve it, philosophical analysis is insufficient. Only poetry, which shares the same foundation as music, rhythm, can reveal the meaning of musical language.

"Symbolism and Immortality" was addressed to young poets, primarily to those Pasternak could meet at the Anisimov home. (Not one of the older symbolist poets came to the talk.) But the Anisimov soirées had changed since 1909–1911, the years of Serdarda. Then a semi-Bohemian salon with ever-changing membership, toward the beginning of 1913 the Anisimov group evolved into a literary circle with a smaller but more stable number of participants, determined to found their own publishing house. Dependence on Musagetes and the symbolist mentors was much less unconditional than it had been in 1910.

From all appearances, the circle was formed in the spring, after Pasternak's report in Krakht's studio. As a poet Pasternak seemed much less mature than other members of the circle. Yulian Anisimov's poems had already appeared in the journal *Sovremennik* (The Contemporary), and in the spring of 1913 he had published his first poetry collection. Semen Rubanovich and Sergei Durylin had published some time before. Alexei Sidorov, who was studying at Moscow University and who was later to become a major Soviet art historian, had by 1910 published his first book jointly with Alexei Baranov, another member of Musagetes.

The presence of Sergei Bobrov changed the nature of the Anisimov gatherings. He played a prominent role in the development of the Russian literary avant-garde, but, with the exception of Vladimir Markov's monograph,[26] he is rarely mentioned by scholars of this period. Sergei Bobrov (1889–1971) was born in Moscow into the family of a comptroller of the Moscow State Fund, who also was a famous chess player. His parents soon divorced. Sergei later told of his unhappy childhood in the autobiographical novella *The Boy*. The misfortunes and deprivations he had endured made him envious and argumentative, but at the same time ambitious and stubborn in the pursuit of his established goals. He studied at the Moscow School of Painting, Sculpture, and Architecture, in the "department of general education," which had been specially designed for children from indigent families. In his youth he was attracted equally by poetry and painting. As an artist he had ties to the most radical segments of the Russian avant-garde, and he was friendly with Goncharova, Larionov, and Tatlin. At the exhibition of the Donkey's Tail group in Moscow, his *Nature morte* hung next to their works and some by Marc Chagall and Kazimir Malevich. On December 31, 1911, as a representative of Donkey's Tail, Bobrov read a paper on modern Russian painting.[27] He made his debut in print as a poet with "Spiritus," which was published at the end of 1908 in N. Shebuev's journal *Vesna* (Spring).

His acquaintance with Biely and Briusov gave a powerful impetus to Bobrov's literary activities. Starting in 1910 he became one of the most zealous participants in Biely's metric seminars. Here he proved to be the most capable of Biely's pupils. The metric studies he began at that time were continued throughout his life, and they won high praise from specialists. Along with other members of the Young Musagetes, Bobrov contributed to the *Anthology* of 1911. At this time he began to visit the Anisimovs' salon. As Pasternak states in his second autobiography, Bobrov's appearance "was preceded by his reputation as a newly-hatched Russian Rimbaud."[28] Bobrov was infatuated with Rimbaud's poetry and (on Biely's advice) had begun to translate it. But Pasternak's comment contains some sarcasm as well, hinting at Bobrov's pretentiousness, his quarrelsome character, and the series of scandals that accompanied his early literary career. In the end, Bobrov did not excel in either painting or literature. His poems were not published after the beginning of the 1920s (when he wrote his best, unpublished, book *I Breathe*). From 1922 to 1931 he turned out three adventure novels that enjoyed no success and were quickly forgotten.

It was Bobrov who became the driving force for the publishing projects in the Anisimov group. Feeling himself a pariah among his well-to-do and better-educated contemporaries, he nevertheless possessed the temperament and ambitions of an organizer and leader; his contemporaries compared him in this regard with David Burliuk, "the father of Russian futurism." In order to win himself a reputation, he needed his own literary group much more than, for example, Anisimov or Durylin, who already had strong ties to the literary world. Bobrov's loyal associate was Nikolai Aseev, a novice poet from the provinces. Bobrov met him at a soirée in 1911 at the Shebuev home, and they became close friends.[29] The poems that constituted Aseev's first book, *Nocturnal Flute*, were well-received in the Anisimov circle. The group's first publication, the almanac *Lirika* (Lyrics), appeared in May 1913. It contained five poems each by Anisimov, Aseev, Bobrov, Pasternak, Raevsky (this was Durylin's pseudonym), Rubanovich, Sidorov, and Vera Stanevich. The collection was produced on a cooperative basis, and the publishing house was given the same name as the almanac. Bobrov designed the cover of the book and the publisher's logo. There were no introductions or manifestos in the book, but the epigraph was from Viacheslav Ivanov, and one of Bobrov's poems was taken to be a tribute to symbolism. Otherwise there was no symbolist content whatsoever. Judging by its verse techniques and themes, much of the collection is a pale imitation of clichéd poetry of the presymbolist period. Least typical, and least understandable, were the poems by Pasternak, who was appearing in print for the first time. Immediately after the almanac, Bobrov's first collection, *Gardeners over the Vines*, was released.

The first books published by Lirika did nothing to distinguish it from the other publications of the time. Around 1910 there was an epidemic of poetry writing. "Statistics will show that never before has there been such a harvest of poets in Russia," wrote one poet-satirist. "Do you think that hearts have become more sensitive, springs more beautiful, and that nightingales sing more sweetly than ever before? Nothing of the sort. It is a case of neurasthenia, on the one hand, and the terrible laziness of our age, on the other. You must study in order to play the violin. You must take lessons in order to decorate porcelain. But to write poetry you simply need ink and paper." [30] The works making their debut with Lirika were particularly inconspicuous against the background of the stormy and sensational performances by the new literary groups of 1912–13 (ego-futurists, cubo-futurists, acmeists) with their impudent slogans and scandalous demands to overthrow the old idols.

Announcements appearing in Lirika's first books give valuable information about the group's plans. An interesting fact emerges: in catalogues from May 1913, a long list of books being prepared for publication mentions Aseev's *Nocturnal Flute* but makes no mention of Pasternak's first book of verse, *Bliznets v tuchakh* (A Twin in the Clouds), which appeared simultaneously in December. The catalogue does list, however, a collection of articles, *Symbolism and Immortality*, which was never published. Evidently the majority of poems in *A Twin in the Clouds* were written in the summer of 1913. But there may be another reason: Anisimov and Bobrov, the leaders of the group, were still skeptical about Pasternak's poetic work, and they thought of him much as they did his university classmate, Konstantin Loks, as more of a theoretician than a poet. Those with less influence in the group—Durylin, Loks, Aseev—had more sympathy for Pasternak's early poems.

Meanwhile it was announced that Pasternak would contribute (along with Anisimov, Stanevich, and Sidorov) to the second Lirika anthology, which was to be devoted to translations of modern German poets: Stefan George, Rainer Maria Rilke, Richard Dehmel, and others. This miscellany was scheduled for the fall, but it never appeared. It was evidently supposed to contain Pasternak's translations from Rilke's *Buch der Bilder;* rough drafts of these translations were found in the 1960s and were published by Elena Pasternak. [31] In the Anisimov circle, it was Pasternak who was the most ardent admirer of this German poet. But, as a translator, Pasternak lagged behind his comrades at Lirika. By this time Anisimov had already prepared one book of verse and one of prose by Rilke. At the end of the year Alexei Sidorov published his translation of Goethe's *Geheimnisse;* Bobrov's translation of Aloysius Bertrand's *Gaspard de la nuit* was ready and scheduled for publication, as were Loks' translation of "Isid and Osyris" by Plutarch of Chaeronea, and *Catholic Hymns of the Twelfth, Thirteenth, and Fourteenth Centuries* in Durylin's translation.

What prompted the group to choose the name Lirika not only for their first book but for their publishing house? Given the garish titles of the time (Scorpio, Libra, Musagetes, Apollo, Hylaea, the Mezzanine of Poetry), it seemed particularly unpretentious. That the name was carefully selected is shown by the fact that lyricism was a central theme in articles published by the group's members in various places at the time. Thus Durylin's review of Anisimov's *Cloister* was given the title, "Lyrical Agitation." [32] But if for Durylin (and for Anisimov) the concept of lyricism or "lyrical fire" was identical to the concept of poetic inspiration or sincerity, Sergei Bobrov invested lyricism with a more detailed and technical meaning. He was influenced in his thinking by the recently published article by Ivanov, "On the Essence of Tragedy," whose concluding passages were devoted to the specific characteristics of lyrical poetry. Ivanov introduced here the concept of the lyrical theme in a new sense: not as a synonym for a poem's content but as an element of its *formal* structure (that is, as this term is used in musical terminology).[33] Depending on whether a given poem is built on two or three themes (according to Ivanov), it can be attributed either to the Dionysian or to the Apollonian type of art. In his article "On the Lyrical Theme," written in the fall of 1913, Bobrov amended Ivanov's conception. In every poem there are three themes: of content, form, and lyricism. In their turn, the themes of form and content are composed of a multitude of minor themes. The lyrical theme, however, is indivisible and it permeates the other two. A lyrical poem is understood by Bobrov to be the unceasing and multidirectional movement of monads (that is, of form and content themes) throughout the entire text of the poem. It is through this motion that the poem's "lyrical expanse" comes into being, and this expanse unites the poet and the reader (here Bobrov cites Mallarmé).

Bobrov's article is remarkable because of the huge gap between the audacity and sophistication of his theoretical ideas and the epigonic character of his poetry during this period. But even more notable is the fact that these ideas are akin to the peculiarities of Pasternak's poetry, and there is some reason to think that the article appeared as a result of Bobrov's reflections on Pasternak's poetics. Moreover, there is no doubt that the article was formulated in the course of conversations with Pasternak. Direct evidence of this dialogue is the poem "Lirichesky prostor" (Lyrical Expanse), written by Pasternak in September 1913. Unlike Bobrov, Pasternak explains lyrical expanse without any connection to the concept of "reader": it is simply the realm of the pure movement of lyrical monads .[34] One can therefore trace the evolution in Bobrov's and Pasternak's writings of an idea originally introduced by Ivanov. One can also see the magnitude of the distance separating the interpretation of lyricism within the group's two different wings: Anisimov and Durylin on one side, Bobrov and Pasternak on the other. Taken in such a strictly technical sense, the term lyricism made it irrelevant whether a given poem was symbolist or not or, more broadly, whether its author was a symbolist. It is worth noting that the concept of lyricism surfaces throughout Pasternak's early prose works, long before the name Lirika was chosen and even before Pasternak began to write poetry. But he was attributing the property not to verbal, literary texts but to all objects in the real world, and it became a synonym for "free subjectivity" (later a theme in his talk "Symbolism and Immortality"). All of this compels us to acknowledge that Pasternak's role in formulating the theoretical positions of Lirika was quite formidable indeed.

4

In the Futurist Camp

The increasing similarity between Pasternak's and Bobrov's theoretical positions coincided with changes in the Lirika circle. In the summer of 1913, after his graduation from the university, Pasternak wrote the poems that would comprise his first book. At this time Aseev and Bobrov became the members of the circle who were closest to him. Bobrov liked Pasternak's new poems more than the earlier ones, and it was he who suggested publishing them as a separate book. He and Aseev selected the material for *A Twin in the Clouds*.

After the publication of the first miscellany, tensions arose within Lirika over attempts to start a journal. It became clear that in the complex literary situation of the time it would be impossible to work out a united position, without which a journal was unthinkable. All the members of the group were then critical of, if not disgusted with, the futurist group Hylaea (Burliuk, Kruchonykh, Mayakovsky, Khlebnikov) and rejected not only the stylistic innovations in their poetry, but also the vulgarity of their public behavior and the outrageous nature of their manifestos and pronouncements. But there was no such unity with regard to the older generation of symbolist poets. Whereas Bobrov reacted ecstatically to Briusov's newest poems, Anisimov was shocked by Briusov's betrayal of the ideals of theurgist symbolism, as well as by Briusov's favorable evaluations of the newly formed antisymbolist groups. Even sharper disagreements emerged over attitudes to their former teachers, Biely and Ellis, who had turned to anthroposophy. During their travel abroad, the Anisimov couple had met with Ellis and Biely and were themselves attracted to Rudolf Steiner's teachings.[1] As a result, anthroposophic problems began to replace literary themes in the evening gatherings at the Anisi-movs'. Bobrov had an instinctive hatred for the occult and mysticism. Anthroposophy was just as alien to Aseev, with his interest in ancient rural culture and folk poetry. The solid training Pasternak had received in critical philosophy fostered in him, as well, a skepticism toward the fashionable Steiner craze.

The assessment of anthroposophy was not the only issue that produced divisions within Lirika. All its members were of course shaken by the lukewarm, if not outright negative, reception given its first publications. But Bobrov was especially troubled. Partially due to the influence of Pasternak's idiosyncratic style, and partially due to the swiftly changing literary situation in Moscow in 1913 and the ever greater triumphs of the most radical modernist groups, Bobrov's poetry "moved to the left" and from the autumn began to take on more clearly expressed avant-gardist overtones. Bobrov made contact with Ivan Ignatiev, the leader of the Petersburg ego-futurists, and received an invitation to join in their publishing efforts. This alliance was supposed to start with their seventh almanac, *Vsegdai* (The Alwayser), which was published in the early autumn; Bobrov entered into the coalition not alone, but with Pasternak: it was proposed that the almanac publish Pasternak's poem "Vokzal" (The Station), which Bobrov particularly liked. But evidently because of opposition from the Moscow ego-futurist Vadim Shershenevich, who was an avowed enemy of Lirika, neither Bobrov nor Pasternak appeared in *The Alwayser*. One article and a few poems by Bobrov were printed only later, in December 1913, in the ninth almanac published by the Petersburg ego-futurists, which bore the name *Razvorochennye cherepa* (Shattered Skulls); Shershenevich boycotted this issue. Bobrov's appearance in the organ of the Petersburg futurists and Pasternak's near-appearance is evidence of their dissatisfaction with the situation at Lirika and of their search for new allies. It is noteworthy that traces of ego-futurist diction in Pasternak's poems are more strongly felt at this time than in Bobrov's work, and these elements survived right up to 1916.

The schism within Lirika occurred in the winter. On January 22, 1914, six of its members—Anisimov, Stanevich, Durylin, Rubanovich, Loks, and Sidorov—were sent a letter signed by the Provisional Extraordinary Committee of Centrifuge. The letter announced the dissolution of the Lirika publishers. The name of the new group Tsentrifuga (Centrifuge), was suggested by Bobrov, who headed the rebellion. In answer to the letter, the five addressees who were in Moscow met and passed a resolution expelling the rebels, Aseev, Bobrov, and Pasternak. This resolution proved to be a purely symbolic gesture, since the group was never again reconstituted. But passions ran high, and the conflict became so heated that Pasternak was forced to challenge Yulian Anisimov to a duel.[2] The last books published by Lirika came out just before Christmas: Aseev's *Nocturnal Flute*, Pasternak's *A Twin in the Clouds*, and Goethe's *Geheimnisse* in Sidorov's translation. Although only a minority left the group (three against six), in the publisher's overall production of 1913 the books of the "left opposition" clearly outweighed those of their opponents.

Many years later in *Safe Conduct* Pasternak emphasized the absence of clear-cut boundaries between the "innovators" and the "epigones" in the period in question. The history of the emergence of the innovative Centrifuge out of the epigonic Lirika is a good illustration of this observation. Centrifuge was conceived as a deliberate break with the symbolist past. Even a short while before, in the spring of 1913, such a concept would have been unthinkable for Bobrov: symbolism was still for him the most advanced and innovative school in art. The tempestuous changes in literary life during the intervening months, marked by the feverish regrouping of participants in the various literary camps, forced him to move outside the waning symbolist school, to seek allies among its young and audacious opponents.

As is well known, the word "futurism" was first used in Russia in the term "ego-futurism," coined by Igor Severianin and the group of young poets he headed in 1911. In January 1912 they founded the Academy of Ego-Poetry (Universal Futurism) and the newspaper *Petersburg Herald*. In the fall of 1912 Severianin left the group around *Petersburg Herald* and its leader became Ivan Ignatiev. The more radical group of poets and artists, which had existed from 1910 and was known by the name Hylaea—the Burliuk brothers, Benedikt Livshits, Velimir Khlebnikov, Vasily Kamensky, and Elena Guro—avoided the label "futurism" for a long time because of their unwillingness to create the impression that they were related to the Italian futurists. In the fall of 1912 the Hylaeans were joined by Vladimir Mayakovsky, a classmate of David Burliuk at the Moscow School of Painting. In December 1912 this group published its notorious manifesto and miscellany *Poshchechina obshchestvennomu vkusu* (A Slap in the Face of Public Taste), whose violent slogans prompted the Russian press to draw a parallel with Marinetti's group in Italy. Russian critics began to apply the term "futurism" equally to the Burliuk group and to ego-futurism. It was precisely in this way that Briusov used the term in March 1913 in his annual survey of current Russian poetry. A few months later, in August 1913, in the almanac *Dokhlaia luna* (The Croaked Moon), the Hylaeans finally adopted the name "futurists." At the same time, they began to be called by a new name, "cubo-futurists", whose prefix reflected the participation of the Bur-liuk brothers and Mayakovsky in art exhibitions influenced by French cubism. In his public lectures Mayakovsky drew an analogy between the principles of cubist painting and the verbal experiments of the Hylaeans.[3]

Relations between the two wings of Russian futurism were hostile. In essence, their aesthetic positions had little in common. The plat-form of the ego-futurists was based on the propagation of extreme individualism and "intuitionism", while for the cubo-futurists it was primitivism and "liberation of the word."

A new ego-futurist group emerged in Moscow in the middle of 1913. The twenty-year-old poet Vadim Shershenevich (son of the Moscow University law professor) decided to found, together with the artist and poet Lev Zak, his own group, the Mezzanine of Poetry, which was soon joined by several novice poets. The most talented and promising of them was also the youngest, eighteen-year-old Konstan-tin Bolshakov, who had already published two booklets of poetry. Toward the end of 1913, the influence of Mayakovsky's urbanist style began to be strongly felt in the writing of Shershenevich and Bol-shakov. In December, the Mezzanine of Poetry decided to unite with the group of cubo-futurists. Igor Severianin also joined this alliance for a few weeks. These changes created an unprecedented situation: instead of disparate groups, there was a united futurist front.

These sensational successes achieved by Mayakovsky and the cubo-futurists coincided with the disintegration of Lirika. Bobrov jealously followed the changes in the futurist champ, which now united his two powerful enemies, Shershenevich and Mayakovsky. Back in the spring of 1913, it was he who had blocked Shershenevich's acceptance into Lirika. In the first issue of his own almanac, Shershenevich sought revenge against the group that had rejected him by accusing its poets of epigonism.[4] This deeply offended Bobrov and Pasternak (whose poetry Shershenevich compared with that of Nadson, a second-rate poet of the nineteenth century, who personified, in the epoch of sym-bolism, all that was mediocre and banal in literature).

Partially in order to counterbalance this attack, Bobrov decided that the first books by Aseev and Pasternak, due to be published in the winter, should have prefaces stressing the independence of these young poets from symbolism and their devotion to artistic innovation. He wrote the foreword to Aseev's collection himself and asked Aseev to write the one to Pasternak's book. These prefaces, which took the place of the scandalizing manifestos in the futurist miscellanies, were filled with vague rhetoric, offered no concrete analysis of the authors' works, and in general lacked any connection with the contents of the book. They were subjected to ridicule in the press and thus were only harmful to the three founders of the future Centrifuge group. In her review of Pasternak's *A Twin in the Clouds* Marietta Shaginian wrote:

> This volume is published with a foreword by Nik. Aseev. Usually, forewords are written by people who are more or less known in readers' circles; a foreword then plays the role of a recommendation, and we learn in advance about the book, about its character, and about the significance of the author. But what would a reader say if, in an unfamiliar place, an unfamiliar person introduces another unfamiliar person? That's exactly what the unknown Aseevs together with the unknown Pasternaks are doing to us in the unknown Lirika.[5]

His embarrassment was so great that for the rest of his literary career Pasternak flatly refused to allow any forewords to his books, and he never wanted to write them for anyone else's books.

Bobrov allied himself with the group of Petersburg ego-futurists, Petersburg Herald, headed by Ivan Ignatiev, which had declined the invitation to enter into an alliance with the cubo-futurists in Hylaea. In November 1913 Ignatiev had already sent two of his poems to Bobrov for publication. Ignatiev's support was important not only because the rebels in Lirika had no other allies, but even more because of the unquestionably futurist, innovative, and antisymbolist reputation of Petersburg Herald. But on January 20, 1914, just when Centrifuge was announcing its break with Lirika, Ignatiev committed suicide (on the day after his wedding).

The Centrifuge publishing house was founded on March 1, 1914. Its first release was Sergei Bobrov's pamphlet *Lyrical Theme*. Following it, at the end of April, was the almanac *Rukonog* (Brachiopod). This strange name clearly meant to suggest its futurist character, although none of the three founders of the group had decided to apply the term to himself. The problem of futurism had become acute for

them because in March there appeared the first (and only) issue of
Pervyi zhurnal russkikh futuristov (First Journal of the Russian Futurists), a publication that arose as a result of the alliance between Hylaea and the Mezzanine of Poetry. To be more precise, it was a product of the union of Mayakovsky with Shershenevich and Bolshakov:
the other Hylaeans who were named as editors, David Burliuk and
Vasily Kamensky, took no part in preparing the issue. The review section (headed by Shershenevich) contained extremely abusive assessments of the publications from Lirika. The recently published books
by Aseev and Pasternak, as well as Bobrov's *Gardeners over the Vines,*
were called typical examples of symbolist epigonism, which the newly
united front of futurist innovators rejected with noble indignation.
Thus the entire coup d'état that had occurred in Lirika was simply
dismissed.

Meanwhile, judging both by the list of its contributors and the nature of the material it contained, *Brachiopod* had moved far away
from the *Lyrics* of 1913. A large portion of the poetry section was
devoted to the works of the Petersburg ego-futurists, including posthumous publications of Ivan Ignatiev and poems by Riurik Ivnev and
Vasilisk Gnedov. The poems of the founders of Centrifuge also differed decisively from their works of the previous year. In terms of
style, they were on a par with the work of their ego-futurist partners.
The radical poetic technique of Pasternak's three poems impresses
critics even now, and some scholars have gone so far as to compare
them to Khlebnikov's. This parallel does not seem convincing. These
texts are striking because of the abundance of lexical archaisms,
along with colloquialisms, the use of neologisms, recourse to specifically folkloric idiom, and also a play with sound repetitions that deliberately aims at obscuring meaning. But all these features more
likely stemmed from competition with Aseev—with whom Pasternak
was now sharing an apartment in Moscow—rather than from any
imitation of Khlebnikov. Besides verses by members of Petersburg
Herald, *Brachiopod* also contained the poetry of two unexpected
guests: Elizaveta Kuzmina-Karavaeva, a member of the Petersburg
Poets' Guild whose presence gave a slightly acmeist tinge to the miscellany, and the young Kharkov poet Bozhidar (Gordeev), whose experimental poem here was his first—and last—appearance in print as
a poet during his lifetime. He committed suicide at the age of twenty
on September 7 of the same year.

The greatest stir, however, was caused not by the poems but by the critical section and the manifestos of *Brachiopod*. The first manifesto, "Turbopaean," was written in verse by Bobrov[6] and looked incongruous because of its comical tone, self-glorification, and bombastic style. It was followed by "Charter," which was an unusually vicious (even for the futurist epoch) attack on the *First Journal of Russian Futurists*. "Charter" declared the journal's editors to be renegades, pretenders, cowards, and betrayers of the genuinely futurist doctrine of the dead Ignatiev. Following Marinetti, who had recently visited Russia, "Charter" labeled them "passéists." There were four signatures beneath the "Charter": Nikolai Aseev, Sergei Bobrov, Ilya Zdanevich, and Boris Pasternak. Even more unrestrained in tone were the anonymous chronicler's notes in *Brachiopod* concerning the *First Journal of Russian Futurists*. The main target of Bobrov's attacks was Shershenevich, who was not only accused of imitativeness but of direct plagiarism.

Much different in tone from these clamorous notes was Pasternak's article "Vassermanova reaktsia" (Wassermann Test), which occupied a central place in the almanac. This was his first openly polemical article, and it proved the last. Never again did Pasternak resort to personal critical attack, and abstention from direct polemics became one of the main principles of his literary conduct. That is why he never referred to this article. That is also why it was not included in the four-volume American edition of his writings edited by Gleb Struve and Boris Filippov, begun while the poet was still alive.[7] Still it is an extremely valuable document not only within the context of the history of futurism, but also for understanding the evolution of Pasternak himself. The point is not only that the negative assessment of Shershenevich's works is much more profound, calm, and well-grounded than Bobrov's cheap feuilleton witticisms. What is important is that for the first time Pasternak gives (however reluctantly) his own explanation of futurism, a term that had only recently gained widespread currency, that still contained contradictory meanings for his contemporaries, and that had not been acceptable for Centrifuge itself up to the last moment (even during the preparation of *Brachiopod*).

Pasternak begins by declaring the existence of two futurisms, one genuine and one false. As an example of true futurism he names without reservations Khlebnikov and "with a few reservations, Mayakovsky, and only to a certain degree Bolshakov and the poets from the Petersburg Herald group." This unexpected hierarchy testifies to

the poet's close attention to the futurist movement and to his understanding of its internal differences. Khlebnikov was singled out not
only because his work had appeared in more complete form than the
writings of any other futurist,[8] but because it was in Khlebnikov that
Pasternak saw an original and self-nurtured source of futurist ideas,
fostered by a man who refused to adapt to public tastes. As opposed
to the other futurists with their bizarre and clamorous public appearances, Khlebnikov impressed Pasternak with his self-absorption and
inward focus. Evidently Pasternak discovered a special enchantment
in Khlebnikov's poetry at that time. Josephine Pasternak recalled (in
a personal conversation with me) that her brother came into the children's bedroom at night and read her Khlebnikov's grasshopper poem
"Krylyshkuia zolotopismom" (Glitter-letter wing-winker)—which
was first published in *A Slap in the Face of Public Taste* and then in
Khlebnikov's *Works*.[9] This attraction is all the more significant in
view of the lack of any palpable evidence of Khlebnikov's influence
on Pasternak's work. In the context of early 1914, the characterization of Khlebnikov as a genuine futurist seemed to be a polemical
challenge: in the camp of the futurists, and particularly for Mayakovsky, Shershenevich, and Bolshakov, the theme of the big city
crowded out primitivist tendencies, and in this regard Shershenevich
considered Khlebnikov to be more of an anachronism than an example of innovation. By singling out Khlebnikov, Pasternak was
stressing not the popular but the timeless and eternal content in futurism.

An example of false futurism for Pasternak was Shershenevich. Pasternak mocks Shershenevich's painstaking and fussy turn to the motifs of everyday city life; he sees in this nothing more than a concession to the demands of the reading market. He criticizes not only the
content of Shershenevich's poems, but also his poetics. In analyzing
the most conspicuous traits of Shershenevich's style—the overabund-
ance of tropes, the deliberate cacophony of images from modern technology—Pasternak asserts that the root of all evil here is by no means
the shocking antiaestheticism of the metaphors (indeed this feature is
characteristic of genuine poets such as Mayakovsky and Bolshakov),
but the fact that the endless series of metaphors has no core or "lyrical theme." The very structure of the tropes exposes the absence of
artistic talent in Shershenevich's works. The only form of metaphor
available to him is the metaphor of similarity, whereas only the met-

aphor of contiguity, to use Pasternak's words, "has the trait of imperativeness and inner intensity which might justify the very use of metaphors."

We have here the essence of Pasternak's argument: besides the extremely perceptive characterization of Shershenevich's futurism, the article contains an oblique characterization of Pasternak's own method. To the metaphor of similarity Pasternak counterposes, as a more sophisticated lyrical device, metaphor by contiguity. Two decades later, the very same juxtaposition lay at the heart of the remarkable interpretation of Pasternak's literary method by Roman Jakobson.[10] The contents of "Wassermann Test" go beyond, therefore, the polemical goals set by Centrifuge. In general, the significance of the article is that, without rejecting any of the innovations of futurist poetry, it subordinates them to the inner demands of the lyrical work and not to the satisfaction of the reader's tastes or expectations. The juxtaposition of genuine and false futurism rests upon the implied juxtaposition of true poetry and its imitations.[11]

On May 2, 1914, immediately after the publication of *Brachiopod*, the editors of the *First Journal of Russian Futurists* sent Bobrov an angry letter (signed by Bolshakov, Mayakovsky, and Shershenevich) which demanded a face-to-face meeting within four days for negotiations over the slanderous insinuations in the almanac. The authors of the letter insisted that the delegation include Bobrov and Pasternak. Whereas Bobrov was inclined to talk his way out, it was Pasternak who insisted on arranging a meeting. The timing was far from opportune for Centrifuge. Nikolai Aseev, one of its founders and one of the four signatories of "Charter," had just abandoned Centrifuge. In addition, it soon emerged that one more signature beneath "Charter" was invalid: that of Ilya Zdanevich. In his search for support for the projected almanac, Bobrov turned for advice to his friend, the artist Mikhail Larionov, who assured him that Zdanevich's hatred for the Hylaeans guaranteed his solidarity with the Centrifuge manifesto. But Larionov either forgot to request direct authorization from Zdanevich or else received a categorical refusal.[12] Bobrov as editor of *Brachiopod* was forced to announce publicly in the newspaper *Nov* (Virgin Soil) that Zdanevich's signature was not authorized. As a result, besides Bobrov and Pasternak, Centrifuge had no other representatives to meet with the three editors of the *First Journal*. The delegation was forced to complement its ranks with the young poet Boris Kushner, a friend of Pasternak's who had no connection either with *Brachiopod* or with *Lyrics*.

The meeting of the two groups was held in the Café Grec, a favorite meeting place for Moscow's bohemians. In the course of the discussions Bobrov argued with Shershenevich, Kushner with Bolshakov, and Pasternak with Mayakovsky. As Pasternak explains in *Safe Conduct*, the representatives of Centrifuge suffered a resounding defeat. In 1967 Bobrov recalled that he and Pasternak left the meeting absolutely crushed, and for a long time afterward Boris remained angry at his friend for drawing Centrifuge into a senseless scandal. On the next day Pasternak accidentally met Mayakovsky at the same café, and the latter read him his tragedy *Vladimir Mayakovsky*. If on the day before Pasternak had for the first time discovered Mayakovsky and gained respect for him as a man, then on this occasion he discovered the full force of Mayakovsky's poetic genius.

As with other incidents involving Pasternak, it is difficult here to distinguish victory from defeat. As a result of the May meeting, several dramatic changes took place: the collapse of the fragile alliance between the Mezzanine of Poetry and the cubo-futurists, the separation of Mayakovsky from Shershenevich, and the rapprochement of Bolshakov, who was then Mayakovsky's close friend, with Centrifuge and, more important, with Pasternak.

In the literary circles of Moscow and Petersburg, *Brachiopod* was unquestionably considered another species of futurism. It was therefore with malicious relish that reviewers described the attacks of Centrifuge on the *First Journal of Russian Futurists*. The only one who turned his attention to the originality of Centrifuge's positive platform was Valery Briusov, whose evaluations of young poets carried enormous weight at that time. He devoted one of his articles in *Russian Thought,* to poets who had avoided the cubo- and ego-futurist extremes but who had, to one extent or another, been tainted by futurist experimentation. He called these poets "borderlanders" and included Centrifuge among them. Briusov referred to their break with Lirika[13] and stressed that the impact of futurist ideas on the Centrifuge poets was undeniable. Their futurism, however, was of a special type, insofar as it also respected previous literary traditions.

Briusov proceeded to analyze the books of poetry by the three founders of Centrifuge. Of the three he singled out Pasternak as "the most original." While noting that originality by no means signified that Pasternak's poems were of better quality or more mature than the poems of his fellow group members, Briusov also wrote: "Nevertheless, with Pasternak one feels the greatest power of imagination; his strange and at times awkward images do not seem artificial—the poet indeed felt and saw just that way; the 'futuristicity' of B. Pasternak's poems are not a matter of subordination to theory, but his own special kind of mentality." [14] In conclusion Briusov announced that, of all the futurists, he considered that Centrifuge had taken the most correct path.

After the humiliating dispute with Mayakovsky and Shershenevich, Briusov's review signified a victory for Centrifuge, all the more so since a year earlier he had felt that the poetry of Lirika was weak and eclectic. Pasternak was particularly moved by this article. Quite possibly it was Briusov's unexpected encouragement that made Pasternak refrain from breaking with Bobrov after the May meeting with Mayakovsky. Referring to this article, Pasternak tried to impress upon his friend that he should soften the polemical tone of his articles in order to attract other young poets to Centrifuge. [15] It is clear that Pasternak, who remained Bobrov's only close supporter after Aseev's defection, succeeded in his arguments.

External factors also aided the reinforcement of conciliatory tendencies within the avant-garde camp. On July 19 (August 1), 1914, World War I broke out, and tragic events soon pushed literary debate into the background. The declaration of war found Pasternak in the village of Petrovskoe on the Oka (not far from Tarusa), where he was living in a cottage rented by the Lithuanian-Russian poet Yurgis Baltrushaitis, one of the founders of the Russian symbolist movement. Pasternak was a tutor for the poet's eleven-year-old son. Nearby Konstantin Balmont was vacationing with his family, and Baltrushaitis was often visited by Viacheslav Ivanov, who lived in the neighborhood. For the first time since his literary debut, Boris Pasternak was in direct contact with leading figures of the symbolist generation. Baltrushaitis helped Pasternak to break out of the closed circle of young avant-garde poets and introduced him to the literary establishment. He read Pasternak's recently written "Tale of the Carp and Naphtalain," which was partially in prose and partially in verse, and recommended it for publication in the journal *Zavety* (Testaments), where he had great influence.

Although this *skazka* (fairy tale) was never printed and its text is lost, [16] it is possible to speculate about its role in Pasternak's literary development. First of all, much like the fragments of his early prose, the narration had markedly non-Russian, "European" overtones. Second, as for genre, it was evidently connected not with folklore and not even to the fairy tales of the Brothers Grimm, but to a literary form cultivated in Germany during the romantic era: the fantastic tale (Wieland, Tieck, Hoffmann). Pasternak's friends in Lirika, notably Aseev and Bobrov, also turned to this genre (in books that were written but not published). They shared their attraction to German romanticism with the older literary generation of symbolists. It was, in fact, precisely at this time that literary critics began to emphasize the German romantic "genealogy" of Russian symbolism in contrast to what had earlier been considered the decisive influence of French decadence. Russian symbolism was now declared the descendant of German romanticism,[17] and the book that promulgated this idea, Viktor Zhirmunsky's *German Romanticism and Modern Mysticism* (1914), became very popular. But the symbolists and Centrifuge were separated by important differences: in the work of Bobrov and Pasternak, the motifs and poetic devices that originated in romantic poetry acquired much more eccentric futuristic features.

It was Baltrushaitis who suggested that Pasternak translate Heinrich von Kleist's comedy *Der zerbrochene Krug* (The Broken Jug). Three years before that, in 1911, Pasternak had started to write an essay about Kleist. Kleist had only recently, about a hundred years after his death, been rediscovered in Germany, and he remained unknown in Russia. A translation by Fyodor Sologub of his best drama, *Penthesilea,* was published (with an accompanying article by Zhirmunsky) in the journal *Russian Thought* just as Pasternak began to translate *The Broken Jug.* Not long before this, Baltrushaitis had become friendly with two young stage directors, Konstantin Mardzhanov and Alexander Tairov, and had taken a very active part in the new experimental theater they founded in Moscow, the Free Theater. The Free Theater survived only a single season and collapsed in the summer of 1914 owing to friction between the directors and financial difficulties. But in the fall of 1914 Tairov created an enterprise of his own out of the shambles of the old. This Kamerny (Chamber) Theater lasted until 1950 and left an indelible trace in the history of Russian art. During the early period of the Chamber Theater's existence, Baltrushaitis was Tairov's consultant in literary matters. He recruited Balmont to the theater,[18] as well as Briusov and Sergei Gorodetsky. Scriabin's hopes for the realization of his grandiose project of the

"Prefatory Act" were bound up with the Chamber Theater's premier actress Alisa Koonen and with Tairov's artistic ideas. Pasternak was commissioned by the Chamber Theater to translate *The Broken Jug*.[19]

We can therefore see how the circle of Pasternak's literary acquaintances widened immediately after his first appearances in print. In addition, his relations with Mayakovsky took a new turn in the fall of 1914. Mayakovsky invited Pasternak to participate in the "Literary Page" he had organized in the newspaper *Virgin Soil*. The publisher of the newspaper was Alexei Suvorin, "who had gained the stubborn reputation of being a rebel, madman, dare-devil, sometime populist and sometime slavophile, but in any case a genuine and passionate patriot."[20] He advocated yoga, Indian mysticism, and fasting as a medical cure. Political editorials in the paper were written by the prominent anarchist and lecturer at Moscow University, Alexei Borovoy. The editors included P. D. Uspensky, the author of *Fourth Dimension*, and Vladimir Durov, a clown and animal trainer at the circus. The paper also opened up its pages to young poets.[21] Suvorin's inclination toward eccentricities and his interest in new art led him to entrust Mayakovsky with the "Literary Page." The first issue was devoted to the war, and among the items appearing under the general title of "Funeral Hurrah" were poems by Mayakovsky, Bolshakov, Aseev, David Burliuk, and Pasternak (who contributed "The Artilleryman Stays at the Helm"), as well as prose works by Burliuk and Mayakovsky. This issue of "Literary Page" proved to be the last: the editor of *Virgin Soil* was dissatisfied with the incomprehensibility of the material chosen by Mayakovsky, and as a patriot he was also disturbed by the pacifist ethos of the poems by Mayakovsky and Pasternak.

Despite all his fascination with Mayakovsky, Pasternak remained loyal to Centrifuge. At this time Bobrov was compiling the group's *Second Miscellany*. It was published only in the spring of 1916, but the greater part was not only collected but also typeset by the winter of 1914–15. In contrast to *Brachiopod*, the polemical aspects were greatly muted (owing to Pasternak's pressure), and the positive content of the group's literary platform was emphasized.

Pasternak's article "Chornyi bokal" (The Black Goblet) served just this purpose. Like the "Wassermann Test," it deals with the theory of futurism. But it contains not a single personal attack, and in general there are no references to individual literary figures. It is charged with a strong message nevertheless. "The Black Goblet" was written as a response to events from the end of 1913 through 1914, when Pasternak, much to his own surprise, found himself inside the futurist movement. In this regard the article must be viewed as a kind of sequel to the "Wassermann Test."

But if the first article dealt with the difference between genuine and false futurism, then the second addressed the relationship of futurism to the schools that had preceded it: symbolism in poetry and impressionism, and even the Wanderers, in painting. For all the other futurists at the end of 1914, this question was of little importance, and even more so in 1916 (when the article was actually published): their period of *Sturm und Drang* had drawn to a close. Pasternak ran counter to the main current of the futurist manifestos not only by his choice of the questions but in the way he answered them. The article defends the idea of the close continuity of generations at a time when the most provocative feature of futurism, no matter what its stripe, was its break with past traditions. In 1913 Mayakovsky had declared that "our poetry has no predecessors." [22] The tortuous path followed by Centrifuge, which led to the acknowledgment of its innovative character, resulted in the group's stress on its respect for tradition. As we have already seen, in Briusov's article (June 1914), only that form of futurism was considered genuine. [23] Without mentioning Briusov by name, Pasternak makes a transparent reference to him when he states that the term "futurism" was applied to the younger generation by its "mentors," the symbolists. It actually was Briusov who sanctioned the use of the term both with regard to Hylaea and to Centrifuge.

But Pasternak's remark is not simply a factual statement. It reveals his ambivalent attitude to futurism, especially when he explores the teleological meaning of the term. He says that it was only after the appearance of the term "futurism" that the symbolists were *first* able to reconsider the fundamental tenets of their aesthetics, as well as to understand art as a whole. In other words, futurism is art's "self-consciousness" (a favorite word and theme for Pasternak). What previously had existed unconsciously and unrecognized for the first time became conscious. The future is a goal of art and gives it meaning. Another allusion to Briusov forms one of the leitmotifs of "The Black Goblet": in speaking of the futurist poets, Pasternak uses the formulation "their own special kind of mentality," [24] which is an exact quotation from the passage about Pasternak in Briusov's article in the June issue of *Russian Thought*.

There was no attempt in "The Black Goblet," however, to smooth out all differences in literary ideology. While paying tribute to symbolism, Pasternak at the same time subjects it to merciless analysis. He first of all attacks it for "overloading the sky," in other words, for the extreme devotion to mysticism that was evident not only in the Steinerism of Biely and his followers in Lirika, but also in the grandiose projects of Pasternak's childhood idol, Scriabin. Pasternak was of course informed about the course of his work, "The Mysterium," since Baltrushaitis and Ivanov were at the time Scriabin's closest confidantes, and it is inconceivable that in their conversations over the summer of 1914 the question of the composer's work in progress never arose.

Another major criticism made by "The Black Goblet" of symbolism and impressionism (these concepts are used interchangeably in the article) is concerned not with world view but with style and poetics. Pasternak ridicules one peculiarity in symbolist poetry, which had also become a main target for attack by the acmeists: the absence of concrete content in the "symbols." The conclusion drawn by Pasternak is unexpected and paradoxical, but also perceptive and exact. The actual content of the elusive symbolist symbols, he says, can be found in the poetry of futurism. What appears to be merely a metaphor or cliché reveals itself in futurism as a genuine and profound reality.[25]

But his sarcastic remarks concerning "empty" symbolism were a thrust at the futurist manifestos as well: despite their differences, both the creator of "transrational" poetry, the cubo-futurist Kruchonykh, and the ego-futurist Shershenevich agreed that the essence of modern art consists in liberating word from meaning. Kruchonykh spoke about this in a number of manifestos, and Shershenevich in a book of articles, *Futurism Without a Mask* (1914), and later in the 1919 imagist declaration, where content was called the "caecum of art."

Pasternak also questioned the current theory of futurism, according to which the source of new art lies in the technological civilization of the twentieth century, with its new rhythms, velocities, and means of transportation. Pasternak considered this idea absurd, and he compares it to the behavior of an ape who sees some horses moving on four legs in a zoo and then proceeds to imitate them: "that's just how some ape that had changed from one day to the next would explain its new tricks. As the arrival in the menagerie of a new non-cloven-footed animal." As an alternative, he invites his fellow poets to adopt the viewpoint of man and not the ape.

Against whom is this remark directed? The explanation of futurist poetry by reference to the characteristics of modern civilization became one of the commonplaces of futurist declarations. Marinetti's first manifesto (1909) states: "We affirm that the world's magnificence has been enriched by a new beauty: the beauty of speed. A racing car whose hood is adorned with great pipes, like serpents of explosive breath—a roaring car that seems to ride on grapeshot—is more beautiful than the *Victory of Samothrace*." [26] Vadim Shershenevich echoed him in the book *Green Street*: "Every epoch differs from another not by events, not by anecdotes, not by facts, but by its general rhythm. There was the age of walking, the age of horses, now the age of the auto (the twentieth century), and there will be the age of the airplane." [27] In November 1913, while appearing with Mayakovsky and Burliuk at the Polytechnic Museum in Moscow, the cubo-futurist Vasily Kamensky spoke of the influence of technological inventions on modern poetry: "Giant steamship races, automobile races, and airplane flights which shrink the globe, give us a new conception of the modern world." [28] Opposed to all these attempts to connect modern art with the achievements of technology, Pasternak advances a different conception: futurism is lyricism par excellence, and therefore expresses the spirit not of the times but of eternity. Thus Pasternak returns in "The Black Goblet" to his reflections in the university notebooks and in his paper "Symbolism and Immortality." This once again testifies to the precacious unity of the early Pasternak's literary path and to his unique position within futurism.

During 1915, in the period between the writing of "The Black Goblet" and its publication, the activity of Centrifuge came to a halt. The exigencies of wartime did not allow Bobrov to print books that had been earmarked for publication, or even books that were already prepared for printing. Beginning with the summer of 1914 he became a frequent contributor to the Petersburg journal, *The Contemporary*, which was dominated by left-wing political figures, social democrats (Mensheviks), and populists. The journal had emerged in 1911, and its unofficial leaders were Maxim Gorky and Alexander Amfiteatrov. From that time the editorial board had changed several times, and its literary section rapidly deteriorated. Publication of the journal was frequently delayed by censorship bans. The number of subscribers fell drastically. Gorky repeatedly left the journal and then returned, hoping to save it. At one point the symbolists appeared in the journal and then abandoned it. Even before *Brachiopod* was published, Bobrov had been invited to *The Contemporary* by the head of its fiction department, Evgeny Lundberg, a young prose writer, literary critic, and follower of Lev Shestov. Lundberg reacted skeptically to futurism of any type. He found the vituperative and coarse style of the articles written by Bobrov to be unpleasant, but in this crisis most of the contributors defected from the journal and he had little choice. In the winter of 1914–15, therefore, Sergei Bobrov became one of the most active authors in the literary-criticism section. In January 1915 he published a survey of Russian literature for the past year, according to which the central event was the formation of Centrifuge (naturally its opponents, particularly Shershenevich, were treated disdainfully).

In December 1914 Bobrov sent Lundberg poems that had been written by his friends in Centrifuge, including Pasternak. They were all rejected. Lundberg declared that he absolutely could not understand Pasternak's verses, but at the same time he acknowledged the talent and originality of the poet. After this, the journal was sent Pasternak's translation of Kleist's *The Broken Jug*. Meanwhile a new conflict arose in the editorial board of *The Contemporary* and Lundberg retired. Making one of his periodical returns, Gorky took the reading of literary manuscripts into his own hands. It was evidently he who made the decision to accept for publication the work of an unknown translator of Kleist. Yet he found it necessary to edit the manuscript heavily. Since he did not read German, Gorky corrected the translation without consulting the original. The proofs were not sent to Pasternak, and when the May issue came out, the poet was outraged to see that his work had been subjected to substantial unauthorized changes. Acting on Bobrov's advice, on May 8 Pasternak directed a sharp protest to the editors, with a request to forward it to Gorky. Pasternak knew that Gorky was about to return to the journal, but he had no idea that it was Gorky himself who had made changes. When he found out about this later, an embarrassed Pasternak sent Gorky a belated apology in 1921.[29] This publication in *The Contemporary* was Pasternak's first appearance in the established press and remained his only publication in a thick journal until the early 1920s.[30]

In the winter of 1914–15, Pasternak earned his livelihood at the home of a wealthy Baltic German, Moritz Filipp (who owned fashionable haberdasheries in Moscow), by giving private lessons to his son Walter. This work left much time for literary activities, but we have very little information about them. The reason is that, after the severe defeat of the Russian troops in Galicia, there were pogroms of German trading companies in Moscow from May 27 to May 29, 1915, that were just as savage as pogroms in Russia had always been. An enraged mob attacked the Filipp home, smashing a china collection (worth several million rubles) and barbarically destroying Dutch master paintings. In a fire on May 28 all of Pasternak's manuscripts, which were located at the house, perished in the flames.[31] The destruction of these manuscripts creates a large gap in our knowledge of Pasternak because at this time he was undergoing a profound transformation in literary style. The transformation seemed to consist of a sharp reinforcement of avant-gardist traits (for this reason, perhaps, Pasternak later considered the loss as nothing to be lamented), and it coincided with the poet's rapprochement with Mayakovsky. Pasternak took part in the two main publications of the futurists during this year, the miscellanies *Vesennee kontragentstvo muz* (The Vernal Forwarding Agency of the Muses) and *Vzial: Baraban futuristov* (Took: Futurists' Drum). The rapprochement occurred despite fundamental differences between Pasternak and Mayakovsky over both poetry and life; a detailed account of these differences is given in *Safe Conduct*.

New and unexpected stylistic features had already manifested themselves in the poem "The Artilleryman Stands at the Helm" (printed by Mayakovsky in *Virgin Soil*), Pasternak's first work devoted to a 'civic theme. As with the poems published in the *Second Miscellany* of Centrifuge in 1916 but written, evidently, in the same fall of 1914, Pasternak made his first departure from the traditional metrical patterns of Russian syllabo-tonic verse and turned to free verse. Free verse and accentual verse were already the subject of wide experimentation by Mayakovsky, Khlebnikov, and Shershenevich (as well as by some symbolists). Bobrov was also obsessed with free verse at this time. In August 1914 he published an article in which he predicted an imminent break from traditional types of prosody and the mass transfer of modern poets to free verse.[32] Thus this departure was characteristic not only of Pasternak but of Centrifuge in general, and it conformed to the dominant tendencies of futurist poetry. In the winter of 1914–15, Pasternak filled a whole notebook with free verse (lost in the fire). But of the various forms of free verse, Pasternak preferred more moderate ones than Bobrov did, and he obstinately strived to preserve rhymes, however occasional they may have been.

It was no accident that he attributed the source of this poetic form to "Dernier Vers" by Jules Laforgue, where rhyme is used.[33] Pasternak turned for the last time in his own works to free verse in February 1917, in "Poema o blizhnem" (Poem on the Neighbour). Incidentally Laforgue and Rimbaud were mentioned in passing in his article on Mayakovsky written exactly at this time. But already a year later, in his 1918 article "The Quintessence," Pasternak denounced free verse, and in 1921, taking issue with Bobrov, Mayakovsky, and other proponents of "liberated verse," in the poem "Tak nachinaiut" (So they begin), he declared the perennial validity of iambs.

An attraction to free verse was not the only novel feature of this period in Pasternak's life. In the spring of 1915 he returned to prose and began to write the novella *Apellesova cherta* (The Apelles Mark). It was his first prose work to be completed and published. In narrative style it differs sharply from the fictional fragments of 1910–1913. In place of amorphous composition devoid of action, there emerges a concrete plot, though it borders on the anecdotal. In the early prose fragments, scenery description was inseparably intertwined with philosophical and aesthetic reflection. Pasternak now rejects this, and the complex of literary ideas that prompted the writing of the novella recedes deeply into the subtext.

These changes in narration are all the more striking since Pasternak smuggles into the new novella a character we already know from his earlier prose, Relikvimini, whose name is now slightly modified as Emilio Relinkvimini.[34] Yet it is difficult to say whether he is truly the same character—so dimly is he presented in both instances—or whether he simply bears the same name. Relinkvimini is no longer the hero, merely a peripheral figure. At the center of the story is a "poetic competition" between Relinkvimini and another poet, called Heinrich Heine. The appearance in modern Italy of a character who has the same name as the great German poet and is a poet himself, but who has no family relation, is an expression of a trait we already know: Pasternak's tendency to play with names.

Although the plot is based on a contrast between the two poets, it is difficult to establish what it is that makes them opposite types. As is often the case with Pasternak, the fact of juxtaposition is more important than what is being counterposed. But as Michel Aucouturier has convincingly shown,[35] the content of the novella and its hero, Heine, are indissolubly linked with Pasternak's reflections about the theatrical nature of the poet and the theatrical essence of poetry, as well as with the two conceptions of art offered in most complete form in 1931 in *Safe Conduct*. There one poet's outwardly passive mode of behavior (always characteristic of Boris Pasternak) is contrasted to another type of poet: one who never leaves the stage and is understood as a "visual-biographical emblem." *Safe Conduct* connects the latter poet to the "romantic" conception of art and offers as the clearest example of its realization the works, life, and death of Vladimir Mayakovsky.

With the character of Heine in *The Apelles Mark* we encounter this romantic type of poet for the first time. There is no doubt that the portrait bears the stamp of Pasternak's close acquaintance with Mayakovsky and the opportunity to observe him in an intimate setting. The theatrical element in Mayakovsky's behavior emerged even in everyday life and impressed Pasternak just as strongly as it did in his recitals before large audiences. It should also be mentioned that Mayakovsky's poetry at this time was frequently called "romantic." In February 1914 Gorky spoke of "the hearty notes of future romanticism" in him. In the summer of the same year Ivanov compared Mayakovsky's poetry, in conversations with Pasternak, to the hyperbolic style of Victor Hugo. Journal critics customarily linked Mayakovsky to early German romanticism.[36] Earlier in "Symbolism and Immortality," in the winter of 1913, Pasternak had drawn the analogy between the word in poetry and the actor's word. Thus the features of literary style were projected onto the life of the poet himself.

Just as would be the case in *Safe Conduct*, in *The Apelles Mark* attention is focused on the tenuous borderline dividing art from life, the poet from the man, imagination from truth, and text from reality. Indeed, the very title of the novella points precisely at this fragile boundary.[37] In this sense Relinkvimini and Heine, who are antipodes on the level of plot, actually prove to be doubles or transformations of the same essence. The authorship of the laconic challenge sent to Heine by Relinkvimini, the author of the love poem "Il Sangue," is confirmed by a dried bloodstain from his finger. In other words, Relinkvimini has translated his verbal imagery into material reality. An analogous intersection of text and life is accomplished by Heine: the poetic improvisation he so masterfully plays becomes transformed before the eyes of the reader from a "spectacle" into life's ultimate reality.

This theme leads back to the romantic tradition. But it cannot be said that one of the poets in the novella is a romantic and that his opponent is not. Nor can it be said that the author's attitude toward romanticism is unequivocally negative (as it is in *Safe Conduct*). Nothing in *The Apelles Mark* indicates the sharp condemnation of romanticism that strikes us so forcefully in the later Pasternak. On the contrary, character portrayal and narrative technique both show the clear influence of the romantic tradition.[38]

And yet Pasternak's attitude toward romanticism in the novella is not unequivocally positive. The very choice of name for the main character testifies to this. Heine's place in the history of the romantic movement was somewhat contradictory: a late adept of romanticism, it was he who mercilessly ridiculed and destroyed it. This might explain why, of all the German romantics, the author of *The Apelles Mark* opted for Heine. What mattered for Pasternak was neither romanticism in the pure sense of the word nor its antipode, whatever it might be called (realism, antiromanticism). Of special importance to him was the very possibility of oscillation between the two—romantic and antiromantic—within the same literary system, of the annihilation of the opposite poles within the same person or character. That is why the conflict between the visual emblem and the reality of life within Pasternak's "Heinrich Heine" plays a greater role in the plot of the novella than does the contrast between the two protagonists. Heine's name is both devoid of any meaning in the story (since our hero has no relation to the real Heine) and is imbued with a most profound meaning. He is not just an emblem but a real historical figure, a genuine artist who, like Pasternak himself, questions and demolishes the very foundations of his own art. In this sense, the author's perception of Heine strikingly resembles that of the philosopher Shestov, Pasternak's older contemporary. For Shestov, Heine was one of those tragic figures who, struggling in the search for truth, "disclose that the ground is slipping from under their feet." [39]

Pasternak's position within Centrifuge became just as complicated as this evaluation of romanticism. The group grew much livelier at the beginning of 1916. Oddly enough, this change for the better occurred when its leading members were scattered throughout Russia. Starting in January, Pasternak was living far from Moscow, in the Urals, working in the village of Vsevolodo-Vilva in the office of a chemical factory. In the summer, when Pasternak returned to Moscow, Bobrov was no longer there. And from the beginning of October 1916, Pasternak once again left Moscow and went to the Prikamie. Aseev, who had rejoined Centrifuge after two years away from it, was in the army.

The increased publishing activity of Centrifuge was attributable to two new members. The first of these, Samuil Vermel, was the son of a rich Moscow merchant, an aesthete, a stage director, and an actor. He helped Centrifuge to overcome its financial crisis but exerted no influence on its literary platform. He was closely linked to Tairov and the Chamber Theater. Vermel's literary ambitions (he had written and published a book of imitations of Japanese tankas) led him to an alliance with the futurists. In the spring of 1915 he joined David Burliuk in publishing the miscellany *Vernal Forwarding Agency of the Muses.* In the spring of 1916 he put out the first and only issue of a literary and artistic journal *Moskovskie mastera* (Moscow Masters), which impressed his contemporaries with an imposing typographical elegance never seen before in futurist publications. Vermel's subsidy allowed Centrifuge to publish several books of poetry in rapid succession, and these were the best books brought out by Bobrov during the entire existence of the group. In September 1916 it put out *Gold of Death* by Riurik Ivnev (an ego-futurist who had participated in Centrifuge from the very beginning). In November *Oksana* by Nikolai Aseev appeared, and in the winter–spring of 1916–17 two poetry collections by Sergei Bobrov, *Diamond Forests* and *Lyre of Lyres,* were published. Along with these new publications there was also Pasternak's second book, *Poverkh barierov* (Above the Barriers). Pasternak sent the manuscript to the typesetter in September, and the book came off press in the middle of December 1916. The alliance of Centrifuge with Vermel was, however, short-lived; in February 1917 he and Bobrov went their separate ways.

Relations between Centrifuge and its other new ally, Ivan Aksyonov, followed quite a different course. His ideological solidarity with the group proved to be no less important than his financial support. He was a professional military engineer, but all his life he had a passion for the arts. Fluent in several European languages, Aksyonov was well versed in the most recent cultural developments in Russia and abroad. His article on modern Russian painting appeared in 1913, in a miscellany published by the avant-garde art group Jack of Diamonds. He wrote poetry and worked on translations. In 1914 his name was announced among the collaborators of the *First Journal of Russian Futurists,* but it was only in Centrifuge in 1916 that he found kindred spirits in literature.

Aksyonov and Bobrov became acquainted through correspondence. Since the literary positions of Centrifuge seemed to be closest to his own, Aksyonov proposed that Bobrov publish under its imprimatur three of his own books that were already at the typesetter's. These were a book about Picasso (the first to be published in Russian), a book of original poems, and a collection of his translations of Jacobean dramas by Ford, Webster, and Turner (writers virtually unknown in Russia). On active duty in the army, he needed help because he could not supervise the preparation of the books. In reply Bobrov told Aksyonov about the stalled plans of his publishing house and then, even before the agreement with Vermel, received from Aksyonov the money to publish the *Second Miscellany*. From the spring of 1916 Aksyonov became the group's chief strategist. Unlike Pasternak, but in agreement with Bobrov, he considered that its goal was not the broad consolidation of young poets under the aegis of Centrifuge, but rivalry with competitors—with the group of cubo-futurists headed by Burliuk and Mayakovsky. Aksyonov's literary tastes were of a much more radical character than Bobrov's, and the general direction of Centrifuge under his influence became much more uniformly avant-gardist than ever before. This is especially striking if we study those who were to contribute to the *Third Miscellany*, scheduled for 1917 but never printed because of the rupture with Vermel and the outbreak of the February Revolution. From the old group Petersburg Herald only the most extremist of its members remained, Vasilisk Gnedov. The poetry section was supposed to contain, besides Gnedov's, poems by Khlebnikov, Bolshakov, Mayakovsky, Aseev, Bobrov, Pasternak, and Aksyonov. This would have been the most impressive of the group's collective appearances.

Aksyonov had mixed feelings about Pasternak's words. He liked the poems in the *Second Miscellany*, as well as "The Black Goblet," pleased with its criticism of the cubo-futurists. But he was disappointed by *Above the Barriers*. He felt that, in comparison to Pasternak's poems of 1914, the new book made concessions to traditionalist forms, and these symptoms of a "retrograde" tendency alarmed him. Pasternak himself flaunted this retrograde orientation in his second book. In this sense Aksyonov's evaluation coincided with the author's, however different their starting points were. Aksyonov placed Aseev much higher than Pasternak, since he felt that Aseev's poems were free from passésist tendencies. And yet, despite their substantial differences in literary tastes, Aksyonov and Pasternak respected each other. Pasternak had no doubt that Aksyonov was a valuable addition to Centrifuge.

It is necessary to point out that by 1915–16 the status of futurism in Russian literary life had changed. Ego-futurism, as an organized movement, no longer existed. The cubo-futurist group was losing the militant features that had both frightened and tantalized the public. After Mayakovsky's move from Moscow to Petrograd at the beginning of 1915, he became the focus of favorable attention from literary circles that previously had been hostile to futurism. In February 1915 the almanac *Strelets* (The Archer) appeared, in which the most prominent figures of the symbolist and near-symbolist camp (Blok, Zinaida Vengerova, Fyodor Sologub, Alexei Remizov, and Mikhail Kuzmin) coexisted peacefully with the cubo-futurists (Mayakovsky, Kruchonykh, Kamensky, Livshits, Khlebnikov). The publication of the almanac caused a sensation. The participation of the futurists was not only taken as proof of their greater toleration for the older generation, but as a sign of the social and literary recognition granted to the former rebels and outcasts. An even greater sensation was the public approval of futurism (and of Mayakovsky in particular) bestowed by the dean of the realist movement, Maxim Gorky. Gorky declared that futurism was young, and that the future belonged to it and not to the old guard. Under these conditions, with the cubo-futurists diminishing in oppositional fervor and organizational unity, Pasternak felt that Centrifuge could unite the young poets of various avant-garde shadings. This is why he hailed the publication of poems by Bolshakov and Khlebnikov in the *Second Miscellany,* the return of Aseev to Centrifuge, and the recruitment of Aksyonov. He considered the group's "leftward turn" a beneficial development.

Centrifuge flourished in the period between 1914 and early 1917. With Pasternak, Aseev, and Bobrov as its principal members, the group was able to present alternatives to the reform of Russian poetry carried out by futurism. Aside from Bobrov, Pasternak was the only Centrifugist whose path was inseparable from the group's, no matter what crises arose along the way. It is difficult to imagine how his first literary efforts would have fared in such chaotic conditions of aesthetic ferment and the toppling of old idols had he not enjoyed so much important support from a circle of friends who appreciated the originality of his lyrical style. But Pasternak was not simply a poet. He was at the same time the group's leading theoretician and had taken part in shaping its program. His theoretical articles played a much greater role in the group's self-definition than the writings of its acknowledged leader, Bobrov. Thanks to Pasternak's position and the influence of his works, Centrifuge gradually gained the reputation of a truly serious literary enterprise and won ever greater support among the young avant-garde poets.

But as the leftward drift of the platform and the members of Centrifuge became more pronounced, Pasternak began to distance himself from its goals. It is here that we witness the birth of his consistent noncommitment, so clear throughout his life and works. Pasternak's rejection of the "group"—any group—came out into the open on the very eve of the revolution of 1917.

5

Revolutionary Years

In the autumn of 1916 Pasternak's main occupation was a verse translation of Algernon Swinburne's tragedy *Chastelard,* the first part of his trilogy about Mary Stuart. Having begun this work in Moscow, Pasternak took it with him in early October, when he hurriedly moved to Tikhie Gory on the Kama River, not far from the town of Elabuga in Viatka Province. His hasty departure was prompted by rumors in the newspapers that those who had previously been exempted from military service would have to undergo a reevaluation of their claim to exemption. The poet thus faced the threat of being mobilized and sent to the front. After a brief upsurge of patriotic sentiment early in the war, when he had attempted to volunteer for front-line duty, Pasternak (like Mayakovsky) soon began to see the war in a new light. Pacifist feelings were expressed distinctly in his verse as early as the autumn of 1914.

Tikhie Gory was the site of a chemical plant directed by Lev Karpov, an engineer and member of the Bolshevik Party who in his student days had been an active participant in the revolutionary movement. Later Karpov became prominent in the Soviet government, when Lenin appointed him to head the entire Russian chemical industry. Karpov has hired as director of his factory's research laboratory the young biochemist Boris Zbarsky.[1] Zbarsky had as a teenager also been a member of the revolutionary underground, affiliated with the Social Revolutionaries. It was Zbarsky, after meeting Pasternak in the spring of 1916, who set up a job for the young poet in the factory office; he was put in charge of military registration and draftee mobilization. The fact that he was working at a factory in the defense industry gave Pasternak hope that he would not be sent into action even if the medical commission did declare him fit for service. In addition to his office work, Pasternak tutored Karpov's children.

Despite his full-time employment at the factory, Pasternak's work on *Chastelard* progressed quickly. He finished the translation by December and immediately set to work on *Mary Stuart*. It was apparently his intention to translate the whole trilogy. It is not clear what inspired him to take on this laborious and somewhat quixotic project. Then, as now, Swinburne was virtually unknown in Russia, despite efforts by the symbolist poets Balmont and Briusov to arouse interest in him. Pasternak had first become acquainted with Swinburne's work in 1913 when, as he put it, he "taught himself to read Keats and Coleridge, Swinburne and Poe in the original."[2] It may be that the decision to translate Swinburne's tragedies grew out of Pasternak's increased enthusiasm for the theater, for it was in 1916 that he was introduced into the society of the Moscow Chamber Theater, made the acquaintance of Vermel, and attended a performance of Shakespeare's *Merry Wives of Windsor*. At the same time, Pasternak was rereading Shakespeare, and in his poem "Marburg," written in the Urals in May 1916, he makes mention of a provincial tragic actor rehearsing "a Shakespearean drama." References to Shakespeare's work also surface in the poem "Uroki angliiskogo" (English Lessons), which appeared in *My Sister, Life*. Another poem, written in early 1918 and published in *Themes and Variations*, is also devoted to Shakespeare.

Apparently, in the autumn of 1916, Pasternak also was reading Swinburne's book on Shakespeare, and the two English writers became entwined in his mind. He became particularly absorbed in the development of historical themes in their works, as well as seeming dialogue between separate epochs that was evoked by his simultaneous study of the two poets.[3] For his work on *Chastelard* Pasternak took notes from scholarly monographs on the history of Scotland and the Stuarts; here too what he had learned in seminars with Professor A. Savin, Russia's foremost expert on English history, proved to be particularly useful.

Pasternak's interest in the tragic conflicts of the transitional period between the Tudor Reformation and the Glorious Revolution was to reappear several decades later, when he returned to the theme of Mary Stuart. In the 1950s he translated two other tragedies about her life, those of Schiller and Juliusz Slowacki. There are flickers of themes taken from not only Schiller but from his early Swinburne translations in a longer poem of that same period, "Bacchanalia." [4] In his 1918 article "Kvintessentsia" (The Quintessence), Pasternak mentions the Scottish queen and his own work on the tragedy. It is likely that the experience of working on Swinburne's play was reflected in two other articles from 1917–1919, one on tragedy and the other on Shakespeare. Both articles have been lost, as has the translation of *Chastelard* that Pasternak sent to Gorky's publishing house, Vsemirnaia literatura (World Literature), in Petrograd. But there can be no doubt that Pasternak's perception of the events of 1917 carried the indelible mark of his immersion in European history and his reflections on tragedy.

Distracted by many new plans in early 1917, Pasternak laid aside his work on Swinburne's trilogy. This does not mean that he abandoned his interest in tragedy, however. In the work of Mayakovsky, his companion in the futurist movement, it was the tragic aspects that most appealed to Pasternak. In February 1917 Pasternak wrote an article in which he cited the tragedy *Vladimir Mayakovsky* as the poet's greatest achievement. This article was written upon the publication of a volume of Mayakovsky's selected works, *Simple as Mooing*, by Gorky's publishing house. The book had been sent to Pasternak by Bobrov, who detected in Mayakovsky's new poems a waning of talent and the betrayal of the ideals of pure poetry, along with the demise of cubo-futurism in general. It should also be noted that even some of Mayakovsky's former associates in the futurist movement—Alexei Kruchonykh in particular—objected to the new direction of Mayakovsky's poetry. They saw the simplification of his style as a vulgar concession, a willingness to play to the crowd. To a certain degree this was Pasternak's assessment as well. This is why Bobrov asked Pasternak to write a review for the forthcoming *Third Miscellany* of Centrifuge, on the assumption that Mayakovsky's book would provoke Pasternak into attacking their cubo-futurist opponents as he had in "Wassermann Test" and "The Black Goblet."

But Pasternak did not meet Bobrov's expectations. His review turned out to be one of the most enthusiastic responses to Mayakovsky's book. Moreover, he immediately warned Bobrov that he would refuse to take part in the *Third Miscellany* if it contained attacks on Mayakovsky. Although the vulgar stylistic elements in Mayakovsky's new satirical poems appalled him, Pasternak welcomed his attempts to find a new, simpler style, seeing in this the inevitable consequence of artistic maturation. As can be seen from *Above the Barriers,* Pasternak himself was also feeling the need for greater simplicity in poetic expression, desiring to rid himself of the strained lyrical style of his early work. (Pasternak's review did not appear in print, since the *Third Miscellany* never came out. He intended to include it in a collection of his articles, but decided against publishing it after 1922, when his relationship to Mayakovsky entered a new phase.[5]) Bobrov eventually concurred with Pasternak's evaluation of Mayakovsky, and he even accepted one of the latter's recent poems, "The Last Petersburg Tale," for the *Third Miscellany.*[6] Thus Mayakovsky went from adversary of Centrifuge to a participant in its publishing ventures.

The tendency toward consolidation and compromise in the group was supported in yet another article by Pasternak, this one a review of Aseev's *Oksana.* In comparison to the article on Mayakovsky, this one is far more clearly positive. The direction of Aseev's formal leanings was much closer to Pasternak's than was Mayakovsky's, with the latter's extreme dramatism or, in Pasternak's words, his "demonism." It is also noteworthy that Pasternak enthusiastically defined Aseev's poetic method as the culmination of romanticism. Once again this shows that Pasternak was still inclined to invest the concept of romanticism with a positive meaning.

While accepting Bobrov's request that he review these two futurist works for Centrifuge, Pasternak flatly refused to criticize the symbolists—more specifically, Biely's book on Goethe and Ivanov's *Furrows and Boundaries.* It was not that he disagreed with Bobrov's negative assessment of the older poets' theories, but he no doubt considered symbolism a vanquished enemy, unworthy of further battle. On the whole, the details of Pasternak's life during these months attest to his growing independence from partisan biases and to his unwillingness to subscribe to group tactics.

Pasternak's main artistic concern at this time was to put the lyrical miniature behind him. It was his dissatisfaction with the book *Above the Barriers* that prompted him to make this move. Because the collection seemed uneven, he tried to group the poems in it along thematic lines: first, he placed together the poems about war, then those on urban themes, then those about the "city under snow," and so on.

This organizing principle turned out to be ineffective, not only because the poems did not lend themselves to a thematic classification but also—and especially—because the collection showed stylistic heterogeneity as well. There were poems here which exhibited blatant, idiosyncratic technical experimentation, alongside relatively traditional, "retrograde" texts. Two opposing tendencies were at work. In some poems the author resorted to "spasmatic" shifts in meter in his attempt to express anxiety and nervousness. Elsewhere he avoided such superficial means of lyrical expression; instead, he focused his attention on an externally "objective" scenic depiction. For this purpose he turned to manipulations of metaphor, interweaving complex images and causing fluid transformations of one image into another. Such threading of tropes one into another was accompanied by syntactic complexity, including extensive use of enjambement (which, incidentally, is a hallmark of Swinburne's work).

The book's inconsistency disturbed the author and, unable to correct it, he even considered parodying it with the title, "Gradus ad Parnassum: 44 Exercises." In the end, however, he opted against a title that would emphasize his technical experimentation and chose instead to bring out his peculiar ideological position with *Above the Barriers* (a self-citation from the poem "Petersburg"). This title was, in fact, a double allusion. First it expressed the author's attitude toward the main preoccupation of the day, the war. It thus echoed Romain Rolland's famous slogan, "au-dessus de la mêlée." Second the title alluded to the nonpartisan position Pasternak had consciously adopted vis-à-vis another "war," that between the literary factions of the time.

His inability to solve the internal contradictions of *Above the Barriers* led Pasternak to try his hand at a larger verse form: the epic poem. (Here, his translation of Swinburne's lengthy tragedy had already taught him a great deal.) One of his attempts at an original work in this genre was "Poem on the Neighbour." Pasternak wrote two sections of this work on February 8 and 9, and he sent them to Bobrov for publication in his almanac. Although he continued to work on this long poem, the transition from lyric poetry to the epic proved so difficult that it was never finished. At first Pasternak assumed that success in this genre could come by means of a simple extension of the lyric text—a broadening of the boundaries of lyric narration from within. It seemed to him that the longer lyric poems in *Above the Barriers,* such as "The Ballad" and "Marburg," represented a natural transition toward the epic. It is no accident, therefore, that "Poem on the Neighbour" contains direct citations from "Marburg." Apparently the poet had no intention of introducing a conventional plot into his narration. Pasternak was by that time undoubtedly familiar with Mayakovsky's "A Cloud in Trousers" and saw those experiments with the epic form both as a challenge and a model. For Pasternak, as for Mayakovsky, the concept of the epic genre in poetry was connected with the use of polymetric composition, with rapid shifts from one meter to another, in accordance with the unfolding thematic movement.

Pasternak was also occupied with another project during these weeks, a plan for a collection of prose works. He wrote to Bobrov that this collection could be ready by April. It would include *The Apelles Mark,* which had been fatally ill-received by the publishers of the established journals.[7] It would also include "The Suboctave Story" and "The Duchess' Coach," a novella that has survived only in the form of memoir accounts by Rita Wright-Kovaleva[8] and the author's sister Lydia. All three pieces had a distinctly West European flavor and were apparently united by the theme of art, explored from different standpoints.

The February Revolution put an end to these plans. Pasternak returned to Moscow with Zbarsky at the beginning of March. Konstantin Loks tells of his mood at this time: One day followed another, and on one of those days Boris Pasternak arrived. He was happy; he was satisfied.

> "Just imagine," he said at our first meeting, "if the sea of blood and filth begins to radiate light—" Here an eloquent gesture crowned his delight.[9]

Most of the artistic intelligentsia shared Pasternak's enthusiasm for the changes taking place in the first weeks and months of the revolution. It was not individual parties or political slogans that attracted him, but the general spirit of freedom and unanimity, which he saw as uniting not only inimical groups and classes of society but even the trees and the land—nature itself. A few weeks earlier in Prikamie he had found the people to be drab and depressing. Now it seemed to him that, of all the people who had lived through a revolution, the Russians had been best prepared for it. That was why the events had such a peaceful and bloodless character. This opinion was not unique to Pasternak. The philosopher Lev Shestov wrote from Moscow to relatives in Switzerland:

> All of us here are thinking and talking exclusively about the grandiose events going on in Russia. Anyone who has not seen it himself

would have difficulty imagining what it is like here. Especially in
Moscow. As if by decree from on high, everyone has decided as one
to change the old order. Decided, and done everything in a week. If
Petrograd had some episodes of unrest, Moscow has had nothing
but celebration . . . In less than a week the whole enormous country
has thrown off the old and moved on to a new order, with the calm-
ness characteristic only of great and solemn occasions.[10]

At the same time, Pasternak stubbornly avoided any involvement
in political life or in the numerous social organizations that arose in
the aftermath of the upheaval. His behavior was in sharp contrast to
that of many of his peers. One of the most zealous among them was
of course Mayakovsky, who was struggling in Petrograd to get full
and equal representation for leftist artists and poets in the agencies
governing cultural life. Throughout 1917 he gave speeches at innumerable meetings, speaking with passion on behalf of the futurists.
He also became a regular contributor to Gorky's newly created newspaper *Novaia zhizn* (New Life). Within Centrifuge, Ivan Aksyonov
was exultant over the new political order. From the first moments of
the February Revolution, when he was still at the front, he engaged
in constant correspondence with Sergei Bobrov on political issues,
attempting to draw Centrifuge into the whirlpool of social struggle.
When Lenin returned to Russia in early April and came out with his
"April Theses," Aksyonov immediately suggested that Bobrov enlist
him as a contributor to the journal then being planned by Centrifuge.
Aksyonov was but one of many who felt that the Bolsheviks' program
and tactics were inherently akin to futurism. In May 1917 one journalist wrote: "The Lenin group are political futurists. Just like all the
Burliuks or Olimpovs, who are already half-forgotten, they need publicity above all. In silence they die out; they need a row, they need
swearing. From scornful swearing they draw their inspiration; from
mockery, strength; from malicious spitting, their pathos." [11]

In place of the plans he had nurtured earlier, Pasternak now began
to write a novel, moreover one on a historical theme, the French Revolution. We know nothing about the content of this novel or how
much of it he wrote. But the "Dramaticheskie otryvki" (Dramatic
Fragments) that have survived provide a reliable basis for speculation
about how the poet reworked historical material in the course of his
contemplation of the events of his own time. These fragments were
written in June and July 1917, that is, when the Russian revolution
was reaching its critical stage and revolutionary euphoria was being

supplanted by a sharp polarization of the political camps. It became clear that the road to democracy was by no means as smooth as it had seemed just a few weeks before. In early July, crisis and division within the Provisional Government and mass unrest were followed by a catastrophic military defeat at the hands of the Germans. During these days of reaction (there were threats of a military dictatorship, and several leftists leaders, including Trotsky, were arrested) Pasternak turned to the French Revolution in his "Dramatic Fragments," focusing on its final days. The characters, Saint-Just and Robespierre, seen in the last moments of their lives, carry the mark of doom and self-immolation. What is more, the entire revolution is shown in a tragic light. For Pasternak, the whole history of the republic was a chronicle of its demise. But it was precisely this fatal imprint of doom that Pasternak saw as the most beautiful trait of the revolution.[12] Although "Dramatic Fragments" came as a response to political developments in the revolutionary summer of 1917, they should not be seen as an allegory or as a direct allusion to those events. The poet understood revolution as an expression of the general laws of historical development, in the course of which the will of the individual revolutionary leader is brought into inevitable, tragic conflict with the implacable order of things.

"Dramatic Fragments" was published in 1918, nearly a year after it was written, in the May–June issue of the Social Revolutionaries' newspaper *Znamia truda* (Banner of Labor). The work was never republished during Pasternak's lifetime. In 1920 he suggested that the fragments be included in the first volume of his poetry, then being prepared for publication by the literary section of Narkompros, but the editorial board declined to accept them for the book (which was never issued).[13]

In May 1918 the same newspaper published another little-known work by Pasternak, a short prose piece called "Dialogue." An unnamed Russian, a wandering proselytizer of communism, finds himself in France. Forgetting that he is not at home, the hungry man eats a melon that does not belong to him, for which he is arrested. The situation described is based on an ironic reworking of Proudhon's dictum that all property is theft. In this way the author shows how incompatible Proudhon's philosophy is with the realities of modern France, and he puts forward the idea of Russia's superiority over the west. The protagonist of "Dialogue" is a symbolic figure, called simply "the Character" (*Subekt*). Russia also appears as an abstraction. It is not the country in its historical reality; much less is it the country Pasternak had recently observed from within, from his remote corner in the Urals. It is instead an idealized, utopian country, transferred into an imagined future.

It is not clear whether "Dialogue" was written at the same time as "Dramatic Fragments." The external contrasts between the two works are evident. Instead of following the lofty tradition of verse tragedy, Pasternak creates in "Dialogue" a sort of political pamphlet in dramatized form. Instead of developing a historical theme, he intentionally makes his work ahistorical. In place of the great French revolutionary leaders, he chooses an unknown pilgrim with a vague likeness to a political agitator, a scientist, or a poet. In place of the parting thoughts of tragic heroes, he describes a petty misdemeanor, without indicating its consequences for the plot: the author breaks off "Dialogue" in the middle of a word, and the reader never knows whether the Character is punished or set free.

Nevertheless, for all their differences, there is an undeniable internal connection between "Dialogue" and "Dramatic Fragments." In his meditations on the ongoing Russian revolution, Pasternak appears to be making a twofold mental leap along the temporal axis: one leap into the past and one into the future. Contemporary events are juxtaposed, in "Dramatic Fragments," to the final, critical moments of the French Revolution and, in "Dialogue," to that ideal society whose arrival seemed imminent and could only be reached, the poet believed, through an understanding of the historical lessons of the Russian experience. In both cases, however, Pasternak avoided depicting reality as it stood before him. The concept of revolution was essentially a philosophical or metaphysical category; before it could be analyzed, it had to be purified of anything pedestrian or transient.

"Dialogue" offers the first distinct expression of the philosophy of "natural right," which was to take a central role in all of Pasternak's later work, especially when he reflected on the theme of revolution. He understood revolution as an elemental force that engulfed all human beings whatever their intentions or desires. The fact that people are plunged into nature in times of revolution purges all that is mediocre, base, vapid, or amoral. At such times genius is found not only in selected individuals but in everyone. Revolution is a state of nature and humanity, marked by an encompassing feeling of love. In "Dialogue" the concept of revolution approaches the concept of love, of each person "dissolved" in all others.

The Bolsheviks' accession to power in October 1917 appeared to Pasternak to be a natural continuation of the February Revolution, although he was appalled by the first signs of internecine terrorist acts. Still the leaders of the new regime seemed more understanding of the desires and expectations of the people than was the Provisional Government, which had been paralyzed in the weeks preceding the October upheaval. A year earlier, events had brought Pasternak together with people who were now actively engaged in building a new Russia, such as Karpov and Zbarsky. He never doubted their revolutionary ideals or sympathy for the oppressed. In fact, from this time on, all Pasternak's reflections on the nature of revolution were inevitably linked to the impressions he had formed while in the Urals and in Prikamie.

The theme of Russia now intruded into the poet's artistic conceptions, crowding out the "foreign" overtones that had previously dominated his work. In place of subjective, abstract plots tailored to European settings (Italy, France, Germany), Pasternak now moved the setting of his poetic experiments to Russia. Moreover, he set his works in the remote provinces rather than in Moscow, where he had witnessed the advent of the February Revolution, or in Petrograd, which had been the subject of a poem in *Above the Barriers.*

The first signal of this change is seen in *Pisma iz Tuly* (Letters from Tula). This tale, written in April 1918, is close in subject to *The Apelles Mark;* here too the main theme is that of the relationship between poetry and the idea of "biography as spectacle." The narrative divides into two apparently unconnected parts. In the first, the hero is a young poet who observes the affected behavior of actors "with pretensions to genius." They have come to Tula from Moscow to take part in the making of a historical film about a peasant uprising led by Bolotnikov in the early seventeenth century. Their unnatural behavior in life off stage fills the poet with a sharp sense of shame, for he sees in them the same falseness he has detected in himself. The conclusion he reaches is devastating: he must break immediately with poetry, since it distorts the truth.

The second part of the story puts forward a diametrically opposite idea. Here the main character is an old actor and playwright. He too is repelled by the falseness of film production. So he performs a *mise-en-scène* (reproducing an episode from his own past) not for an external audience but for himself alone, and it moves him to tears. The theatrical theme appears here, as in the first part, not in pure form but in conjunction with the theme of poetry: it is no accident that Pasternak mentions "pentametric lines" (obviously alluding to verse tragedy). Moreover, the "actor" in the second part may well be seen as the transformed "poet" of the first part. It is evident that in *Letters from Tula* Pasternak finds himself unable to give definitive answers to the questions that trouble him. The opposition between poetry and spectacle is more sharply expressed here than in *The Apelles Mark,* but again the author offers no solution.

One element is entirely new in *Letters from Tula* and sets it apart from all of Pasternak's earlier work; that is its moralizing tendency. Both parts of the narrative are set in Tula province, which was the site of Tolstoy's estate, Yasnaia Poliana. Tolstoy's invisible presence, according to Pasternak, causes "the compass needles to dance." Thus the opposition between life and art takes on specifically Tolstoyan, passionately polemical connotations. Tolstoy often spoke of the amorality, falseness, emptiness, and cruelty of modern civilization, which he considered contrary to human nature. In *War and Peace* he explored in depth the question of lies and hypocrisy in human behavior, embodying the "actor with pretensions to genius" in the figure of Napoleon. The road to truth lay not in the political or social sphere but in the moral self-perfection of the individual. Although Pasternak sympathized with these ethical ideas, there were certain aspects of Tolstoy's teaching—in particular, the condemnation of art (including his disparaging attitude toward Beethoven and Shakespeare)—which he could never bring himself to accept. Thus Tolstoy's presence in *Letters from Tula* reflects Pasternak's ambivalent attitude toward the writer who had influenced him most.

There is another polemical subtext in *Letters from Tula*. It is clearly aimed at Vladimir Mayakovsky, who deemed it necessary to take a visible role in revolutionary events. Once when the two met during this period, Pasternak called upon Mayakovsky to "publicly send futurism to hell." Pasternak felt that futurism, which had always expressed opposition to the existing order of things by creating public uproar, had lost its raison d'être in the new social environment. Mayakovsky disagreed: he feared that if leftist artists did not form a cohesive group, they would be pushed into the background. According to the reminiscences of Nikolai Aseev, Mayakovsky in the spring of 1917 even imagined the possibility of putting forward a futurist slate as a separate political entry in the municipal elections in Moscow, adding in jest, "What if they elect me President?" [14] In September

1917, before the October Revolution, Pasternak had his first falling out with Mayakovsky, who had organized a futurist performance entitled "Bolsheviks in Art" and announced, without asking permission, that Pasternak would be taking part in it. Pasternak was clearly upset not only at the unceremonious way in which his name was used, but also at the attempt to tie him to any sort of—however fictitious—literary party. In December 1917 Mayakovsky moved from Petrograd to Moscow for a few months. There, along with Vasily Kamensky and David Burliuk, he announced the resurrection of futurism. In March 1918 they published *Gazeta futuristov* (The Futurists' Newspaper), which marked a return to the old forms of public spectacle. The three men performed as a group in the newly created Poets' Café.[15]

Pasternak saw this cabaret form of literary activity as demeaning to the status of poetry and art. It was doubly unacceptable, in his opinion, during revolution, which should be the time of a radical moral renewal of the human spirit. He saw in the futurists' performances the same vulgar, theatrical behavior that his hero condemned in *Letters from Tula*. The use of a cinematographic motif in the story also related to this polemic between Pasternak and Mayakovsky. In March 1918 Mayakovsky, Kamensky, and Burliuk had begun to act in the film *Not Born for Money*, and Mayakovsky's role was precisely that of a poet with pretensions to genius who starts out unknown but eventually achieves a large following.[16] Like Tolstoy, Pasternak had come to consider film as a profanation of art. In this light it is understandable that Pasternak's argument with futurism should take on a moralistic tone. After all, futurism both in Italy and in Russia had from the start posited amoralism as one of its main slogans.[17] Still Pasternak's earlier attacks had focused on other aspects of futurism, and it was only now, in the aftermath of the revolution, that his attention shifted to the theme of "conscience."

The "café-chantant" aspect of Mayakovsky's behavior never blinded Pasternak to the more serious facets of Mayakovsky as a poet and a person. In January 1918 he first heard Mayakovsky's epic poem "Man" recited by the author. He was overwhelmed, as he had been by the tragedy *Vladimir Mayakovsky* in 1914. Here, in contrast to the cabaret vulgarization of poetry, Mayakovsky's self-dramatization revealed a high level of artistry. The reading took place at a poetry recital entitled "The Meeting of Two Generations," which brought the symbolists together with their young literary rivals. It was against this background that Pasternak concluded that Mayakovsky had no peer. It can therefore be said that, just as the attack on the idea of biography as spectacle in the first part of *Letters from Tula* represented a rejection of the cabaret aspect of Mayakovsky's futurism, so the second part also stemmed from Pasternak's appreciation of the poet's artistry. Once again it is apparent that Pasternak's rejection of theatrical elements was not absolute or immutable. He continued to emphasize (as he had been doing since 1913) that the poet's essence was inseparably linked to that of the actor. Yet the revolution and the peculiarities of Mayakovsky's behavior did force Pasternak to question the moral basis of the theatrical component in poetry.

With the October Revolution came radical changes in the relations between the various literary camps and groups. New forces appeared at the center of literary life: the so-called proletarian and folk poets. These names referred not only to the chosen themes and stylistic features of the two groups, but point also to their members' social origins. The established schools—symbolist and futurist—now found themselves playing an entirely different role. The futurists immediately sided with the revolution and the social changes it promised, although they were concerned about the new regime's conciliatory stance toward the old culture. The symbolists were sharply divided on the question of support for the Soviet regime; they had long since given up the idea of formulating a consistent aesthetic theory and now entered into literary alliances under new ideological banners.

Pasternak's first publication in the postrevolutionary period appeared in the collection *Vesennii salon poetov* (The Poets' Spring Salon), which included a broad and deliberately nonpartisan coalition of literary forces. It was composed of poems written after the outbreak of the First World War and included both previously published and unpublished works. Among the contributors were Baltrushaitis, Briusov, Bunin, Voloshin, Ivanov, Mayakovsky, Tsvetaeva, Ehrenburg, Khodasevich, and Boris Savinkov (a hero of the revolutionary underground and a prominent Social Revolutionary, as well as prose writer and poet).[18] The collection was published by Mikhail Tsetlin, himself a poet and patron of the arts, who had recently returned to Russia from a lengthy political exile in Paris.[19] Many of the contributors to *The Poets' Spring Salon* had also been invited by Tsetlin to take part in the recital "The Meeting of Two Generations," where Pasternak first heard Mayakovsky's "Man."

Although this venture into print was distinctly apolitical in nature,

Pasternak's other publications in 1918 reveal definite political leanings. He published "Dramatic Fragments" and "Dialogue" in the Social Revolutionaries' *Banner of Labor,* and *The Apelles Mark* appeared in a collection produced by the same paper, *Vremennik
znameni truda* (Banner of Labor Miscellany). This group, which supported the Bolshevik revolution, formed a new party, the Left SRs,
and joined the Soviet government. The newspaper's literary section
was headed by Ivanov-Razumnik, the literary critic who had first advanced the idea that Russians were distinguished from Europeans and
Asians by their "Scythian" nature. He saw the February and October
revolutions as an expression of elemental forces with features unique
to the Russian national character. Russia had an unprecedented historical mission: to transform the entire "old world" and save it from
certain doom. He described the revolution in apocalyptic terms, and
Lenin was a new Christ. The poets who wrote for *Banner of Labor*
were among those who enthusiastically welcomed the Bolshevik revolution, and they wrote about it not as a social or political upheaval
but as a "revolution of the spirit." This ideology appealed to many
poets and writers. Blok (whose "The Twelve" and "The Scythians"
first appeared in this newspaper) and Biely were particularly attracted, as was a group of younger folk poets—Kliuev, Esenin, and
Oreshin—who contrasted the eternal elements of Russian village life
to capitalist urban civilization.

In March 1918 the Left SRs broke from the ruling coalition in protest against the Brest-Litovsk Peace Treaty with Germany. Whereas
those who opposed Soviet power had earlier viewed *Banner of Labor*
as a semiofficial organ of the government, after March such accusations could no longer be made. It was at this point that Pasternak's
friends in Moscow—Yulian Anisimov and Vera Stanevich, later
joined by Sergei Bobrov—began to contribute to the paper. Pasternak's own work appeared there shortly before the Left SRs July mutiny against the Bolsheviks, in the wake of which the paper was closed
down along with all other opposition periodicals.

Several factors led Pasternak to contribute to *Banner of Labor.*
First, his views on the revolution as an elemental force echoed those
of the editors. Second, his notion that the Russian revolution was
superior to all others was clearly in concert with the Scythian platform. In contrast to the ideas of Ivanov-Razumnik, however, Pasternak's praise for Russia lacked nationalistic or religious overtones.
Nor did he have sympathy for the idealization of patriarchal peasant

society that characterized the folk poets and made them the butt of
disdain on the part of Russian intellectuals. Pasternak's hero in "Dialogue," the Character, has the features of a typical member of the
intelligentsia and, despite his passionate declaration of love for Russia, there is nothing specifically Russian about him. Thus, however
much Pasternak may have had in common with the Scythian poets in
his attitude toward the revolution, his ideas differed from theirs in
essential ways. Nevertheless, he was in accord with the Left SRs' general readiness to cooperate with the new Soviet government; and he
was attracted by the paper's independence, by the fact that it lacked
the narrowly political dogma and fanaticism he so disliked in the Bolshevik press.

Pasternak's works about the revolution in *Banner of Labor* corresponded to the ideological line of the paper itself. As far as artistic
leanings were concerned, however, the only member of the paper's
editorial board who supported Pasternak was Evgeny Lundberg.
Back in 1914 Lundberg had invited the members of Centrifuge to
contribute to *The Contemporary*. In the Urals in the spring of 1916,
he and Pasternak had become close friends. And now the decision to
invite the Anisimovs, Bobrov, and Pasternak to write for *Banner of
Labor* was also initiated by him. In fact, just after he joined the editorial board in December 1917, Lundberg wrote a review of Russian
literature for 1917 which made favorable mention of the last publications of Centrifuge, in which he saw signs of a "new and important
literary school." [20]

However, the Centrifuge writers were rather uncomfortable about
being grouped with the folk poets. In the spring of 1918 Bobrov
wrote an acrimonious column in the Petrograd journal *Knizhnyi ugol*
(Book Corner), in which he ridiculed their pretensions to the status
of revolutionary poets and labeled them epigones of symbolism. [21]
Ivanov-Razumnik, in turn, was lukewarm toward the members of
Centrifuge and all other "urban" poets; among the latter he singled
out Mayakovsky. In Ivanov-Razumnik's eyes, Esenin and Kliuev were
unmatched in their treatment of the cataclysms of war and revolution
and of Russia's special mission. Although Pasternak's "Dramatic
Fragments" was fully acceptable for his paper, he disliked the poet's
lyric poems. So it is not surprising that not one of the poems that later
made up *My Sister, Life* was printed in *Banner of Labor*. When they
did appear as a book in 1922, Ivanov-Razumnik disparaged them for
their supposed lack of revolutionary spirit. [22]

The closing of most non-Bolshevik papers in the summer of 1918 marked the inauguration of War Communism. Russia embarked upon a difficult period of bitter civil war, revolutionary and counter-revolutionary terror, famine, dictatorial censorship, and the paralysis of publishing activities. Many of those who had earlier welcomed the revolution with open arms now looked upon it with bitterness. Alexander Blok was typical in this regard. Whereas he had previously written about the revolution as "a musical element," now, after the terrible winter of 1918–19, he asked the agonizing question, "Who has destroyed the revolution (the spirit of music)?"[23] Pasternak also started to have qualms about the revolution. His mood at this time can be seen in some passages in *Safe Conduct* and in the epic poem "Lofty Malady."

War Communism eliminated much of the political pluralism that had survived the October Revolution. The non-Bolshevik socialist parties, the Left SRs and the Mensheviks, were outlawed. It was under these conditions that Pasternak began a prose work focusing on the first days of the February Revolution, with one of its main characters a rank-and-file member of the SRs. Its main theme was political volatility and the unpredictability of events in the early stages of revolution: was the monarchy really destroyed, and what form would the new government take? Unlike the works published in *Banner of Labor*, which gave a heroically elevated, romantic aura to the revolution, this one treated it on a lower, mundane level. The extant fragment has a strange title, "Bezliubie" (Without Love). Two men rush off to Moscow from provincial Prikamie as soon as they hear of the revolution, and there is a detailed description of their journey by sleigh. (The two are easily recognizable as Pasternak and Boris Zbarsky, who traveled to Moscow together.) The fact that his protagonists are SR party members suggests that Pasternak's tale was an attempt to understand why the "spirit of music" had disappeared from revolutionary Russia. Since Pasternak saw revolution as synonymous with "neighborly love," the title "Without Love" may suggest that the rest of his planned narrative would have taken up that theme.

The circumstances of the publication of "Without Love" seem as portentous as its theme. It appeared in the Moscow newspaper *Volia truda* (Liberty of Labor), which was an organ of the central committee of the Party of Revolutionary Communism. This was a tiny and short-lived group that had broken off from the outlawed Left SRs in September 1918. It retained the old populist ideology from which the

SR movement had sprung and refused to merge with the Bolshevik Party, thus making an attempt to assert its right to intellectual independence under War Communism. Initially the staff of the newspaper was mediocre, but on the eve of the First Party Congress the editorial board initiated a section on literature and art and enlisted the support of some of the leading writers of the day. It received promises of contributions from Biely, Esenin, Mandelshtam, Khlebnikov, and Shershenevich. The first story it published was Pasternak's "Without Love" (subtitled "A Fragment"), which appeared in two issues, on November 26 and 28, 1918. We have no knowledge of the rest of the work and do not even know if more was actually written or only contemplated. The author's date on the work—November 20—is intriguing because it reveals an unusually short interval between the writing and the publication of the story. It is possible that he wrote this fragment in response to a direct commission from the newspaper.

Through whom was such a request conveyed? It probably was the twenty-seven-year-old Riurik Ivnev (the pseudonym of Mikhail Kovalyov), who had been loosely connected with various wings of the futurist movement since 1913. A second-rate poet, he was a mild and amiable man. As far as politics was concerned, he held no strong positions. One can only wonder why he of all people became a major figure in Soviet literary life in the months after the October Revolution. As early as December 1917 he, together with Blok and Meyerhold, initiated an attempt to reconcile the Petrograd artistic community to the new Soviet regime (although in the preceding winter he had contributed to extremely right-wing publications). Anatoly Lunacharsky, the People's Commissar of Education in the Bolshevik government, asked him to be his personal secretary. Lunacharsky thought so highly of Ivnev that, late in 1918, he invited him to become his deputy. Ivnev declined, not wishing to join the Bolshevik Party or to be drawn too deeply into politics. Nevertheless, when Moscow was made the capital in March 1918, Lunacharsky, still in Petrograd, dispatched Ivnev to Moscow as his permanent representative in the government. This was when the members of Centrifuge became personally acquainted with Ivnev, whom they had known earlier only through his poetry and letters.

Ivnev's arrival in Moscow led to an attempt to resurrect Centrifuge. A petition, signed by Bobrov, Aksyonov, Bolshakov, Ivnev, and Pasternak (Aseev had been in the Far East since the autumn of 1917), was sent to Lunacharsky asking for governmental support for the publishing house. Among the books that were ready for publication, the petition listed the *Third Miscellany* of Centrifuge, a volume of Briusov's entitled *Centrifuge: To Pushkin,* books of poetry by Aseev, Aksyonov, Bobrov, Bolshakov, and Ivnev, and prose works by Ivnev, Pasternak, Bobrov, and Aksyonov.[24] The request had no effect: Narkompros was unable to subsidize private publishing enterprises.

Several ventures into print by Pasternak at this time attest to his growing friendship with Ivnev. First came his decision to contribute to the newspaper *Liberty of Labor.* It was also through Ivnev that Pasternak began to draw closer to the new imagist group in literature which had formed in the winter of 1918–19. Its main proponent and organizer was Vadim Shershenevich who, since breaking with Mayakovsky in the summer of 1914, had been unattached to any literary circle. In contrast to Mayakovsky, who placed increasing emphasis on the content of poetry, Shershenevich advanced a theory of poetry as a blend of images wholly devoid of logic, content, or thematic structure. In 1918 he managed to assemble a group of sympathizers, including Esenin, Ivnev, and Mariengof. Of these, only Mariengof truly shared Shershenevich's theoretical views. But the presence of Ivnev in the circle gave them easier access to Bolshevik-controlled printers at a time when book production (except for propaganda materials) had virtually stopped. The first work this group published was a miscellany entitled *Yav* (Reality), which included works by Pasternak, Kamensky, and Pyotr Oreshin. In spite of his long-standing feud with Centrifuge, Shershenevich had written articles in 1918 praising Pasternak's and Aseev's new poetry, and he greeted Pasternak's contributions with enthusiasm. *Reality* came out in March 1919; two months before that, the first manifesto of imagism had been released, signed by Shershenevich, Esenin, Ivnev, Mariengof, and the painters Boris Erdman and Georgy Yakulov.[25]

In many respects the beginnings of this new trend recalled the debut of the futurists. Imagism lasted until 1924, undergoing major changes in membership and in the slogans it advanced. Its publications encompassed the works of such major poets as Osip Mandelshtam and Velimir Khlebnikov, whose own poetic views and interests were far removed from the imagist platform. Pasternak contributed to imagist miscellanies only in the initial period of the group's existence (1919–20), and he took part only in those projects that included nonimagist poets, such as *Reality, Avtografy* (Autographs), and *My* (We). Among the members of the group, he had the most respect for Esenin and

Ivnev. Otherwise the imagists' declarations were alien to him. He particularly objected to the imagists' penchant for self-promotion and for shocking audiences. He saw the appearance of an extravagant new poetic clique, cast in the futurist mold, as an anachronism.

Yet there were aspects of imagism that attracted Pasternak. For one thing, it was independent of the struggles between the futurists and the proletarian writers to win the support of the Soviet leaders. The only poets who were considered truly revolutionary by the proletarian writers were those who had grown up, as they had, in working-class families. On the other hand, Mayakovsky and his circle, who published their works in the paper *Iskusstvo kommuny* (Art of the Commune), refused to recognize revolutionary qualities in the proletarian writers, keeping that distinction for themselves. With its exaggerated pathos and grandiose use of allegorical language, proletarian poetry recalled the early symbolist tradition (Balmont, Briusov, and Blok).[26] This is why it seemed so anachronistic to the futurists and other modernist writers.

The imagists differed from both groups by their complete lack of propagandistic zeal. Their goal was pure poetry, not its application to the government's political interests. They preferred to discuss the technical features of a literary work rather than the extent to which it reflected proletarian ideals. For this reason, although he disliked various aspects of its literary platform, Pasternak saw in imagism an attractive alternative to futurist or proletarian writing and agreed to take part in its ventures.

In time, however, the imagists became hostile toward Pasternak. Beginning in late 1920, Sergei Esenin's attacks on Centrifuge became even more virulent than those against Mayakovsky, and in the winter of 1920–21 his conflict with Pasternak nearly brought the two men to blows. It was the lack of specifically Russian traits in Pasternak's poetry that particularly aroused Esenin's ire. The more nationalistic (and even antisemitic) Esenin became, the more Pasternak's "cosmopolitan" style and language irritated him. He began to see Pasternak as the embodiment of those traits that were essentially hostile to the development of a national world view and literature. Pasternak was a "poet for the few" and therefore doomed to scorn and oblivion.

The extent to which Pasternak felt alien to all existing literary camps at that time is evident from his article "The Quintessence." It was written in December 1918, when Pasternak's own literary work and Russian publishing activities as a whole had come to a standstill.

He begins his article with a discussion about what now seemed inaccessible: the book. Here the "book" is counterposed to the "stage," a theme reminiscent of *Letters from Tula* and its indirect censure of the futurists' love for public spectacle. But now, in the autumn of 1918, writers had no way to reach their audience outside of recitals in cafés—books were not being published. Hence the motif that appears in the fourth section of the article: art in abeyance.

"The Quintessence" aims its critical remarks not only against futurism but against all of the avant-garde in poetry. Instead of the usual notion of art as a "fountain," Pasternak offers the image of a "sponge" (an image first used in the poem "Poezia vesny" (The Poetry of Spring) in *Above the Barriers*). The very nomenclature of literary movements—symbolism, acmeism, futurism—seems suspicious and ridiculous to him. When he was writing "The Quintessence," Pasternak was certainly aware of the moves to advance imagism as a new literary school. Perhaps the dedication of the article, "To Riurik Ivnev, poet and friend," reflects the fact that Pasternak had discussed with him the platform of this new movement. The first draft of the article had two more sections that addressed topics of particular interest to the imagists, those of free verse and rhythm.[27] When Pasternak had the opportunity to publish his article in 1922, he deleted these sections because the polemic around imagism was no longer relevant.[28]

From the beginning of 1918, Pasternak turned his attention primarily to writing a novel. His topic was family life deep in the Russian provinces, in the Ural region. He worked quickly. In fact he later said that, until he wrote *Doctor Zhivago*, the only time that prose writing had come easily to him was during 1918.[29] The newfound possibilities for "slow," detailed description, for epic breadth of narration, and for gradual character development gave him obvious pleasure. It is this unhurried narrative style that distinguishes this work not only from all of Pasternak's earlier writing but from that of most of his contemporaries. It is reminiscent of nineteenth-century realist novels, whose prose had seemed so hopelessly superannuated in the modernist era, and the influence of Tolstoy is apparent. Pasternak was clearly avoiding anything that would link his new work to the latest fashions in prose: to the stylized ornamentalism of Alexei Remizov or Mikhail Kuzmin or to Biely's "kaleidoscopic" shifts among images and his application of metrical patterns to prose.

This novel has not survived in its original form. Only the first third of it is known to us. It was ready for publication by the summer of 1918 and was apparently supposed to appear in the Moscow miscellany *Epokha* (Epoch). However, because of the general crisis in publishing, the project was canceled. The fragment finally appeared in print as a separate piece, *Detstvo Liuvers* (Liuvers' Childhood), in 1922.

The story is about a young girl, Zhenia Liuvers, as she grows up and comes to understand the world around her. Events that are insignificant from an adult viewpoint take on an unexpectedly profound, "providential" meaning for the adolescent girl. Pasternak shows how fundamental concepts may suddenly crystallize out of the chaos of apparently unimportant impressions and observations. From those concepts Pasternak chose one that was especially engaging at the time, the idea of man.[30] Zhenia Liuvers approaches the idea by way of a chain of accidental associations. These fragments of knowledge, broken and unrelated as they are, together give a generalized understanding of "the Other," of "man in general." In the manuscript of the tale, the philosophical undercurrents are given more open expression than in the published version. Purely philosophical digressions were injected into the original narrative only to be deleted, apparently, by the editors.[31]

Some scholars see in the content of *Liuvers' Childhood* religious— even Christian, Russian Orthodox—elements. Such assertions are unfounded. Pasternak saw Christianity at that time as only one cultural system among many. In *My Sister, Life* he lets slip the jocular comment that a train schedule is grander than the Scriptures. As proof of the Christian content of *Liuvers' Childhood* scholars point to the unquestionably important authorial digression that concludes the tale. Here, citing the Commandments, Pasternak says, "'As a living human individual,' they say, 'you must not do to this featureless generalized man what you would not wish for yourself as a living individual.'"[32] But this sentence is also a paraphrase of the famous admonition of the Jewish sage Hillel the Elder, who said, "What is hateful to you, do not do unto your neighbour: this is the entire Torah, all the rest is commentary."[33] This so-called negative rule of love is generally contrasted to Christian ethics. Thus, if there is any trace of religious thought in Pasternak's story, it is ecumenical or synthetic by nature rather than specifically Christian.

In the winter of 1918–19, Pasternak decided to compile a book of poems written after *Above the Barriers*. Although three of the poems had already appeared in print, this was the first time Pasternak thought of bringing them all out in one volume. The book became a major work of twentieth-century Russian poetry, *Sestra moia–zhizn* (My Sister, Life). Pasternak's decision was apparently influenced by the unprecedented enthusiasm that Mayakovsky showed toward these new poems. He even proposed to publish them himself and in May 1919 included the title in the forthcoming list for Izdatelstvo molodykh (Publishing House of the Young), which he established.

My Sister, Life is subtitled "Summer 1917" but this date is only partially accurate with regard to the writing of the poems. Not everything he wrote during that summer was included, and he continued to add new poems right up to the winter of 1921–22, long after he had developed his first clear idea of the book's structure and submitted the original manuscript to Mayakovsky's publishing house. Unlike *Above the Barriers,* which was hastily prepared for publication and lacked an overarching structure, *My Sister, Life* matured over a much longer period of time and grew as an organically integrated work. The selections were positioned so as to create the impression that they belonged to a common storyline; they were grouped into cycles that resembled the chapters of a novel. Since it was the author's intention to force the reader to see the book as a whole, rather than as a conglomeration of independent texts, some cycles were even accompanied by short prose remarks underscoring their connection to the storyline. At one point in a manuscript copy, the author placed an arrow between two consecutive poems to show that the transition between them should be smooth and unbroken. This was meant to indicate that boundaries between texts within the book were merely relative.

Many of the poems in *My Sister, Life* related to a love affair between Pasternak and Elena Vinograd, which began in spring 1917. The two had become friends in 1909; according to Christopher Barnes, "Along with Ida Vysotskaya, Olga Freidenberg, and Nadezhda Sinyakova, she was one of the most important amorous attachments Pasternak formed in early manhood."[34] Elena Vinograd had been betrothed to Sergei Listopadov, the illegitimate son of Lev Shestov. Her romance with Pasternak began shortly after her fiancé died at the front early in 1917, and it ended a year later. A significant number of poems in Pasternak's *Temy i variatsii* (Themes and Variations) are also addressed to her.

Taken together, the two books *My Sister, Life* and *Themes and Var-*

iations show how radically Pasternak's lyric poetry changed in 1917 and 1918. The latter book, his fourth, was largely composed of works not included in the preceding volume. There were various reasons for their omission, including incompatibility with the "plot" requirements, violation of the stylistic homogeneity of the intended novel in verse, or because the author considered them inferior to the other poems. As a result, despite a tendency to arrange the poems into cycles, *Themes and Variations* has a considerably looser structure than its predecessor.

Whereas *Above the Barriers* had given expression to stylistic traits that Pasternak shared with Bobrov and Aseev, the two later books revealed a highly original, individualized poetic style. Its distinctiveness lay in the poet's eccentric transformations of language. Rejecting the use of neologisms, he concentrated on an unconventional treatment of idioms and syntactical units, dismantling them and placing them (or parts of them) in unexpected contexts, eliminating or transposing their components. Some critics try to subsume the Pasternakian lyrical style under such traditional terms as "metaphor" and "metonymy." The presence of these tropes in *My Sister, Life* and *Themes and Variations* (as well as earlier books) is quite obvious. Yet what is unique to Pasternak is not the abundance of tropes, but the way in which they are used. Paraphrasing Albert Einstein, Pasternak once called his literary method of this period "a general principle of metaphoric relativity." How should we understand this principle, and how does it work in Pasternak's poetry? What we observe so frequently in Pasternak is that a text is deliberately composed in such a way as to make it impossible to determine whether an expression is used figuratively or not. All the vehicles of language at the author's disposal seem, in fact, to be mobilized to blur the distinction between a trope and a nontrope.[35] In most cases, both interpretations are equally valid, suggesting a plurality of readings. As a rule, the elements of a text gain metaphorical force to the same extent and almost at the very same moment that they lose it. The derivation of verse becomes a kind of pendulum, continuously swinging between clarification and concealment of the meaning of a text. As Marina Tsvetaeva put it, "Lyric poetry, let us not forget, elucidates the obscure and obscures the lucid." Each poem in these volumes is thus characterized by a general ambiguity of content and, although the style is incomparably more transparent than in *Above the Barriers,* each phrase is marked by an unprecedented elusiveness.

Pasternak's contemporaries viewed his innovations as more than just an alternative to existing poetic practices. What was new and striking in him was the fact that he did not break with cultural tradition but rather absorbed and transformed it. This was especially apparent in Pasternak's poems about Pushkin, written in 1918, before he began to compile his third book of verse. From the start of the twentieth century, beginning with the symbolists, Pushkin had been regarded not as a museum piece to be venerated but as a living phenomenon, an active participant in contemporary literature. However they may have quarreled among themselves, each of the modernist schools saw in him its own stylistic precursor. There was therefore nothing extraordinary in the fact that Pasternak also chose Pushkin as the subject of these poems. What was extraordinary, however, was the way in which he captured the relativism, indefiniteness, or (as he put it later in reference to the Scriptures) "susceptibility to various similitudes" which permeated Pushkin's entire oeuvre.

It is this trait that led Pasternak to construct his image of Pushkin in the form of a "theme with six variations," in which each variation suggested a different interpretation of the same phenomenon. The principle of variations (obviously borrowed from music) had a dual function here: they not only echoed the principal poem ("Theme") but also played on Pushkin's own texts and motifs. In this regard Pasternak's approach to Pushkin resembles other examples of twentieth-century "transformations" of classical images; suffice it to mention Picasso and Stravinsky. Yet Pasternak's approach to the Pushkinian tradition stood in sharp contrast to that of those twentieth-century poets, such as Vladislav Khodasevich or Boris Sadovskoy, who turned to Pushkin and his epoch as a kind of refuge from the onslaught of modernist culture. They tried to imitate old-fashioned images, genres, and styles. In contrast, Pasternak did not attempt to mimic early nineteenth-century idiom; instead he discovered and revived a more profound quality of Pushkin's poetry—its essential relativism. The leap he made was not into the past but into the future. It was only later, well after Pasternak's "Theme with Variations" had appeared, that Russian literary critics came to recognize this relativism as the central element of Pushkin's art. In one respect it can be said that Pasternak's innovations of this period were strikingly similar to Pushkin's reform of Russian literature one hundred years before: Pushkin also did not invent new means of poetic expression, but found new uses for what already existed.

Given these profound similarities, one might wonder why then, in the spring of 1919, Pasternak decided to dedicate *My Sister, Life* not to Pushkin but to Lermontov, "as to a living man." Does this mean that the two poets were interchangeable, either of whom could be called the precursor of Pasternak's poetics? Are there grounds for terming Pasternak "a lyricist of the Lermontov school," as some of his contemporaries did?[36] Of course not. As an artist, Pushkin was incomparably broader and more multifaceted than Lermontov. The dedication of a book about the summer of 1917 to Lermontov "as to a living man" sets up a biographical juxtaposition between him and Pasternak, not a comparison of their poetic methods. In the Russian cultural consciousness, Lermontov's name primarily evoked the image of a young poet who dies an untimely death. He died at twenty-seven, Pasternak's age at the time of the revolution. The theme of a death that is expected but does not occur plays an important role in the peculiar dedication of *My Sister, Life*. This is confirmed by a poem that Pasternak included as a "preface" to the book, although it has no apparent connection to the rest. The poem is called "Pamiati de-mona" (In Memory of the Demon) and serves as a sort of obituary to Lermontov's hero. It was Pushkin who introduced to Russian poetry the romantic image of the demon, but it was a peripheral theme for him. In contrast, in Lermontov's oeuvre the demon plays a central role and can even be said to represent the author's double. It is Lermontov's, not Pushkin's, demon that Pasternak says farewell to in his book when he dedicates it to the "living" Lermontov at a time when (in the words of another poem) "the very air smells of death."

Pasternak liked to portray authors in conflict with their characters: the creator versus the created. Thus in "Shekspir" (Shakespeare) the bard and his own sonnet meet and argue in a tavern. In "Theme with Variations" Pushkin appears as equivalent to and interchangeable with the characters he has created. In *My Sister, Life,* however, we have the opposite case: Lermontov and the demon are placed at separate poles, and the entire book is a polemic against the "demonic pose," or the demonic approach to the world.[37]

The subtitle of *My Sister, Life,* recalling as it did the summer of 1917, was also internally polemical. The book was compiled during the period of War Communism, when the realities of life offered a sharp contrast to the hopeful and joyful atmosphere that had reigned in the first weeks of the revolution. In place of its romantic ideals came the reality of powerful speculators. In place of overwhelming social unity came the bitter divisions of counterrevolution. The year 1919 was the most difficult one of the postrevolutionary period. The Bolsheviks held less than half of the former Russian Empire, and the outcome of the Civil War was impossible to predict. The country was cut off from the outside world. Famine beset the cities, and unlawful arrests and executions were common. This was the period the poet would later call the Stone Age (*peshchernyi vek*).

It was in these apocalyptic times that Pasternak embarked on his career as a professional writer, something he had dreamed of for five years. It is surprising that he finally achieved his goal now, when printers were closed, journals were not being published, and much more famous authors than he were forced to find other sources of income. Official data indicate that only a tenth of writers were able to earn a living through their writing,[38] while the rest had to find work in government offices.

Pasternak's professional literary work took the form of translations. Two organizations gave him commissions, the Theatrical Department of Narkompros and Gorky's Petrograd publishing house World Literature. He was extremely productive: in 1920 he reported that he had completed a total of 12,000 lines of verse translation for publication. In addition to the works he had translated before the revolution, Kleist's *Der zerbrochene Krug* and Swinburne's *Chastelard,* he translated three more works by Kleist, *The Alchemist* by Ben Jonson, three *Fastnachtspiele* by Hans Sachs, Goethe's *Geheimnisse,* some poems by Rilke from his *Buch der Bilder,* and poems by the Belgian poet Charles Van Lerberghe. This may also be the time when he began to translate Georg Herwegh's *Gedichte eines Lebendingen.*[39]

These translations were of uneven quality, and some were rejected by the publisher. Blok is known to have reacted with condescension to Pasternak's translation of Goethe, and World Literature turned down his translations of Van Lerberghe. In 1926 Georgy Adamovich recalled that the poor quality of Pasternak's translations caused astonishment among Petrograd writers just when praise for his poetry was filtering in from Moscow.[40]

Although the majority of Pasternak's new poems could not find their way into print, the period from 1917 to 1921 witnessed what Marina Tsvetaeva later called "the emergence of the subterranean fame" of the poet. Handwritten copies of his poems were circulated widely. Briusov claimed, perhaps with some exaggeration, that no poet since Pushkin had achieved such popularity on the basis of man-

uscript copies as Pasternak did in those years. His fame was both
remarkably widespread (given the fact that the book market was shut
down) and unusual in nature. Whereas the futurists and imagists had
made a practice of self-advertisement and loved noisy public extrav-
agances, Pasternak was unassuming in manner and agreed to give
readings only before professional literary circles. He received the most
enthusiastic response from novice poets, and it became increasingly
clear that his influence on them was greater than that of the symbolists, Mayakovsky, or Esenin. But there was only one poet of the older
generation who was caught up in the wave of enthusiasm for Pasternak. This was Valery Briusov, the leader of Russian symbolism in the
1890s. He was at first skeptical of the general fascination with Pasternak, but then he underwent a sudden metamorphosis as a poet that
confounded everyone. Nowhere else in the history of Russian literature is there an example of such slavish imitation by an older poet of
a younger one. Briusov had always been an unusually gifted imitator
of other poets' styles, but the influence Pasternak exerted on his writing was without parallel.

Although Pasternak, unlike Mayakovsky, consistently refrained
from making political pronouncements, no one ever questioned his
loyalty to the Soviet government. He was a poet of the avant-garde,
and no avant-gardist would have taken an active anti-Soviet position
in those years. The fact that Pasternak kept silent on the burning political questions of his day was seen as a peculiarity of his temperament rather than as an indication of his opposition to the regime. In
all respects he seemed to be in keeping with postrevolutionary realities, even though he never directly sang the praises of the new government. It was the fact that his poetry had its roots in the turbulent age
of revolution, and not that he made any verbal declarations of fealty,
that attracted Pasternak's contemporaries.

6

Factions in the Twenties

The New Economic Policy (NEP) was introduced in Soviet Russia in March 1921. The resurgence of business and trade led to the legalization of publishing activity. By the end of May 1922, in Moscow alone there were 220 private publishers and, in Petersburg, 99.[1] As if trying to make up for lost time, the publishers began to put out books, miscellanies, and journals in rapid succession. The Stone Age had come to an end. The luxuriant growth of literature in Russia in 1922 can indeed be compared only to the situation in 1913. The feverish publishing activity demonstrated how much valuable material had been written—and especially in poetry—during the years of the revolution, a time when an outside observer might have concluded that art had fallen silent. At the beginning of 1922 a multitude of new poetic schools and groups declared their existence.

Boris Pasternak became one of the primary beneficiaries of this new cultural climate. In December 1921 his manuscript of *My Sister, Life* was accepted by the publisher Z. I. Grzhebin. It was printed in April in Moscow, and nine months later was reissued in Berlin (where the publishing house transferred its quarters). Other works by Pasternak soon followed. The translation of Goethe's *Geheimnisse* was brought out as a separate book. The new almanacs and periodicals carried *Letters from Tula, Liuvers' Childhood,* the article "The Quintessence," and a host of poems. Pasternak's name suddenly became famous and surfaced in the announcements of a wide range of publishers. Never before had his writings appeared with such frequency in the press.

But these publications and the critical responses they triggered failed to clarify the poet's position among the literary groups. On the contrary, they made it more complicated. If in 1914–1917 Pasternak's membership in Centrifuge, and through this group in futurism, was an indisputable fact, now the most variegated and ephemeral organizations claimed him as their own. Sometimes accounts appeared in the press declaring that Pasternak's poetry no longer had any relationship to the avant-garde. This was the opinion of the influential literary critic, historian, and journalist Viacheslav Polonsky. During the period when publishing activity was still frozen, he had founded the Press House in Moscow, where starting in March 1920 he arranged literary evenings. A man of broad cultural interests and free of political fanaticism and prejudices, Polonsky was able to gather around his Press House the best writers and poets. It was then that he became acquainted with Pasternak. In his eyes, Pasternak's literary positions seemed to correspond much more to the role of art in a revolutionary epoch than did the garish slogans of futurism and other avant-garde currents. Indeed he considered Pasternak's works antifuturistic. Polonsky's achievements as head of the Press House and other Soviet establishments led to his appointment in 1921 as the editor-in-chief of a new journal *Pechat i revoliutsia* (Press and Revolution), which was wholly devoted to criticism and bibliography. Evidently it was Polonsky who introduced Pasternak to Alexander Voronsky, editor of the first Soviet literary journal *Krasnaia nov* (Red Virgin Soil), founded with Lenin's and Gorky's support in the spring of 1921.[2] Pasternak was one of the first contributors to this periodical.

The "antifuturist" interpretation of Pasternak's works was most concisely outlined in an article printed in summer 1922 in Polonsky's *Press and Revolution*. Its author, Yakov Cherniak, stated that in *My Sister, Life* one senses an attraction to "Pushkinian lucidity and simplicity of form." Having passed through an artistic apprenticeship with futurism, Pasternak was now absolutely independent of it. Moreover, his book signaled a break from the irreconcilability and one-sidedness of literary "parties."[3]

This characterization was echoed by Pasternak in his own article "The Quintessence," which was printed under a new title, "Several Propositions," in the miscellany *Sovremennik* (The Contemporary) in spring 1922. This miscellany was initiated by a group of young Moscow poets who were strongly influenced by Pasternak's poetry. They declared themselves representatives of a new tendency, "neorealism." The principles of the new school were outlined in a preface written by its patron, Valery Briusov. Unlike the old literature of the nineteenth century, neorealism was supposed to absorb the experience of the latest artistic currents—impressionism, symbolism, futurism, cubism. Their recognition of these achievements was undoubtedly close to Pasternak's position—he had come to the conclusion in 1920 that realism is not a separate school but the nature of art as a whole.[4] A central place in the miscellany was devoted to Briusov's poems (styled in imitation of Pasternak) and to Pasternak's remarkable lyrical cycle "Razryv" (The Break). Although Pasternak does not mention the term "neorealism," both the article and his poems were undoubtedly taken to be a manifesto of the new tendency.

A similar call for realism was advanced by a group of artists operating under the name of Makovets (the birthplace of the holy father Abbot Sergius of Radonezh, ca. 1321–1391). This group rejected the ideas of the futurists and constructivists about the withering away of art and the need of the artist to produce "things" instead of paintings. The artists of Makovets understood realism not as a retrograde tendency, passéism, or the resurrection of the naturalistic traditions of the nineteenth-century Wanderers, but as a synthesis of the achievements of great masters from the Renaissance to Cézanne. At the end of 1921 Makovets decided to publish a journal and invited several poets to its meetings. Among them were Khlebnikov and Pasternak, and both gave their poems to the journal *Makovets* (only two issues of it appeared in January and June 1922). This episode is by no means irrelevant to Pasternak's creative biography. The program of artistic realism, as well as the idea advanced by Makovets about the indivisible unity and continuity of human culture, were especially dear to him at this juncture.

Another ephemeral and traditionalist poetic group, Lyrical Circle, appeared in March 1922. A little later it printed an almanac consisting of works by poets who called themselves "neoclassicists" (Sergei Solovyov, Vladislav Khodasevich, Anna Akhmatova, Konstantin Lipskerov, Osip Mandelshtam, Sofia Parnok, Abram Efros). This group was opposed to leftist tendencies in art and pledged to strive for clarity, harmony, and simplicity. Although Pasternak did not contribute to their almanac, he felt it necessary to announce publicly his solidarity with the group.[5]

Pasternak's antifuturist tendencies during these months were offset by no less formidable futurist inclinations. Throughout 1922 Pasternak's name continued to be associated with Centrifuge, which was vainly trying to resurrect its publishing activity. Pasternak's books also figured in the announcements of the Moscow Association of Futurists organized by Mayakovsky. In an article reviewing Russian poetry from 1917 to 1922, Briusov named Pasternak and Mayakovsky as the central figures in futurism. Other critics classified *My Sister, Life* as an unquestionably futurist work. Osip Mandelshtam compared Pasternak's reform of poetic language to Khlebnikov's and declared that the changes introduced by both were irreversible.[6]

Personal relations between Mayakovsky and Pasternak in this period were very warm. Mayakovsky and Brik viewed Pasternak as a full-fledged member of their circle. He was invited, for example, to a meeting of futurist poets with A. V. Lunacharsky, the People's Commissar of Education. The meeting took place at Mayakovsky's flat on May 1, on the eve of Mayakovsky's first trip abroad (to Riga). Others taking part were Khlebnikov, Kamensky, Aseev, Kruchonykh, Kushner, and Brik. While acknowledging that "gathered in this room are the most colorful and melodious representatives of our generation,"[7] Lunacharsky spoke sharply against futurism and naturally encountered stiff opposition. When the discussion began, Pasternak sided with his futurist opponents against the commissar.[8] But if Lunacharsky criticized the other futurists for their anticultural positions and their revolutionary nihilism, in Pasternak he saw the opposite danger—an excessive refinement and scholasticism that was incompatible with the needs and character of the proletarian state.

The complex and nebulous position that Pasternak occupied with regard to existing literary groups made it difficult to answer questions about how "modern" the poet was and to what extent his works corresponded to the nature of the times. Despite his undisputable acceptance of the Russian revolution in both of its stages and his sympathy toward the Bolshevik authorities, his attitude to the realities of the Soviet state was much more ambiguous than, for example, that of Aseev and Mayakovsky, who went to work for the new regime and were energetically engaged in its propaganda efforts. At the end of 1919 Pasternak flatly rejected Mayakovsky's proposal to collaborate with him on·posters for the Windows of ROSTA (the Russian telegraph agency) and later sarcastically referred to this work in his poem "Lofty Malady" (1923–24).

To a certain extent, the detached attitude shown by Pasternak toward contemporary Soviet life corresponded to the position of Boris Pilniak. Pasternak had become friendly with him in 1920 and helped

Pilniak to publish his first novel, *Golyi god* (The Naked Year): he mentioned the work to Gorky, who arranged its publication. The appearance of the novel marked the beginning of Pilniak's reputation, and he began to be viewed as one of the most brilliant figures (along with the Serapion Brothers in Petersburg) in postrevolutionary Russian prose. Pilniak was the first writer to make a trip to the west as a representative of nascent Soviet literature. His sojourn in Berlin at the beginning of 1922 was a genuine triumph: he was able to convince many émigrés that Russian culture under the Bolsheviks was flourishing.[9] Pasternak valued Pilniak very highly as a prose writer and ranked him above all other contemporaries, including the Serapion Brothers. In his 1956 autobiography Pasternak named Pilniak first among those who had created the new Soviet prose.

Like Pasternak, Pilniak greeted the revolution of 1917 enthusiastically. But he understood it differently. Pilniak felt that it bore a peasant, rural imprint, and that it expressed the elemental traits of the Russian national character. It followed then that the communist order was a superficial and temporary phenomenon, and for this reason Pilniak accentuated the differences between his position and the ideology of the leadership. In September 1923 he wrote:

> I am not a communist, and therefore I do not acknowledge that I should be a communist or write in a communist manner—and I assert that the communist regime in Russia is determined not by the will of the communists, but by Russia's historical fate, and insofar as I want to trace (to the extent that I can and that my mind and conscience allow me to) this Russian historical fate, I am with the communists, that is, insofar as the communists are with Russia, I am with them ... I recognize that the fate of the RCP [Russian Communist Party] is much less interesting to me than the fate of Russia, and the RCP for me is only a link in the history of Russia.[10]

Pasternak of course also never considered himself a member of the Communist—or any other—Party, and he too was not prepared to subordinate himself to its directives in his writing. But his conception of communism differed decisively from Pilniak's. In response to declarations expressing opposition to the Soviet regime, Pasternak loved to say that he was a communist. He would add then that he was a communist in the same sense that Peter the Great and Pushkin were communists, and that in Russia now, thank God, these were Pushkinian times.[11] This stance was in opposition not only to that of Pilniak or staunch opponents of the Soviet regime, but also to those at the other end of the spectrum, such as Mayakovsky and the proletarian poets. If Pilniak saw in the Russian revolution only a spontaneous peasant rebellion, while Mayakovsky praised the organizational role of the Bolsheviks within it, then for Pasternak the actual revolution signified primarily a *cultural* transformation. He would state this clearly in *Safe Conduct,* when he claimed that there is no genuine revolution when culture is replaced by a surrogate. With these views Pasternak obliquely replied to the reproaches of "excessive refinement" that had been directed against him. In addition, by defining Pushkin as a true communist, Pasternak rebuked the accusations that he was insufficiently in touch with modern life.

In February 1922 Pasternak applied for permission to travel to Germany.[12] His parents and sisters had been in Berlin since August 1921. At about this time, his life underwent significant changes. In the fall he had met Evgenia Vladimirovna Lurie at a party; she came from Petersburg and was studying painting with Robert Falk at the Moscow Art College. In January the couple traveled to Petersburg and were married there. But besides a desire to see his parents, Pasternak had other reasons for setting out on a foreign journey. Travel abroad was a type of escape from his sudden fame. He was irritated by notoriety not only because of his inherent shyness, but also because it came to him at a time of profound creative crisis. Since the winter of 1918–19 he had done little but translations. The large prose work to which he once again returned was progressing slowly.[13] The poet thought that a change of setting and seclusion would return him to normal creative activity.

Pasternak left Russia at a time when the liberalization of economic and cultural life was in full swing. The NEP brought about striking changes in Soviet Russia, and observers—some with joy and others with trepidation—saw in it a waning of the revolution. Pasternak was one of those who greeted the normalization of life and who did not consider the NEP a betrayal of revolutionary ideals. On December 22, 1921, he was present at the opening of the Ninth All-Russian Congress of Soviets and heard the speech in which Lenin surveyed the accomplishments and goals of the NEP. The speech made an indelible impression on the poet; in 1928 he made mention of it in the poem "Lofty Malady." The appearance of the revolutionary leader, his unbending determination, the magnetic force of his arguments, his readiness to sacrifice familiar doctrines to life's demands—all this remained etched in Pasternak's memory. The following words in Lenin's speech must have made a particularly strong impact on the poet: "Materially—economically and militarily—we are extremely weak; but morally—by which, of course, I mean not abstract morals, but the alignment of the real forces of all classes in all countries—we are the strongest of all."[14] On the other hand, in the summer of 1922 there were symptoms that the party was going on an ideological offensive. This could be seen in hostility to dissident voices and cruel persecution of them. These tendencies were expressed most clearly in the show trial of the Social Revolutionaries.

In August 1922, on the eve of his departure for Berlin, the poet was summoned to meet with Lev Trotsky. In the Soviet hierarchy, Trotsky was second only to Lenin. Since Lenin, seriously ill, was not taking part in government affairs during these months, everyone considered Trotsky to be the most likely candidate for his post. The meeting was arranged because of the party's increased interest in the mood of the Soviet intelligentsia and in literary matters.[15] The administration wanted to find out what attitude Pasternak would take abroad. Konstantin Balmont, one of the first poets to receive an exit visa, had begun to slander life in the Soviet republic as soon as he reached the west. On the other hand, Ilya Ehrenburg (who left in the spring of 1921) praised the modern art in revolutionary Russia. Trotsky had read *My Sister, Life,* which had become a literary sensation, but neither this book nor any other of Pasternak's publications of 1922 nor, finally, the poet's position among the existing literary groups clarified the poet's view of the Bolsheviks and the Soviet regime.

Trotsky's conversation with Pasternak lasted for more than half an hour and, according to the poet's account of it in a letter to Briusov on August 15, 1922, Trotsky "charmed and delighted" him.[16] Trotsky was remembered with similar feelings many years later by the artist Yury Annenkov, who lived in emigration from the mid-1920s on and who in the end lost all sympathy for the revolution and the Soviet regime. He had been able to get to know Trotsky thoroughly in the course of working on his portrait (as well as the portraits of other party leaders) in 1923. Annenkov recalled: "Trotsky was an intellectual in the real sense of this word. He was interested in and always up to date on artistic and literary life not only in Russia, but on a world scale. In this regard he was a rare exception among the 'leaders of the revolution' . . . The cultural level of the majority of Soviet leaders was not high."[17] Trotsky charmed Pasternak because in him the poet saw an indissoluble link between the spirit of the Russian revolution and the culture and traditions of the Russian intelligentsia. The only thing he regretted after the meeting was that he had been less able to listen to Trotsky than to talk himself.

The main question Trotsky asked Pasternak was why the poet refrained from dealing with social themes. The same question—often in the form of accusations—was addressed to Pasternak by Soviet critics for the rest of his life. But Trotsky was evidently satisfied by the poet's response. Pasternak declared that "genuine individualism" is an integral part of every new "social organism." His defense of individualism corresponded to his deep conviction that the times, without the will of the author and even in defiance of it, express themselves in works of art, and that therefore there was no sense in the efforts (of the futurists, for instance) to appear modern. Pasternak even advised Trotsky that he should not expect any social themes or responses to the contemporary scene from him in the future: his next works might even be more individualistic than *My Sister, Life*. In principle this position found an appreciative audience in Trotsky. It was with great interest that he followed the young nonparty writers who objectively recorded the conflicts of revolutionary Russia. He called them the "fellow travelers of the revolution" and, as writers, placed them higher than those who tried to go out of their way to prove their revolutionary spirit. In particular (and much like Pasternak), he placed Mayakovsky's works of the Soviet period on a much lower artistic plane than his prerevolutionary longer poems, and in his article on futurism he compared Mayakovsky to a circus strongman who "makes an heroic effort and lifts a hollow weight." [18]

Boris and Evgenia Pasternak left Petrograd for Berlin on August 17. They stayed abroad for seven months. In the years 1921–1923 Berlin became, along with Moscow and Petrograd, the third capital of Russian culture. The Russian population there was marked by pluralism and a diversity of political groupings. [19] Russian literary life and publishing activity were especially intense. Some have even claimed (somewhat preposterously) that the Russian publishing houses in Berlin in 1922 printed more books than were printed in the German language during the same year. [20] In Berlin Pasternak saw friends and acquaintances—emigrants or semi-emigrants—whom he had met not long before in Moscow or Petrograd: Viktor Shklovsky and Evgeny Lundberg, Roman Jakobson and Boris Zaitsev, Ilya Ehrenburg and Vladislav Khodasevich, Andrei Biely and Alexei Remizov. Gorky was also in Germany at the time, trying to organize a journal for distribution in Soviet Russia that would be absolutely independent of party authorities.

Pasternak's name was not totally unknown in Europe. Ehrenburg (whom Pasternak had first met in 1917) had gone to the west a year and a half earlier. Shortly before his departure, he became familiar with the as yet unpublished *My Sister, Life*. From that moment on, and for the rest of his life, Pasternak was his favorite poet (along with Marina Tsvetaeva). Ehrenburg's articles were the first accounts of contemporary Russian culture to come to the west. During the first few months of his stay in Western Europe, Ehrenburg published several surveys of recent trends in poetry in revolutionary Russia,[21] the anthologies *Poety bolshevistskikh dnei* (Poets of the Bolshevik Days) and *Portrety russkikh poetov* (Portraits of Russian Poets), and the book-manifesto of modern art *A vse-taki ona vertitsia* (And Yet It Moves). No one could deny the enthusiasm with which he declared that poetry was flourishing in Russia and that the most lively literature was to be found there rather than in emigration. Many people listened to his assurances both because he had once been critical of the October Revolution and because in his literary evaluations he was guided by purely aesthetic criteria. Ehrenburg found evidence of the vitality of Soviet poetry in the works of a wide variety of poets: Mayakovsky, Pasternak, Akhmatova, Mandelshtam, Esenin, and Tsvetaeva. One might even say that poetry reconciled him to the revolution. With somewhat excessive zeal he declared that nowhere in Europe could poetry compare with that of contemporary Russia (and this included French poetry, which Ehrenburg knew well and cherished).

Ehrenburg had a number of friends among the left-wing poets and artists of Europe. In the beginning of 1922 he joined the Russian suprematist painter, El Lissitzky, in publishing the avant-garde international journal *Veshch* (The Object). On the pages of this journal propaganda for the art of revolutionary Russia occupied a central place, and Pasternak's lyrics were declared to be its highest expression. Pasternak's poems, as well as those of Mayakovsky and Esenin, were for the first time presented here as a part of a cosmopolitan, modernistic milieu, which included Jules Romains, André Salmon, Charles Vildrac, Pablo Picasso, Charlie Chaplin, and Igor Stravinsky. Although Ehrenburg engaged in literary criticism only for a very short period, in 1921–22, his publications played an enormous role in familiarizing the west with Russian literature of the postrevolutionary period, which included Pasternak. Incidentally, they caught the eye of Rainer Maria Rilke, who always had great interest in Russia and yearned for information about its recent cultural life.

Pasternak was well informed about the situation in Russian literary Berlin even before his departure: Boris Pilniak, who had visited there, undoubtedly shared his impressions with him. At first Pasternak thought about settling down in some quieter place, in Marburg or Göttingen. But these plans were not realized, and he spent almost his entire time abroad in Berlin, living in the same hotel where his parents were settled. He was immediately drawn into the Russian literary community. On September 22 he read his poetry at the House of Arts, which convened in the café Leon (on Nollendorfplatz); at the same gathering Alexei Tolstoy, one of the most prominent and controversial figures in the Russian emigration, read two chapters from his new novel *Aelita*. At the previous meeting of the House of Arts, the first of the season, Viktor Shklovsky (who had recently fled from Petersburg) gave a report on the life of writers in Soviet Russia, and the poets Vladislav Khodasevich and Nikolai Otsup (who had also just arrived from Petersburg) read their poems. Pasternak was present at a poetry reading by Mayakovsky at the House of Arts on October 20; Igor Severianin, who had emigrated to Estonia after the revolution, was also there. According to Ehrenburg's memoirs, Mayakovsky read his poem "The Backbone Flute" while turned directly to Pasternak. On January 19, 1923, a reading by Pasternak was arranged at the House of Arts, and before that, on January 15, at the Writers' Club, a literary organization that was in competition with the former and was much more conservative in its political orientation. Not long before his departure, on March 7 he (and Andrei Biely) took part in the discussion following a report of his old mentor in Musagetes, the philosopher Fyodor Stepun, who lectured on "The Nature of the Actor's Psyche."

In December and January in Berlin, two of Pasternak's books were published: a new edition of *My Sister, Life* by the Grzhebin publishing house and a new, fourth book of poetry, *Themes and Variations,* by Helikon, whose owner was close to Ehrenburg (they also proposed to bring out a separate edition of *Liuvers' Childhood*). Two sympathetic reviews of these books were written by the young literary critic Alexander Bakhrakh (Bacherac) and published in *Dni* (Days), a newspaper recently founded by Kerensky. In his analysis of Pasternak's poetry, Bakhrakh basically repeated what Ehrenburg had said, but he was more restrained in his praise.

During the same winter, Biely's Berlin journal *Epopeia* (Epopee) carried a major article by Marina Tsvetaeva about *My Sister, Life*. In June 1922 she and Pasternak had exchanged emotional letters after the two poets had suddenly discovered how much they shared, at least in terms of their writing. At that time Pasternak was still living in Moscow, and Tsvetaeva was in Berlin.[22] *My Sister, Life* made a very strong impression on Tsvetaeva and forced her, for the first time in her life, to sit down and write a critical piece. Her article was one of the earliest responses to the book, and perhaps the most enthusiastic.[23] To a certain extent it embarrassed Pasternak with its lavish praise. But of all that was written about him at this time, Tsvetaeva's piece contained the most profound and comprehensive appreciation of his poetry.

Despite his readings, Pasternak was inconspicuous in Berlin literary life. With the exception of the reprinting of his poem "Matros v Moskve" (Sailor in Moscow) in a "nonpartisan" almanac, *Grani* (Facets), Pasternak avoided the Russian-language press. What is particularly remarkable is that he did not contribute to the newspaper *Nakanune* (On the Eve), whose literary supplement (edited by Tolstoy) propagated the works of Soviet writers: it published the poems of Akhmatova and Esenin, Mandelshtam and Ivnev, Mariengof and Aseev, the stories and articles of Vsevolod Ivanov, Valentin Kataev, Boris Pilniak, Mikhail Bulgakov, Konstantin Fedin, Sergei Bobrov, and others. In 1922, when he was visiting Berlin, Mayakovsky concluded a contract with the publisher Nakanune for the publication of his poetry. *On the Eve* was the organ of Smena vekh (Change of Landmarks), a group that emerged among Russian emigrants in 1921. With the introduction of the NEP, the members of this group, political leaders of the White Guard movement, renounced their struggle against the Soviet regime and called upon the Russian émigrés to cooperate with it and even to return to their homeland. Change of Landmarks had a major impact on the intelligentsia both in emigration and within Soviet Russia. But when it became known in the summer of 1922 that the Soviet government had been subsidizing *On the Eve,* the paper became odious not only to anti-Soviet émigrés but to many independent Soviet authors as well. Boris Pilniak and Anna Akhmatova declared a boycott of the paper, and Gorky firmly advised Tolstoy to resign as editor of the literary supplement.

Against this background, the participation of Mayakovsky and Aseev in *On the Eve* was as much a political declaration as was Pasternak's nonparticipation.[24] It is noteworthy that well before his departure for Berlin Pasternak had become a close collaborator of another Change of Landmarks journal, *Novaia Rossia* (New Russia), which was published not in emigration but in Soviet Russia from 1922 to 1926; Pasternak remained loyal to it until the end.[25] Yet nothing in Pasternak's statements would indicate his sympathy for the ideological doctrine of the Change of Landmarks group. On the contrary, he repeatedly made sarcastic comments about it. It was not political philosophy that attracted him to the journal, but something else. Whereas *On the Eve* was sustained by Soviet money and served as an organ of the administration, *New Russia* was subjected to severe persecution at the hands of the censors and remained one of the last private publications in the Soviet state to survive. This explains why Pasternak kept contributing to it while he vehemently rejected *On the Eve,* the Berlin publication that would certainly have been eager to tout him as a poet of the new Russia.

The months Pasternak spent in Berlin convinced him of the inauspicious future for Russian culture there or in the emigration as a whole. If, in the winter of 1921, it had seemed that Soviet and émigré culture might "meet" in Berlin, by the fall of 1922 one could detect the first symptoms of the decline of Russian Berlin, which was wracked by political squabbles and economic hardships. Pasternak came to the conclusion that conditions in Soviet Russia were much more propitious for art. As he wrote at the time, against the background of emigration, "we" (Mayakovsky, Aseev, and himself) "look like gods." This evaluation of the emigration was shared by many other writers (regardless of their political views) who happened to be outside Russia at the time, including Biely, Tsvetaeva, and Esenin. When compared to the tempestuous literary situation in Soviet Russia at the beginning of the 1920s, Russian Berlin appeared "featureless" to Pasternak. That is why, despite the interest shown in him by emigrant circles, Pasternak decided to return to Moscow.

During Pasternak's absence, the situation in Soviet literature had changed beyond recognition. In the summer of 1922 the party initiated an ideological offensive against "bourgeois influences," and one of its consequences was the expulsion from Russia of the best and most independent representatives of the intellectual elite—philosophers, journalists, writers, and scientists. Russian literature underwent an ideological polarization that was no less severe than in Russian Berlin. Political servility increasingly became the norm in the cultural realm. Esenin, who was wavering at that time over whether to return to his homeland, wrote to his close friend Alexander Kusikov:

> It is sickening for me, a *legitimate* son of Russia, to be a stepson in my own land. I am fed up with the bloody condescending attitude of those in power, and even more sickened by having to put up with the fawning behaviour of my brethren towards them . . . I am ceasing to understand what revolution I belonged to. I can see only one thing—that it was evidently neither the February nor the October.[26]

One of the expressions of these new tendencies in Soviet literary life was the activity of the group Lef (Left Front of the Arts), which was headed by Vladimir Mayakovsky. The editorial nucleus of its journal was initially composed of Nikolai Aseev, Sergei Tretiakov, Osip Brik, Boris Arvatov, Boris Kushner, and Nikolai Chuzhak. Despite its small size, Lef became one of the most important groups in Soviet literature of the 1920s. This was not because of the particularly high quality of its literary production, but because of its extremely militant and provocative theoretical platform. Lef considered its goal during the revolutionary epoch to be the creation of literary genres that differed from those of prerevolutionary culture. Such a goal was in natural opposition to the reigning tastes of the party leadership: for example, at this very moment Lunacharsky was calling for a return to the realism of the nineteenth century and the classical tradition. Lef not only advocated rupture with the classical past, but rejected the very principle of realism, of the reflection of life in art. Nikolai Chuzhak, the main theoretician of Lef, advanced the slogan that art was not the reflection but rather the "building" of life. According to his theory, the art of the past was aimless, idle, and passive; its aesthetic qualities lulled the attention of the reader and spectator, distracting them from the class struggle by an illusory world of fantasy. In contrast, the new art would renounce traditional aesthetic values and serve the needs of socialist production and construction. The traditional forms of art—lyrics, novels, symphonies, paintings—were not needed in the new social conditions. The genuine artist was now expected to turn to genres based not on fantasy but on the real facts of life: to newspaper sketches, reportage, memoirs, feuilletons, and biographies.

Much that was contained in Lef's theories was a logical outgrowth of the futurist conceptions that had been advanced by the group around Mayakovsky and Brik in the newspaper *Art of the Commune* in 1918–19. But with the arrival of Sergei Tretiakov, and even more so Nikolai Chuzhak (both came from the Far East), the group became much more sectarian and fanatical.

The journal *Lef* soon split into two opposing wings. Although Chuzhak championed the notion of literature as production, the journal still printed transrational verses by the old-guard of futurists (Vasily Kamensky and Alexei Kruchonykh), who saw literary work as individual expression. Mayakovsky's position as editor of the journal was ambivalent. On the one hand, he shared the extremist slogans of Tretiakov and Chuzhak, and on the other hand, far from renouncing his old futurist allies, he tried to prove that their works were indispensable to the tasks of socialism. In addition, as a poet he did not have an easy time at Lef: just when the official line of the group was condemning lyrical themes, he proved incapable of breaking with them, and his longer poem, "Pro eto" (About That), which appeared in the journal, is direct evidence of this.

The first issue of *Lef* appeared in March 1923, and it contained Pasternak's poem "Kreml v buran 1918 goda" (The Kremlin in the Snowstorm of 1918) from *Themes and Variations,* which had recently been published in Berlin. Immediately after returning to Moscow, Pasternak contributed to the second issue by writing, at the request of the editors, a poem devoted to May First. What now compelled Pasternak to join Mayakovsky's group, when shortly before he had stressed in every way possible his independence and antifuturist position? In the first place, the destructive and nihilistic aspects of Lef's aesthetics, as well as the influence of Chuzhak and Tretiakov within the group, were still not completely clear to him in the spring of 1923, when he returned from Berlin. He thought that the journal was the home enterprise of his close friends Mayakovsky and Aseev, and he had no qualms about his ability to reach an understanding with them, no matter what their past differences had been. In addition, at an early stage, Bobrov had been invited to join Lef, and this allowed Pasternak to believe that the role of the Centrifuge members would be decisive in the journal. And even Lef's flaws, the polemical exaggerations of its declarations, still seemed more attractive to Pasternak than the featureless Berlin literary press.

From the very beginning, however, it became clear that Lef was interested in Pasternak only selectively. From his works the journal chose only those in which it could discern a civic theme; his lyrical poems were rejected. Nor did Mayakovsky like Pasternak's prose. Meanwhile Lef declared that the value of Pasternak's poetry lay not in its content (which was too obscure and difficult for the general reader) but in its formal virtuosity. By praising Pasternak's "verbal experiments," Lef reserved for him a role somewhat similar to that played by Kruchonykh's transrational poetry. This attitude did not shock Pasternak, despite the fact that he had long been critical of Kruchonykh. The position to which Lef relegated Pasternak satisfied him because it allowed him to avoid the "excessively Soviet loyalty" (as he later put it) which was becoming more and more palpable in the writings of Mayakovsky and Aseev.

In the meantime, because of its theoretical articles, regarded as a call for the liquidation of art, and the publication of transrational verses in its first issues, *Lef* came under extremely hostile attack in the Soviet press, including the newspaper *Pravda* (Truth). Thus, despite its concerted efforts to represent itself as the most revolutionary group in Soviet art, Lef was unable to gain governmental support. The critics were particularly upset by transrational language, and in opposition to it they pointed to the example of Demian Bedny's newspaper verse, which was accessible, comprehensible, and enjoyable to any semiliterate reader. The Soviet press condemned Mayakovsky and his group for not breaking with their old methods of scandalizing the public.

It is quite possible that these attacks on *Lef* in the press were one of the factors that kept Pasternak in the group. It probably seemed to him that the most valuable features of prerevolutionary futurism—its nonconformist and antagonistic spirit—still persisted in Lef. That is why, despite the fact that Bobrov soon abandoned Lef (not willing to coexist with Kruchonykh and declaring that "futurism is an anachronism"), Pasternak did not quit Mayakovsky's group. No matter how much he disagreed with its views, he preferred to be not with the majority, but with the minority under attack.

Another symptom of the sharp change in the literary climate was the emergence of the powerful organization of "proletarian writers," RAPP, which held its first conference in March 1923.[27] The majority of its members were novice writers and autodidacts of proletarian background who first took up the pen after returning from the civil-war fronts. Their professed goal was to defend the class interests of the proletariat in literature. They declared that literary works were a component of party ideological activity, and insisted that the party bureaucracy have full control in the cultural realm. The works of fiction by members of RAPP were even more impotent than the proletarian literature written during the first years after the revolution. This became obvious as soon as they began publishing their literary journals. The extremely low level of their artistic work forced the group to shift its center of attention to the realm of literary polemics and criticism. The principal organ became the journal *Na postu* (On Guard), which began publication in June 1923 and was entirely devoted to attacks on everything that appeared to be unorthodox. The main target of attack was Soviet writers who idolized the revolution but who, like Pilniak, refused to subordinate their work to the demands of the Communist Party. Following Trotsky's lead, everyone now began to call such writers "fellow travelers of the revolution." In the spring of 1921, the communist leadership had begun to publish the journal *Red Virgin Soil,* with the express intent of attracting the fellow travelers to the Soviet regime. Alexander Voronsky, a prominent party literary figure, was named editor of the journal. By attacking Voronsky and the fellow travelers in 1923 and demanding full orthodoxy from writers, RAPP was essentially challenging the political course established by the Politburo. Among the writers who were persecuted by the On Guardists were Anna Akhmatova and Pilniak, Ehrenburg and Khodasevich, Alexei Tolstoy and Mayakovsky, Aseev and even Gorky. Although the On Guardists received solid backing in the lower and middle echelons of the party bureaucracy, they did not enjoy much support at the very top, in the Politburo. In fact there was no consensus among party leaders as to whether the very concept of proletarian culture was legitimate. Whereas Lenin and Trotsky especially considered the slogan of proletarian culture to be a nonsensical and detrimental invention, Lunacharsky and Nikolai Bukharin supported the proletarians. But even they dissociated themselves from the On Guardists. This only made the On Guardists' denunciations of those holding differing views, and their demands for party intervention in literary matters, even more persistent and clamorous.

The main opponents of the On Guardists were Trotsky and Voronsky. In 1922, after a long interval, Trotsky once again began to write about literature. In the fall of 1923 he intervened directly in the unfolding literary struggle. In September he published three articles in *Pravda:* on Lef, on the journal *On Guard,* and on party policy in art.

While sharply criticizing the extremist assertions of Lef's program, Trotsky nevertheless tried to defend the group against the kind of persecution launched in the Soviet press. He declared that it was wrong to dismiss futurism as "charlatanry" and that futurism's services in the field of poetic form were valuable for Soviet culture. In this sense Trotsky demonstrated much more flexibility than Lenin, who harbored negative views about modernism. Much like Briusov, Trotsky stressed that all modern poetry directly or indirectly felt the influence of futurism. He did not mention Pasternak in this article. His personal meeting with the poet had shown him how unusual Pasternak's place was in literature, and the publication of one or two poems on social themes in *Lef* evidently were not enough to prove that Pasternak shared the group's platform. But he did say that the futurists were weakest as poets in those works where they expressed themselves most ardently as communists. Mayakovsky's best work was therefore his prerevolutionary "Cloud in Trousers," and his worst was "150,000,000" (a poem Pasternak called "unimaginative" in *Safe Conduct*). Trotsky's liberalism in the realm of cultural policy was clearly expressed in his statement: "Art cannot live and cannot develop without a flexible atmosphere of sympathy."[28]

Trotsky's position toward the On Guardists was much more hostile. He saw in them a real threat to Soviet culture. He decisively rose to the defense of the fellow travelers and scorned the slogan "proletarian culture." It was ridiculous, he declared, to think that revolutionary art could only be created by workers; on the contrary, the very fact that the revolution was proletarian left too little energy and time for workers to take up art. The intelligentsia was much better suited for reflecting the revolution than were the people who had carried it out. Trotsky reiterated the principle he had formulated previously about the party's nonintervention in questions of art. He rejected the pretensions of the proletarian writers to the leading role in Soviet literature, declaring that such hegemony could only be justified by genuine achievements in literature and their works were strikingly mediocre, crude, and aesthetically illiterate. The works of the proletarian poets, as he put it, not only failed as proletarian poetry but as poetry of any kind at all.

If the Soviet leadership had officially adopted Trotsky's views on art, the entire course of literature in the ensuing decades would have been different: Soviet literature would not have been as doleful, empty, and desolate as it became under Stalin. But these articles appeared at a time when Trotsky's position in the party hierarchy was being challenged by his rivals. His statements on the principles of Soviet literary policy not only failed to become party directives, but, as he was edged out of the party hierarchy, they became increasingly distasteful. Thus, despite Trotsky's devastating criticism, the proletarian writers were able to strengthen their position in literature.

Their first success was the conclusion of a pact with Mayakovsky's group, Lef, in October 1923. The initiative came from the leaders of RAPP, who needed to widen their front in response to accusations that the proletarian writers had no genuinely talented authors and poets in their ranks. But for Lef the pact was a clear capitulation to political demagogy, an attempt to win an orthodox reputation and to prove its irreproachable political reliability. The agreement was published in the journals *Lef* and *On Guard*. On behalf of Lef it was signed by Vladimir Mayakovsky and Osip Brik; on behalf of RAPP by Leopold Averbakh, Yury Libedinsky, and Semen Rodov. The thrust of the new alliance was directed against Alexander Voronsky and the camp of fellow travelers he represented. By entering into the alliance, the two sides pledged to refrain from mutual polemics and to seek out new literary groups.

In discussing the alliance, Rodov demanded that Lef do away with transrational poetry and that they cease collaboration with Boris Pasternak and Viktor Shklovsky (who had just returned from emigration). Mayakovsky accepted the first demand and decisively rejected the second, stating that Shklovsky and Pasternak might still be of use to Soviet literature.[29] Then *On Guard* published—in the same issue containing the agreement with Lef—an article by Viktor Pertsov entitled "A Negligible Figure," which was entirely devoted to Pasternak.[30] Pertsov aimed his fire against *My Sister, Life,* assuring the reader that Pasternak's book not only had nothing to do with revolutionary literature but was utterly counterrevolutionary. At a time when the revolution demanded an art that was comprehensible to the masses, Pasternak's "nonsense" was detrimental to proletarian literature. This article provoked the wrath of Aseev and Mayakovsky, for they both regarded *My Sister, Life* as the best book of modern Russian poetry. Yet they were prevented from taking issue with RAPP by the pact they had just signed. Mayakovsky's fury was further intensified because Pertsov was personally closer to Lef (especially to Chuzhak) than to RAPP (later, in 1927, he formally joined Lef). Although the Soviet press had previously contained statements faulting *My Sister, Life,* for obscurity (assessments by Sergei Klychkov in *Red Virgin*

Soil and by Valery Pravdukhin in *Sibirskie ogni* [Siberian Fires] and *Red Virgin Soil*), the article in *On Guard* was the first attack on Pasternak from a position of political demagogy. Later (especially in the 1930s) such diatribes became common, but in 1924 it was a novelty. The same Pertsov would proudly remember his old article in *On Guard*—during the campaign against Pasternak over the Nobel prize in 1958.

This period, the end of 1923 and the beginning of 1924, marks the beginning of the development of Pasternak's conviction that lyrical poetry was untimely and superfluous. He was led to this by Lef's theory about the withering away of art and by RAPP's attacks on writers. If in 1922, before his trip to Berlin, Pasternak firmly believed that it was precisely individualistic poetry which most thoroughly expressed the spirit of the revolutionary age, then the new social atmosphere showed how inappropriate this hope had become.

Tragic reflections on the superfluity of poetry lay behind several statements made by Pasternak during this period. One of them was the poem he read at the jubilee for Valery Briusov's fiftieth birthday on December 15, 1923. Pasternak had never before been known to write versified salutations, and the somber overtones of his poetic greeting seem most inappropriate in an atmosphere of celebration. Although Pasternak always showed little enthusiasm for Briusov's works, he decided to participate in the celebration for a number of reasons. First, he was personally indebted to the older poet: Briusov had welcomed Pasternak's literary debut in the summer of 1914 and supported the poet during the civil-war years from prominent posts in the Commissariat of Education. In an article of 1922 he had called Pasternak's lyrical poetry the most fascinating poetic phenomenon of the last decade. Second, Briusov meant a great deal to all the members of Pasternak's generation (he was seen as a forerunner by a wide range of literary schools—acmeists and Centrifuge, imagists and the Proletcult.) Third, and most important, throughout the entire postrevolutionary period Briusov was subjected to vicious political attacks from both the right and the left. Some accused him of prostituting himself to the Soviet regime and, after entering the Communist Party, of having become a bureaucrat instead of a poet. Others declared that he had proved incapable of being a genuine proletarian writer and that his membership in the party was merely a cover for vestigial decadence.

The atmosphere of the birthday celebration was dampened by a major literary scandal. RAPP protested in the newspaper *Rabochaia Moskva* (Workers' Moscow) against Lunacharsky's proposal to award Briusov the Red Banner of Labor (the only writer to have been awarded the order was Demian Bedny). On the very day of the jubilee it became known that the Central Executive Committee of the USSR had agreed with their assessment and denied Lunacharsky's request. These events explain why Pasternak decided publicly to salute Briusov and to clothe his salutation in the form of a lyrical poem. In 1920, in the preface to his 1917–1919 verse collection *Poslednie mechty* (Last Dreams), Briusov had declared that lyrical poetry was incompatible with the modern era. Pasternak's recital now was a double-edged response to this idea.

The theme of the superfluity of poetry appears also in the epic poem "Vysokaia Bolezn" (Lofty Malady), written in the winter of 1923–24. It differed from Pasternak's earlier epic conceptions in both its historicism and its contemporary theme. Its main subject was life during War Communism. In describing the recent past, the author was profoundly ambivalent: he simultaneously praises the revolution and shows the tragic side of the aftermath. The tragedy did not altogether lie in the unbelievable hardships that were so prevalent. Pasternak never—during the Civil War or World War II—complained about such burdens. On the contrary, he found in these difficulties, which fell equally on everyone, something beneficial and morally uplifting.[31] The tragic collision as Pasternak saw it grew out of the dual historical role of the intelligentsia: on the one hand, its desire to merge with the modern age, to dissolve itself in the revolution, and, on the other, clear symptoms of its historial doom, its "stepping off the stage." There is no resolution of this antinomy in "Lofty Malady."

Just as elusive are other, more fleeting motifs in the poem. With no noticeable connection between them, recollections emerge about the first days of the February Revolution before the abdication of Nicholas II, about the Ninth Congress of Soviets in December 1921, whose opening session Pasternak attended, and about a recent earthquake in Japan. Regardless of how haphazard and arbitrary these motifs appear to be, taken together they reveal the author's ambivalent, if not ironic, attitude toward current events. This is particularly evident in the Japanese episode. In the beginning of September 1923 Japan was shaken by an earthquake so terrible that it was compared to World War I in Europe. The Soviet propaganda machine accordingly declared it to be the harbinger of social revolution and called upon Japanese workers to meet the impending upheaval with the rapid formation of a communist party and powerful trade unions. The absurdity of these prognoses and slogans was obvious, and Pasternak introduced the episode to contrast the forces behind the revolution of 1917 to the empty rhetoric of the party agitators.

Another aspect of the revolutionary theme was revealed in the novella *Vozdushnye puti* (Aerial Ways). Here Pasternak sought to emphasize the nonpartisan, universal nature of the revolution. This was expressed in a passage glorifying the moral power of Lenin and Karl Liebknecht. But the novella's plot contradicts this thesis. A father and son, who know nothing about each other and who do not even recognize each other, turn up on opposite sides of the barricades during the Civil War; the father learns that it is his son who is being shot at the very moment he is trying to avert the execution. As with "Lofty Malady," the collisions described here remain unresolved. The novella was apparently conceived while Pasternak was still in Berlin and it was intended for the Berlin journal *Beseda* (Colloquy), which was founded by Gorky in order to offset the splitting of Russian literature into two hostile camps, Soviet and émigré. Such a position was inherently close to Pasternak's, and it is no accident that it was in such a nonpartisan context that Gorky's name was mentioned in an early variant of "Lofty Malady." Gorky expressed this view particularly clearly in his public protest over the trial in the summer of 1922 of the Social Revolutionaries, who now faced the death penalty. His protest was supported by Romain Rolland, Henri Barbusse, and Anatole France; it gained international attention and led to Gorky's prolonged conflict with the Soviet government. By intending to place *Aerial Ways* (with its implicit statement against the institution of the death penalty) in Gorky's Berlin journal, Pasternak was of course underscoring his solidarity with Gorky's stance.

But when, in February 1924, a new journal named *Russky sovremennik* (Russian Contemporary) appeared in Leningrad, Pasternak sent his manuscript there. This was because Gorky, who remained abroad, played a major role in this journal, and it could be expected that its nonparty profile would be no less distinct than that of the Berlin *Colloquy*. *Russian Contemporary*, which was published in 1924, was the best Soviet journal of the NEP period. Its editors besides Gorky were Alexander Tikhonov, Evgeny Zamiatin, Kornei Chukovsky, and Abram Efros. The four issues that were published contained pieces by the best prose writers and poets both in Soviet

Russia and in emigration. Gorky printed his reminiscences about
Lenin there; other contributors included Alexei Tolstoy, Tsvetaeva,
Esenin, Khodasevich, Pilniak, Fedin, Tynianov, and Shklovsky. The
journal was purely literary and lacked the sociopolitical section typical of other Soviet organs. But despite its political neutrality, it was
declared hostile, a symptom of the growing threat of bourgeois influence in literature. At the beginning of 1925 *Russian Contemporary*
was closed down, and its publisher, Tikhonov, was arrested.

Besides *Aerial Ways,* Pasternak published several poems in *Russian
Contemporary* (including some that had been rejected by *Lef*). Articles written for the journal by Tynianov and Sofia Parnok spoke of
his works with reverence.[32] At the same time, Efros attracted Pasternak to another journal, *Sovremennyi zapad* (Contemporary West),
which was a satellite of *Russian Contemporary* and was closed down
at the same time (they had the same editors). It printed Pasternak's
brilliant translations of several poems by the German expressionists
Johannes Becher, Paul Zech, and Jakob van Hoddis.[33]

The attacks in the Soviet press on *Russian Contemporary* made Pasternak dream about his own publishing venture—a journal of the
"three Borises," edited together with Boris Pilniak and Andrei Biely
(Boris Bugaev)—which would be just as much opposed to the official
journals as *Russian Contemporary*. But the literary situation made
such plans unfeasible. Pilniak and Biely were perceived to be much
more vulnerable to ideological attack even than Pasternak. In addition, the difficult financial situation that Pasternak found himself in
after his return from Berlin and the birth of his son, in September
1923, led him to consider stopping professional literary activities altogether. His attempt in the summer of 1924 to have the Leningrad
Gosizdat publish a new edition of *My Sister, Life* proved to be unsuccessful: Gosizdat at that time was headed by the proletarian poet Ilya
Ionov, who hated the fellow travelers, and the recent article on Pasternak by Pertsov in *On Guard* was a poor recommendation in his
eyes. Whereas during the difficult years of War Communism Pasternak could survive on literary contracts signed with various publishers,
now he was forced to the verge of abandoning literature. In the fall
of 1924 Pasternak's friend Yakov Cherniak found him a more or less
regular income. The poet was hired for the project of compiling a
bibliography of foreign publications about Lenin, and until December, Pasternak went each day to the library of the Commissariat of
Foreign Affairs to peruse the latest foreign journals.

Pasternak's consistent refusal to engage in the struggles raging in Soviet literature at this time is striking. In May 1924 the Central Committee convened a special meeting devoted to questions of literature in an attempt to reconcile the warring camps and to defuse the tense atmosphere. A large group of writers sent a petition to the Central Committee asking it to protect them from the attacks of RAPP and to defend the rights of the fellow travelers headed by Voronsky. Among the signatories were Boris Pilniak, Maximilian Voloshin, Sergei Esenin, Osip Mandelshtam, Alexei Tolstoy, Abram Efros, Vsevolod Ivanov, and Nikolai Tikhonov. Although Pasternak had close personal and literary ties with many of those signing the letter, and although he had been one of the victims of the On Guardists' attacks, his name is not to be found on the document. And this was no accident. Unlike most of his colleagues, Pasternak did not consider the party echelons to be the supreme arbiter in artistic disputes, and he did not believe that their defense of the fellow travelers would in any way be a crucial factor in literary life.[34]

Regardless of how distant Pasternak was as a writer from the proletarian poets, and no matter how much he was sickened by the demagogical slogans of their leaders, he never made derogatory remarks about their works or about the concept of proletarian literature. On the contrary, he did what they themselves were incapable of doing: he tried to find them predecessors and drew a parallel between them and Hans Sachs, a German poet (and a shoemaker) of the sixteenth century. Such a parallel was unusual during those years: it ran counter to all the disparaging evaluations of proletarian culture. Yet it was also a blow against the pretensions of the proletarians to the historical uniqueness of their mission.

It might appear that Pasternak's refusal to issue a public declaration of solidarity with the fellow travelers at this dramatic moment was dictated by the demands of group discipline observed by Lef: indeed Mayakovsky's group had decisively taken the side of RAPP in the struggle against Voronsky. But Pasternak did not hesitate to contribute to *Russian Contemporary,* a journal that was much more unacceptable to Lef than Voronsky's. He demonstrated his disdain for caution. In fact, within Lef, Pasternak adopted a line that was just as independent as the one he had outside the group. And just when Mayakovsky demanded in 1925 that Lef do away with the prerevolutionary traditions of futurism, and with transrational verse in particular, Pasternak suddenly, for the first time in his life, offered public support to Alexei Kruchonykh, who was the sole remaining founder of futurism to ignore Lef's efforts to politicize literature and who stubbornly continued to cultivate transrational language.

Taken together, these facts show how consistently Pasternak stood apart from all literary factions during these heated struggles. This distinctly individualistic position was reflected as well in his writings of the second half of the 1920s.

7

Against Romanticism

In 1925–1927 the book market was flooded by literary works devoted to the anniversary of the Russian revolution of 1905. Among them, two of Pasternak's poems, "1905" and "Lieutenant Schmidt," attracted special attention. Pasternak wrote the first poem from the summer of 1925 to February 1926, and immediately turned to "Lieutenant Schmidt," which he finished in March 1927. The two works differ sharply in their poetic features. The poem "1905" has neither a separate hero nor any identifiable plot. It is simply a "chronicle" (as it was called by the author) of the well-known events of the revolutionary year: troops firing into the peaceful mass demonstration on January 9 in Petersburg, the assassination of the Grand Duke Sergei Alexandrovich, uprisings and strikes, the mutiny of the battleship *Potyomkin,* and so forth. But the poem also has personal overtones and includes references to the author's adolescence, the Moscow School of Painting, Sculpture, and Architecture, Scriabin, and the poet's parents. Pasternak had always been reluctant to use autobiographical details in his verse. So in this regard his historical poem about the revolution proved to be more autobiographical than all his previous lyrics. "1905" stands apart from Pasternak's earlier attempts at epic literature in that it is an immediate story about definite events; as we remember, his earlier efforts were devoid not only of a developed plot but even of episodes that were in any way clearly delineated.

His second poem also marked a departure from previous endeavors. For the first time Pasternak constructed his poetic narrative not around himself but around an external persona: the most legendary of the 1905 heroes. Lieutenant Schmidt's psychological profile and his tragic situation are surprisingly reminiscent of that aspect of the revolution which Pasternak discussed in the "Dramatic Fragments" of 1917. Absolute moral purity, fearlessness in the face of death, lofty idealism, self-sacrifice, a feeling of doom—all these features link the hero of Pasternak's poem with Saint-Just and Robespierre as Pasternak had depicted them ten years before. But, in contrast to these heroes, Schmidt displays shades of character that subtly tie him to Shakespeare's Hamlet and to the Chekhovian type of fin-de-siècle intellectual. The appearance of these new traits was no accident: a few years before Pasternak had reread Chekhov and virtually rediscovered his prose,[1] exactly when he was first trying to translate *Hamlet* (in 1923–24). Apparent weakness, lack of resolve, and reticence, combined with boundless humanity and active sympathy for the oppressed, conscientiousness, and acute yearning for justice, a belief in the eventual triumph of good—all these qualities, traditionally linked with the image of the Russian intellectual of the nineteenth century, attracted Pasternak to Schmidt. The mixture of traits reminiscent of Chekhov and Hamlet, which first appears in Pasternak's work in the figure of Lieutenant Schmidt, would later become a chief characteristic of his other heroes—Spektorsky and Doctor Zhivago.

The sources of "Lieutenant Schmidt" were genuine historical documents that had only recently been published. Pasternak followed them so scrupulously that a few sections of the poem appear to be an almost verbatim exposition in verse of these documents.[2] In the fall of 1905, during the height of the revolutionary upheavals in Russia, a young naval officer, Pyotr Schmidt, who had long sympathized with revolutionary ideals and socialism, became leader of a sailors' mutiny in the Black Sea Fleet. Later, during the 1917 revolution, many officers of the army and navy sided with the revolution, but in 1905 this was unheard of. Schmidt was swept along by the revolutionary wave quite unexpectedly. It was not he who initiated the mutiny, nor was he one of its unswerving supporters.[3] He was fully aware that all of its participants were doomed: a slow, unarmed cruiser stood alone against the entire fleet and had no chance to flee punishment. Despite the fact that Schmidt realized the futility of the uprising and believed he could have accomplished more for the revolution at another post, he could not refuse the sailor's invitation to lead the uprising. Until the very last minute he hoped that his presence, as an officer and a nobleman, would ensure a peaceful outcome, mitigate reprisals, and prevent bloodshed.

Schmidt was an unusual political figure in still another respect. He never joined a revolutionary organization or belonged to a political party. His political beliefs were so broad and amorphous that it is impossible to define any party orientation. Schmidt seemed to consider himself closest to the Social Revolutionaries, although he unequivocally rejected terror, one of the main planks of their program. At the same time, he talked of his sympathy for the Social Democrats and about his intention to join the Constitutional Democratic Party. It was precisely the vagueness of Schmidt's political convictions and the absence of dogmatism, coupled with unquestionable devotion to the ideals of socialism and a readiness for self-sacrifice, that constituted his appeal for Pasternak. Schmidt said that he represented not some party but the entire Russian people, one hundred million strong. This comment discloses the hidden polemical meaning of the poem and hints at why, instead of writing about the October Revolution or the Civil War (which Mayakovsky and Aseev were then doing), Pasternak turned to 1905. By 1927 not only had all other socialist parties been outlawed in Soviet Russia, but even within the Bolshevik Party a fierce struggle for power was taking place. The former heroes and leaders of the revolution—Trotsky, Zinoviev, and Kamenev—were now, one after the other, branded as having been its most insidious enemies from the very beginning. History was rewritten and falsified, and emphasis was placed exclusively on the role of the Bolsheviks. Citing the poem "1905" Pasternak wrote to Gorky that his intention in it was "to take the revolutionary theme historically, as one chapter among many, as one event among many, and elevate it to a rather flexible (*plasticheskaia*), nonsectarian, all-Russian level."[4]

Schmidt's lofty idealism was also revealed in the story of his love affair. Pasternak's poem is based in part on Schmidt's almost daily letters to a woman whom he first saw in August 1905 at the hippodrome in Kiev and then, on the very same day, accidentally met on a train. Their forty-minute conversation in a railway car was their only meeting before the uprising; the next time they met was in jail, a few weeks before Schmidt's trial and execution. Thus their entire affair unfolded in correspondence.

Pasternak refused to draw a heroic halo around his central character. His deliberately ordinary, matter-of-fact portrayal of Schmidt repulsed poets who were artistically close to the poet (though with divergent political views), such as Mayakovsky and Tsvetaeva. A revolutionary hero whose main qualities included Hamlet-like indecision, rejection of bloodshed, and submission to spontaneity seemed too unheroic as far as they were concerned. Tsvetaeva's opinion carried particular weight for Pasternak, since they maintained an intense dialogue in personal correspondence and poetry throughout the 1920s.

After 1922, when she emigrated, Marina Tsvetaeva experienced an unprecedented creative outburst, which was to a significant extent prompted by her acquaintance with *My Sister, Life* and *Themes and Variations*. Under the direct influence of Pasternak's lyrics, her poetic style changed radically. During these years she became the best poet of the Russian emigration. Pasternak, who was undergoing a noticeable crisis in his lyrical work during this period, and who was seeking refuge from it in epic poetry, eagerly followed Tsvetaeva's development. He placed her new poems on a much higher level then his own or Mayakovsky's, and generally above everything else that was being produced in Soviet literature. Toward the beginning of 1926, their correspondence grew particularly intense.[5] It turned into an ecstatic romance, and Pasternak was prepared to abandon his family in Moscow and rush off headlong to Tsvetaeva in Paris.

It was precisely at this time that he began writing "Lieutenant Schmidt", and one senses that the author was not so much "constructing" a hero on the basis of historical sources as he was becoming "infected" with his hero's features. In Schmidt, Pasternak discovered his own double. There was a certain relation between the story of Schmidt' romance and the one between Pasternak and Tsvetaeva: in both instances a love affair unfolded through an exchange of letters.

Although Pasternak did not join Tsvetaeva, the emotional uplift that accompanied the composition of "Lieutenant Schmidt" left an indelible mark on his life and works. The very fact that he could have thought of emigrating, the possibility that he could have such a close tie with an émigré poet, no matter how fantastic his plans of going to Paris or of her returning to Moscow might seem in hindsight, must have made Pasternak's position within Soviet literature appear ambiguous and false in his own eyes. It is significant that at the beginning of 1926, following the publication in émigré periodicals of a number of antirevolutionary works by Tsvetaeva, the attitude toward her in official Soviet circles grew openly hostile. She was labeled a White Guard, counterrevolutionary author, and the Soviet press carried numerous malicious comments about her. Thus, when Pasternak decided to dedicate "Lieutenant Schmidt" to Tsvetaeva, disguising this dedication in the form of an acrostic when publishing the poem in the Moscow journal *Novyi mir* (New World), he committed a provocative and defiant act.[6]

The epistolary romance with Tsvetaeva took an unexpected turn when Rainer Maria Rilke suddenly came on the scene. Pasternak had only seen the German poet once—in 1900, when Boris was ten years old. That meeting had taken place on a train when Rilke was on his way to visit Leo Tolstoy. The subsequent reading of Rilke's poetry made a very strong impression on Pasternak. Twice—in 1911–1913 and in 1920—he tried to translate *Buch der Bilder*. But his veneration of Rilke reached heights of genuine exultation in the spring of 1926, when he learned from his father that the great German poet knew a few of his poems. Rilke had quite a good command of Russian and translated Russian epics, lyric poetry, and dramas. During his stay in Paris in 1924–25 he met with émigré Russian writers and artists. Since the young Rilke had believed that the essence of the Russian national character lay in pastoral life, idyllic humility, and piety, revolutionary Russia struck him as a somewhat inscrutable phenomenon. He sought to discover from the Russian emigrants in Paris how the revolutionary events were being reflected in Russian poetry. Among his acquaintances there were Mikhail and Maria Tsetlin; the leading representatives of Russian émigré literature often gathered at their home.[7] Here he may have heard that among the most noteworthy figures of recent Russian poetry was Boris Pasternak, son of the artist with whom he had become friendly during his trips to Russia. It was now in Paris that Rilke first read a few of Pasternak's poems—in the original Russian in Ilya Ehrenburg's *Portraits of Russian Poets* (Berlin, 1922) and in the French translation by Hélène Iswolsky published in *Commerce,* the best French journal of the time.[8] He referred to these publications in his letter to Leonid Pasternak, written on March 14, 1926.

When Pasternak's parents sent him an excerpt from this letter, he decided to write directly to his idol. The letter, sent on April 12, contains ardent expressions of his love for Rilke's poetry. At the same time, Pasternak felt it necessary to address Rilke's exaggerated assessment of Russia[9] with a warning about his own profound disillusionment with the present stage of the revolution. He wrote:

A great thing is most full of contradictions when it takes an *active* form; in its reality, it is also *small* within its magnitude, and sluggish

within its activity. Such is our revolution, which is a contradiction
in its very appearance: a fragment of gliding time in the form of an
immobile, fearful tourist attraction. Of such a nature are our personal fate, too, *immobile* temporal *subjects* of the somber and ex-
alted historical portent, tragic even in its smallest, even ludicrous
detail.[10]

In the same letter Pasternak describes how shaken he was by Tsvetaeva's "Poem of the End." Declaring that she is his greatest if not his
only friend, he asks Rilke to send his *Duineser Elegien* to her in Paris,
with a gift inscription. Rilke immediately fulfilled this request, and as
a result there arose another ecstatic correspondence. What developed
as a result was something of a romantic triangle. Tsvetaeva from the
beginning tried to separate her contacts with Rilke from her epistolary relations with Pasternak. Having initiated the correspondence
with Rilke, Boris fell silent and did not answer the German poet's
letter, since he did not want to intrude on the epistolary affair between Rilke and Tsvetaeva. As she herself would later say, Tsvetaeva
"set a limit" to her relationship with Pasternak and discouraged him
from traveling to see her in Paris. Beginning in August, their intense
correspondence stopped completely. At the same time, Tsvetaeva's letters to Rilke took on an entirely different character. She repeatedly
asked to meet the poet, who was seriously ill and had only a few
months left to live.[11]

Besides the erotic aspect of Pasternak's relationship with Tsvetaeva,
there was an important, purely literary dimension. Tsvetaeva's presence in Paris strengthened the polarization among the young Russian
poets there. A group of enthusiastic admirers of Pasternak (Boris Po-
plavsky, Daniil Reznikov, Vadim Andreev, Dmitry Kobiakov) was opposed by a group of "neoclassicists," who proclaimed adherence to
literary traditions, sharply rejected Pasternak's style, and considered
Khodasevich their mentor.[12] With the appearance of a new journal,
Versty (Mileposts), in the summer of 1926, the debates over Pasternak, and Soviet poetry in general, sharpened in émigré circles. The
editors of the journal were the philosopher and musicologist Pyotr
Suvchinsky, Tsvetaeva's husband Sergei Efron, and the literary critic
Dmitry Sviatopolk-Mirsky; the main contributors were Marina Tsvetaeva, Alexei Remizov, and Lev Shestov. Suvchinsky, along with the
geographer Pyotr Savitsky in Prague and the linguist Nikolai Trubetskoy in Vienna, was a founder of the "Eurasian" movement. This
group, which stressed the uniqueness of the Russian national charac-

ter and of Russia's historical path, saw in the Bolshevik revolution a
manifestation of this national particularity. It also believed that the
Soviet state, with its autocratic principles, would encourage a genuine
flowering of culture. Unlike the majority of those in emigration, the
Eurasians felt that Russian culture in the Soviet Union was flourishing, whereas in emigration it could only decline and decay. *Mileposts*
was immediately condemned by the rest of the emigrant community
in Paris.

It was the *Mileposts* circle that began to advance Pasternak as the
most important poet of the day. Such an evaluation was offered, in
particular, by Prince Sviatopolk-Mirsky, one of the few Russian emigrants who had close contacts with western literary figures and who
moved in academic circles. He taught Russian literature at London
University and collaborated in two prestigious literary journals, T. S.
Eliot's *Criterion* and *Commerce* in Paris. Pasternak's lyrical poetry appeared to him to be among the highest achievements of European
culture, equalled only by the work of Eliot. He was no less enthusiastic about Pasternak's prose and revolutionary poems.

Whereas the young Russian poets in Paris saw Pasternak as a model
of modern technical virtuosity, *Mileposts* hailed his treatment of social themes and the theme of the revolution. A section of his poem
"1905" was reprinted in the first issue of the journal. In the second
issue, the editors intended to publish the first part of "Lieutenant
Schmidt," but for some reason these plans never materialized. Instead
it appeared in another émigré journal, *Volia Rossii* (Freedom of Russia), which had long maintained close ties with Tsvetaeva. This was
the organ of the Social Revolutionary Party in Prague; its literary section was edited by Mark Slonim.[13] The decision to transfer "Lieutenant Schmidt" to this periodical was evidently made after the publication in Moscow of the acrostic-dedication to Tsvetaeva had caused
problems for the editor of *New World* and for Pasternak: it was necessary to weaken the impression of a too close relationship between
the poet and Tsvetaeva and her Parisian milieu. It is plausible to assume that the text printed in *Freedom of Russia* originated from the
manuscript Pasternak had sent to Tsvetaeva. Evidently it was handed
over to Mark Slonim on December 31 when he met Tsvetaeva in Paris
on the way to Prague from America; it was on this occasion that he
informed her of Rilke's death. "Lieutenant Schmidt" was published
in *Freedom of Russia* in February 1927, in an issue that also contained sections of Evgeny Zamiatin's novel *We*.

Thanks to his contacts with Tsvetaeva, Pasternak must have been able to follow the debates in émigré literature. He knew about the scandal that had erupted over the publication of *Mileposts* and about the fierce attacks its publishers encountered. Of the various intellectual currents in emigration, the Eurasian movement appealed to him the most. In the spring of 1929 he wrote to a young Russian poet in Paris: "I am glad to know that you love Tsvetaeva. Her circle is the closest to me." [14] If in 1923 Boris Pasternak had felt that émigré literature in Berlin was "featureless", he could never have applied it to Russian Paris.

The vicissitudes of the trilateral correspondence between the poets in 1926 left a bitter aftertaste for both Pasternak and Tsvetaeva. Tsvetaeva could not get over the terrible shock of Rilke's death. The lyrical outburst that had begun for her in 1922 waned and was never to return. Rilke's death led her to renew the correspondence with Pasternak, but the former closeness between the poets was gone.

For Pasternak, the emotional maelstrom of this year heralded a "second birth" after, as he put it, "seven years of moral slumber." [15] Under the dual influence of Rilke's invisible presence and his intensive correspondence with Tsvetaeva, he felt a surge in creativity for the first time since 1917. It was now that he began work on "Lieutenant Schmidt." Tsvetaeva was his first reader: he sent the poem to her in manuscript, section by section. Her critical remarks were more valuable to him than those of anyone else. But it was precisely her reaction to the poem that now showed Pasternak the fundamental differences in their intellectual makeup and creative temperaments. Those differences could be seen in the opposition of Pasternak's antiromantic conception of life and creativity to the romantic conception that dominated Tsvetaeva's world view. Whereas she saw the revolutionaries of 1905 (as well as the White Guard during the Civil War) as sublime heroes, Pasternak consciously tried to play down or eliminate any idealization of revolutionary themes.

But Pasternak directed this condemnation of romanticism against himself as well. He now reevaluated the recent course of his relations with Tsvetaeva—their possible effect on his family, his naive plans of a reunion with Marina in Paris or of her repatriation to Soviet Russia, his introduction of her to Rilke and the project of a joint meeting with him—as fruitless and romantic dreams. Pasternak also reviewed his attitude toward real life in Soviet Russia, and in this Pushkin served as an unfailing role model. As is well known, Pushkin's early enthusiasm for revolutionary ideals gave way to an acceptance of the tragic contradictions in life. For Pasternak, as for Pushkin, the process of "overcoming romanticism" took the form of a "reconciliation with reality." And as with Pushkin, it never signified a justification of the evil aspects of the existing order. Pasternak said that the modern world posed the following dilemma: "to suffer without any illusions, or to prosper by deceiving both oneself and others." [16] Whereas Mayakovsky and Aseev appeared to lean toward the second variant, Pasternak in the late twenties firmly chose the first.

Such a "reconciliation with reality" would not have been possible if Pasternak had not received timely support from Viacheslav Polonsky. In January 1926 Polonsky had been appointed coeditor of the literary journal *New World,* which under his leadership quickly became one of the most influential organs of the fellow-traveler camp. Cordial relations between Polonsky and Pasternak went back to 1920–21. Unlike Voronsky, who considered Pasternak's poetry too esoteric for the Soviet reader, Polonsky did not consider complexity of poetic language to be a deficiency. He felt that the future culture of socialism would be based on more refined, not more simplified, means of artistic expression.

Polonsky enthusiastically supported Pasternak's historical poems on the revolution. His journal published a fragment of "1905" and the complete text of "Lieutenant Schmidt." Thanks to these publications, as well as to the publication of *Two Books* (combining *My Sister, Life* and *Themes and Variations*) that soon followed, Pasternak managed to get out of his financial difficulties.

Polonsky and his circle repudiated statements that Pasternak's poetry was cut off from social interests and themes. They said that, in contrast to the period of War Communism, when the country needed immediate response to events of the day in the form of agitational posters and verses, social themes now required more profound treatment. In their view, although Pasternak spoke less frequently about contemporary matters, because of their depth and poetic merits his contributions carried more weight than those of Esenin or Mayakovsky, Aseev or Tikhonov. With genuine "realism" and sincerity Pasternak was able to transmit the tragedy of the intelligentsia during the revolutionary epoch. Immersion in this theme had led to changes in Pasternak's style, making it clearer and more transparent, without, however, eliminating its original distinctive features. In his recent historical poems about the revolution, Pasternak remained loyal not only to his moral and civic convictions, but to the fundamental characteristics of his poetics. This secured for him the pivotal role in modern Russian poetry.[17]

In his turn, Pasternak saw in Polonsky one of the "people of the revolution." "Here I received my political education," the poet later said.[18] A rejection of political servility and a conviction that the true essence of the revolution excluded fawning before superiors, time-serving and submissive behavior—this is what primarily united the poet with the editor of *New World*.

His closeness to Polonsky affected Pasternak's relations with Mayakovsky and his circle. After the journal *Lef* ceased publication in 1925, Pasternak continued to maintain close ties with the entourage at the Briks' salon. While sharply condemning Mayakovsky's attempts to subordinate poetry to the utilitarian needs of the party, Pasternak still considered him the "premier poet" of the modern period, the true voice of their generation. And, whatever its disagreements with Pasternak, Lef was still proud of his participation in their circle. They considered Pasternak's poetry a great achievement of revolutionary art, on a par with Meyerhold's new theatrical productions or Eisenstein's films. In the fall of 1926, when discussions were begun about publishing a new journal, Pasternak took part in the meetings. When *Novyi Lef* (New Lef) appeared in January 1927, he was listed among its principal collaborators, and a fragment of "Lieutenant Schmidt" was published in the first issue.

The publication of the monthly *New Lef* aroused just as sharp a controversy as the publication of *Lef* had four years before. But this time its chief ideological opponent was Viacheslav Polonsky. His views on literary policy were always similar to those of Voronsky, Trotsky, and Lenin: he advocated a liberal line and considered the extremism of RAPP and Lef a threat to Soviet literature. But until he came to *New World* he had not been directly exposed to literary battles. Now, as editor of this journal, the role of chief defender of the fellow travelers passed to him, especially because Voronsky's position in the party hierarchy and the Soviet literary establishment had steadily weakened. Polonsky's furious attacks on Mayakovsky and his group did not originate in any kind of personal hostility; on the contrary, in 1926, before the appearance of the *New Lef* Mayakovsky and Aseev were published in Polonsky's journal even more frequently than Pasternak was. But Polonsky considered any literary grouping harmful, since he felt that sectarian instincts within a group always outweighed literary interests. As people and as poets, Pasternak,

Aseev, and Mayakovsky triumphed when they acted as individuals. Conversely, their individuality was compromised when they saw themselves as a unified group and when they tried to lay theoretical foundations for the transitory existence of a transitory group. Polonsky said that *New Lef* was an unnecessary formation. Unable to make any real contribution to Soviet art, Lef had turned to cheap self-advertising, something that was justified before the revolution but absurd in Soviet circumstances. Polonsky firmly contrasted Pasternak and Lef: "An enemy of publicity and sensationalism, an extremely modest and well-focused man, and one of the most refined masters of our time, Pasternak was not a futurist during the first years of the futurist brawls, nor is he one now, when the disintegrating corpse of futurism is beginning to emit a rotten stench. And can *New Lef* boast of anyone else?" [19]

The literary dispute quickly assumed political overtones when, in response to the declaration that Lef was unnecessary under socialism, the members of Lef maliciously recalled a serious mistake that Polonsky had made during his first year as editor of *New World*. In May 1926 he had published "The Tale of the Unextinguished Moon" by Boris Pilniak. The story depicts in disguised form the murder of the Soviet leader Mikhail Frunze, which had been accomplished with Stalin's sanction. The editorial board quickly acknowledged its error (and that issue of the journal was confiscated), but now the members of Lef felt it necessary to recall the incident in order to neutralize criticism directed their way. This action angered Pasternak, and he declared to Mayakovsky that he was leaving the group. In the collision between Lef and Polonsky, therefore, Pasternak firmly took the side of the latter. Pasternak suffered greatly from the break with Mayakovsky, whom he continued to love and value as a poet. In the course of 1928–1930 he carefully avoided any public statements about Mayakovsky and Lef, and he tried to find ways toward a personal reconciliation with his old friend.

Pasternak's support for Polonsky proved to be particularly important, since in the summer of 1927 his position in the Soviet literary establishment was severely shaken. He lost his main ally in the literary struggle, Voronsky, who was dismissed from his post as editor of *Red Virgin Soil* a year after he joined the Trotskyist opposition in 1926. Polonsky himself was on the verge of being expelled from the party: at the height of the struggle against Trotsky and Zinoviev, RAPP accused him of belonging to the opposition. While his case was being investigated, he was suspended from editorial duties at *New World*.[20] During the months Polonsky was off the editorial board, Pasternak drew even closer to him and boycotted the journal.

If Polonsky had originally attacked Lef and Mayakovsky for "bohemian" conduct that was anachronistic in the Soviet state, under Pasternak's influence his criticism became more serious. The emphasis shifted to attacks on the concept of "social command," which had become the main component in the aesthetic program of Lef toward the end of the 1920s. It had first been advanced in 1922 in an article by Nikolai Aseev in *Press and Revolution*.[21] He declared that as a result of the October Revolution the function of the artist had sharply changed. The artist must now turn into a voluntary executor of the urgent and pressing tasks set before him by the revolutionary state. The production of agitational posters and cartoons during the Civil War became just such an emergency social command. Mayakovsky's activity at Rosta (the Russian telegraph agency) was described by Aseev as an example of the proper socialist relationship of the artist to art. The concept of social command became the cornerstone of Lef doctrine; all its other propositions—the call for "literature of fact" and the liquidation of imaginative literature, the rejection of the novel and poetry in favor of journalistic writing, the rejection of Raphael and Rembrandt for photography—were based on this fundamental idea.

Pasternak saw in Lef's slogans a direct threat to art, especially if it were to receive official sanction. While the animus of Lef against "easel painting," the novel, and the epic was not supported in other camps of Soviet culture, the idea of social command was seized upon by everyone, and even such a principled opponent of Lef as Voronsky dared not place it in doubt. Polonsky was the first—at Pasternak's urging—who decided to speak out against it. In articles published in *New World* and *Press and Revolution*, Polonsky proposed that the notion of social command be discarded, insofar as it implied that the artist must cater to the tastes of the "client" (the state), and this in turn implied an insincere attitude of the artist toward his own work. Servility to the whimsical tastes of a client precluded the truly serious transition of a genuine artist to the positions of socialism. Such a transition was inconceivable without painful internal struggle and vacillation, and for Polonsky an example of such sincerity and honesty was Boris Pasternak. In *Safe Conduct* Pasternak returned to the discussion of social command and developed Polonsky's argument.

In the fall of 1927 an intensive, though short-lived, correspondence began between Pasternak and Maxim Gorky, who was still residing in Sorrento. After 1925 Gorky became increasingly involved in Soviet literature. He gave it preference over the work of older writers who had settled in emigration and he tirelessly propagated the new works of young Soviet authors in Europe. His authority among the government leaders allowed him to be an effective advocate of liberal forces in Soviet literature. Many talented writers who came under attack found in him a defense against the RAPP bureaucracy.

Gorky, who believed in the early 1920s that the best contemporary poet was Vladislav Khodasevich, reacted unfavorably to Pasternak's lyrical poetry. *My Sister, Life* he found simply incomprehensible. But he liked Pasternak's book of prose that came out in 1925. He even arranged for the publication of *Liuvers' Childhood* in America and wrote a foreword to the English translation by Maria Budberg, his de facto wife at the time.[22] Pasternak found out about this project in October 1927 in a letter from Gorky himself.

The pretext for their correspondence, however, was not Pasternak's publications but the fate of Marina Tsvetaeva. During the summer her sister Asya was a guest at Gorky's residence. On the way from Moscow to Sorrento, she had visited Marina in Paris and, even with her knowledge of the difficulties of life in Soviet Russia, was shaken by the poverty in which her sister was living. At Gorky's she discussed the possibility of his giving financial assistance to Marina. Gorky's generosity was well known, and he heeded requests even of people who were far removed from him in political convictions or literary affiliations. But this was an awkward situation. Direct financial assistance from Gorky to Tsvetaeva and her family would have placed all of them in an intolerable position. It would have reinforced suspicions among the emigrants in Paris that the journal *Mileposts,* as well as the activity of the Eurasian movement in general, was being funded by the Bolsheviks. On the other hand, in Moscow Gorky's assistance to Tsvetaeva, the author of counterrevolutionary poems, would be interpreted as political duplicity.[23] He therefore asked Asya to find an intermediary through whom he could channel money to Paris unofficially. Asya decided on Pasternak, who immediately agreed to help. In the course of discussing the matter, misunderstandings arose that severed Gorky's correspondence with Pasternak.

From Pasternak's letters it is clear that he attached great significance to the life and works of Gorky. In the fall of 1927 he read the first part of the novel *The Life of Klim Samgin* and was struck by Gorky's emphasis on the decisive role of the intelligentsia in the revolution, his understanding of its broad national character transcending caste and class divisions, and his humanism. The very possibility that Gorky was prepared to offer assistance to Tsvetaeva served as confirmation of his political tolerance and broad-mindedness. That is why Pasternak wrote in those days: "I don't know what would have remained of the revolution for me, or where its *truth* would have been, if you had not existed in Russian history." [24]

Gorky valued Pasternak's striving toward artistic integrity and sincerity. He responded warmly to the book *1905* (although he liked "Lieutenant Schmidt" much less than "1905"), and he welcomed the poet's turn to social themes. [25] But he criticized *Dve knigi* (Two Books, the reprint of *My Sister, Life* and *Themes and Variations*) in the same severe terms that he had always used for Pasternak's lyrical poetry. He condemned it for being too abstruse and for the excessive complexity of the poetic thought and expression, in which Gorky saw a "struggle with the language, with the word." This reproach touched an extremely tender nerve in the poet. "I always strived for simplicity and I never will stop striving for it," he answered Gorky in a letter on January 4, 1928. Pasternak was not being the least bit hypocritical when he made this statement. From his earliest steps in poetry, he was convinced that his means of verbal expression were aimed at making his thoughts lucid, not obscure. But the "fatal originality" of his thinking and his intellectual profile, which all his critics acknowledged, made it difficult for many of his readers, especially those who remained true to the old poetic canons, to understand him. Even the poet's close friends often did not understand his poems, and this created a kind of inferiority complex in him. That is why Pasternak unexpectedly switches in this letter to Gorky to the peculiarities of his origins: "With my place of birth, with my childhood circumstances, with my love, instincts, and inclinations, I should not have been born a Jew." [26]

This is an extraordinarily strange statement. Like Blok, Pasternak always believed that a poet's "foreign blood" did not diminish his contribution to culture but, on the contrary, made it more valuable. With his "Hamitic" origins, Pushkin served as a striking illustration. What compelled him now, in answer to the reproach of incomprehensibility and "struggle with the language," to complain about his origins? From other passages in the letter it becomes clear that the answer lies not in the circumstances of his own life, but in the social atmosphere of the moment: Pasternak felt that the attention being paid to him by the press (after the publication of his poem about 1905) was to be explained not so much by the quality of his poetry as by the fact that the literary establishment (as well as the government) was largely composed of Jews and that they sympathized with him primarily for that reason. This undeserved, privileged status seemed shameful to him and, in his own words, prevented him from publicly venting the anger he felt for the "idiocies" of Soviet reality.

Today we find it difficult to comprehend the reasons for such conclusions. The entire later history of the Soviet regime reveals an undeviating and systematic exclusion of Jews from the spheres of power in all areas of life. Against his background Pasternak's statements are nonsensical. But if we take into consideration the fact that the year 1927 in literature was characterized by a struggle against "Russian patriotism," and that the newspapers were filled with a campaign against Esenin's pernicious influence on Soviet poets and against the cult of Esenin (he had committed suicide in December 1925) as a "great national poet"—then Pasternak's guilt in connection with the positive attention he was receiving becomes more understandable. Not long before, Valentin Parnac had mentioned that Pasternak "descends from the illustrious Sephardic family of the Abravanels" in his article about Jews in modern Russian literature.[27] And earlier, Parnac's sister, the poet Sofia Parnok, had stated that Pasternak was "organically devoid of nationality."[28] The tragic sensation of being divided from his country continued to haunt Pasternak. It is in this context that we must appreciate Pasternak's strained and exaggerated attempts to introduce into his prose low colloquialisms and elements of "common vernacular," which seemed false and shocking to admirers of his lyrical poetry. Nor was it accidental that Pasternak made Sergei Spektorsky, the hero of his *Tale* (1929)—and his alter ego— half Jewish.

Pasternak tried to continue the dialogue with Gorky even after their correspondence stopped. In April 1928, for the first time since 1921, Gorky returned for a few months to Russia (on the occasion of his sixtieth birthday). Like many other fellow travelers, Pasternak expected much from his visit. He believed that Gorky's more active participation in Soviet literary matters would be beneficial. Polonsky was suspended from editorial duties at *New World* at this time, and the fate of his journal and his literary policies was not clear. Despite his shyness, Pasternak decided to take the floor at a meeting between writers and Gorky at the editorial offices of *Red Virgin Soil* in June 1928. Judging from the short newspaper account of this gathering, it is evident that his remarks had sharply polemical overtones. In accordance with his perception of Gorky as the connecting link between the Soviet and the prerevolutionary periods, the poet ridiculed those who offered to "know and remember" only the last decade, "as if history had only begun with October, and as if the revolution were not only one of the episodes of history." [29] This remark was of course directed at RAPP and Lef, and endorsed Gorky's position.

A desire to see the threads connecting the modern period to the prerevolutionary epoch may explain Pasternak's sudden return to his earlier poems in the collections *A Twin in the Clouds* and *Above the Barriers,* and his reworking of them for new publication in the journals. Back in 1922 the republication of both books—evidently without major changes—was announced by Centrifuge, but the project was never realized. Why did Pasternak now undertake to rework his older poems? Some critics see in it an attempt to "simplify" the earlier style in accord with the poet's new aesthetic inclinations. But the new versions are not really simpler than the older ones, and a few poems have clearly become even more esoteric. It is certainly impossible to find in them the same clarity of expression that excited Gorky in the poem "1905." The reasons for the revision lay elsewhere. His contemporaries sensed a special, nostalgic note of reunion with the past and a "bidding farewell" to it in Pasternak's writings of these years. The turn to his two prerevolutionary books was the author's own peculiar way of escaping from the dictates of the contemporary social and cultural situation.

Pasternak also returned now to "Lofty Malady," his only work from the 1920s that dealt with the October Revolution. The most substantial change he introduced in the poem was to include Lenin's speech at the Ninth Congress of Soviets (although he does not mention Lenin by name). The tradition of paeans to Lenin went back to the first months of the revolution and increased dramatically immediately after the leader's death in January 1924. But except for one fleeting reference to Lenin in "Aerial Ways," this is the first time Pasternak includes a discussion of the leader of the revolution; he did this much later than most Soviet poets. It is worth noting that in his portrait of Lenin the main concern is with the force of his intellectual activity: "He directed the [people's] stream of thoughts, / And only then—the country." The full meaning of this comment becomes obvious if we recall that the struggle for power being waged in the Kremlin at the time led to the elimination of free thinking and to the crushing of all opposition.

No less evocative was the new ending of the poem, with its aphorism: "A genius comes as a harbinger of betterment, and his going is avenged with tyranny." [30] The poet was hinting here at the ominous signs accompanying the retreat from the New Economic Policy and the return to the norms of War Communism at the beginning of 1928. In the spring, notice was given about the impending trial of mining engineers from the Donets coal basin who were accused of sabotaging the first five-year plan. Later, during the 1930s, such show trials became a common occurrence, but this "Shakhty" trial in Moscow was the first to take place. A few days before the beginning of the trial, when the newspapers began to carry in issue after issue the official text of the indictment, Pasternak responded with gloomy sarcasm. He wrote to his cousin, contrasting the present repressions to the early 1920s: "As you know, terror has resumed, this time without the moral grounds or justification that were found in it earlier, in the heat of commerce, careerism, and unsightly 'sinfulness.' These men are far from being Puritan saints who then emerged as avenging angels." [31]

Changes in the political climate were directly reflected in literary matters. After Stalin's speech about the "rightist danger" in the party, RAPP immediately applied his thesis to the domain of culture. The journal *Na literaturnom postu* (On Literary Guard) declared that a right-wing danger existed in literature also, from the fellow travelers, who were an even greater threat than such "internal émigrés" as Mikhail Bulgakov or Nikolai Kliuev. Abram Efros and Boris Pilniak, the leaders of the fellow travelers in Moscow, tried to defend the independence of writers, but they were confronted with a coalition of RAPP and Mayakovsky.

Pressure on literature at the end of the 1920s was maintained through two channels. The first was censorship. The second and more effective means was RAPP, which constantly altered its program and slogans, depending on shifts among the party leaders. RAPP was the only literary organization whose leading bodies were constituted not through elections but through directives of the Central Committee. These two channels for controlling literature were joined in the middle of 1928 by a new one. At this time the GPU (the secret police) initiated the systematic infiltration of literary organizations, private circles, and salons, thereby creating a network of espionage within the Soviet intelligentsia. The mastermind of this system was the assistant to the director of the Secret Department of the GPU, Yakov Agranov. One of his tasks was the recruitment of writers as informers for the GPU, and those who refused such missions often encountered insuperable barriers in their literary career. Agranov began to feel quite at home in the salon of Lily Brik, and many of the zigzags in Mayakovsky's literary positions during the last period of his life can be understood by taking into account the major role played by behind-the-scenes pressure from the Soviet bureaucracy.

One of these strange twists was Mayakovsky's unexpected declaration in the fall of 1928 that he was leaving Lef and "rehabilitating the novel and Rembrandt." Insofar as Lef had been Mayakovsky's offspring, his exit together with his close friends Aseev, Brik, and Kirsanov struck a mortal blow to the group. It would seem that this was the same decision that Pasternak had so impatiently awaited in the summer of 1927, since he felt that the first to leave Lef should not have been himself, but Mayakovsky and Aseev. But Mayakovsky's motives for leaving Lef were diametrically opposed to Pasternak's. Mayakovsky sought not greater individual independence, but even greater subordination to party control. Thus the chief goal of Ref (Revolutionary Front of Art), the new literary group he formed, was declared to be journalistic writing. This was understood to be the best guarantee against "apolitism" (political indifference) in literary affairs. Several times a week Mayakovsky placed versified editorials in the newspapers, which were nothing but rhymed rewordings of party propaganda material. The "rehabilitation" of Rembrandt was prompted not so much by a reexamination of his attitude toward the classical heritage as by his desire to please party functionaries, who looked askance at futurist nihilism. Ref was unable to carry out any real activity: the social and literary situation changed so rapidly that the group reached senility before it could justify its existence.[32]

Dramatic changes in Soviet literature occurred in August 1929 when, as if at the command of an invisible director, several Moscow newspapers simultaneously published malicious articles against Boris Pilniak and Evgeny Zamiatin. Both writers were accused of publishing their fictional works abroad, in circumvention of Soviet censorship. Written in 1920, Zamiatin's We had come out in an English translation in America in 1924, and in the beginning of 1927 sections of it were published in the Prague émigré journal Freedom of Russia.

Pilniak's novella *Mahogany* was printed in the spring of 1929 by the pro-Soviet publishing house in Berlin, Petropolis. It was abundantly clear that the campaign unleashed by the leaders of RAPP was directed not only against Pilniak and Zamiatin, but against the entire camp of fellow travelers.[33] The attacks quickly widened, and every day new names were mentioned—Platonov and Bulgakov, Klychkov and Mariengof, Vsevolod Ivanov and Ehrenburg. An atmosphere of uncertainty and dismal fear arose: at any moment any of the fellow travelers might expect to become the next victim of accusations that he had slandered Soviet reality, secretly sympathized with Trotskyism, or showed political indifference.

The inquisitional atmosphere plagued other cultural areas as well: the Academy of Sciences, the theaters, and the universities. On September 1, Lunacharsky was removed from the post of Commissar of Education because he had maintained too soft a line in cultural policy. RAPP demanded in print the rescinding of the Central Committee's 1925 resolution on literature, which shielded the fellow travelers from attack. After Bukharin was removed, the Politburo contained none of the old guardians of the fellow travelers, and the demands by RAPP for a new party document to replace the resolution of 1925 might have been successful had it not been for Gorky's opposition. During the winter of 1929–30 the personal attacks against Pilniak and Zamiatin quieted down. But this led neither to the improvement of their personal situation nor to the weakening of RAPP's influence. On the contrary, on December 4 an article appeared in *Pravda* that officially declared for the first time that RAPP was *the* vehicle of party policy in literature.

During this witch hunt of the best writers among the fellow travelers, Mayakovsky unhesitatingly stood on the side of their persecutors. The overzealous loyalty expressed in his public statements disguised a profound crisis in his writing and personal life. Nor did it dissipate the authorities' skeptical attitude toward his ideological orthodoxy. While in Paris in the fall of 1928, Mayakovsky had fallen in love with a Russian émigré, Tatiana Yakovleva. The Soviet organs that directed literature had to contend with the fact that their greatest poet might be wavering, precisely when impassable barriers to emigration had been erected by the state. In the fall of 1929, for the first time in his life, Mayakovsky was refused permission to travel abroad. This public demonstration of mistrust deeply wounded him. The last months of his life were filled with attempts to prove his unswerving loyalty to the Soviet state: he organized an exhibition entitled "Twenty Years of Work" announced the disbandment of Ref, and joined RAPP. He joined alone, relinquishing the support of his closest friends. But even this step failed to shield him from the blows that fell upon him from the party echelons and the press. His last play, *The Bathhouse,* was declared a slander against Soviet reality. On April 14, 1930, the great poet of the revolution committed suicide.

The years 1928–1930 marked profound upheavals in the very foundation of Pasternak's thinking. In terms of power of expression, this period can be compared only with the creative upsurge during the revolutionary years. But judging from his basic mood, the two epochs were quite different. He was crushed by the certainty that moral values were disappearing from Soviet life, particularly the very values he had found inseparable from the idea of the revolution: personal independence, magnanimity, honesty, humanity. And the flexible (as Trotsky had called it) atmosphere around art also ceased to exist.

Pasternak's reaction to the increased ideological pressure in literature took diverse forms. Initially, during the first systematic attacks on the fellow travelers in the fall of 1928, he stopped writing. But in January 1929, driven by forebodings of the imminent end of all real literature, and envisioning an impending abandonment of literary activity, Pasternak hastened to finish all the works previously conceived or begun.

One of these works was the novel in verse *Spektorsky,* started in 1925. The appearance then of the first chapters had immediately aroused the interest of his contemporaries and prompted discussions about the role of Pushkin in Pasternak's works. Parallels between Pushkin's *Eugene Onegin* (the first Russian verse novel) and Pasternak's new work engendered speculation about what the hero would be like and how recent events would be treated by the poet. Rumors began to circulate that the novel would encompass the prerevolutionary years, the revolution, and the initial Soviet period. The new chapters both disappointed and intrigued readers. The plotline and the character of the hero were ill defined. It was as if the events narrated and the main characters were dissolved in landscape description. The lyrical elements in Pasternak's verse novel clearly dominated the epic elements.[34] In this regard, the new work was reminiscent of his earliest prose fragments of 1911–1913.

The novel was printed in scattered segments as they were written.

Pasternak wrote slowly and was often distracted by more urgent projects, such as the historical poems "1905" and "Lieutenant Schmidt."
During the course of work on the novel, its plan evidently changed.
In the first three chapters from 1925 the narrative content was focused on erotic themes, and the action was set in the years preceding
the war. But the fourth chapter, which appeared in 1926, gave
grounds for assuming that a social theme would also be presented:
the passive and idle main character is juxtaposed to his sister, who is
actively drawn into revolutionary work. It is possible that in order to
correct the unfavorable impression of Spektorsky in the fourth chapter, Pasternak set him up against an unequivocally negative character,
Balts, in the fifth chapter (1927). Whereas Balts is portrayed as an
amoral cynic and buffoon, Spektorsky is endowed with positive characteristics: humanism and sympathy for the oppressed.

This chapter was followed by an unexpected shift. A fragment published in July 1928, corresponding to the sixth and seventh chapters
of the final edition of the novel, introduced a new heroine, Maria
Ilina. This section describes how Spektorsky meets her and how their
love affair is suddenly interrupted by a dramatic twist of fate. This
fragment differs so radically from the preceding chapters that one
feels that the author wrote it spontaneously, without worrying about
whether it was in harmony with the previous parts. Pasternak was
particularly fond of this chapter and was obviously inclined to attach
independent significance to it. In it, in a modified way, he attempted
to recreate the story of his relations with Marina Tsvetaeva.[35] Of
course the real upheavals of 1926 only faintly resemble the events
depicted in *Spektorsky*, but the motif of the separation of two characters who are fated to turn up in different countries recalled for Pasternak a main aspect of his ties with Tsvetaeva.

When this portion was published in *Red Virgin Soil* it was accompanied by the notation: "End of the first part." Evidently the second
part (which was supposed to be devoted to the war, revolution, civil
war, and War Communism) should have been more or less equal in
size to the previous chapters taken as a whole. But it did not turn out
that way. The next portion of *Spektorsky* was written in the fall of
1929, at the height of the Pilniak scandal, and it appeared in December in the same journal with the indication that the novel had been
completed.[36] The patent disproportion of the parts can be explained
only by a sudden change in the author's intentions. For some reason,
the development of the plot in the originally selected genre of a novel

in verse struck Pasternak as untenable. In January 1929 he decided to transfer part of the plot to a prose narrative with the same main protagonist, Sergei Spektorsky. Completed in May, this new work was published in July in *New World*. There it bore the strange title "A Tale," although originally the author had proposed to call it "Revolution." [37] It was here that he intended to transfer all the motifs and episodes connected with the war and revolution. As often happened with Pasternak, in the course of work his plans changed, and the text that appeared in July in the journal was viewed as only the beginning of a future prose novel.

The events of 1929 prevented Pasternak from continuing his work as planned, and he once again returned to his novel in verse. Pasternak knew all the main victims of the witch hunt taking place. But he was closest of all to Boris Pilniak who, in the winter of 1928–29, had been chosen chairman of the fellow-traveler organization in Moscow (the All-Russian Union of Writers) and headed the opposition to the new attacks by RAPP. Pasternak was a frequent guest at his home, where literary readings were held. Here he read his *Tale*. There is no doubt that he was acquainted with Pilniak's *Mahogany* while it was still in manuscript form. Pasternak had always considered Pilniak the best of the Soviet prose writers. The apocalyptic circumstances at the end of 1929 forced the poet to hurry, and instead of a major prose novel about the revolution, he wrote a few stanzas in a verse narrative, an idiom much more familiar to him than prose.

Thus stanzas appear in *Spektorsky* where the revolution is depicted as an uprising of women, as if the participation of men were negligible. As opposed to a heroic and masculine interpretation, the poet singled out a passive and feminine element in the revolution. The entire notion of the revolution is reduced to the protest and revenge of women for centuries of outraged dignity. These stanzas from *Spektorsky* echoed in a succinct form the central theme of *A Tale*. The theme of humiliated and oppressed women and the author's acute compassion for them had appeared for the first time at the height of the correspondence with Tsvetaeva during the summer of 1926. Pasternak wrote to her then: "I . . . could love neither my wife nor you, neither myself nor my life, if you were the only women in the world, if your sisters were not legion." [38] This theme showed the obvious influence of Lieutenant Schmidt's letters, in which it was expressed with particular force and passion.

It is clear, then, that Pasternak's conception of the revolution at the end of the 1920s grew out of his work on the historical poems. We also see that *A Tale* and *Spektorsky* complement each other, since they can hardly be understood when taken separately. In this regard, the motif of authorship had a profound and ironic meaning in both works. Whereas in *A Tale* the hero Spektorsky is shown at the moment of potentially becoming a writer, at the end of the novel in verse (set during War Communism) he is shown as a full-fledged, professional man of letters, even a member of the Writers' Union. This is the same organization that Pasternak helped found in 1919 and that Pilniak became chairman of in 1929. But it is referred to in a strange way: instead of being engaged as writers, a brigade of its members is dispatched to warehouses in order to sort old junk discarded by emigrants. The author ironically calls them the "Roman decemviri." The hidden meaning of this designation and of the entire episode becomes transparent when we recall that the Writers' Union, created to defend the independence of writers, was forced to violate its charter in the fall of 1929 by acting against its chairman and ousting him from his post.

Additional poignance in this episode comes from a motif that Pasternak often repeated during this period: his imminent rupture with literature. We find similar moods in Osip Mandelshtam (in his "Fourth Prose") and in Mikhail Bulgakov (in *The Master and Margarita*). With Pasternak, these feelings led to the general reinforcement of autobiographical themes. It is a sharp about-face in his writing, since prior to this time the basic feature of his lyrical poetry, usually the most intimate and confessional of literary genres, was the consistent obliteration of the authorial "I."

Safe Conduct, his other main project at the end of the 1920s, is also related to the sudden increase of autobiographical features in his writing. Pasternak began work on it in 1927. The news of Rilke's death led him to attempt to formulate a conception of art. This was the period of his agonizing break with Lef and Mayakovsky. In addition, his relations with Tsvetaeva remained unresolved, though correspondence with her did resume after Rilke's death. The work he began did not immediately take on definite form, and the author himself did not know where he was headed: would he write an essay (the first since "The Quintessence" of 1918) or fictional prose or, last of all, memoirs? Toward the end of 1928, with a major portion of the new work already written, Pasternak called it "autobiographical fragments." Indeed, there is no cohesive narration. Although the author mentions

some of the most important events of his childhood and adolescence—the chance meeting with Rilke on a train, the horse accident
in 1903, his study of music, his fateful meeting with Scriabin in 1909,
Moscow University, the decision to travel to Marburg—given the
structure of the narration, the new work violates all the traditional
conventions of the memoir or autobiography. The boundary between
real events and their poetic reflection is effaced in a text saturated
with lyrical ruminations.

But even this feature expresses the work's deep polemical intent.
The heart of the matter was that Lef had declared that "literature of
fact" was not only the most progressive literary form, but the only
appropriate one given the new Soviet conditions. Memoirs, reportage, diaries, travel notes, and newspaper accounts were advocated,
as against traditional literature based on imagination and fancy. So
Pasternak turned to a recommended form, but he deliberately cast it
so that the boundary between fact and fiction was blurred.

The title of his new book was also polemical in character: *Okhrannaia gramota*. This term went back to the vocabulary of the first years
of the revolution, when the Soviet government issued documents confirming the inviolability of valuable private cultural collections and
thus saved them from being plundered by mobs and from nationalization. By using this term, which at the end of the 1920s was already
anachronistic, Pasternak was drawing an eloquent parallel between
the first years of the revolution, when even under harsh conditions art
had not been degraded, and the current situation, when art seemed
defenseless before the attacks of Lef and RAPP.

The first part of *Safe Conduct* appeared in the Leningrad journal
Zvezda (Star) in August 1929. Simultaneously Pasternak published
his translations of Rilke's two "Requiems." These were his first translations of Rilke to appear in print. One "Requiem" immediately followed the text of *Safe Conduct* in *Star* and formed a kind of dialogue
with it; the second was published in *New World*.

It was precisely during these days that the campaign against Pilniak
and Zamiatin began. Pasternak did not write the second and third
parts of *Safe Conduct* until 1930. These sections bore the imprint of
the changed climate in literature and social life and, in particular, of
Mayakovsky's suicide in April. In the second part, describing the author's trip during the summer of 1912 to Marburg and Italy, there are
cryptic allusions to recent events; the third part is entirely devoted to
Mayakovsky and the fate of his (and Pasternak's) generation. In com-

parison with the first part, the polemical forays are more prominent and complex. If in the first part of *Safe Conduct* the "Rilkean" core of Pasternak's philosophy had been counterposed to the theories of Lef, now these theories are counterposed to the fate of Mayakovsky as a poet. During the campaign against Soviet writers in 1929–30, Lef was defeated and dissolved (as were all literary organizations except RAPP). For the first time it was affirmed, with cynical openness, that the state had the right to control both literary texts and their authors. The old, aggressive theories of Lef had seemed dangerous, but absurd and utopian. Now they became governmental policy, and with irresistible logic they were turned back upon the heads of the creators. The tragic meaning of Mayakovsky's death became abundantly clear in connection with the cataclysmic changes in Soviet Russia. Pasternak discovered tragic irony in the fact that in death the first poet of the revolution simultaneously displayed resistance and helplessness, rebellion and resignation. Pasternak thus called Mayakovsky's death an act that was both voluntary and forced.

Mayakovsky's death affected the treatment of all past events in *Safe Conduct*. Before the suicide, the book was to contrast Mayakovsky's path to Pasternak's, treating them as two alternative systems. Romanticism is first closely analyzed by Pasternak as a negative concept in *Safe Conduct*. Against the romantic conception of the poet as a "visual-biographical emblem," devoid of real living content, Pasternak proposed his own notion of the poet as a person consumed by moral strivings. We should recall that the definition of Mayakovsky as a romantic (in his relation to the revolution) was first elaborated by Trotsky in his analysis of the poem "150,000,000." [39]

The debate with Mayakovsky and his circle also prompted the passages about art and its patron in the second part. Pasternak indirectly refers here to the theory of social command advanced by Lef. Citing the example of Renaissance Venice, Pasternak says that art always deceives its patron, the state. An example of such a deception was Mayakovsky's death, which in Pasternak's view was provoked by an outburst of anger and rebellion against the same political reality to which the poet had seemed to be so selflessly devoted.

But in this death Pasternak also saw elements of the same romanticism that had always repelled him in Mayakovsky. In *Safe Conduct* Pasternak defines art as "resistance to the inevitable." From this point of view, the rebellious, heroic side of the artist is indivisible from another, nonromantic, more pedestrian side—or "collaboration with real life." Here Pasternak brings in another poet-futurist, Mayakov-sky's antipode, Velimir Khlebnikov, who ignored existing social insti-tutions as if he had fallen out of time. Pasternak's new program united "rebellion," understood as the eternal function of art, and "collabo-ration with real life," which went far deeper than the servitude of Mayakovsky's romanticism.

This program was dictated not only by the poet's outlook and char-acter, but by the constantly changing political and literary situation in Soviet Russia. One cannot expect from *Safe Conduct*—his most important work—firm and precise declarations, categorical state-ments, or clear slogans. For Pasternak life was elusive and enigmatic: all truths could turn into untruths, all concepts into their opposite. And it is this ambivalence, with the author's bewilderment in the face of it, that makes *Safe Conduct* one of the great literary works of our century.

8

The Thaw of the Thirties

Even before the publication of the first section of *Safe Conduct* in
August 1929, Pasternak might well have expected to receive the same
critical cudgels being aimed against all fellow-traveler literature. He
was already just a hairbreadth away from danger because the same
issue of *Freedom of Russia* that printed a fragment of Zamiatin's
novel *We* had also contained a portion of "Lieutenant Schmidt," with
a note, moreover, indicating that it was published from a manuscript
copy.[1] By this time the scope of politically motivated attacks had generally widened, and the victims were not only those who, like Bulgakov, Pilniak, or Zamiatin, stubbornly defended an author's right to
political neutrality, but also staunch advocates of the party's politici-
zation of literature, such as Mayakovsky and even the RAPP poet Alexander Bezymensky. The production of Ilya Selvinsky's play
Komandarm-2 was halted in January 1930 after a charge that it exaggerated the role of the intelligentsia in the revolution. This accusation could easily have been directed against Pasternak as well. But in
October his new verse collection, *Above the Barriers,* augmented with
revised versions of his early poems, appeared without problems, and
in December the journal *Red Virgin Soil* published the last part of
Spektorsky.[2] Pasternak wrote to one poet: "My reclusive and difficult
way of life protects me from unpleasant occurrences . . . Time and
circumstances are most indulgent toward me."[3]

Quite plausibly there was another factor at work here: the hermetic
character of Pasternak's poetry and prose, the difficulty of his style.
Incidentally, one village teacher in the provinces decided to conduct
an interesting experiment: he began to read the best examples of lit-

erature to peasants, who were sometimes illiterate. Among the works he read was the fifth chapter of *Spektorsky*. The listeners were so irritated after only the first two quatrains that one of them immediately declared himself ready to strangle the author with his own hands, and others called for the confiscation of all the poet's property as punishment for publishing such verses in the Soviet press.[4] Of course prominent Soviet literary figures, even in RAPP, were more sophisticated, but even for them Pasternak's works after "Lieutenant Schmidt" were a riddle.

Pasternak finished *Spektorsky* in the summer of 1930, reworking it for a book edition and writing an introduction for it. He spent these months, with the family of his brother Alexander, at a dacha in Irpen, outside Kiev. This summer proved pivotal for both his life and his works. Two others also staying at the dacha, the philosopher Valentin Asmus and the pianist Genrikh Neuhaus, became his lifelong friends. Through Neuhaus, Pasternak renewed his ties with the musical world. A man of great refinement, Neuhaus was one of the leading Soviet pianists of the time. He had received an education similar to Pasternak's, and fundamentally different from that of most of the new Soviet intelligentsia. It was also here in Irpen that a stormy romance arose between the poet and Genrikh's wife, Zinaida Nikolaevna Neuhaus. She soon left her first husband and married Pasternak, after his divorce from Evgenia. The radiant moods connected with new friends and new love stood in stark contrast to the gloomy events in the outside world. That is why, in one of his poems of this time ("Summer"), Pasternak evokes motifs from Pushkin's tragedy, *Feast in the Time of Plague*.

While Pasternak was at Irpen, rumors began to circulate about widespread arrests of prominent scholars, economists, engineers, and agricultural experts, all of whom were accused of sabotaging the five-year plan. These accusations were followed in September by an official announcement of the impending trial of the mythical "Industrial Party." Trials were also being prepared for the equally mythical "Agricultural Party" and for former Mensheviks.[5] In the phantasmagoric atmosphere of these months, pressure on the intelligentsia assumed unprecedented forms. Throughout the country, endless meetings were held to demonstrate unanimous support for the Soviet government and to demand the death penalty for the arrested criminals (who had not yet appeared before a court). These meetings became a way to test the loyalty of the intelligentsia, and writers were expected to prove their devotion to the regime. Among those who spoke at the meetings were the best of the fellow travelers, including such leaders of the writers' opposition in the 1920s as Abram Efros and Boris Pilniak. Despite the humanistic traditions of Russian literature, the writers now called not for clemency but for severe repression against those arrested. Failure to express the most active support for punitive measures began to be interpreted as duplicity and, by extension, as sympathy for enemies of the Soviet regime. These months witnessed the forging of a new political phenomenon: Soviet unanimity, the principle of unconditional support for any and all steps taken by the Soviet leadership, no matter how contradictory.

Although the writers closest to Pasternak were drawn into this campaign, during these months the poet himself remained inconspicuous (and aloof from the campaign). It should be noted that silence was interpreted as politically suspicious and potentially hostile. Pasternak emerged from seclusion in the spring of 1931 when *Red Virgin Soil* printed the last two parts of *Safe Conduct* and when the publication of *Spektorsky* as a separate book was planned. In these days there emerged symptoms of a sudden and unexpected "thaw." Stalin delivered a speech that was seen as a call for a more attentive and discriminating treatment of the "technical intelligentsia" (engineers). At the same time, rumors abounded about his dissatisfaction with RAPP, whose reign since 1929 had seemed unshakable. Fellow-traveler writers took heart when they learned of his disparaging remarks about the literary qualities of the proletarian writers. The possibility of a liberal turn in literary policy was demonstrated by an unexpected about-face in the authorities' attitude toward Boris Pilniak. Plunged into deep poverty since the fall of 1929 and driven to the verge of suicide, Pilniak received permission directly from Stalin in January 1931 for a visit to the United States.[6] At this time foreign trips were almost unheard of and were taken to be a sign of the regime's special confidence. Although Pasternak's own requests for a foreign journey did not succeed (Gorky refused to intervene in the matter), Evgenia Vladimirovna and their seven-year-old son were allowed to visit the Pasternak family in Germany.

In the spring of 1931, upon finishing *Safe Conduct*, Pasternak returned to lyrical poetry. Among the poems written in April was a paraphrase of Pushkin's "Stanzas" (1826). Pushkin's poem had been directed to Tsar Nicholas and appealed for clemency toward those who had participated in the Decembrist uprising. Several radicals of that time were inclined to see, in the very fact of such a dialogue with the tsar, the poet's betrayal of his old revolutionary ideals. For Pasternak, this was by no means the kind of political poetry that Lef advocated or the type of poetry calculated to delight the authorities. The poem was an entreaty not to use force against opponents of the regime and—somewhat prematurely—an expression of certainty that positive changes were already taking place. It was clearly the poet's response to the signs of liberalization in the country and an attempt to express support of Stalin for these moves.

The fact that Pasternak's poem paraphrased Pushkin's "Stanzas" drew sharp historical parallels on two levels. Stalin's leadership is contrasted simultaneously with that of two Russian tsars, Peter the Great and Nicholas I. While the first parallel could only flatter the leader,[7] the second was much less panegyric in character: Soviet historians always viewed the thirty-year reign of Nicholas as the incarnation of reaction. Moreover, references to absolutism within the context of a new socialist Russia were highly inappropriate. The censors had just removed from *Safe Conduct* the author's major argument about Russian and West European autocracy, although it contained no allusions to the modern era. The presence of the dual historical parallel added a profoundly ambivalent note to Pasternak's poem, despite its outwardly complimentary form. It was therefore published only a year later—in the spring of 1932, during a tumultuous and brief literary thaw—and it was never again printed in the poet's lifetime.

Nevertheless, despite its ambiguity, this poem, like other works of the period, indicated Pasternak's readiness to accept Soviet reality as an inevitable and lawful model of socialism. No matter how much this model differed from the utopian prognoses expressed by the poet in his "Dialogue" of 1917, he gave the benefit of the doubt to this unprecedented social experiment. The positive elements in the poet's attitude toward the Soviet regime were reinforced by the influence of Zinaida, his new wife. He emphatically acknowledged this himself in one of his letters to her. Whatever the exaggeration here, we should recall that in *Spektorsky* and in *A Tale* of 1929 the author had interpreted the revolution in terms of the feminine principle. His meeting with Zinaida Neuhaus probably also bolstered the changes in Pasternak's diction. She barely understood Pasternak's earlier poems and preferred Mayakovsky. But of course one cannot attribute the shift to greater stylistic simplicity to this factor alone. Even before their meeting, in May 1929 Pasternak declared his intention to seek a new poetics because the language developed by himself, Khlebnikov, and Tikhonov had become common currency.[8] Be that as it may, Pasternak's poetic style changed sharply at the beginning of 1931, becoming more lucid and simple, with a direct expression of the personal "I."

In June 1931 Pasternak made a short trip to the Urals. Viacheslav Polonsky asked him to join a brigade of writers that was being dispatched to new construction sites in order to praise the achievements of the five-year plan. Such writers' trips—individual but especially collective—became increasingly common at the beginning of the 1930s. The authorities saw them as a decisive means of reeducating the fellow-traveler writers. Although Pasternak could not fail to be skeptical about the official goals of this campaign, he decided to join the excursion. The fact that it was organized and headed by his old friend and ally, Viacheslav Polonsky, led him to believe that this time the enterprise would be more serious than usual. He also understood that his participation in the brigade would strengthen the position of Polonsky and *New World,* both under unrelenting attack from the leadership of RAPP. Finally, the poet's literary curiosity was excited. He had not been to the Urals for fifteen years. The contents of both his large unfinished prose pieces—*Liuvers' Childhood* and a novel about the revolution with Spektorsky as the main character—were bound up with this area, and Pasternak was ready to continue work on both of them. He felt that the dull rhetorical clichés permeating Soviet propaganda speech in the capital would reveal their true meaning when brought into contact with real life in the provinces.

Pasternak was shaken by what he saw. He was overwhelmed not by the truly immense, "cyclopean" scale of the construction, but by the merciless deindividualization of the people. What he now saw in the Urals seemed in no way better than the depressing picture he had witnessed in Tikhie Gory during the last prerevolutionary winter. Pasternak cut short his trip and returned to Moscow earlier than the other members of the brigade. The journey found no response in his poetry and thus, from the point of view of its agitational goals, proved fruitless.

The destructive effect of this journey on the poet's attitude toward Soviet life might have been much more powerful had these impressions not been partially offset by his subsequent travels with Zinaida in Georgia in the fall of 1931. They went there at the invitation of the Georgian poet Paolo Yashvili, whom Pasternak had met in Moscow

through Andrei Biely. During this trip Pasternak began a life-time
friendship with the Georgian poets who were members of the group
Blue Horns. Their works were strongly influenced by the symbolist
and postsymbolist currents in European (and especially French) poetry; they knew well the Russian literature of the 1900–1920 period.
Before Pasternak arrived in Georgia, the poets of Blue Horns had
been visited by Mandelshtam, Mayakovsky, Esenin, and Biely. Here
Pasternak discovered what he had been unable to find in the Urals: a
refined culture coupled with genuine faith in socialism, prosperity
(unthinkable in Russia), and personal independence. Here there was
none of the hypocrisy, fawning, and blind fanaticism that reigned in
the literary circles of Moscow. Starting in the fall of 1931, the poet's
repeated attempts to accommodate Soviet reality always occurred
through the mediation of his contacts with Georgia: thus they became
a kind of litmus test for his political opinions and principles. In Georgia he found warmth and unwavering support during the most difficult moments of his life, and he felt free from the stifling pressure of
the central bureaucracy. For the Georgian poets, friendship with Pasternak was valuable because it allowed them to overcome their provincial isolation and to find a road to a wider reading audience. From
his very first acquaintance with the Georgians, Pasternak was struck
by the idea of translating several of their poems into Russian, although he generally translated verses only from languages he knew
well. Personal contact with the authors showed how much he shared
with them—and particularly with Titsian Tabidze—with regard to
views on lyrical poetry. Pasternak's translation plans were realized
two years later, and translations from the Georgian became one of his
greatest achievements of the 1930s, making an unexpected impact on
his standing in Soviet literature.

These Georgian impressions were so intoxicating that, on his return
to Moscow, Pasternak was moved to deliver a seditious speech at one
of the literary discussions. Its content can be summarized by the declaration that "not everything has been destroyed by the revolution"
and that art had remained "mysterious and eternally ineradicable."
Pasternak insisted on freedom of creativity for poets and protested
against the tiresome instructions issued to literature. Paraphrasing the
words of Jesus about the Sabbath, he said: "Time exists for man, man
does not exist for time." [9]

This speech coincided with the beginning of a campaign by the
RAPP critics against *Safe Conduct,* which had just been published as a

book. It was condemned for the customary sins of the time (idealism, "bourgeois restorationism," and so forth). The book received not one sympathetic response in the Soviet press. By that time Pasternak had lost his closest ally in the Soviet literary leadership, Polonsky, who was dismissed from *New World* at the end of 1931, demoted to a less significant post, and died a few months later of typhus. Ivan Gronsky, who replaced him at the journal,[10] was in no way Polonsky's equal. He was an obedient party functionary who happened to be in Stalin's good graces, and his knowledge of literature was limited. But he lacked the bloodthirsty fanaticism of RAPP's administrators and, since he was more tolerant and good-natured than they, instinctively took a relatively liberal line in Soviet literary policy. In the winter of 1930–31, before Pilniak's trip abroad, he extended a helping hand to him and, in fact, saved him from suicide. Pasternak continued to collaborate with *New World* under the new editor, but his relations with Gronsky never became as warm as those between him and Polonsky.

In the spring of 1932, the clouds above Pasternak continued to darken. He became one of the chief targets of RAPP. His new poems written in the spring of 1931, including "Volny" (Waves)—which contains an unprecendentedly strong declaration of the author's readiness to accept Soviet socialism—were greeted with derision by the leadership of RAPP. Much against his will, the poet ceased to be an inconspicuous and neutral figure for the regime. At this time any author targeted by RAPP was in a hopeless position, condemned to relentless "reeducation." Even entry into RAPP was insufficient to save a writer from systematic slander (Mayakovksy's fate serves as an example of this). Nor could the sympathy of some of RAPP's members for Pasternak's poetry shield him from persecution; on the contrary, it led to redoubled ferocity against the poet and his defenders.

During this period, the poet's family situation became extremely difficult. After his first wife and son returned from Germany, Pasternak gave them his room in a communal apartment and wandered among his friends with Zinaida Nikolaevna. To make a complete break with Evgenia Vladimirovna was just as hard for him as to abandon Zinaida, leaving her without a husband and with two small children. All this led Pasternak to attempt suicide in the spring of 1932.[11]

On April 23, 1932, however, the general atmosphere changed suddenly and drastically. On this day the newspapers contained a decree of the Central Committee, "On Restructuring Literary Organizations," which struck writers like a bolt from the blue. With one stroke of the pen, the declaration drove from the literary arena those who only yesterday had seemed the omnipotent arbiters of writers' destinies. All blame for the stagnation in literature was placed on the leaders of RAPP and their military-bureaucratic methods of controlling the intelligentsia. The "fellow travelers" were proclaimed the best representatives of Soviet literature, and this very term, which had implied a certain ideological inferiority, was now officially replaced by a new one—"Soviet writer." The decree ordered the formation of a new Writers' Union, without classifications of writers into more or less orthodox categories. Ivan Gronsky and the literary critic Valery Kirpotin were placed at the head of the organizing committee.

No resolution by the party leaders during the interwar period was met with such genuine enthusiasm by the Soviet intelligentsia as the decree of April 23. Rejoicing was greatest among those writers who had shortly before been the object of RAPP's attacks. But it is striking that the exhilarated chorus was not joined by the voice of Boris Pasternak. Like a few other astute observers, he was clearly worried about the crudely administrative character of the liberal upheaval, which once again only demonstrated the absolute power of the party in the realm of art. Pasternak's skeptical attitude toward the reform was not mitigated by signs of increased attention toward him on the part of the new literary authorities. In the summer a collection of his new poems, *Vtoroe rozhdenie* (Second Birth), was published. He and Zinaida were provided with a new apartment in a wing of the headquarters of the Writers' Union. *Literaturnaia gazeta* (Literary Gazette) printed a long and benevolent article about him, one of the goals of which was to repudiate RAPP's earlier assessments.[12]

The regime's favorable attitude toward Pasternak was expressed in the organization of a new journey to the Urals in the summer of 1932. Unlike his trip of the previous year, Pasternak and Zinaida with her two sons spent more than a month at a tranquil cottage near Sverdlovsk, as honored guests of the government. He was not sent this time to "shock" construction sites as a reporter dispatched by the administration. This generosity was one of the many examples of the paternal "warmth" displayed by the party leadership for former fellow travelers. Bribing the intelligentsia became a cornerstone of Stalinist cultural policy.

The impressions from this trip proved to be even more distressing than in 1931, however. For the first time Pasternak saw with his own eyes the results of the collectivization of the countryside. He was shaken by the poverty of the peasants and workers and by the general ruination and irreversible degradation of centuries-old economic traditions. He was even more repulsed by the cynical inequality, by the attempt to place him, a celebrated guest from the capital, in a privileged position, replete with abundant meals at a time when the surrounding population was in a state of dire poverty. In the summer of 1932 came the first symptoms of the terrible famine that seized even the traditionally wealthy regions of Russia.[13] Unlike 1921, when social activists in Russia and the west were broadly mobilized to fight the hunger, this time the plight of millions of peasants was shrouded in complete secrecy, and the newspapers let it pass unmentioned. There is evidence from Zinaida Nikolaevna's memoirs that Pasternak, on his return to Moscow, wrote an indignant letter about what he had seen to the presidium of the Writers' Union. He received no reply. The Writers' Union was in the process of formation during these months, and internal literary matters concerned it far more than troublesome social problems.

The dimensions of the euphoria that seized Soviet writers in the summer and fall of 1932 had no precedent. This could be felt most clearly at the first plenum of the Organizational Committee of the Writers' Union, held at the end of October. The joyous atmosphere was reinforced by a private meeting of poets, prose writers, and journal editors with Stalin and a few other leaders at Gorky's apartment. Such meetings, in an unofficial setting over a cup of tea, had never been held before. Here, the first discussions took place about a newly proposed artistic method for Soviet literature, defined by Stalin as "socialist realism." Pasternak did not attend either of these two important meetings. Whereas writers had been invited to Gorky's in strict confidentiality from a special list of particularly trustworthy people, the plenum was open to everyone, and Pasternak's refusal to join in the general exultation is noteworthy. But there is no doubt that he was well informed about what took place at both gatherings. He probably was able to find out about the meeting with Stalin (which was not reported in the press) from one of his friends, the critic Kornely Zelinsky.

Pasternak could not help reacting seriously to the slogan "socialist realism," which had not yet acquired its ominous and numbing content. At that time, in fact, it generally lacked a content, since no one— neither Stalin or Gorky nor Gronsky—was in a position to explain to the writers what lurked behind the phrase. It seemed clear, however, that the term had a liberal aura since it was proposed by Stalin as an antidote to the noisy demands of RAPP that the fellow-traveler writers adopt the "method of dialectical materialism." Stalin, who himself read with great difficulty (even in translation) the philosophical works of the founders of Marxism, quite reasonably noted at Gorky's that a poet might entirely forget how to write poetry if he was forced to study *Capital*. Thus socialist realism in the fall of 1932 had liberal, not restrictive, overtones. But this in itself gave it no positive meaning, and when the anxious writers at the plenum turned to Gronsky for explanations, he answered simply: "Write the truth, comrades."

Pasternak sincerely tried to understand how this call for unadorned truth, issuing from Stalin and the leaders of literature appointed by him, would affect his own situation and his conceptions about the role of the writer. The criterion of realism certainly seemed appealing: at the beginning of the 1920s he had come to the conclusion that realism is the very nature of art in any epoch. In *Safe Conduct,* having rejected the romantic conception, he asserted that art is "realistic as activity." If the call for naked, honest truth was sincere, could he expect an answer to his letter to Writers' Union about what had shocked him in the Urals? Or did these questions lay outside the sphere of their competence and have to be redirected to higher government authorities? The gathering at Gorky's seemed to be a reassuring sign of that Stalin himself was concerned with art, instead of relying on the mediation of bureaucrats, and that he was prepared to engage in direct contact with writers.

Such were Pasternak's thoughts, apparently, during those days. But he was experiencing a creative crisis. He was not writing any new poetry, and his collection *Second Birth* deeply dissatisfied him. Outwardly nothing had changed since 1931, when the majority of the poems making up *Second Birth* were written: not his love for Zinaida or his magnanimity to his first family, not his enthusiastic reminiscences about Georgia or his fundamental belief that socialism might eventually bring freedom and happiness to millions. Although there was nothing that was actually untrue or deceitful in the collection, Pasternak thought it contained a certain degree of compromise and falsehood, and he never became fond of it. This was his first book of verse since *My Sister, Life* and *Themes and Variations,* and comparisons with them led to depressing conclusions. The optimistic mood expressed in the collection, underscored by its title, did not correspond to the gloomy and tormented impressions he brought back from the Urals in the fall of 1932. His old plans for prose also lost their attractions. Instead of facilitating work on his novel about the revolution and civil war, the summer trip to the Urals only paralyzed him. What he had seen in the backwaters of Russia led the author to an impasse and forced him to question how beneficial and liberating an act the revolution had actually been. His former hopes and plans now seemed naive. That is why Pasternak not only stopped trying to continue his novel about Spektorsky, but also burned the manuscript of the sequel to *Liuvers' Childhood*.

On November 10 an announcement was made that struck Pasternak just as powerfully as it did most of his contemporaries. During the night of November 8, Stalin's wife, Nadezhda Allilueva, died suddenly at the age of thirty-one. The cause of her death was not mentioned in the press, but according to rumors that immediately spread in Moscow, she committed suicide. Along with responses in other Soviet newspapers, the *Literary Gazette* published on November 17 a collective letter from writers expressing their condolences to Stalin. This was the first letter to him from writers ever to appear in the press. Among the signatories were Leonid Leonov, Viktor Shklovsky, Yury Olesha, Vsevolod Ivanov, Boris Pilniak, Valentin Kataev, the poets Eduard Bagritsky (whose poems Stalin had commended at Gorky's meeting) and Ilya Selvinsky, as well as prominent former members of RAPP who knew Stalin personally—Alexander Fadeev, Vladimir Kirshon, and Leopold Averbakh. Separate from the others, but in the same letter, Pasternak added the following note:

> I share the feeling of my comrades. On the eve [of Allilueva's death] for the first time I thought as an artist about Stalin profoundly and persistently. In the morning I read the news. I am as shaken as if I had been there, and had lived through and seen everything.   Boris Pasternak.[14]

In an article in 1958, the émigré literary critic Mikhail Koriakov was right to call this note "unusual and mysterious."[15] It was first of all unusual that Pasternak did not simply sign the collective letter, but stood apart and, as if it were, juxtaposed his own reactions to the official and impersonal clichés of his literary colleagues. The "clairvoyant" overtones of the poet's declaration were also strange, especially given the mystery that surrounded the death of Stalin's wife. But something else is suspicious. Pasternak declared that "on the eve"—in other words, during the triumphant celebration of the fifteenth anniversary of the October Revolution (and, thus directly connected with it)—he had first thought *as an artist* about the leader. Some critics suggest that this phrase should be understood in the context of the tradition of singing paeans to Stalin. But these would emerge in Soviet literature only a few years later, and thus Pasternak's words would have to be interpreted as an anachronistic promise to embark on this genre in advance. I think there is a much more convincing explanation. In the spring of 1958, a western journal published an anonymous note, the author of which recalled meetings with Pasternak in the years 1945–1950. The reminiscences mention one unrealized project the poet had contemplated:

> Pasternak once told me of an idea he had for a poem on a political theme. It would take the form of a mental soliloquy by Stalin as he drove by night through some villages which had been ruined by the "dekulakization" of 1930. The headlights pick out the blackened shells of houses one after another, and Stalin ruminates on the monstrous cost of his policies in terms of human suffering. And against that he sets the final result, the building of a strong, rich Russia. The net result was that Stalin justified himself, but, as Pasternak said, such a poem, by suggesting that there was a debit column at all, disqualified itself for publication, and it had never got beyond the planning stage.[16]

It is possible that the words in Pasternak's addendum to the letter on Allilueva's death were related to the conception of such a poem. The origin of the idea could have arisen from the poet's reflections on the new role it appeared that Stalin was playing in literary life, and from his thoughts about the demand to write and speak the unadulterated truth.

The poem was never written, and Pasternak found no escape from his crisis. A period began that both he and his biographers have called the interval of silence. Until 1940 Pasternak wrote only a handful of lyrics. But to think of this entire time as barren would be wrong. Pasternak's mood was not fixed. On the contrary, these years are remarkable for the contradictions and dramatic shifts in the poet's behavior and in his place in Soviet society. His silence was not a political demonstration, as is sometimes imagined. It was prompted by attempts to find an answer to questions that were tormenting him. But during all the sharp fluctuations, which were not accompanied by the kind of creative surge that had led to the creation of *My Sister, Life* and *Safe Conduct,* and during which he sometimes "deceived himself" and even involuntarily "deceived others," Pasternak remained true to his fundamental convictions.

The poet himself attributed the beginning of his silent period to the worsening political climate. The feeling of freedom that had intoxicated writers in the spring of 1932 now seemed "inappropriate." How inappropriate it actually was he was soon to find out for himself. At the beginning of March 1933 he learned that his most important work, *Safe Conduct,* had been banned by the censors. It was a paradoxical situation. During RAPP's domination, the book had been freely published. Now that the leaders of RAPP had been toppled at the initiative of the highest echelons in the party, *Safe Conduct* was prohibited. Moreover, old reviews, which should have been anachronistic after RAPP's dissolution, served as the basis for the censorship. As soon as the news reached him, Pasternak wrote to Gorky in Sorrento; the writer had reacted ecstatically to the appearance of *Safe Conduct* in 1931 and had even volunteered to arrange its English translation. Gorky was infuriated, but his protests led to nothing and the book was not republished in the Soviet Union for fifty years. In a letter to his parents, written during the same period, the poet likened the internal situation in Russia to the changes taking place in Germany. National socialism, which had come to power there, and Soviet Bolshevism seemed in his mind to be related phenomena.[17] This attitude explains why Pasternak deliberately avoided the tumultuous activity of the writers' organization that had been created by a resolution of the Central Committee and was feverishly preparing for its first congress.

Meanwhile, toward the summer of 1933, other changes were occurring in the literary life of Soviet Russia. With his return to Moscow on May 19, Gorky began to take a more active role in the everyday affairs of the Writers' Union. He agreed to this partially at Stalin's insistence and partially because of his own concern over the apathy and lethargy that gripped Soviet writers after the auspicious beginning of liberalization a year before. This indifference was particularly upsetting to him because in Italy he had witnessed the triumphant spread of the "brown plague" in Europe. He was struck by the ease with which the Nazis came to power in Germany and by the direct consequences of their rise in the sphere of culture—the arrests of writers, the fleeing of the best thinkers from the country, and the book burning in city streets. He believed that only culture, and particularly the culture of socialism, could serve as a barrier against the fascist contagion in Europe. But the situation in the recently created Writers' Union and the way it was preparing its first congress distressed him. That is why he agreed to become the chairman of the organizing committee (a post previously held by Gronsky) and why he arranged the postponement of the congress for one year.

According to Gorky's plan, the impending congress would, along with other tasks, set the "friendship of peoples" and the flourishing of minority literature in the Soviet Union against the wild outburst of chauvinism in Germany. It would also be necessary to create a broad international aura around the congress itself and Soviet culture as a whole. Thus invitations to the congress were extended not to the full-blooded "proletarian" writers of the west favored by RAPP during the 1920s, but to leftward-leaning intellectuals who did not necessarily belong to the communist movement.

Gorky felt that his most urgent task was to arouse the social activity of the Soviet writers. One way to do this was to form writers' brigades in Moscow and Leningrad to be sent to the union republics in order to assist the provincial literary organizations in preparing for the congress. Such brigades were established at the beginning of September. Pasternak was included in a team bound for the Urals. Evidently this was a result of purely bureaucratic, routine procedure, without the poet's sanction, for the simple reason that he had recently visited the Urals twice. The officials were caught by surprise when they heard Pasternak's objections and his unexpectedly insistent requests to be included in the brigade assigned to Georgia. His requests were buttressed by his translations of several poems by his Georgian friends Paolo Yashvili and Titsian Tabidze. These translations made a tremendous impression on Gorky and his associates. Pasternak even convinced his Leningrad friend Nikolai Tikhonov (who enjoyed the sympathies of the authorities and Gorky) to join the delegation and to undertake the translation of Georgian poetry as well. The group's trip to Georgia turned into a genuine triumph: it was widely reported in the Soviet press, and accounts even appeared in western newspapers.

What was the reason for the sudden change in Pasternak's attitude to the Writers' Union, an organization he had boycotted not long before? Merely the attempt to avoid a new trip to the Urals is insufficient to explain the poet's "creative gusto" which so pleased the literary establishment. The reasons were, of course, more profound. Optimistic notes again began to sound in the poet's comments about the Soviet regime. The conviction that Soviet reality concealed within it the seeds of a better future was strengthened in Pasternak's mind as ever more troubling news arrived from Germany. Under the direct impact of a story about the humiliations suffered by the Jews there, Pasternak sent a telegram to his parents proposing their immediate return home. But changes within Russia also prompted the poet to feel more favorably disposed toward the Soviet system. From the summer of 1933 on, a definite relaxation could be felt in political life; several prominent oppositionists were returned from exile and prison. Rumor attributed this nascent democratization of the Soviet regime to the influence of Gorky on Stalin; relations between the two men were very cordial at this time.

The organizers of the "Georgian brigade" hoped that Pasternak would return to Moscow with poems praising socialist construction in Georgia, poems similar in their power to the "Waves" of 1931. But he wrote no poems, and art once again deceived its patron. A surge in the poet's creativity found expression in his work on translations from Georgian poetry. In Georgia, Pasternak discovered that the poems he had selected for translation did not suit the local administration. Vestiges of ill will and political distrust still remained from the RAPP period in the Georgian authorities' treatment of the Blue Horns poets. The close relations of the guest from the capital, who had come as an official envoy of the Writers' Union, with this group of poets was not seen by the administrators as an entirely positive situation. They bore an even greater grudge because Pasternak was exclusively interested in "pure lyrics" whereas they felt that a repertoire of civic poetry would be much more appropriate for translation into Russian. They revealed their dissatisfaction by reproaching the poet's selection of Georgian material for its "subjectivity."

Upon his return to Moscow, Pasternak decided to make some concessions and agreed to translate several poems on civic themes. Among them were two odes to Stalin written by his Georgian friends, Mitsishvili and Yashvili. Both odes were written within the framework of the propaganda campaign preceding the seventeenth Party Congress. In January 1934, on the threshold of this "congress of victors" (as it was then called), *Pravda* published a long article devoted to Stalin by Karl Radek (formerly a prominent member of the Trotskyist opposition). This article, entitled, "The Architect of Socialist

Society," inaugurated that unrestrained cult of personality that from this time on became the norm in the Soviet press until Stalin's death in 1953. The poems by Mitsishvili and Yashvili translated by Pasternak were the counterparts to Radek's article; never before had such poems about Stalin appeared in the Russian language. That is why their appearance provoked a major response in society.

These translations were, of course, a political compromise. But they cannot be considered a complete political or moral capitulation. Pasternak would not have had hidden behind the screen of translations if his main goal had been to please the leader and to stand out among other Soviet poets. The initiative for the translation of these poems came not from Pasternak but from others, and he would not have undertaken them if he had been coerced through bureaucratic channels. The translations should be seen as a friendly gesture toward his Georgian friends, not as an example of zeal to carry out orders. Pasternak shared the convictions of the authors of both odes that Stalin was the cementing force in the country, that the period of terror was drawing to a close, and that the Soviet Union was witnessing the inexorable triumph of the principles of social justice and reason. (Similar views were held by leaders of the former opposition at this time.) Pasternak had no doubts about the sincerity of the Georgian poets— it was precisely his trip to Georgia and his meeting with them in 1931 that had led him to embrace socialism in the form he observed there. The hyperbolic formulas of glorification in the odes were alien to Pasternak's style, but this seemed irrelevant in comparison with the sincerity of the author's feelings, and he considered the bombastic style to be one of the national peculiarities of the leader's homeland.

In this light, it becomes clear why Pasternak reacted so sharply to the derogatory (and underground) political verse satire against Stalin written by Osip Mandelshtam in the fall of 1933.[18] Unlike Pasternak, Mandelshtam saw in Stalin not a revolutionary leader but a political usurper and tyrant. He recited his poem to Pasternak on the street (fearing "even the walls have ears"). "This is not a literary fact, but an act of suicide, which I do not approve and in which I have no desire to take part," Pasternak said to him in reply.[19] It might be possible to conclude that the author of *Safe Conduct* and *Second Birth* was excessively cautious in reacting to the deed of his fellow poet. Yet in calling this an act of suicide, Pasternak had in mind not only the possibility of police repression, but also Mandelshtam's lack of any positive program at a time when even many of Stalin's bitter enemies

Boris Pasternak, 1908.
Collection of Mr. and Mrs. Irwin T. Holtzman

Inscription on a copy of the miscellany *Lirika* (1913) presented to Emile Metner, head of the publishing house Musagetes. All the contributors signed, including Pasternak. *Collection of Mr. and Mrs. Irwin T. Holtzman*

Pasternak reading Rainer Maria Rilke's *Buch der Bilder,*
1920s. *Gleb Struve Collection, Hoover Institution
Archives, Stanford University*

Marina Tsvetaeva, 1922. *Gleb Struve Collection, Hoover Institution Archives, Stanford University*

Vladimir Mayakovsky and Vsevolod Meyerhold, 1929. *Joseph Freeman Collection, Hoover Institution Archives, Stanford University*

Boris Pilniak, ca. 1929.
*Joseph Freeman Collection,
Hoover Institution
Archives, Stanford
University*

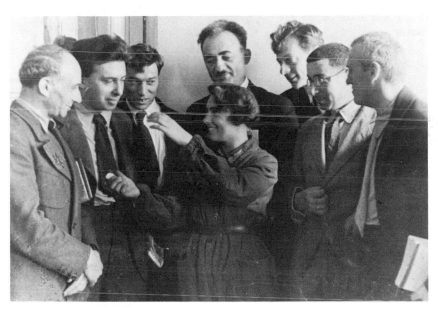

Parachutist Kaisheva with delegates and foreign guests (left to right: Jean
Richard Bloch, Ilya Ehrenburg, Pasternak, Paolo Yashvili, two unidentified
men, Nikolai Tikhonov) at the First Congress of Soviet Writers,
August 1934. *Joseph Freeman Collection, Hoover Institution Archives,
Stanford University*

To dear C. M. Bowra
as sign of my deepest
acknoledgment with
my warmest Thanks for
his rare and profound
articles on Blok, Rilke
and on myself —
whole heartedly

Пастернак

10 апр 1941
Roma
Show it please, to my other
and others

Author's inscription on the typewritten manuscript of
poems from *Doctor Zhivago,* sent to C. M. Bowra,
April 10, 1948. *Collection of Mr. and
Mrs. Irwin T. Holtzman*

Pasternak, 1957. *Gleb Struve Collection, Hoover Institution Archives, Stanford University*

The poet's funeral, June 2, 1960.
Collection of Mr. and Mrs. Irwin T. Holtzman

in the party and the nation believed that, because of the threat of fascism and a possible invasion of the USSR, the leadership was preparing sweeping liberal reforms in order to placate the people. The Seventeenth Congress appeared to be compelling confirmation of these prognoses. But Pasternak had poetic objections to Mandelshtam's anti-Stalin poem as well. He felt that rhymed invective was just as much a betrayal of art as the newspaper poetry of Mayakovsky. Although Pasternak himself never would have written odes like those by Mitsishvili and Yashvili, he nevertheless found them to be superior to underground verse satire.

One of the results of the Seventeenth Congress was the appointment in February 1934 of Nikolai Bukharin as editor-in-chief of *Izvestia* (News), the second most important newspaper in the USSR. This marked the first time since 1929 that Bukharin had available to him the means of publicly expressing his views. Bukharin—like Gorky—felt that the most crucial task of the hour was to effect a real transformation in art, education, and science. This activity, in his opinion, would ensure the victory of a new socialist humanism over fascist barbarism. Like Gorky, Bukharin considered culture the sole bastion against the onslaught of the fascist plague. His arrival at *Izvestia* completely changed the profile of the newspaper. Before he took over, industrial, economic, and international political issues overshadowed cultural ones; Bukharin, however, emphasized the latter.[20] In quantity, variety, and artistic quality, the literary works printed in *Izvestia* were superior to those in all other Soviet periodicals. Bukharin attracted to his daily the best literary talents of the time. The brightest star in this galaxy was Boris Pasternak.

A close collaboration between him and Bukharin began from the very start. Pasternak's debut at the newspaper took place two weeks after Bukharin's appointment—in the same issue of March 6, in which (for the first time during his editorship) Bukharin himself published an article. This article, "The Crisis of Capitalist Culture and Problems of Culture in the USSR," presented the ideological platform of the newspaper and of its editor-in-chief. It established the basic direction of the new editorial policy: a critique of fascist ideology. Accompanying the article was a selection "From Georgian Poets" consisting of Pasternak's translations of Yashvili and Tabidze. Significantly, the works chosen were not the civic verses suggested to Pasternak by the literary authorities, but intimate, contemplative, clearly apolitical verses.

As a rule, throughout his literary career Pasternak avoided contacts with newspapers. His rare appearances in the daily press (mainly in the revolutionary years) confirm the idea that the poet considered such publications incidental and insignificant. As opposed to his comrades in Lef—Mayakovsky and Aseev—he felt that placing one's poems in newspapers (not to speak of working regularly for one) was demeaning to the status of poetry and the poet. Thus Pasternak's active association with *Izvestia* under Bukharin is a fact of particular literary and historical importance. During 1934 his translation appeared there a number of times, giving them an audience they would otherwise not have had. Other translations from Georgian—by Nikolai Tikhonov, Benedikt Livshits, and Pavel Antokolsky—also appeared in *Izvestia* in 1934 and 1935. Pasternak's translations were also published in the *Literary Gazette* and in journals. And yet Pasternak's publications in *Izvestia* had a special social-cultural value: they created a kind of antiphony together with the editor-in-chief's own statements. Certainly no other paper or journal gave so much attention to Pasternak as did *Izvestia*. (In *Pravda* he was completely ignored.)

The rapprochement between Bukharin and Pasternak was not based on any deep appreciation of Pasternak's lyric poetry. As we know, other high-ranking former party authorities in literary matters, such as Lunacharsky and Trotsky, also were perplexed by Pasternak's obscure poetic style. The rapprochement came about, rather, because in the specific circumstances of the years 1934–1936 the poetry and position of Pasternak embodied for Bukharin the ideal of a courageous and honest acceptance of the existing order, combined with the preservation of personal independence. Bukharin's moral and political program required a figure who would embody these values. Thus the editor of *Izvestia* and Pasternak became literary allies, and Bukharin was closer to the poet than were the editors of the purely literary journals, such as *New World, Red Virgin Soil, Molodaia gvardia* (Young Guard), and *Tridtsat dnei* (30 Days), which also published Pasternak's Georgian translations.

Two months after Pasternak began his association with *Izvestia,* his relation with the paper's editor underwent an unexpected test in connection with the arrest of Osip Mandelshtam on May 13, 1934. From the memoirs of Anna Akhmatova and Nadezhda Mandelshtam, we know that the alarmed Pasternak turned to Bukharin for help, and Bukharin noted in a letter to Stalin: "Pasternak, too, is very upset."

All memoirists and historians agree that the situation of Mandelshtam was alleviated thanks to the efforts of Bukharin and Pasternak, and to the intercession of Avel Enukidze, the chairman of the All-Union Executive Committee, who agreed to hear out Mandelshtam's old friend, Akhmatova. As a result of these actions the GPU investigators came to regard his anti-Stalin poem not as a terrorist act but merely as counterrevolutionary propaganda, and the poet received a relatively mild sentence. But one should not forget that the weight of these two channels of intercession was not equal: if Enukidze was the ordinary channel for appeals, Bukharin's protest was a much more dramatic gesture. Nor could Akhmatova, who was by then severed from official literary life, have had the same impact as Pasternak, who had demonstrated his readiness to accept Soviet reality. We therefore have firm grounds for believing that the joint actions of Bukharin and Pasternak played a decisive role in saving Mandelshtam. Stalin's subsequent phone call to Pasternak serves to corroborate this.

The spring and summer of 1934 were the eve of the First Soviet Writers' Congress, and in May, the month Mandelshtam was arrested, a great upheaval in literary policy occurred. In the light of subsequent events this sharp change has been forgotten, but at the time it caused a sensation. What happened was that the designated official speaker at the Writers' congress, Nikolai Aseev, was replaced. This marked the failure of the former members of Lef to promulgate Mayakovsky's poetry as the canonical model of socialist realism. At that time Aseev occupied the top position in the official hierarchy of Moscow poets. In his talk at a pre-congress meeting of poets in Moscow, on the same day Mandelshtam was arrested, Aseev presented a general survey of contemporary Soviet poetry against the background of Mayakovsky's poetic legacy. His evaluation of Pasternak's work was highly negative, with decisive overtones of political denunciation: Aseev declared that all of Pasternak's recent work (including his collection *Second Birth*) was out of tune with, and even hostile to, socialist art. This speech had a definite sectarian flavor—a Soviet poet was seen as worthy of praise only insofar as he could be proclaimed a follower of Mayakovsky. As a result of this speech, which attacked not only Pasternak but many other poets, Aseev was excluded from the list of official speakers at the congress. On May 23 it was announced that the newly appointed congress speaker on poetry would be Bukharin. It is clear that all speakers (and their speeches) had to be approved by the party

Central Committee. The choice of Bukharin, who not so long before had been a leader of the opposition, required the special approval of Stalin. It is difficult to know which came first—Bukharin's intervention on behalf of Mandelshtam, which earned him the appointment as the official speaker on poetry, or his knowledge of his upcoming appointment, which emboldened him to turn to Stalin.[21]

The paradoxical character of Bukharin's appointment should not be underestimated. Although Bukharin was one of the party leaders of the 1920s who took a keen interest in problems of culture, he hardly stood out as a connoisseur of poetry. On the other hand, the fact that he, a former member of Politburo, was to give a keynote speech indicated the special importance accorded poetry at the congress. His position as editor-in-chief of *Izvestia* and his appointment as speaker at the congress transformed Bukharin in the eyes of his contemporaries into one of the main, if not the main, spokesmen for the party line in the field of literature. For the first time since the 1920s, Bukharin was returning to an active role in literary policymaking, and his oppositional past lent his new appointment particular meaning. The initiative for this appointment evidently came from Gorky. Bukharin's platform clearly aimed at strengthening the views of Gorky and his supporters, who wanted to see higher artistic quality, greater mastery, more culture from Soviet writers—in opposition to the efforts to homogenize Soviet literature, to place it under the day-to-day control of party watchdogs and turn it into a tool of party functionaries. The appointment of Bukharin was immediately understood as blocking the efforts to canonize the poetry of Mayakovsky at the congress.

It is within this play of literary-political forces that we must consider the mysterious phone call of Stalin to Pasternak in June 1934. The immediate reason for the call was Mandelshtam's attempted suicide soon after his arrival at Cherdyn. This act nullified the whole effect of the clemency granted him, which was expressed in the phrase "to isolate but preserve"—to keep him alive—as the GPU interrogator summed up his orders before the poet's exile to Cherdyn. In order not to dissipate the aura of miracle and clemency surrounding Mandelshtam's punishment, a more dramatic act was needed than a simple administrative decision to transfer the poet to a new location, Voronezh. One of the purposes of Stalin's call was to provide precisely that: to use the "Mandelshtam affair" to demonstrate the influence of the liberal political wing in connection with literature. This is why the Leader decided to let people know about the clemency being shown to the dangerous poet. To do so he used Pasternak.

Yet the talk evidently strayed into somewhat less noble territory as well. Its content is now well known from the memoirs of Akhmatova, Nadezhda Mandelshtam, and a whole series of other sources, including unwritten reminiscences by Pasternak himself. Having related his decision regarding Mandelshtam's transfer to Voronezh, Stalin reproached Pasternak for displaying unpardonable indifference to the misfortune of his friend. To this Pasternak responded that, if he had made no appeal, Stalin would be totally unaware of his role in the matter. During this exchange, neither Pasternak nor Stalin ever referred directly to Bukharin's letter. Stalin also rebuked Pasternak for not having turned to the Writers' Union, which would have been a more natural channel. Pasternak replied by noting that since 1927 the writers' organizations (since the defeat of the innerparty opposition) had been afraid of making appeals for their own arrested members. Indicating that Pasternak had acted incorrectly, Stalin let him know how inappropriate it had been to turn to Bukharin. It was a blatant violation of protocol: until May 23, when the sudden announcement was made that Bukharin was to give a main report at the congress, Bukharin officially had nothing to do with the affairs of the Writers' Union. Stalin also asked Pasternak whether Mandelshtam was a good poet and a genuine master.[22] Pasternak replied: "That's not the point." The meaning of this reply (which Akhmatova interpreted as a sign of cowardice and professional jealousy) is that poets should never be treated—regardless of whether they are "master" or not—like criminals. Pasternak discerned in Stalin's question an attempt to find out whether he knew about Mandelshtam's underground poem and what he thought about it.[23]

Thus the leader's conversation with the poet served not only to show clemency, but also to carry out hidden police functions. In returning to this conversation many years later in his memoirs, Pasternak came to the conclusion that Stalin's goal was to "check up" on Bukharin. But it is possible that Stalin was also checking up on Pasternak himself. Mandelshtam had given his interrogator the names of most of the people to whom he had recited his poem. According to Soviet law, failure to denounce a crime was considered complicity in the crime and was subject to no less severe punishment. Although Pasternak did not know whether he was among those named, he would have had to take such a possibility into account. Stalin had to notice the two Georgian odes dedicated to him that had just appeared in Pasternak's translation. Naturally the question arose: when was the poet being sincere, in the translations of the Georgian odes or in his "complicity with terror"?

The dialogue with Stalin was left hanging. As soon as Pasternak proposed that they meet face to face in order to talk about life and death rather than about mundane things, Stalin hung up. His one and only conversation with the leader, which proceeded and ended in such a strange manner, left Pasternak for the rest of his life with a nagging feeling that much had remained unspoken and unresolved—and possibly that he had made some kind of mistake with regard to Mandelshtam. Later he was inclined to reproach himself publicly for this. Akhmatova and Mandelshtam's widow declared that he had conducted himself in a good but not outstanding manner and gave him a solid "B grade." [24] It is now clear that this evaluation is insufficient. Pasternak could not have obtained greater clemency for Mandelshtam not because he was indifferent to his fellow poet's fate, but because it was simply not within his power.

How widespread were the rumors concerning Stalin's phone call to Pasternak? Much later, in the 1950s, Zinaida Nikolaevna claimed that, within several hours after the call, all of Moscow knew about it. [25] This seems an exaggeration. Right up to the second half of the 1940s the conversation was never mentioned in the western press, neither in connection with Pasternak nor in connection with Mandelshtam. One of the reasons for the call—to inform the public about the softening of Mandelshtam's punishment—should have guaranteed its becoming known to the widest possible audience, with a subsequent leaking of the news to the western press. But this did not happen. In the west, Mandelshtam's arrest and exile to Voronezh went unnoticed until the late 1940s (when hundreds of thousands of Soviet refugees flooded Europe in the second wave of Russian emigration), and the names of Pasternak and Stalin never came up in this regard. By contrast, the "miraculous" role of Stalin in the fate of Pilniak in 1930 was reported quite fully by Max Eastman in his book *Artists in Uniform* (1934), and the call of Stalin to Mikhail Bulgakov on March 18, 1930, was mentioned in the émigré periodical *Sotsialistichesky vestnik* (Socialist Herald) in October 1933. Since rumors about the call were supposed to have originated with Pasternak and not with his interlocutor in the Kremlin, it follows that Pasternak did not rush to spread the word about the conversation.

It is my guess that Ilya Ehrenburg should be given credit for circulating the news about the phone call to a fairly limited audience. As Nadezhda Mandelshtam noted, on the day of the call Pasternak visited Ehrenburg and told him what had happened. Ehrenburg had just come from France with André Malraux to participate in the First Writers' Congress, and their arrival coincided with the announcement of a new date for the congress and the determination of its final program. The new program clearly revealed a dramatic increase in the influence of Gorky and Bukharin, and it would have been only natural for Ehrenburg to connect the call of Stalin to Pasternak with these changes. While for Pasternak the conversation would continue to be darkly enigmatic for the rest of his life, for Ehrenburg it was an obvious indication of Stalin's intent to set a liberal course for Soviet literary life. The very fact that the leader called the most prominent Soviet poet could well have seemed an indication of trust and sympathy. Ehrenburg helped make known the fact rather than the content of Stalin's conversation with Pasternak, and this led to a perceptible change, a warning of attitude toward the poet on the part of the literary establishment. Since the early 1920s Ehrenburg had been hailing Pasternak's lyrical poetry in both European and Soviet literary circles; now he had reason to hope that the "Pasternak line" would emerge triumphant in the struggle of various cultural-political forces before the congress.

In this struggle Ehrenburg had an extremely powerful ally, Malraux, who was visiting the USSR for the first time and who also esteemed Pasternak. Not long before Ehrenburg's and Malraux's arrival in the Soviet Union, on April 25, 1934, the French magazine *Marianne* published an essay by Malraux about his meeting (at the end of July in the previous year) with Trotsky. With unconcealed surprise and criticism, Malraux noted Trotsky's indifference to Pasternak's poetry:

> In the domain of the mind, this man had created his own world and lived in it. I remember the way he spoke of Pasternak:
> "Almost all the young Russians follow him at the moment, but I don't care for his work. I don't care very much for an art of technicians, an art for specialists." [26]

This disparaging evaluation by Trotsky of the poetry of Pasternak, attested to by one of the best-known representatives of revolutionary literature in Western Europe, undoubtedly brought increased attention and a more positive attitude to Pasternak from the Soviet literary establishment.

The campaign against Trotskyite propaganda just before Stalin's call to Pasternak became one of the main components of Soviet literary policy. It grew out of the appearance of Eastman's *Artists in Uniform,* which accused the Soviet regime of homogenizing literature, robbing it of any individuality. Eastman specifically linked this tendency to the series of suicides of Soviet poets, first Esenin in 1925 and then Mayakovsky in 1930.[27] In the summer of 1934, before the congress, the appearance of Eastman's book was seen as a crushing ideological blow. He was one of the most knowledgeable authorities abroad in the field of Soviet literature. If Mandelshtam's suicide attempt had succeeded, the accusations in Eastman's book would have been confirmed at a most inopportune moment. One can appreciate the concern of the authorities from the fact that two leading Soviet ideologists were sent into action to counter the book: Valery Kirpotin and Karl Radek, who was at that time Stalin's personal adviser on foreign policy. In addition, one of the main examples in Eastman's book, Boris Pilniak, was also mobilized against it, and his response was published not in the USSR but in the American leftist journal *Partisan Review* (the June-July issue of 1934). The appearance of Eastman's book thus affected the consolidation of the liberal faction in Soviet literary politics.

It is within the context of this liberal "offensive" that one should view the appreciation of Pasternak as the "premier" Soviet poet by the literary establishment close to Gorky and Bukharin. Although this opinion was nowhere stated explicitly, it was expressed in giving Pasternak an honored (and hitherto unimaginable) place in the official surveys of Soviet literature published before the congress, and in the atmosphere of demonstrative attention paid to him at the congress itself.

9

Premier Soviet Poet

Two antithetical concepts were on a collision course when the First Writers' Congress opened on August 17, 1934. Coming from the upper echelons of the party was a demand for ideological orthodoxy and unquestioning obedience to the constantly changing policies of the party. From Gorky's side came the assertion of the artists' right to diversity and autonomy. This contradiction permeated all aspects of the congress. The negative evaluation of contemporary Soviet literature in Gorky's address shocked the audience. It stood in striking contrast to the atmosphere of elation that prevailed at the congress, and it reflected Gorky's concern about the direction Soviet literature was about to take. This speech was the high point of the first five sessions, which were entirely devoted to official reports.

Emil Mindlin's memoirs reveal Pasternak's disappointment at the start of the meeting:

> Pasternak said that he earlier had high hopes for the Congress; he had hoped to hear something entirely different from what the speakers had been saying. He was expecting speeches with important philosophical content; he had believed that the Congress would become a meeting of Russian thinkers. Maxim Gorky's address seemed to him to stand alone at the Congress. The things Pasternak considered to be most important for the fate of Russian literature had not been discussed. Pasternak was discouraged.[1]

However, when the debates began, Pasternak's attitude changed. On August 22 he wrote to his wife: "The opening of the Congress frightened us with its tedium: it was too solemn and official. But now each day is more interesting than the last: the debates have begun."[2]

During these debates Pasternak was frequently mentioned as the greatest contemporary poet in the speeches of various Soviet writers and foreign guests. There is not doubt that the congress was a personal triumph for Pasternak: this is confirmed by everyone who was present. But the acclaim has often been attributed to the praise for Pasternak in Bukharin's speech. Although that speech was a remarkable episode in the history of Soviet literature, the section devoted to Pasternak can hardly be considered an encomium for the poet. Bukharin's main goal lay elsewhere. Following Gorky's lead, Bukharin emphasized the urgent need to raise the level of artistic complexity in literature. To understand the full significance of this exhortation we must remember that Soviet culture was in fact moving in the diametrically opposite direction, toward primitivism and homogeneity. Bukharin addressed the problem of literary *quality* and artistic experimentation. He linked this directly to cultural pluralism and competition among different stylistic tendencies. His report was the most concentrated and polemically pointed expression of the position of the Gorky camp.

In contrast to Gorky's speech, which had been devoted to Soviet literature as a whole, Bukharin spoke only about poetry. With a poem it was easier to demonstrate that, no matter how party-oriented was the thematic content of a text, it could not stand as a guarantee of quality. Bukharin chose two poets who were very popular in the 1920s, Demian Bedny and Vladimir Mayakovsky, in order to show that genuine art is a matter not of orthodox ideas but of formal complexity and subtlety. In the new cultural and political climate of the thirties, their work already seemed obsolete. The true criteria for Soviet art, in Bukharin opinion, should lie not in the plane of current party politics or in the latest fiats from the upper echelons of the government. Soviet art should take as its standard of comparison the highest achievements of world culture, such as Shakespeare and Goethe.

Bukharin judged the garish style of Mayakovsky's and Bedny's propaganda poetry in terms of the ancient Indian teaching that the essence of poetry lies in the "double"—ambiguous, enigmatic— meaning of its language. Against this criterion the so-called Komsomol poets, who held a respected position in poetry in the 1930s, appeared ridiculous. For Bukharin, true Soviet poetry, genuine poetic art, was embodied in the work of three poets: Pasternak, Selvinsky, and Tikhonov. The leader of the former opposition called for artistic experimentation, autonomy, independence, creative activity, and works unfettered by official decrees.[3]

Bukharin's speech stood out sharply from the mass of insipid official addresses at the congress, not only in its content but also in its sarcastic and taunting style. No other speaker except Gorky received so tumultuous an ovation. Foreign observers saw the address as decisive proof that the Soviet regime was sincerely interested in freedom of competition in artistic endeavors, that this concept had the official support of the government, and that the period of RAPP dictatorship was over. Yet it became almost immediately obvious that the official sanction enjoyed by Bukharin's speech was not absolute. His caustic remarks created a strong coalition of adversaries, including the Komsomol and proletarian poets along with the former members of Lef. Alexei Surkov, a minor poet and a seemingly negligible figure in Soviet literature, was the first to be given the floor to rebut Bukharin's address. He claimed that there was no such thing as abstract artistic mastery, that mastery must have a Bolshevik tinge, and that Pasternak was an inappropriate model for Soviet poets to emulate. The fierce attacks on Bukharin and the attempts to undermine his and Gorky's positions compelled the Georgian poet Sandro Euli, a party member and one of the old proletarian poets, to declare that Bukharin's report had the full support of the Georgian delegation.

In his short address to the congress, Pasternak did not explicitly side with either of the declared positions. It is obvious that he regarded heated arguments about his role in Soviet literature to be unnecessary and tried to avoid the impression that he spoke for any of the literary groups. Yet his sympathy for Bukharin's views on literary policy could be seen from the fact that his poem "Waves" in the second edition of *Second Birth* (1934) carried a dedication to the former leader of opposition. (This is Pasternak's only text with a formal dedication to a political figure.) And the content of his speech left no doubt that his stance in the literary battles was close to the liberal camp of Gorky and Bukharin. The strange definition he gave to poetry indicated this position: "Poetry is prose, prose not in the sense of the aggregate of someone or other's works, but prose itself, the voice of prose in action, not in narration." This statement was directed against the stilted rhetoric that permeated official Soviet propaganda and the speeches of many writers at the congress. There was a deeply polemical subtext in the call with which the poet closed his address: "Don't sacrifice your personality for the sake of your status . . . Given the immense warmth with which nation and state are surrounding us, there is all too great a danger of becoming a literary dignitary. Keep away from such favor in the name of its direct sources, in the name of a great, active and fruitful love of country and of the greatest men of our day."[4] This appeal was all the more poignant because Pasternak found himself on the verge of being declared "the premier poet" during the congress. He felt it necessary to warn that, no matter what official status might be granted to him, he should not be expected to become a politically engaged writer. Instead he summoned his fellow writers to be loyal to the rebellious values of Tolstoy's ethics.

In the polemical discussion that followed Bukharin's speech, neither side won a clear victory. The tumult it created resulted in his banishment from the affairs of the Writers' Union just after the congress. This was largely due to the general moral and philosophical import of his speech and not to his praise of Pasternak. This can be seen from the fact that Bukharin's removal in no way harmed Pasternak's status, who after the congress—in 1934–35—was still considered the central figure in contemporary Soviet literature. The poet was also elected to the Board of the Writers' Union.

Pasternak never felt as close to the Soviet regime as he did during these first few months after the congress. On December 25, 1934, he wrote to his father in Germany: "I have become a part of my times and the state, and its interests have become my own." Such a statement would have been unthinkable coming from a poet who had considered the essence of art to be its "noncoincidence" with the epoch. This change in thinking is striking when compared with 1932. Then Pasternak had been seemingly indifferent to the liberal trend sweeping over literature. Now the liberal forces in literature were confronted with a no less powerful conservative camp, but this did not prevent Pasternak's rapprochement with the leadership of the Writers' Union. What can explain this apparent inconsistency? In 1932 the liberal shifts were confined to literature. But now, after the Seventeenth Congress, the party had set its course on consolidating its various political wings. Broad democratization seemed irreversible, and the situation in literature simply mirrored more general changes in the life of the state. Indeed, the liberalization seemed so real that in behind-the-scenes discussions the idea of legalizing a social organization independent of the Communist Party was considered. Such a group would be outside party control and able to work out its own alternative conceptions, although it would remain loyal to the Soviet regime. One of the main proponents of the idea of a legal opposition was (along with Bukharin) Gorky. The very idea of a writers'—and nonparty—congress reflected these moods. In the Writers' Union he saw the embryo of such a future social organization and perhaps even a second party, a party of the intelligentsia. For him, this would be an experimental laboratory in which the spontaneous activity and independence of artists could be forged.

Meanwhile, the assassination of Kirov on December 1, 1934, led to a palpable change in the political atmosphere. On December 17 an announcement was made about the arrest of Zinoviev and Kamenev and their responsibility for terrorist activity in the country. A wave of mass shootings, arrests, and deportations rolled across the Soviet Union. Gorky, who had previously exercised great influence in many spheres of Soviet life, was subjected to insulting attacks in *Pravda,* something that would have been inconceivable a few months earlier. After the Writers' Congress his personal relations with Stalin became noticeably strained, and they deteriorated further at the beginning of 1935. He was denied a trip abroad for medical treatment. In the Writers' Union that he headed, he was surrounded by dull-witted, semiliterate apparatchiks appointed by the party. Gorky's depression and his indignation, bordering on despair, can be felt in his correspondence from this period and in memoirs about him. The signs of Gorky's fall from favor, along with Bukharin's removal from literary matters, signaled imminent changes in cultural policy.

Evidently these shifts led to a sharp change in Pasternak's mood in the spring of 1935. In a letter to Titsian Tabidze he complained about the "gray and enervating emptiness" that was paralyzing work on his novel.[5] This depression developed into a deep spiritual crisis, marked by the complete cessation of writing and an agonizing six-month bout of insomnia. During the height of this crisis, it was proposed that Pasternak travel to Paris. He had not been abroad since 1923, and he had never been in France. But this new indication that he enjoyed the authorities' confidence only plunged him further into depression.

The proposed trip was connected with the International Writers' Congress in Defense of Culture, which was being organized in Paris. Its initiators were André Malraux, André Gide, and Ilya Ehrenburg, who was living in France at the time. In their eyes the congress was to demonstrate that the ideas of communism—unlike fascism—and sophisticated culture went hand in hand. Besides having a propagandistic effect in the world arena, Ehrenburg hoped that the success of the conference would have a beneficial impact on the disposition of forces inside Soviet literature: it would reinforce the liberal camp that enjoyed particular sympathy in the west.

These hopes were dealt a serious blow when the organizers in Paris learned about the composition of the Soviet delegation to the congress. With two or three exceptions, it was composed of colorless mediocrities and literary functionaries. The selection of candidates followed the directives of Stalin himself. For some reason, Gorky, who had eagerly awaited the congress and who was to have headed the Soviet delegation, was unable to travel to Paris. The official explanation was his illness, but western journalists treated the announcement with skepticism. Whatever the reason, the composition of the Soviet delegation sent to Paris in no way confirmed the claims by the organizers of the congress about the unprecedented flourishing of the arts in communist Russia.

Malraux and Gide set off for the Soviet embassy and insisted on the urgent dispatch to the congress of two more writers: Isaak Babel, who had lived in Paris for many years and was well known in the west, and Boris Pasternak, who had been at the center of the discussion at the First Congress of Soviet Writers. On June 20, Stalin's personal secretary Poskrebyshev telephoned Pasternak and conveyed the leader's command that the poet prepare to travel immediately. Against the background of the telephone conversation with Stalin a year ago, this order seemed crude and humiliating. All of Pasternak's excuses about illness and unrelenting insomnia were flatly rejected. The poet was unable to fathom the reasons for such an unexpected order delivered in such an unceremonious way. Why was he now being added to the delegation when he had not been originally included? Why was this being done at the last moment, after the delegation had already left for Paris? Why were his references to illness dismissed at a time when Gorky's illness prevented him from going abroad? How could he represent Soviet literature, from the depths of a crisis in creativity and his bleak depression?

Pasternak and Babel traveled together to Paris by train. Along the way they stopped for a few hours in Berlin, and Boris was able to see his older sister Josephine and her husband.[6] He arrived at the congress on June 24, the day before it closed. He entered the hall in the middle of Nikolai Tikhonov's report about Soviet poetry and was met with a standing ovation. We do not know whether Pasternak attended the following session (on the morning of June 25), which discussed freedom of thought. This discussion upset the relatively peaceful course of the congress and caused severe embarrassment for the Soviet delegates. The representatives of the west's left-wing intelligentsia demanded the immediate liberation or open trial of the revolutionary and writer, Victor Serge, who had been accused of Trotskyism and was in internal exile since his arrest in 1933 in Leningrad. Gorky and Romain Rolland, who knew him personally, and Gide, Malraux, and Vildrac were drawn into the appeals for his release. No doubt Pasternak felt a burning sense of shame as he observed the deceitful and demagogic responses of the Soviet writers (including his friend Tikhonov) to the questions of the western intellectuals. The reaction of the Soviet delegation, not to mention the very fact of Serge's arrest, showed the lack of divergent opinions and freedom of mind in the socialist state. The issue was all the more poignant for Pasternak since he (and Tikhonov) knew Serge personally. Upon returning to Moscow, he sent a petition to Mikhail Kalinin, the chairman of the All-Union Central Executive Committee, adding his voice to the foreign demands for the liberation of the revolutionary.[7]

Pasternak spoke from the rostrum of the congress only once, on the same day he arrived. He declined to read the text that Ehrenburg had prepared for him. The speech he gave was strikingly laconic: he spoke only a few sentences, and then fell silent for a long time. "This made a devastating impression," Tikhonov wrote in a letter to Pyotr Pavlenko. "Everyone began to respect him very much for this silence, which was greatly amplified by the microphone."[8] Pasternak had not said what might have expected from an emissary of Soviet literature. There was no word about the superiority of Soviet democracy or Soviet culture to that of the west. Nor did he even mention the threat of German fascism. According to Malraux's account, the central idea of Pasternak's speech was that happiness and poetry lay not in conferences and meetings. Writers had no reason to unite; writers' organizations and unions made no sense. What mattered was the personal independence and ethical principles of each individual writer. By saying this, Pasternak opposed the principle on which the very idea of the International Congress in Defense of Culture had been based. His position sharply differed both from Gorky's views about the Writers' Union as the embryo of a loyal opposition in socialist society and from the Stalinist interpretation of the union as a means of controlling the intelligentsia. Despite his appeal for the writers "not to unite," Pasternak was chosen a member of the directing body of the

International Association of Writers in Defense of Culture (which dis-integrated in 1937).

On the day of his arrival in Paris, Pasternak met with Marina Tsve-taeva. They had not seen each other since the spring of 1922. On December 31, 1929, Tsvetaeva had written to him: "If I should die without meeting you, my destiny would not be fulfilled, I would not be fulfilled, because you offer the last hope of preserving the whole me, that me who now exists and could not go on existing without you." [9] In the intervening years their tempestuous epistolary romance had subsided. But there was still no person in Paris who was closer to Pasternak than Tsvetaeva, since so much had linked them in literature during the 1920s. Now they were both in a state of profound crisis, and both had stopped writing poetry. In the political sphere, they were poles apart. Pasternak was in Paris as an official emissary of the state, and this alone created a certain barrier between them. But prob-lems in Tsvetaeva's family made contacts between the two poets even more strained. Tsvetaeva's husband and daughter cherished the hope of returning to the Soviet Union and were actively preparing to take this step. Since 1932, Sergei Efron had been an official member of the Union of Friends of the Soviet Homeland and was gradually drawn into the NKVD's terrorist activity in Europe. Their daughter Ariadna worked for the communist press. Even Tsvetaeva herself was becom-ing more inclined to think about returning to Russia. But the vehe-mently expressed political passions of her family and the crisis tor-menting Pasternak precluded any candid discussion of whether Tsvetaeva should go back to her native land. In 1927, in a letter to Gorky, Pasternak said it was necessary to "return Tsvetaeva to Rus-sia." Now in his every sentence Tsvetaeva sensed an inexplicable un-certainty. And in her home Pasternak felt himself an even greater pris-oner of his false official status, "premier Soviet poet," than he was in Moscow or even at the Paris congress. The people who were closest to him in Paris were much more pro-Soviet than he was, and to tell them about what was plaguing him or to transmit his doubts about the regime, with the arrests and deportations (including news about Mandelshtam, with whom Tsvetaeva had had a love affair before the revolution), was simply behind his powers.

The trip to Europe deepened Pasternak's depression. He returned to Russia in a state of near-hysteria and wept incessantly. The net of inescapable lies surrounding him caused him great suffering. Later he wrote that he was haunted by "a sensation of the end without any visible approach of death." [10] But after a few weeks, at the beginning of September, he found the strength to resume his work. The trip to Europe had not made Russian reality any better in his eyes, but it did suggest the need to make a choice, however undesirable and tentative it might be. The poet once again came to a conclusion about the inevitability of a "reconciliation with reality." But what was now most important for Pasternak was not "becoming a part of the times and the state," but maintaining his personal independence in light of the profound falseness of the official status he had been accorded.

That is why he greeted with such relief, if not joy, the publication on December 5, 1935, in *Pravda* of Stalin's verdict that "Mayakovsky had been and remained the best Soviet poet." Pasternak even wrote a letter of thanks to the leader. Although it was clear that this pronouncement represented a further erosion of the conception that had served as the foundation for the congress of Soviet writers, and directly lashed out at Bukharin's report, Pasternak nevertheless found it attractive. In a poem he wrote in 1930 soon after Mayakovsky's death, he had said that the post of premier poet is a threat to culture if it is filled. Now that the leader had filled it with the dead Mayakovsky, Pasternak was reassured because it might free him from those awkward, and perhaps dangerous, situations in which he had been placed (for instance, the trip to Paris). Besides his posthumous praise for Mayakovsky, Stalin's intervention during these months played a major role in the fate of another poet, Anna Akhmatova. In the fall, her husband and son were arrested. In response to a letter she wrote to the leader (accompanied by a note from Pasternak), both were set free. Pasternak learned of this immediately: during this trip to Moscow, Akhmatova was staying with the Pasternaks, and Stalin's secretary called their apartment to relay the good news. Pasternak saw a connection between the leader's concern for the dead poet and his concern for one who was alive. [11]

The end of 1935 witnessed astonishing changes in Soviet life. The American journalist Louis Fischer later wrote: "Despite the Kirov assassination, 1935 marks the high-water mark of personal freedom in the Soviet Union." [12] The system of food rationing introduced in 1929 was rescinded; restrictions on people of nonproletarian background (so-called *lishentsy*) were eliminated; western newspapers carried reports (apparently reflecting Soviet rumors) that the new constitution would introduce a parliamentary system on the European model, allowing legal opposition. A striking manifestation of this spirit was the restoration of the New Year's celebration, which had been banned since 1929 as a religious custom, and the Christmas tree was permitted once again. Even more important was the feeling that the Soviet state was entering a new phase, that the proletarian dictatorship was about to be superseded by a "state of the whole people" (*obshchenarodnoe gosudarstvo*). This conception underlay the new constitution that Bukharin had been assigned to draft and that was supposed to give legal muscle to the democratization of Soviet society. When he met with B. I. Nicolaevsky in Paris in March 1936, Bukharin stated with satisfaction that the prospective constitution was to grant the people far greater freedom they had ever had before.[13]

It was in response to these dramatic developments that Pasternak wrote two poems, "Ia ponial: vse zhivo" (I realized: all is alive) and "The Artist" ("Mne po dushe stroptivyi norov"—I am fond of the obstinate character), which were published in the *Izvestia* New Year's issue of 1936. As Pasternak himself revealed twenty years later, these poems were written at Bukharin's request.[14] Some critics today are inclined to censure Pasternak for these poems, which are taken to express the author's servile acceptance of Soviet reality and Stalin. The situation was extremely complex, however, and it would be inaccurate to see the writing of these poems as the fulfillment of a social command dictated by the editor of *Izvestia*. In his remarks in 1956 Pasternak stressed that the poems were "a sincere and very strong attempt (the last during this period) to live with the thoughts of and in tune with the times."

The entire holiday issue of the newspaper was devoted to the general idea of the radical change that the new year (1936) promised for all areas of Soviet life. It contained the answers of the "best people" of the country to questions posed about their plans for the future. Among these people were prominent scientists, artists, musicians, outstanding (*znatnye,* as they were then called) workers and collective farmers, writers—and only two poets: the Georgian Titsian Tabidze and Boris Pasternak. In his article published in this issue Bukharin declared that the outgoing year had marked the beginning of the "flowering of socialist humanism." He wrote that "Stalin's words about *concern for man* have become the most important slogan, the banner of our whole epoch." Bukharin was referring to a speech of Stalin at the beginning of 1935 which had proclaimed a doctrine that was new for Soviet society—humanism. This marked an essential turnabout in ideology: previously the very term "humanism" was considered hostile to the class morality of the proletariat, and it was first rehabilitated in articles by Gorky and Bukharin just before the Writers' Congress of 1934.

The initial version of Pasternak's poem "The Artist" consisted of two parts: the first was devoted to the artist with his "obstinate character" and the second to Stalin, not mentioned by name but as the Kremlin "recluse." A parallel was thus suggested between the two figures. When compared with the odes, hymns, and eulogies to Stalin created by the folk poets of Central Asia and the Caucasus, the suggestion of an analogy between the leader and an obstinate poet appears an act of daring. As noted above, poems about Stalin began to appear only in 1934, from the time of the Seventeenth Party Congress, but all of them, whether individual (like those by Mitsishvili and Yashvili) or in the "folklore tradition," were translations from *Eastern* languages. Most of them were created by minor national poets of distant Soviet regions writing in the spirit of their oriental poetic traditions. Previous attempts to create something similar in a western style had not succeeded. The book *Stalin* by Henri Barbusse had not yet appeared in Russian.[15] At the Writers' Congress Stalin's favorite, Alexander Fadeev, stated that Soviet prose writers had not yet gained the necessary maturity and craftsmanship to deal with such an important task as the depiction of Stalin in literature. In Russian-language poetry there were still no original works devoted especially to Stalin. Herein lay Bukharin's task: to publish a work that would supplant bombast with a genuinely lyric discourse on the leader. Pasternak's role was to raise the artistic level of the new panegyric genre and to lend it prestige. The tone adopted by Pasternak with regard to Stalin would serve, Bukharin believed, as a model for others.

The comparison of the obstinate poet and the leader in the poem emphasized the human, rather than the superhuman, nature of the ruler. This was in clear opposition to the clichés of the Eastern verses. It also corresponded to the doctrine of humanism proclaimed in 1935 as a counterpart to the antihumanistic principles of Nazi Germany. The content of "The Artist" reflected the poet's hope for the establishment in his country of "socialism with a human face" (to use a term that became current thirty years later in Czechoslovakia). Pasternak's hopes related to the social changes that were supposed to be embodied in Bukharin's draft of the constitution. At this time it seemed that the fate of the nation would depend on Stalin's support of the draft.

Did the publication of Pasternak's poem serve its purpose? We have no grounds to think that Stalin was pleased with the Pasternak-Bukharin experiment or with the image of himself in "The Artist." Although it was the first Russian poem about Stalin (besides Mandelshtam's 1933 underground verse satire), it did not appear in the anthology of "best poems about Stalin" which was released soon after the *Izvestia* publication, and after 1936 it was never reprinted in its entirety. In Pasternak's book of poems *On Early Trains* there appeared only the first part of "The Artist," the one about the obstinate poet; the second half, devoted to Stalin, never found its way into print again. It seems that both sides were responsible for this omission— the author and the censor.

Pasternak's turn to lyrical poetry in the winter of 1935–36 coincided with a decision to give up translation. After 1933, when he and Tikhonov had begun working on the Georgian poets, translating the verses of minority poets became an epidemic, not only a source of high earnings for translators but evidence of their political loyalty. Precisely because translation work had become a propaganda campaign, Pasternak publicly announced that he would no longer participate in it.

The question of poetry moved to the center of the literary discussions of this period. A special plenary meeting of the executive board of the Writers' Union was devoted to it. Preparations for the meeting lasted the entire winter. The appearance of Stalin's pronouncement about Mayakovsky lent a particular sharpness to the plenum. Later, in his second autobiography, Pasternak wrote: "Mayakovsky began to be introduced forcibly, like potatoes under Catherine the Great. This was his second death. He had no hand in it." [16] But in the first weeks after the publication of Stalin's comment, it seemed that there would be favorable conditions for experimentation in the arts. This, at least, was how Stalin's statement was interpreted by such convinced advocates of the avant-garde as Meyerhold, Ehrenburg, and Aseev.

These expectations were dealt a sudden blow when the January 28, 1936, issue of *Pravda* published an unprecedentedly sharp attack on the opera *Lady Macbeth of Mtsensk* by Dmitry Shostakovich. This signaled the beginning of a full-scale campaign against so-called formalism. In its scope the new campaign by far exceeded the 1929 campaign against Pilniak and Zamiatin. Whereas then the excuse for the attacks had been the anti-Soviet positions of the authors and the alleged ideological defects of their works, now the accusations were based on aesthetic flaws: formalism and naturalism. The atmosphere was particularly ominous because these attacks originated not from some literary group with pretensions to orthodoxy (as had been the case with RAPP in 1929) but from *Pravda*, a newspaper that was considered the official organ of the party. In addition, its disparaging articles were anonymous and supposedly expressed a state-licensed evaluation of the criminal works. Rumors that Stalin himself sanctioned the *Pravda* articles immediately gained wide currency.[17] Apparently the decision to apply direct administrative pressure on art was taken by the authorities, following the lead of Hitler's Germany. If in 1932 the explanation of the newly coined term "socialist realism" had been reduced to the suggestion to "write the truth," then it now turned out that this concept contained aesthetic prescriptions (although they were not formulated in any positive way). *Pravda* quickly demanded that other newspapers join the campaign, and it snowballed. It destroyed the platform on which Gorky's attempts to "raise the culture" of Soviet writers and stabilize their union had been based.

Under these conditions, on February 10, the plenum of the executive board of the Writers' Union opened in Minsk. Most poets speaking at the plenum ignored the articles that had just appeared in *Pravda*. Not supposing that the new campaign would touch literature, Alexei Surkov made only passing reference to it. A second-rate poet, he was appointed to give the official report as a reward for having initiated the assault on Bukharin at the congress in 1934. He was taking the first steps in his career as a literary functionary, and clearly he was afraid of making a mistake in his assessments. In accord with Stalin's pronouncement, pride of place in his report was given to Mayakovsky as an example of the genuine Soviet poet and of socialist realism in poetry. He also mentioned Demian Bedny and Boris Pasternak as the most significant poets of the modern period. Surkov rejected Bukharin's claims that Bedny was anachronistic, but he reproached Pasternak for adopting Soviet positions too "timidly."

The antithesis between Mayakovsky and Pasternak became the center of discussion at the plenum. The former proletarian and Komsomol poets supported Stalin's declaration on Mayakovsky in order to repudiate Bukharin's attacks on political poems. One of them, Dzhek Altauzen, interpreted Stalin's words as a directive aimed against pure lyrical poetry of the Pasternak type. He censured Surkov for being too soft on Pasternak's non-Soviet position. The speech of another Komsomol poet, Alexander Bezymensky, also bordered on a political denunciation. It was filled with demagogic political accusations, although they were cloaked in the form of well-meaning, comradely advice. He suggested that Pasternak emulate Mayakovsky and write not for a few selected readers but for millions.

But the support offered Pasternak was strong. The most courageous of the speeches in his defense was that of the young Leningrad critic, Evgenia Mustangova. A member of RAPP during the 1920s, she named Mayakovsky as the leading Soviet poet long before Stalin's dictum, and she considered that all poetry of the thirties originated directly from his works. However, the place Mayakovsky had occupied now unquestionably belonged to Pasternak. Thus she did not contrast the two poets but pointed to their inherent similarity. Mustangova rejected the characterization of Pasternak as a timid poet in Surkov's report. She emphasized the courageous and genuinely active element in Pasternak's poetry, and it was precisely this quality that was responsible for his enormous influence. Pasternak, she said, was not only a highly sophisticated and refined master—he was undoubtedly a Soviet poet, and his works served as the most authentic expression of Soviet culture. Dmitry Mirsky voiced solidarity with her views. After his return to the Soviet Union in 1932, he had become one of the most prominent figures in Soviet literary criticism. His opinions carried special weight because he enjoyed the full support of Gorky and was seen as his mouthpiece.

Pasternak's speech at the Minsk plenum was printed in the *Literary Gazette* under the title "On Modesty and Daring." This referred to the opposing characterizations given the poet in Surkov's report and in Mustangova's reply. A careful analysis of Pasternak's speech allows us to discern a veiled polemical response to new tendencies arising in literary and social life. While outwardly it might seem to be "modestly" agreeing with the trite statements in the Soviet press, in fact it calls for a decisive break with established conventions. Thus, for instance, Pasternak *for the first time* publicly addressed the question of socialist realism, but he gave the term a thoroughly unorthodox content. He proposed that this method originated not in the work of Gorky (an accepted truth of Soviet criticism) but in that of Leo Tolstoy, with his "storm of unmaskings and blunt outbursts." Thus Pasternak reiterated one of the central propositions of *Safe Conduct* (which had been banned by the censors): the rebellious essence of art.

The actual conditions of cultural life in 1936 by no means corresponded to such appeals. The campaign against formalism had begun to institute the automatic repetition of government slogans as the sole criterion for civic loyalty. It was against this background that Pasternak proclaimed the "morally suspect character" of all noisily exaggerated rhetorical phrases and ideological clichés. Moreover, he called explicitly for insubordination toward "deductive" orders coming from above: "Art is unthinkable without risk and spiritual self-sacrifice; freedom and boldness of imagination have to be gained in practice . . . don't expect a directive on this score." [18]

Despite the sharp debates, the Minsk plenum as a whole remained loyal to the spirit of the First Writers' Congress. This provoked the dissatisfaction of the authorities and led to the call for a new writers' forum—for a "discussion of formalism." It opened on March 10 and lasted for three weeks. On the eve of the discussion another editorial appeared in *Pravda,* attacking the production of Mikhail Bulgakov's *Molière* at the Moscow Art Theater II. The play was quickly banned. At the same time, the productions of any plays by Bulgakov throughout the country were removed from the stage (just as in 1929). Thus the campaign against formalism entered a new phase: the purge has shifted to the realm of literature. Although, before they began, the March meetings at the Writers' Union were officially defined as "discussion," no real debate was supposed to take place. The authorities' assumption was that everyone would be eager to support the official denunciations of those who came under fire. The task of the meetings was to enforce uniformity in the writers' behavior, ensuring their unwavering obedience to whatever orders they were given. The official report delivered by the secretary of the board of the Writers' Union, Vladimir Stavsky (an untalented journalist and former RAPPist), mentioned a variety of new "criminal" names and works. There was no logic in these denunciations: some writers were accused of formalism, and others were just as ferociously condemned for naturalism. The arbitrary selection of names was obvious. The true goal of the entire campaign was to spread confusion and uncertainty among the intellectuals. Vsevolod Ivanov sarcastically told Gorky, who was in the Crimea: "Our capital is filled with rumors about the two enemies of Soviet power—imperialism and formalism."

Unlike most of the other contributions at the conference, Pasternak's speech, delivered on March 13, was never printed. It was never even coherently summarized in the newspaper accounts. But from the angry responses to it we can reconstruct its general content. With unprecedented sharpness Pasternak spoke against the editorials in *Pravda* and the campaign on formalism as a whole. In these articles, he said, one could sense no love for art. And it would be better to reject the pejorative labels "formalism" and "naturalism" altogether and replace them with the concept of "artistic failure." The term formalism was preposterous. "What do we have to do," he asked rhetorically, "accuse Gogol and folklore of formalism?" Writers in general should never be presented with any demands about either content or form: "You cannot tell a mother: give birth to a daughter and not a son." Pasternak angrily spoke of bureaucrats "with insultingly insensitive hands," knowing nothing about art and crudely meddling in it, who in everywhere cry in unison about the "struggle with formalism." To those newspapers, headed by *Pravda,* which had unleashed the campaign, Pasternak declared: "Don't yell. But if you must yell, at least don't do it in unison." [19] With these words Pasternak assailed the most important principle of Soviet society during the Stalinist period: complete unanimity.

In this speech Pasternak announced that he had realized what collectivization (begun in 1929) was all about only in 1934. The newspapers reporting these words indignantly noted how strange it was for a Soviet citizen to be so slow and caustically asked whether he would also be so slow in understanding the processes now taking place. But the poet's remark contained a more profound meaning. On the one hand, he was drawing a parallel between the collective farms and the Writers' Union, which had been formed in 1934. On the other hand, 1934 was a year of real liberal reforms, and now, in 1936, the country's leaders faced a dilemma: to abandon the reforms or extend them.

But the audience at the conference was most stunned by a moment in Pasternak's speech which received particularly vague treatment in the press accounts. To the "bureaucrats with insensitive hands" he counterposed the Kremlin leader himself, the man whose authority they all persistently invoked. Pasternak insisted on direct contact with him, without the mediation of a third party. This was the most daring—and most puzzling to the audience—section of his speech. But for the poet it was a natural continuation of the "dialogue" that was begun in June 1934 on the initiative of Stalin himself and continued in Pasternak's poems in the New Year's issue of *Izvestia.*

Pasternak was among the very first speakers at the conference. He was apparently roused to battle by the appearance of a *Pravda* article about Bulgakov. This editorial revealed that the special status afforded this author, who had been protected since 1930 by the personal (albeit secret) patronage of Stalin, had come to an end. Although this article was (as we now know) the last in the series of attacks on formalism in 1936, in March it was still possible to expect new blows. In particular, the attacks on Pilniak in Stavsky's report gave cause for concern that he again, as in 1929, would become a victim of an unrestrained witch hunt. Pasternak's speech was a passionate and bold protest against attempts to turn back the clock of literary policy.

The day Pasternak selected for his speech was no accident. On March 3, André Malraux, the secretary of the International Association of Writers in Defense of Culture, arrived in Moscow. On March 5, before traveling to see Gorky in the Crimea, he met with Meyerhold at the latter's home. Pasternak joined them for dinner. The discussion centered in particular on the campaign against formalism. Evidently the three men were puzzled by the relationship of this campaign to the heartening signs of liberal changes: that very day the interview Stalin gave to the American editor Roy Wilson Howard was published.[20] Here for the first time Stalin announced that the Soviet Union was being transformed from a proletarian dictatorship into an all-people's state. This would mean sweeping democratic reforms in society and clearly testified to the leader's involvement in them. After his visit to Gorky, Malraux returned to Moscow. Before leaving for Paris, he visited the Writers' Union on March 13, just as the conference was taking place at which Pasternak spoke. He even looked into the hall during one of the sessions. There is no doubt that Pasternak decided to time his protest for Malraux's appearance, in order to give his position maximum publicity. There is firm reason to believe that Malraux received ample information about how the discussion on formalism was proceeding.[21]

Pasternak's speech had a profound impact on the course of the discussion. The conference lost momentum. No new names to be denounced were introduced, and the purge simply fizzled. Even Pasternak's heretical speech, as if by command, was forgotten by the newspapers. They tried to present his second speech at the meeting as an act of repentance. But it is clear that the poet did not capitulate; otherwise his statements would have been published. The last sessions

were marked by a softer and more conciliatory atmosphere, and at
the end of March the campaign was halted just as suddenly as it had
begun. Its abrupt conclusion was explained by several contemporary
observers as the result of behind-the-scenes pressure on the part of
liberal intellectuals in the west. Stories circulated about a certain letter from France expressing concern over what was happening in Soviet culture.

On April 9, after the campaign was already over, Gorky published
an article "On Formalism." Until then he had maintained an eloquent
silence throughout the winter. Although he never mentioned the
Pravda editorials and confined his article to literary aspects, the attentive reader had to feel how much his anger had been provoked by
recent events. He drew a comparison between the discussion on formalism and the intellectual enslavement of the individual in fascist
states. This article—the last major piece he wrote—reveals Gorky's
despair over the social climate that had developed in the Soviet Union
and his indignation over the apathy of writers who could not defend
their right to independent thought. Until the very last, Gorky hoped
for the creation of an active opposition force, a "nonparty bloc" with
a list of candidates for elective office or even a second political
party—a party of the united intelligentsia.

But the draft of the Stalinist constitution published a few days before Gorky's death dashed the hopes of the Bukharin-Gorky camp. It
proclaimed the emergence of a state of all the people and free elections, without the restrictions against nonproletarian social groups
which had been in effect previously. Yet in the listing of the various
freedoms granted by the new constitution, there was no "freedom to
form unions." As a contemporary émigré observer put it, "the thing
comes down to a presentation of the *forms* of real democracy without
its *substance,* i.e., without political freedom." [22] Immediately upon
publication of the draft, the newspapers started to run articles and
letters expressing readers' ecstatic support for the constitution and
suggesting minor amendments. As a part of this campaign Bukharin
invited Pasternak to share his reaction to the draft. *Izvestia* placed his
article "New Coming-of-Age" first among the writers' responses. [23]
Bukharin did not hesitate to inaugurate the discussion of the constitution with Pasternak's reflections, despite the rebellious speech at the
March meeting.

In contrast to the lofty rhetoric abounding in the Soviet press, the
comments of Pasternak are ambivalent, and certain phrases reveal a

skeptical wait-and-see attitude. He begins by emphasizing the crucial role of future amendments, which would be made in the process of discussion by all the people, and he attributes particular significance to the nomination of candidates. In other words, Pasternak attaches more importance to what might happen in practice than to what was outlined in the draft, to the possible substance of the future rule rather than to its proposed form. What mattered for him was not the legal formulas and verbal declarations, however triumphant they sounded to some or disillusioning to others, but how the proposed changes would actually be carried out.

In his note Pasternak gives a compelling definition of Soviet society: its "body" had been created by twenty years of postrevolutionary history, and now the task was to create its "soul." According to him, the new constitution did create the opportunity to develop the soul of the future society—which was a "freedom" for him. He used this term in a highly polemical fashion, as the following passage indicates:

> I have never envisaged it [freedom] as a thing which one can obtain or seek from someone else, whether by demanding or by whining. There is no force on earth which could grant me freedom if I do not already have the potential for it and if I myself do not take it—not from God nor from an authority but from the air and from the future, from the earth and from myself, in the form of goodness and courage and fully productive work, in the form of *independence*, independence from weaknesses and secondary calculations. This is also how I envisage socialist freedom.[24]

This paragraph obviously represents a response to those moods of depression so prevalent among the intelligentsia owing to the omission of an article about the right to form associations. The main thing in Pasternak's view was personal, individual independence rather than the granting or nongranting of political freedom.[25] He believed that the draft marked a clear turn for the better; the rest could be achieved by the independence and courage of the people themselves. The absence of the long-awaited (at least by many) article was in his eyes compensated for by the inevitable democratization that would necessarily follow from the very fact that a new constitution existed.

Subsequent events introduced substantial corrections in Pasternak's prognoses. After Gorky's death, which coincided with the publication of the draft constitution, the atmosphere in Soviet society and in literature changed rapidly. With no elections, Vladimir Stavsky was appointed head of the Writers' Union; this was the same literary bureaucrat who had been entrusted in the spring with organizing the discussion on formalism. In August an announcement was made about the impending open trial of Zinoviev and Kamenev (who had been in jail since December 1934 and had already been sentenced in a closed trial to prison terms). The new trial evoked memories of 1930–31. As during the old trials of the Industrial Party and the Mensheviks, the language of the Soviet press was radically transformed. The newspapers, in chilling unison, were filled with bloodthirsty slogans and clichés. The published testimony and speeches of the accused were filled with the same clichés. The verbal techniques that had proved so effective in the campaign against formalism were applied on a larger scale in this new sphere.

The same style permeated the note "Wipe Them from the Face of the Earth!" which was printed on August 21 in *Pravda*. The note, demanding the death penalty for the "terrorists," was signed by the sixteen members of the board of the Writers' Union, including Leonid Leonov, Konstantin Fedin, Alexander Afinogenov, and Boris Pasternak. Pasternak's signature shocked Tsvetaeva, who had seen him the year before in Paris. Not suspecting that her husband Sergei Efron was at that time a full-fledged participant in the NKVD's network in Europe, she wrote to her friend in Prague: "Instead of a letter, here is Rilke's last elegy for you; no one beside Boris Pasternak has ever read it. (And B. L. read it poorly: otherwise how could he, after such an elegy, place his name beneath a plea for the death penalty [in the trial of the sixteen]?!)."[26] There is no doubt that Pasternak's signature shocked many. Can this fact, which has no precedent in the poet's life and contradicts the entire spirit of his works, be explained? Of course Pasternak had no part in the *composition* of this note. It would be easy to declare that his name was placed there without his permission, since such a practice had become the norm in the Soviet Union. Besides showing a cynical contempt for principles, this custom had a practical function: it implied the unconditional confidence and favor of the authorities toward a given individual. In August 1936 Pasternak was not in Moscow but in Peredelkino, in the recently constructed writers' village.[27] Since he was so far from Moscow (Pasternak never had a telephone at his dacha), it is highly probable that his signature on the petition for the death penalty was not authorized by him.

But another assumption can be made. Besides being a bloodthirsty declaration, this document served as a kind of self-defense. Among the sixteen accused at the trial of Kamenev and Zinoviev were two writers who had been expelled from the Writers' Union only after the trial had begun. This placed the writers' organization as a whole in trouble. It was during those same days that several other members of the Writers' Union (including Galina Serebriakova) were accused of illegal anti-Soviet activity and of Trotskyism. The leaders of the union and in particular its new head were in a panic. The refusal of any of the writers selected in advance to give a signature would have been taken as a demonstration of disloyalty toward the organization as a whole. The great terror had just begun, and nobody could imagine how it would grow. It is worth noting that even such impartial observers as the Russian émigré newspaper in Paris, *Poslednie novosti* (Latest News), while condemning the violation of traditional judicial norms, nevertheless came to the conclusion that the guilty activities of the accused had actually taken place. The longstanding personal hatred of Kamenev, Zinoviev, and Trotsky for Stalin was not secret. On the other hand, everyone knew that in December 1930, despite unanimous appeals for the execution of the members of the Industrial Party, they not only were all pardoned but were even given the chance to continue work in more or less satisfactory professional conditions. In the same way now, many assumed that the trial would not lead to executions. Even the NKVD investigators did not believe that Stalin would insist on death sentences; they assumed he would be satisfied with the public humiliation of the former leaders of the revolution.[28]

On the same day that the writers' note was published in *Pravda* the course of the trial took a dramatic turn. Kamenev announced that former leaders of the opposition, including Bukharin, Tomsky, and Rykov, had also participated in terrorist activities. Tomsky immediately committed suicide. On August 24 a death sentence for all sixteen defendants was published, followed by an announcement on August 25 that the sentence had been carried out. Parallels with the past were no longer valid.

On September 10 newspapers announced that an investigation of Kamenev's evidence at the trial by the office of the public prosecutor had not yielded sufficient grounds to initiate a criminal case against Bukharin and Rykov. A few months later, everyone would come to understand the treacherous and sadistic meaning of this gesture from Stalin. But at the moment it was generally taken as a good sign. Romain Rolland and Pasternak reacted to the prosecutor's announcement by sending greetings to Bukharin: the first by telegram, the second by letter.[29]

Whatever the reasons for Pasternak's signature on the August writers' petition, his position deteriorated in conjunction with the campaign unleashed in the Soviet press against the book by André Gide, *Retour de l'U.R.S.S.* Since the fall of 1932, when this famous advocate of personal freedom had made the sensational declaration that he was sympathetic toward communism and the USSR, he had become one of the most popular western writers in the Soviet Union. He visited Soviet Russia for the first and only time in the summer of 1936, arriving in Moscow on the day before Gorky died. His book, which came out in Paris in November 1936, was immediately declared a betrayal and a "slanderous attack" on Soviet society. Soviet readers learned about its contents from an article published in *Pravda* on December 3. The newspaper angrily listed criminal statements by the French writer: he insisted on a legalization of the opposition in socialist society, he was sarcastic about Soviet "unanimity," and he sharply criticized *Pravda*'s articles on formalism and the cowardly reaction of the Soviet intelligentsia to them. There is no doubt that Pasternak in many ways shared Gide's position: nonconformism, protest against the persecution of dissident thinkers, inability to see in modern Russia a revolutionary spirit, and affirmation of the rebellious essence of art. He became personally acquainted with Gide in June 1935 at the International Congress in Defense of Culture. They met again during Gide's visit to the USSR. According to later memoirs of the French writer, Pasternak "opened his eyes to what was happening around him, and warned him not to be drawn in by the 'Potyomkin villages' or 'exemplary kolkhozes' they had showed him."[30] On Pasternak's advice, Gide met in the Caucasus with Titsian Tabidze and considered undertaking in Paris an edition of French translations of Georgian poetry and prose. All this can explain why, when Pasternak was asked to issue a protest against Gide's book, he categorically refused, on the grounds that he had not seen it. Other Soviet writers unquestioningly complied with this request, seeming satisfied with the exposition of Gide's views given in *Pravda*.

Revenge for this disobedience came swiftly. In his speech before a conference of Moscow writers on December 16, 1936, Stavsky mentioned the "antipatriotic" behavior of Pasternak. He condemned the poet for his solidarity with foreign slander against the Soviet people and offered the recently published poems by Pasternak in *New World* as proof. This accusation was particularly striking because, in 1936–37, the concept of the "people" took a central place in the Stalinist political doctrine.[31] In the same spirit an editorial appeared in the newspaper *Vecherniaia Moskva* (Evening Moscow), which was meant to demonstrate that all Pasternak's works were inherently hostile to the October Revolution and to the Soviet Union.

On January 23, 1937, a new open trial began, the Trial of the Seventeen. Pasternak knew three of the accused well—Radek, Serebriakov, and Sokolnikov. A week before the beginning of the trial, Nikolai Bukharin was dismissed from his post as editor of *Izvestia,* and it was clear to everyone that he had fallen from favor. The reports by Radek and Bukharin at the 1934 writers' congress were declared to have been enemy attacks. Unlike the August trial, the new judicial proceedings were accompanied by the publication of an enormous quantity of collective and individual appeals for execution of the criminals. Among them were declarations by good and honest writers, such as Yury Tynianov, Isaak Babel, Andrei Platonov, and Yury Olesha. Their friends and admirers abroad were unable to understand such a strange metamorphosis. In this flood of writers' statements, Pasternak's name does not appear. His signature is missing from the collective resolution of the board of the Writers' Union issued on January 25. It is true that he sent a letter after this to the union, in which he attributed his absence at the meeting to illness and declared his readiness to add his signature to the resolution. But the letter was composed in such a provocative tone, undermining the very basis of the propaganda campaign, that there was no question of publishing it.[32] Even before this, he sent Bukharin at the Kremlin a short letter in which he declared that "there are no forces that can compel me to believe in your treachery." [33]

In this light it is clear why Pasternak became one of the chief targets at the plenum of the board of the Writers' Union which convened at the end of February. The goal of the plenum was to eliminate the last vestiges of Bukharin's influence on Soviet literature.[34] Until the last day of the meeting, Pasternak was absent. Such conduct seemed patently defiant insofar as the plenum coincided with the hundredth anniversary of Pushkin's death and was devoted mainly to poetry. Because of their position, the board members of the Writers' Union were required to attend it *ex officio.* Pasternak appeared only at the final session, where the crude attacks on him and Selvinsky were quickly replaced by conciliatory notes in the speeches. To a significant degree this change occurred because of the intervention of Fadeev, whose influence was becoming more noticeable in the Writers' Union and who a year later replaced Stavsky as its leader. His public criticism of Pasternak had the character of a gentle admonition. There is no doubt that Pasternak finally agreed to come to the plenum only in response to Fadeev's personal entreaties.

Still he came not in order to declare his agreement with the accusations made against him (as was demanded by the Soviet ritual of "self-criticism"), but to dispute them. In particular, he denied the reproaches that he set himself against the masses. "With all my heart I am with you, with the nation, and with the party," he said. This statement produces a strange impression today: Pasternak, throughout his entire life, stressed his lack of accord with any party. Why then did he make this declaration, couched in the conformist rhetoric that had always been anathema to him? I suggest that the reason was the specific atmosphere of those months. The "Great Terror," begun in the fall, appeared directed first of all against the party apparatus, and this reveals a second level to the poet's professed loyalty. Pasternak's long-awaited announcement on André Gide seemed to be just as outwardly reliable. By the end of February, he evidently was able to familiarize himself with the contents of *Retour de l'U.S.S.R.*, and it became clear to him that the author had made no mention of their conversations. Therefore Pasternak, having acknowledged the fact of seeing Gide during the latter's trip to the Soviet Union, could stress at the same time that his French guest did not receive any kind of anti-Soviet information from him.[35]

Yet Pasternak's speech at the plenum bore no resemblance to repentance. The literary authorities were not pleased with him, and the speech was never published. In a *Pravda* editorial devoted to the results of the Pushkin plenum, a new line in literary policy was officially proclaimed. The newspaper incriminated Bukharin for attempting in his report of 1934 to introduce into Soviet poetry the doctrine of the hermetic and esoteric nature of poetic speech. This was now assessed as a pernicious appeal for political double-dealing. As a positive antipode and example of genuine Soviet poetry, *Pravda* counterposed political and agitational verse to Bukharin's theories. These new tendencies were viewed as toppling Pasternak from the literary Olympus. Rumors circulated that the attacks against him were personally inspired by Stalin, who had supposedly read the 1936 collection of Pasternak's poems and had been disgusted by them.[36] There is no evidence to support these rumors. But the very fact of the campaign against formalism leaves no doubt that Pasternak's poetry could never have satisfied Stalin's aesthetic tastes.

On February 27, Bukharin and Rykov were arrested. In the subsequent purge of the Writers' Union, the main victims unexpectedly were the former leaders of RAPP, who had always been regarded as the most faithful executors of party directives. Leopold Averbakh and Vladimir Kirshon were arrested. The playwright Alexander Afinogenov and the poet Alexander Bezymensky were subjected to violent accusations at a number of meetings, and their arrest seemed imminent. During the hysterical campaign against the former members of RAPP, Nikolai Aseev blamed them for the death of the "best poet of the Soviet epoch," Mayakovsky. Events became truly grotesque: not long before, during the Pushkin plenum, Bezymensky had condescendingly lectured Pasternak; now he proved to be in a worse situation than Pasternak had been.

It was during these dark days that Pasternak became friendly with Afinogenov, who was his next-door neighbor. The times had brought together two people who had been absolute opposites just five years before. In the beginning of 1932, the leaders of RAPP saw Pasternak as a class enemy. Now, in this tragic hour, Afinogenov, the former favorite of Stalin and Yagoda, abandoned by all his old friends and awaiting arrest from day to day, found his only support and consolation in conversations with a poet who at one time had seemed inexcusably remote from socialist reality.

At the height of the purge of the Writers' Union, Pasternak's fate underwent a strange shift. In May 1937, in the journal *Oktiabr* (October)—from which Pasternak had always been distant—there appeared a major article about him which could be interpreted as a signal that the pressure was subsiding. The article was signed by a second-rate literary critic, N. Izgoev, but the author's relative anonymity during these days of the sharp reshuffling of the bureaucratic apparatus was a rather encouraging sign. No matter how insignificant the reputation of Izgoev among literary circles, it became clear that the evaluations contained in the article originated in the most powerful echelons. Its generally sarcastic and derogatory tone left no doubt that attempts to elevate Pasternak to the pedestal of "premier poet" in 1934 had been misplaced. But the article also protected Pasternak from accusations that would have seemed quite natural during those days. It drew a distinctive line between him and Bukharin, who was in prison awaiting trial. "Bukharin's attraction to Pasternak does not signify Pasternak's attraction to Bukharin, their closeness or ties," wrote Izgoev. The article acknowledged Pasternak as a poet (rather than a counterrevolutionary) and did not advance the relentless demand for political verse. However, it gave a disparaging assessment of Pasternak's poetry and proclaimed the fading of his talent (which, objectively speaking, was justified with regard to the 1930s). Izgoev added that only the poet was to blame for the withering of his talent, and not the revolution, which was able to value and protect artists. Pasternak's greatest achievement had been his translations of Georgian lyrical poetry; he was a much better poet there than in his own work. Thus Izgoev's article served as an unequivocal prescription for Pasternak: he was assigned the role of translator, more precisely as translator of the poetry of national minorities, an occupation he had publicly rejected in January 1936. From now on, Pasternak was allowed to play but a peripheral role in Soviet literature.

10

The Trials of Hamlet

In the nightmarish atmosphere of the spring and summer of 1937, Izgoev's article should have been seen as a signal heralding the softening of official attitude toward the poet. But Pasternak refused to meet the authorities halfway. This is shown by his conduct in June 1937, during the trial of Tukhachevsky, Yakir, and other prominent Soviet generals. According to later memoirs, Pasternak flatly refused to add his name to the petition of a large group of writers supporting the death penalty for the convicted men. Pasternak had not displayed such obstinacy either in August 1936 during the Kamenev-Zinoviev trial or in January 1937 during the Piatakov-Radek trial. Why did it emerge now? Is it possible that the fate of professional soldiers concerned the poet more than the fate of party and government figures? Unlike the first two trials, which preserved the (fictitious) semblance of regular judicial procedures, this one was carried out with lightning speed by a military tribunal.[1] The sentence seemed all the more cruel because, unlike Zinoviev and Piatakov, the generals had never competed with Stalin for leadership or opposed him politically.

Pasternak's refusal to sign the petition was provoked, however, not so much by these considerations as by a radical change in his overall relations with the authorities. The poet was not so naive as to assume that the fate of the condemned hinged in any way on whether his name appeared with the others. His decision was prompted not only by his protest over the terror. It was first of all an act of resistance against the attempts to turn human beings into soulless marionettes who would submit to any action by the regime. Now, when repression raged in the Writers' Union too, it was clear that even unwavering Soviet loyalty was no shield from ostracism or a guarantee of personal sincerity. It was during these days that the purge threatened Paolo Yashvili, one of Pasternak's closest friends. A year before, during the campaign against formalism, their paths had diverged for the first time: Yashvili, who had made a brilliant career as a public figure in Soviet Georgia, tried to adhere faithfully to the official line and was dismayed at what seemed to him Pasternak's childish behavior. Now, in June 1937, Lavrenty Beria, all-powerful in Georgia, publicly accused Yashvili of contacts with "enemies of the people" and demanded a full confession of guilt. This was a sure sign that the terror's pincers were closing in. Another factor in Pasternak's change of attitude was Nikolai Bukharin's imprisonment. The poet was convinced of Bukharin's innocence, as he stated in his letter to Bukharin shortly before the latter's arrest. If even the most loyal people could not be safe from the guillotine of arbitrary terror, then there was no sense in pretending to be the obedient executor of the authorities' commands. In extreme situations, when death lurked around the corner, the poet realized more strongly than ever before that there is no higher value than the preservation of dignity and personal independence.

Even the head of the Writers' Union, Vladimir Stavsky, made an effort to persuade Pasternak to add his signature to the writers' petition. He met with him in Peredelkino. Pasternak answered all entreaties and threats with a decisive refusal, despite the fact that Zinaida Nikolaevna, who was pregnant, begged her husband not to doom her and their child. On the advice of his friends, Pasternak then wrote a letter directly to Stalin, explaining the reasons for his refusal. He referred to Tolstoyan convictions that had been instilled by his family. Although Stalin might be able to decide his fate Pasternak said that he did not consider himself to have the right to be a judge in matters of the life and death of others. Nowhere else did Pasternak's fearlessness and readiness for self-sacrifice reveal itself so strongly. Not only did the poet's refusal to do what he had been ordered appear reckless, but his stubborn defense of his right to act in such a manner could only make the situation worse. Later Pasternak said that he had expected to be arrested the very same night.

Yet this story of the writers' petition demanding Tukhachevsky's execution has another, less heroic, side. Pasternak's stubborn refusal notwithstanding, his signature was affixed to the publication of the petition in *Izvestia* and the *Literary Gazette*. In his own experience he had now seen that any display of personal independence was impossible in the Soviet state. The episode dispelled the last illusions he held about socialist law and order and about Stalin himself. Pasternak's anger and shock were so great that, from now on, he avoided adding his signature to *any* collective letter, regardless of content.

During the period of the "Ezhov terror" there was hardly a person in the Soviet Union who did not lose friends or relatives. In Leningrad, Pasternak's cousin Alexander Freidenberg and his wife were arrested. On July 22, Paolo Yashvili committed suicide; until the very last moment he had unsuccessfully tried to prove his political loyalty. Pasternak learned about his death on August 17. On August 28, when the rumors were finally confirmed, he wrote a letter to Yashvili's widow in Tiflis and drew a parallel between his dead Georgian friend and Vladimir Mayakovsky, who was rewarded with greater glory posthumously than while he was alive.[2] But the most severe blow for the poet was the arrest in the fall of 1937 of Titsian Tabidze in Tiflis and of Boris Pilniak, who had been Pasternak's neighbor for the last year in Peredelkino. In this "time of absolutely unbearable shame and grief, I was ashamed that we kept on moving about, talking and smiling," Pasternak confessed in January 1939 in a letter to Georgy Leonidze, a Georgian poet and friend of Tabidze and Yashvili.[3] The fate of those who had been arrested remained unknown. Pasternak did not guess that Titsian died from savage beatings and torture in prison two months after his arrest; nor did he know that Pilniak, who was accused of spying for Japan, was shot in 1938. Until the middle of the 1950s, evidence of these deaths alternated with rumors that someone had seen them alive in the camps. Pasternak devoured the rumors, continuing to believe in the imminent release of his friends. These two factors—torment over the suffering of his friends and the hope of seeing them live—determined the poet's behavior during the years of terror. These feelings are most clearly reflected in the translation of Shakespeare's 66th sonnet ("Tired with all these, for restful death I cry"), which Pasternak did at the time.

We cannot know why Pasternak himself was not arrested during the Ezhov terror (1937 to the fall of 1938); nor is it possible to explain, for example, why Pilniak's wife was arrested while Tabidze's wife was not touched. The speculation that someone intervened to save Pasternak from arrest or execution has no basis. Nor is there any reason to suspect that Pasternak enjoyed the personal protection or sympathy of Stalin. It is just as pointless to assume that he was shielded from arrest by the intercession of Alexander Fadeev: such problems lay outside Fadeev's sphere of competence even when he replaced Stavsky as head of the Writers' Union in 1938. Within the realm of literature, Fadeev did try as hard as he could to guard Pasternak from attacks by envious fellow poets and bureaucrats, but to influence orders regarding the arrest or liberation of writers was beyond his powers. In the summer of 1937, his own life hung by a thread. Meanwhile, rumors of Pasternak's arrest circulated in Soviet society and reached the west. Herbert Read wrote in his essay "The Necessity of Anarchism" in 1938: "The recent fall of Radek and Bukharin has not brought to an end the persecution of poets and artists. At the present moment, Pasternak, since Mayakovsky's death the most important poet in Russia, languishes in prison, and Shostakovich, one of the few modern composers with a European reputation, is in disgrace." [4]

From 1936, Pasternak's main creative work was a novel about the revolution. This was the same project that had occupied him since the 1920s, but that had met with little success. It is difficult to say which is more striking about the poet's stubborn intention to write this prose work—his commitment to the chosen theme or his inability over such a long time to bring the idea to life. If in the beginning the author thought of the novel as a sequel to *Liuvers' Childhood,* which would also include components of his *Tale* of 1929 and *Spektorsky,* then by the middle of the 1930s he had come to the conclusion that it was necessary to begin everything fresh from the beginning. The new stage of his work on the novel is reflected in fragments printed in the *Literary Gazette* and in journals between 1937 and 1939. [5] The extant chapters of the novel were published only in the 1970s. This does not provide enough material to judge what the whole text was supposed to be like, but it does allow us to see the direction in which Pasternak's prose evolved during those years.

The sharp break with the past involved here is astonishing. In comparison with his complex and exuberant narrative forms of the 1920s, Pasternak's new prose is striking for its deliberately unprepossessing style, neutrality, restraint, and complete rejection of lyricism, including even landscape descriptions. The author carefully restricted himself to a recording of bare facts. Closely connected with this feature was the fact that the novel was written from the viewpoint of the main character, Patrick, in the form of his notes and recollections of adolescence. Pasternak had never before used such a narrative mode in his prose. He removed himself from the scene in order to transfer the narration to a professionally inexperienced person. That all the events in the novel were to be presented through the prism of a single narrator, the protagonist, attests to a radical transformation of Pasternak's diction. Suffice it to recall how vague and indistinct Relikvimini, the main hero, was in the first prose attempts (1911–1913) and how difficult it was to distinguish him from the author.

The intended chronological boundaries of the new novel embraced the period between the revolutions of 1905 and 1917. Some sections introduced Evgenia Istomina, whose maiden name was Zhenia Liuvers. Besides her maiden name and passing references to her father's death, however, her fate and character had nothing in common with the heroine of Pasternak's earlier novella. But Istomina reveals some traits that would later become part of the biography of Lara Antipova, the heroine of *Doctor Zhivago* (including indications that her husband, a schoolteacher in Yuriatin, volunteered during the war and allegedly perished at the front). The extant prose fragments from 1936 contain, in embryonic form, the romantic intrigue that figures prominently in the future novel: we find the hero torn between love for his wife[6] and his infatuation with Istomina.

But precisely against the background of these similarities, we can clearly see the differences between the prose of the late 1930s and *Doctor Zhivago*. The finished chapters by no means allow us to detect in the hero the spiritual profundity and restless moral striving characteristic of Yury Zhivago. As opposed to the latter, Patrick is not a poet (even a nonprofessional one). Nor is he a doctor. He is the embodiment of the "superfluous man," a traditional image from Russian literature of the nineteenth century, considered obsolete in the Soviet period. Educated as an historian, he complains that his professional training is of no use whatever. There are no attempts to show his superiority, either intellectual or moral, to those around him. Nor do Patrick's family origins recall Zhivago's (although it is stated that they are both orphans). Such important characters in *Doctor Zhivago* as the philosopher Vedeniapin and Yury's step-brother Evgraf are also missing. The explanation of the revolution's consequences and its significance for Russian history, as well as the evaluation of the Bolsheviks and Marxism, did not yet receive full treatment.

During the period of the Great Terror Pasternak made several attempts to resume the work he had begun in 1936. But the tragedy unfolding before him destroyed the foundation on which he had hoped to base a novel dedicated to the Russian revolution. All previ-

ous historical explanations and evaluations acquired new and unstable meaning in light of the repression directed against the old
guard of revolutionaries, and in light of the unprecedented, bloody
catastrophe that the great revolution turned out to be for the entire
population of 1937. These events dramatically changed Pasternak's
attitude toward Russia, the revolution, and socialism. In the summer
of 1936 he had still believed in the inevitability of the regime's evolution toward greater humanism, tolerance, and democracy—otherwise, what was the use of proclaiming a new, more liberal constitution? But now this constitution looked like a farce; all the freedoms
and rights declared in it were distorted or crushed. The country was
seized by a wild outburst of terror more ferocious and senseless than
that during the Civil War. It was perhaps more cruel than any event
in Russia's history. The people became paralyzed by insane fear, and
human dignity was trampled at every step. It was precisely at this
moment that the authorities announced that socialism had finally
achieved complete victory in Russia.

Reflecting on the past twenty years, Pasternak did not question the
historical necessity of the 1917 revolution and the superiority of the
socialist ideal over tsarism. But his belief in the historical justification
of the Russian revolution was dashed: instead of liberating the
people, it had led to indiscriminate executions and grief in every family; instead of the triumph of eternal moral principles, their crude and
cynical violation; instead of the universal transformation of the
people into geniuses (as Pasternak had predicted in his "Dialogue" of
1917), the merciless elimination of everything that was the least bit
elevated above the mediocre norm.

All these doubts impeded the writing of "Patrick's Notes" and
eventually compelled the author to abandon the work. In his reflections about the historical mission of Russia, he began to stress not the
beneficial aspects of the revolution of 1917, but the preservation
among the people, in pure and undistorted form, of fundamental human traits and traditional values. What was now most important for
him was not what had been wrought by the revolutionary cataclysms,
but the imperishable aspects of life which no upheavals could eradicate. It was in this context that his seclusion in Peredelkino began to
acquire special meaning for him. After the arrest of Boris Pilniak in
the fall of 1937, Pasternak felt uncomfortable in his dacha and moved
to a new one in the same village of Peredelkino. Here his neighbor on
one side was Konstantin Fedin and, on the other, Vsevolod Ivanov.
He lived in this house from 1938 until his death. In his eyes it was an

oasis, counterposed to all that was happening around him in the nation. It seemed to retain those traits that in Russian literature (and life) of the nineteenth century were characteristic of the gentry's country estates: it was a place where a person could be close to the soil and escape the deadening power of government institutions, an island of family continuity, independence, and stability in a sea of insecurity and anxiety. The dacha in Peredelkino became for him the embodiment of what the country estate used to be during the time of Chekhov—the last repository of a cultural *tradition* doomed to extinction.[7]

Despite the fact that Pasternak abandoned work on his novel, the uncompleted prose of this period played an important role in the evolution of his literary style. For the first time he turned to a simple, terse, and unadorned mode of writing, which posed special difficulties: complexity of thought, as well as inherent ambivalence and verbal paradox, were from the very beginning Pasternak's intrinsic features both as a thinker and as a poet. The new work reflected a profound reorientation of an entire aesthetic system: now the primary model of a literary and moral position for him became not Leo Tolstoy, but a writer who lacked any "prophetic" traits, one who had rejected any preaching or ambitions to change the world, a man who was inconspicuous and modest but firmly dedicated to the highest human ideals: Anton Chekhov. What had most attracted Pasternak to Tolstoy before—the uncompromising moral unmasking, the rebellious bluntness, the prophetic pathos—now, during the gloomy days of the Ezhov purge, lost its validity.

In the course of Pasternak's work on his novel, Patrick increasingly acquired Chekhovian features. But even more important is the fact that from now on Pasternak perceived his generation and his epoch in terms of "the autumn twilight of Chekhov, Tchaikovsky, and Levitan" (as he later would say in his poem of 1943, "Zima priblizhaetsia" [Winter Approaches]), in terms of the "epoch of immobility" (*epokha bezvremenia*), as Chekhov's time has been called. The literary trends that had influenced Pasternak's early poetic development— symbolism, futurism, the avant-garde as a whole—now became completely alien to him, whereas the art of Chekhov, their predecessor and antipode, seemed genuinely contemporary. Pasternak transferred the features of the superfluous hero from Patrick onto himself and his generation, which under conditions of Soviet life at the end of the 1930s began to look increasingly anachronistic.

Reality reminded Pasternak at every step just how unnecessary and superfluous he actually was. Not long ago he had been touted as the premier poet; now he did not figure in the press at all, and only sporadic, isolated publications in random places, consisting largely of prose fragments and translations (of Johannes Becher, Rafael Alberti, and others), reminded readers that he was still alive and that the rumors of his arrest were unfounded. But the fact that he was no longer in favor was clearly demonstrated with the February 1939 publication of a long list of Soviet writers who had been awarded medals and orders. This mass decoration of writers was undertaken for the first time in Soviet and Russian history: the list named 172 people, and the majority of them could not hold a candle to Pasternak.[8] This act was essentially a declaration of who now belonged to the Soviet literary elite and who did not. The fact that no place was found for Pasternak indicated how greatly the picture had changed in a few short years, and how unacceptable the behavior of the obstinate poet was. Considering his inherent indifference to official awards and honors, Pasternak probably did not feel slighted. But the recognition that he was out of step with the times could not have brought him any joy. The change in Pasternak's fortunes and outlook in the late 1930s found no direct reflection in the surviving chapters from the novel about Patrick. The lyrical reflections and moods of the poet at this time appeared in another, completely unexpected, place—in his translation of *Hamlet*.

Pasternak never parted with Shakespeare, and in 1924, when he began work on *Spektorsky,* he had tried to translate *Hamlet*. But only now did he dare to immerse himself fully in this work. It was undertaken at Vsevolod Meyerhold's initiative. All his life the great artist of the theater dreamed of producing *Hamlet,* and he once even proposed in a half-joking manner the following epitaph for himself: "Here lies an actor and director who never played and never produced *Hamlet.*" He envisioned a theater, the entire repertoire of which would consist of only one play—*Hamlet*—as produced by various directors: one evening Stanislavsky's version would be shown, the next evening Max Reinhardt's, then Gordon Craig's, and finally his own.[9] Meyerhold said that fragments of his future production of *Hamlet* were contained in all of his works of the last twenty years. The problem of the inner integrity of Shakespeare's hero seemed especially challenging as he thought about the production. He hoped that in his staging two actors would play Hamlet: one filled with doubt and a second who would be bold and decisive. In the fall of 1936, Meyerhold negotiated with Pablo Picasso about the possibility of his participation in the production. But Meyerhold was never able to stage *Hamlet*. On January 8, 1938, his theater, which had long since come under vicious attacks for formalism, was closed down in the most insulting and unceremonious way. Left without a job during these gloomy days, Meyerhold continued to think about Hamlet and intended to write a book about him.

Pasternak, who had never been an aficionado of the theater, nevertheless idolized Meyerhold. He was most of all delighted by the vigorous and fearless way in which this great innovator treated classical works of art: Meyerhold saw them not as petrified museum items, but as living and contemporary artistic phenomena. His goal was not to achieve an archaeologically exact, pedantic reproduction of the past, but a profound reappraisal in the context of the present. In 1928 Pasternak wrote that, although he had seen productions by such outstanding stage directors as Konstantin Stanislavsky, Vera Komissarzhevskaia, and Mikhail Chekhov, only from Meyerhold did he understand what the art of the theater was and begin to believe in its existence. One of Pasternak's best poems about art, written in the late twenties, was addressed to Meyerhold and his wife, Zinaida Raikh, an actress in his theater. When he learned that Meyerhold's theater had been closed, Pasternak was one of the few who rushed to his home to express sympathy and support.[10] Evidently it was then that he talked Meyerhold out of writing a letter to Stalin; from his own experience Pasternak knew that such a step would be useless.

A year later, in January 1939, Meyerhold was invited to work in Leningrad at the Pushkin Theater. He decided to produce *Hamlet* there, and he immediately commissioned a translation of Shakespeare's tragedy from Pasternak.[11] He made this decision despite the fact that two new translations of *Hamlet,* the first in the Soviet period, were available.[12] Neither of them satisfied him: Mikhail Lozinsky's seemed dry, stiff, and slavishly meticulous, inappropriate for the stage; Anna Radlova's translation seemed tasteless and coarse, eliminating the philosophical ambivalence of the original. He believed that nobody but Pasternak could adequately transmit the spirit of Shakespeare's tragedy.

Meyerhold never got to read the commissioned text of Pasternak's *Hamlet*. In June 1939 he was arrested as an enemy of the people, and Zinaida Raikh was assaulted (her eyes were put out) and killed at her home by intruders who were never caught or identified.[13] Writing about these events to his cousin in Leningrad, Pasternak added: "It is indescribable, and all of it touched me closely." He finished his translation at the end of 1939, when it had become dangerous even to mention Meyerhold's name. The director's arrest forced him to hurry rather than break off the project. He revealed this in the same letter: "For the past few months I have been haunted by the fear that some contingency might prevent my finishing the translation. It was this fear that kept me from answering letters from Papa as well as from you."[14] The contingency Pasternak refers to is undoubtedly his own arrest, which he expected from day to day during these months. Here again Pasternak's foresight is striking. It became known much later that the investigation files contained a list of Meyerhold's accomplices in "sabotage" from among the artistic intelligentsia, including Boris Pasternak, Yury Olesha, and Ilya Ehrenburg (who was still in Paris). The young prosecutor, who studied the material from the investigation and trial of Meyerhold in 1955, and who was working on his rehabilitation, was astounded when he learned that Pasternak had never been arrested (nor had Olesha or Ehrenburg). In reply to a request to characterize Meyerhold's political views, Pasternak wrote the investigator that Meyerhold was always "more Soviet" than himself.[15]

In this extreme situation, anticipating arrest, the poet's work on the translation focused all his lyrical and creative energy. Everything he had been unable to express in his abandoned novel he poured into his work on Shakespeare. Every time he could, Pasternak stressed that this translation must be seen as an independent and original Russian text. It was precisely in the course of this work that Pasternak developed his own conception of poetic translation. The task of the poet-translator is not to reproduce the original with all its details; it lies not in slavish fidelity to the text, but in the attempt to assure that the new text turns out to be a recreation of its model in a new cultural and historical context. In this sense, his theory of translation is remarkably close to Meyerhold's interpretation of classical art: Pasternak carried over the dramatic principles of the director and transferred them to the realm of poetic translation.

Like Meyerhold, Pasternak imbued Shakespeare's *Hamlet* with enormous personal significance. As a result, it was not Patrick of the unfinished novel but Hamlet who became his alter ego, assimilating features of Pasternak himself, of Vsevolod Meyerhold, and of their entire generation. Pasternak called his work on *Hamlet* not only "happiness" but "salvation." What made it salutary? First of all, of course, there was the contrast to Pasternak's own fate and to the fate of the one who had commissioned the translation. What was also salutary was the involvement with great art, which was impossible in any other form during this terrible period of repression. But most important was the fact that Pasternak was reassessing the historical role of the superfluous man in modern society. Later, in an article about Shakespeare written soon after the war, he emphasized in *Hamlet* not inner bifurcation, not "lack of will"—a trait he claimed was generally unknown before romanticism—but self-sacrifice, which was characteristic of Christ: "Hamlet is not a drama of weakness, but of duty and self-denial." Pasternak places the accent on the courageous resistance of the superfluous hero to evil, on his readiness, even in the face of his own inevitable death, to face a cruel world alone. For Pasternak, Hamlet's reflections, his tortuous search for the meaning of life, were not the antithesis of decisive and heroic action. Rather, they were its inescapable precondition. This interpretation of Hamlet was in accord with the stoic pathos contained in Shakespeare's 66th sonnet, which was published in the same issue of the journal with *Hamlet*.[16]

Having begun his work on *Hamlet* at Meyerhold's initiative, Pasternak conceived of the translation as a piece to be staged, not as a book to be read. When it was finished, he read it to his close friends. Among them was a great actor of the time, Boris Livanov.[17] Livanov was one of the premier actors of the Moscow Art Theater (MKhAT), which enjoyed Stalin's special favor and was officially considered the best and most exemplary theater in the country. Through Livanov, Pasternak established contacts with this theater, which he had previously been indifferent to. Now, in connection with the poet's estrangement from the traditions of avant-garde art and his turn to the cultural values of prerevolutionary Russia, MKhAT suddenly proved to be artistically appealing.[18] Livanov had long dreamt of playing the role of Hamlet, and, like Meyerhold, he was never able to fulfill his dream. He and two of his friends, Vitaly Vilenkin and Leonid Leonidov, showed Pasternak's translation to Vladimir Nemirovich-Danchenko who, since the death of Konstantin Stanislavsky, had become the sole director of the theater. The decision to stage *Hamlet* had been made by the MKhAT earlier, in 1938, and the administration had signed a contract to use Anna Radlova's translation. But once Nemirovich-Danchenko read Pasternak's text, he quickly expressed his preference for it and nullified the contract with Radlova.[19]

Nemirovich-Danchenko, the eighty-two-year-old patriarch of the realistic theatrical tradition, intended to direct *Hamlet* himself. He saw this production as his swan song. It was all the more significant because up to this time none of the stagings of Shakespeare at the Moscow Art Theater had been successful. Nemirovich-Danchenko said that Pasternak's translation opened his eyes to a new Shakespeare. In the winter of 1939–40 the poet began working with the theater company. He would come every other day from Peredelkino to Moscow to discuss the text and to rework it according to the requirements of the directors and actors. Nemirovich-Danchenko and his assistants were delighted with Pasternak from their first meeting.[20] Vilenkin felt that Pasternak was the real-life embodiment of everything Hamlet was on the stage, and Leonidov believed that Pasternak had been born in order to play this role at the Moscow Art Theater. Despite all his enthusiasm, Nemirovich-Danchenko felt somewhat uneasy over the language of the translation; he was not quite sure that such a close approximation to modern, idiomatic, colloquial Russian and the deliberate lowering of the style was artistically justified. Defending himself from reproaches of "modernization," the poet claimed that the language of his translation was the vernacular not of the Soviet period but of Russian society at the end of the nineteenth century—the language of Chekhov's time that was subsequently distorted by the false profundity of the symbolist poets. It was precisely the everyday language of prerevolutionary Russia which seemed to him vital to this work.[21]

Although rehearsals began, *Hamlet* was never performed at the Moscow Art Theater. In the spring of 1941 at one of his banquets, Stalin, in answer to a question from Boris Livanov, expressed no enthusiasm whatsoever for the theater's plan to produce *Hamlet* and called the play "decadent."[22] Rehearsals were immediately suspended. It is difficult to say what the leader had in mind when he gave such an assessment. Maybe *Hamlet* seemed decadent from the point of view of the aesthetic tastes of fascism, which exerted a strong influence on Soviet ideology during this period of the rapprochement with Hitler in 1939–1941.[23] MKhAT did not abandon the idea of performing *Hamlet* however, and continued to announce it as forthcoming. Only the outbreak of the war forced Nemirovich-Danchenko to suspend preparation permanently: he understood that there would be no place on the Soviet stage for "poetry of doubts and skepticism" during the troubled times. As soon as the situation at the front began to improve, he renewed rehearsals in early 1943. But he died in April 1943, and his assistants proved unable to complete the production.

Pasternak never stopped working on *Hamlet*. Twelve versions of the translation have survived. It seems that he subjected no other text to such endless revisions. In his earlier translations (Kleist, Swinburne, Jonson, Rilke, Goethe, the Georgian poets), Pasternak selected works that were practically unknown to the Soviet reader. In turning to translations of Shakespeare, Pasternak had to compete with an imposing literary tradition of Russian Shakespearism. Between the time he first became acquainted with the English author and the beginning of his work on the translation, a long period passed that was marked by the poet's constant rereading and study of Shakespeare. His contemporaries felt that Pasternak's translation of *Hamlet* was an exceptional phenomenon in current Soviet literature.

Pasternak recited his translation of *Hamlet* publicly at two evening gatherings in Moscow in the spring of 1940. These readings were a great triumph, a surprise for their organizers and for the poet himself. Many listeners were overjoyed by the simple fact that Pasternak had emerged from the shadows. These were encounters not with a translator but with a poet, not with a translation but with art.

A similar reunion between Pasternak the poet and his readers occurred with the publication of his book *Izbrannye perevody* (Selected Translations), at the end of 1940. The texts included in this book were translated by Pasternak at various times, and there seemed no pattern to the works included. The only section displaying any real unity was the one consisting of lyrical poems by Shakespeare, Byron, Keats, Becher, and others, translated by Pasternak during the 1937–1939 period. In reading them one can clearly feel not only the hidden reflections and moods of Pasternak himself, which did not find expression in this period in any other place, but also a new poetic style.

Renewed contact with an audience was uplifting for Pasternak, and in the summer of 1940 he returned to writing verse. This was also related to the political situation in Europe. After the dark events of the fall of 1939 and spring of 1940, when one European country after another fell to the onslaught of Nazi Germany, the stubborn resistance of the British showed that it was still possible to halt Hitler's offensive. Everyone believed that the Soviet Union would be drawn into the world war, but on whose side was impossible to predict during those months. Pasternak anxiously followed the military reports from the fronts (he regularly listened to the BBC). Great Britain's steadfastness led him to believe that in 1941 things would improve everywhere. These feelings were accompanied by family concerns: his father and sisters were living in England (his mother having died a week before the outbreak of World War II in Europe).

On the eve of worldwide catastrophe, pressure in the realm of literature and culture in the Soviet Union noticeably weakened. There were new editions of books by those twentieth-century Russian authors who once were obliterated from memory: Annensky, Sologub, Khlebnikov. A collection of poems by Anna Akhmatova was released and sold out on the same day. This was her first book since 1923. It contained, in particular, her poem from 1936 dedicated to Boris Pasternak. The success of her work was all the more striking because, during the years of her poetic silence, a new generation of readers and poets had come onto the literary scene, people of different social background, education, thinking, and language, with new tastes and attitudes. The fact that Anna Akhmatova proved not to be an anachronism convinced Pasternak that his generation had not exhausted itself, that it was premature to declare it superfluous. In addition, Akhmatova's unexpected success demonstrated the profound changes Soviet poetry had undergone during the 1930s. Her poems were now perceived not within the context of acmeism or other avant-garde tendencies from the beginning of the twentieth century, but as a manifestation of the enduring traits of Russian and European classical literature. The measure of poetic mastery had shifted from innovation and the complexity of stylistic devices to "bareness," laconic precision, coupled with density of word meaning.

Pasternak's new lyrical poetry shared these features. His style was now even simpler than in *Second Birth*. Like Akhmatova's new verse, it seemed to be a radical renunciation of the entire modernist stage of Russian literature. Pasternak turned to this style not under Akhmatova's influence but for his own reasons. As early as 1933, in a letter to his friend Spassky, Pasternak spoke of his intention to plunge into the "common vernacular," rejecting tropes and all the other special devices of poetic language, thereby achieving such a freedom of expression that even dull, colorless, and simple words would turn into music in his poetry.[24] An example of such verbal bareness in Russian literature was the later poetry and prose of Pushkin. In his new poems, Pasternak completely avoided the use of tropes and of what had once been the core of his lyrical poetry—elusiveness of utterance. In verse and in prose, he was searching for a new style along the same paths.

During this period Pasternak unexpectedly found links with the new generation of young Soviet poets represented by Alexander Tvardovsky and Konstantin Simonov. These poets counterbalanced the poetic tradition of Mayakovsky, who had been canonized by Stalin's pronouncement in 1935. Pasternak was one of the first to recognize Tvardovsky's exceptional talent and supported him even when Gorky in 1935 reacted disdainfully toward the new writer. Thanks to Pasternak's support at this time, Tvardovsky's first epic poem, "The Land of Muravia," was published. Tvardovsky remained grateful for the rest of his life. The poems written by Tvardovsky and Simonov during the war became especially popular. In her memoirs, Nadezhda Mandelshtam somewhat caustically cites Pasternak's declaration in a letter from the mid-1940s, that in contemporary literature he was interested only in them and that he was trying to discover the secret of their success. She sees the poet's confession as a mark of vanity. But in Tvardovsky's and Simonov's poetry Pasternak found immediacy and purity of expression, qualities that had been suppressed in other officially sanctioned literature. The fact that his own diction was starting to approach this tendency in Soviet poetry compelled his attention. Pasternak's adoption of a new style was extremely difficult, whereas for them such traits seemed innate. He saw nothing shameful in the fact that he could learn from young poets, no matter how much they differed from him in other ways.

Pasternak's quest for a different literary style originated in his new desire to be accessible to the widest possible circle of readers. Earlier the opinions of his readers had been, in general, a matter of indifference; like Pushkin, he felt that a poet was his own supreme judge. But the feeling he had in 1937–1939 of belonging to a superfluous generation forced Pasternak to reconsider. The new idea of the poet's unity with the people crowded the sensation of being a "superfluous" hero out of Pasternak's consciousness. This idea was prompted by oppositional political motives; it is no accident that it coincided with the poet's increased interest in the heritage of the Russian Slavophiles of the nineteenth century, who had frequently been a bastion of antigovernmental opposition.

It was with great relief that Pasternak greeted the war with Germany, which began on June 22, 1941. At one stroke, the disgraceful alliance concluded between Stalin and Hitler in the fall of 1939 was shattered. No matter how catastrophic the events of the first days and weeks of the war were for Soviet Russia, Pasternak believed that these most difficult trials would, when all was said and done, lead to the moral rejuvenation of the people, eliminating everything base and cruel that the authorities had inculcated by means of mass terror. During these months, when some yielded to panic or despair and other gloatingly awaited the collapse of the Soviet regime under the blows of the rapidly advancing German troops, Pasternak firmly believed not only in the inevitable final victory of the people but in the renewal of the Soviet regime, which, in his opinion, would never again be able to return to the methods it had employed in 1937–1939. As early as February 1936, addressing his fellow writers at the plenum in Minsk, Pasternak had said that not everything is imposed from above by higher authorities: we ourselves are responsible for our lack of freedom, and the blame lies not so much with the rulers as with the ruled.

The disarray and helplessness of the Soviet authorities, who were taken completely unaware during the first months of the war—and the wave of patriotic self-sacrifice, the inspiring manifestations of heroism, and the need for millions of individuals to make independent decisions and to act on their own in dire circumstances—all this created extraordinary conditions for the expression of the people's strength. The greater the sacrifices exacted by catastrophic events at the front, the more this seemed to the poet a guarantee that there would be no return to the old ways. These hopes were reinforced by the military, political, and economic alliance that was concluded with the western democratic nations after the German invasion. This was accompanied by remarkable shifts in the internal policies of the Soviet state.

Yet the climate surrounding Pasternak during these weeks by no means served to confirm his optimistic prognoses. In July 1941 he wrote with surprise and indignation that literary and publishing circles were dominated by the same obsequiousness and cowardice, fostering lies, empty verbiage, and duplicity of literary language. This seemed especially intolerable now when the fate of the whole nation hung in the balance. He yearned to go to the front, where he expected to find different moral standards, but he was not given permission to make the trip. Matters grew worse every day. The Red Army was in full retreat, and the front relentlessly drew closer to the capital. German planes bombed Moscow and surrounding areas from the night of June 23 on.[25] When the evacuation of the civilian population from the capital to the east began, Zinaida and her children left on July 8 with a group of writers' families bound for the city of Chistopol (in the Tatar Republic). There she lived with her two younger sons, Stanislav and Leonid; her older son (from her marriage with Neuhaus), the sixteen-year-old Adrian, had fallen ill with osseous tuberculosis a year before. He was in need of constant medical attention and was sent to a sanatorium in the Cheliabinsk region in the Urals.

For many weeks the poet was cut off from his relatives. His lack of information about his family in Oxford, which had troubled him since 1939, was now coupled with a similar lack of any information regarding his cousin and aunt in Leningrad, a city that was surrounded by enemy troops and had been subjected to a particularly savage bombardment. Upon graduating from school, Pasternak's eldest son, Evgeny, was sent straight to the front to dig trenches.[26] At the end of July, he returned to Moscow and on August 8 was evacuated with his mother to Tashkent (where he was able to enroll in the university). The first news from them reached Pasternak only in January 1942. Everything became enveloped in a cloud of uncertainty: his family, his own fate, their home. No one could tell how long it would continue. Pasternak was not allowed to travel to Chistopol in order to join his wife and children, and it seemed that he would be forced to stay the winter in Peredelkino.

At the start of the war, Pasternak was mobilized with other writers in a civilian antiaircraft brigade. He spent the night of July 23 under heavy fire from German planes on the roof of the twelve-story building on Lavrushinsky Street where his city apartment was located. Along with other writers, Vsevolod Ivanov, Viktor Shklovsky, Ilya Selvinsky, the poet Utkin, and the playwright Glebov, he used a shovel to throw incendiary bombs that had been dropped onto the roof to the street below. The attacking planes swooped so low that the pilots' faces could be seen. Pasternak had never been called for military duty during World War I, but now he was in the thick of things. According to various witness accounts, Pasternak displayed great courage during these hours. At the end of August, he and several writers, including Fedin, Leonov, and Panfyorov, were mobilized for a two-week course of accelerated military training. Pasternak was proud that he was the best marksman in his detachment.

His literary affairs also developed favorably. The poems he wrote during the initial period of the war were accepted for publication. But even more heartening was the fact that a project he had begun before the war, which seemed infinitely remote from contemporary events—the translation of Shakespeare's *Romeo and Juliet*—was considered desirable under the new conditions, and Pasternak was asked to continue the work. This request appeared to promise the possibility of staging the play in theaters and, consequently, financial stability. At the same time, Pasternak received another commission—to translate a verse collection by the Polish romantic poet, Juliusz Slowacki, who was still virtually unknown in Russia.

Amid these encouraging developments, on September 9 Pasternak learned of Marina Tsvetaeva's suicide. She had returned to Russia with her son in the middle of June 1939; her husband and daughter had been living in Moscow since 1937. Tsvetaeva's meetings with Pasternak were few, and it was impossible to restore the intimacy that had once characterized their relations. As we now know, Tsvetaeva and Akhmatova also failed to communicate well when they met in Moscow. Everyone was occupied with personal concerns, and Pasternak, who was in disfavor, could not serve as the powerful protector Tsvetaeva needed so badly during these months. Having broken her ties with the emigration, Tsvetaeva was living in a kind of vacuum in the Soviet Union. Neither the content nor the style of her poetry could attract a broad Soviet reading public or the support of literary authorities, and her ethical and political positions fundamentally clashed with Soviet views. Her only chance of survival lay in translations. Thanks to Pasternak, she was commissioned to translate the poems of second-rate poets, and this form of livelihood could hardly inspire her. To make things worse, her family was dealt a series of devastating blows: in 1937, before Tsvetaeva returned, her sister Anastasia had been arrested, and Marina's daughter and husband, for whom she had returned to Russia, were arrested soon after her arrival: Ariadna on August 27 and Sergei Efron on October 10, 1939. It was during these weeks that Pasternak was hastily finishing his *Hamlet* and awaiting his own arrest. Little help could be offered to Tsvetaeva even by more influential men, such as Aseev and Tikhonov, who had admired her poetry since the 1920s. Although they now enjoyed official recognition, they were unable to exert any real influence on literary policy. Nevertheless, just before the war broke out, the question of publishing Tsvetaeva's selected verse was raised, and a circle of young poets formed around her, including her fervent admirers Arseny Tarkovsky and Semen Lipkin. Pasternak later said that the impression was that Tsvetaeva was "coming into vogue," and this forced him to step aside.[27] In August 1941, when the Germans began to approach Moscow, Tsvetaeva and her son were evacuated to the Tatar Republic. Pasternak saw them off at the riverside station. She was sent to the little town of Elabuga, where she faced loneliness, isolation, and the absence of all professional prospects.[28] She was unable to move to Chistopol, where most of her Moscow literary acquaintances and influential friends were settled, and on August 31, ten days after she arrived in Elabuga, she hanged herself.

The tragedy of Tsvetaeva and her family haunted Pasternak for the rest of his life. He blamed himself for her return to Russia, and for not having talked her out of such a move when he saw her in Paris in 1935. He also blamed himself for her death, since he assumed that had he been in Chistopol during those days he would have been able to save her. But Pasternak was not allowed to leave Moscow. One could obtain a railway ticket only with special permission and with an assignment that guaranteed not only passage on the train but a place to stay upon arrival. Such permission was granted neither to Pasternak nor to his Peredelkino neighbors Fedin and Leonov, despite their persistent requests during these weeks. Then, in the middle of October, with the German army at the gates of Moscow and with civilian disturbances breaking out that threatened to turn into a full-fledged uprising against the authorities, the panic-stricken evacuation of Soviet institutions was begun. On October 15 Pasternak, together with other members of the board of the Writers' Union, was ordered to leave for Chistopol immediately. On the next day, when it seemed that the fall of Moscow was inevitable, he left by train for the Tatar Republic, accompanied by Fedin, Shklovsky, Akhmatova (who had just been evacuated from Leningrad), and other writers.[29]

Pasternak thought that the eleven months he spent in Chistopol were one of the best times in his life during the Soviet period. In this remote, unattractive, and unremarkable provincial town, he felt much better than in the capital. The poet's ever-present notion that the provinces provided a much more meaningful life than Moscow found unexpected confirmation. Although the Pasternak family was destitute, the poet experienced a feeling of spiritual liberation, independence, and creative activity, impossible since 1936. In Chistopol, a local branch of the Writers' Union was formed, headed by Pasternak's close friends (Fedin, Aseev, Leonov, and Trenyov) and himself.

They guided the life of the writers' organization without the supervision of its leading figures[30] and without the constant meddling of the party bureaucracy. Thus what had been envisioned on the eve of the First Writers' Congress in 1934 suddenly proved possible in the fall of 1941. Pasternak was also inspired by the feeling that he was needed by his country during these difficult times. His translations of Shakespeare were considered by the upper echelons to be a politically important undertaking. Evidence of this attitude is contained in Konstantin Fedin's report on the activity of the writers in Chistopol, which was sent to Fadeev on May 6, 1942: "Pasternak recently translated *Romeo and Juliet*. Judging from the favorable reaction of the Committee on Art Affairs, this was a very opportune step, and I am very glad for Boris. The translation is brilliant! And it really is timely: our British allies will be pleased by our *unflagging* interest in Shakespeare." [31] Similar political overtones accompanied the collection of Juliusz Slowacki's poems that Pasternak prepared. It fit in well with the pan-Slavic tendency in Soviet propaganda and diplomacy during the wartime period.[32]

Pasternak's main undertaking in Chistopol was an original play. He intended to express the new freedom felt by himself and (as he assumed) by the people as a whole during the war. Pasternak not only announced to his friends that his goal was to write "in a new way, freely," but he also declared this in applications to government officials. He had conceived of the play while still in Moscow, in the middle of July 1941, but he had not been able to concentrate on this work there. Now that he was in the provinces, and the translation of *Romeo and Juliet* was finished, he could turn to his own play. He sent a proposal to the Committee on Art Affairs of the RSFSR at the end of January 1942. On February 10 it was accepted, and the committee signed a contract that gave the author an advance. As the application said, the author intended to express in his play what he experienced in Moscow in the first weeks of the war, as well as in the middle of October 1941 (when it seemed that Moscow would fall in a matter of days). The action was to take place in a major Soviet city under siege. Pasternak saw his play as the combination of two literary traditions: one went back to Shakespeare's historical chronicles, the other to the "harmonious realism" of Chekhov and Ibsen.[33] He singled out two aspects in the purposed drama. The first of these was psychological—the demonstration of how, under the threat of mortal danger, human courage comes to the fore. Insofar as the only difference between a genius and an ordinary person was, according to Pasternak, fearlessness, the events of the war created millions of geniuses.[34] The second major aspect of the play was supposed to be a comparison of the people's heroism in current war with their heroism in Russia's past: it was important to show universal qualities of character that had not been eliminated by the revolution.[35]

Rumors about Pasternak's new work spread rapidly and aroused great interest in literary and theater circles. In July 1942 Alexander Tairov, the director of the Chamber Theater in Moscow, asked Pasternak to give him this play for staging. At the same time, the poet Pavel Antokolsky wrote to Pasternak: "Your success is badly needed by the Soviet theater."[36] Pasternak saw his future play as a major work in which he would gather all his reflections about the twenty-five-year history of Russia since the revolution. Meanwhile, the bureaucrats of the Committee on Art Affairs recommended that the poet focus on showing the people's heroism and in no way dwell on the negative aspects of Soviet life.

Work on the play went slowly. By the fall of 1942, Pasternak became convinced that he had overestimated the dimensions of the newly obtained liberties and the readiness of his fellow writers to defend them. On September 16 he sadly wrote to his first wife in Tashkent: "Everything remains the same—double-dealing, double-thinking, a double life."[37] And purely technical difficulties also impeded work on the drama. This was Pasternak's first attempt since 1917 to write a dramatic work in prose, and no matter how instructive the experience of translations of Shakespeare had been, to transfer this mechanically to a play about modern Soviet life was impossible. By the very nature of the genre, action should be developed through the dialogue of the protagonists, and direct speech had always been the weakest element in Pasternak's art. But the greatest difficulty lay elsewhere. For the first time in his life, Pasternak was attempting to write about recent events—about modern Russian life, about the Soviet regime, about collective farms, military events, and so forth. Temporal distance, which he always needed, was absent this time.

Little is known about the contents of what he completed. The play apparently centered on the actions of its main characters under conditions of anarchy, when the city was changing hands.[38] In order to invigorate his work, Pasternak repeatedly asked to be sent to the front, but he was not allowed such a trip until the summer of 1943.

As late as the winter of 1943–44, the poet intended to finish the play. But as the military successes of the Red Army became more secure, the liberal tendencies in Soviet internal life began to shrink. Evidently, in the summer of 1944, Pasternak decided to abandon this venture once and for all. In the poet's family archive, only two scenes have survived, and we do not know to which act they belong. A few characters bear names that reappear in *Doctor Zhivago,* and one of the two scenes was used in writing the novel's epilogue. It is likely that the second scene survived because the author believed it would be possible to rework it in another context. The rest of the completed text was discarded because Pasternak had grown cold to the idea of the play, both ideologically and artistically.

When he traveled from Chistopol to Moscow in the fall of 1942, Pasternak gave the Sovetsky Pisatel (Soviet Writer) publishing house the manuscript of a slim collection of poems, *Na rannikh poezdakh* (On Early Trains). It came out in the summer of 1943. Its first section contained poems about the war written in the summer of 1941, before the poet's evacuation. They were meant to prove that he was not an ivory-tower recluse. The two remaining sections consisted of poems from 1936[39] and poems written in Peredelkino before the war, at the beginning of 1941. Evidently the initiative to publish this book—his first new verse collection in ten years—came from the literary authorities. Its task was to demonstrate that the old pronouncements of 1936–37 no longer applied and that Pasternak was rehabilitated as a lyrical poet. According to Alexander Gladkov, the book caused its author more distress than joy: he was embarrassed by its meager size and by the somewhat haphazard combination of poems written at various periods on different themes.[40] *On Early Trains* revealed Pasternak's new style. But the miscellany seemed lightweight to the author himself, insofar as his broad reflections about Russia's history and its modern-day life, which he had tried to express in his extensive prose narrative and in his play, found almost no place.

In the spring of 1943, even before their publication, the poems from this book, together with the translations of *Hamlet* and *Romeo and Juliet,* were nominated for the highest Soviet literary award, the Stalin Prize. By itself such a nomination indicated that Pasternak enjoyed solid support among the top literary officials. But he was not awarded the prize, neither then nor two years later in 1945, when his candidacy was again discussed by the Committee on Stalin Prizes.

Reviewers greeted *On Early Trains* warmly. Among them was Konstantin Simonov, the twenty-eight-year-old poet and playwright whose works appealed to Stalin himself and who had become a celebrity. In an article called "The Correct Path" Simonov applauded the very qualities in Pasternak that had brought the poet under fire at the end of the 1930s: the honesty and independence of his position and his refusal to yield to external pressure. Simonov also hailed Pasternak's new simplicity, interpreting this turn to a broad audience as a sign of the author's internal growth rather than his creative decline.[41] This assessment was important not only because Simonov had become a rising star in the literary leadership (while still managing to retain his reputation as a decent and courageous man), but also because he personified the new generation in Soviet poetry, whose stylistic traits were in accord with Pasternak's new efforts.

Just as sympathetic, although less panegyric in tone, was the review by Pavel Antokolsky, a poet close to Pasternak in literary tastes and from almost the same generation.[42] Although the article was ostensibly confined to a discussion of *On Early Trains,* it advanced a new characterization of Pasternak's work as a whole. Antokolsky defined Pasternak as an artist of remarkable, but never fully realized *potential.* He claimed that, as with Leonardo da Vinci, Pasternak's finished works are inferior to his beginning attempts. "Pasternak merely outlines a theme, and points the way where someone else, perhaps, may follow. But he himself is not going to move any farther ... A strikingly sincere poet, [Pasternak] has amazed us with his lightning bolts of insight, and yet he has often immediately relinquished what he has just begun."[43] Antokolsky was the first to say in public that the poet's oeuvre was incommensurate with the enormity of his genius. This assessment happened to correspond with the author's own persistent self-deprecation, with a profound dissatisfaction that grew stronger as the years went by. Pasternak could not help feeling that he was a pretender ("I live with the constant, nagging sense of being almost an impostor"), and that his fame and popularity had been achieved on credit ("I've been living on credit").[44] This dissatisfaction embraced not only his earlier works, which had lost all significance for the author, but also his new creations, whose unevenness he could readily see.

During this same year, in 1943, at the height of the war, a voice of support came from completely unexpected quarters. In February the English journal *Life and Letters Today* published an article, "The

Duty of the Younger Writer," by Stefan Schimanski. It was written on a totally unrelated subject: the stance of some younger British poets toward the war. Their immersion in lyrical poetry or complete silence, and their refusal to supply anti-German propaganda poems, was regarded by many as a desire to remain aloof from contemporary life. Schimanski denied that the poets' inactivity in the domain of public service and their lack of patriotic response to political events meant that they were defeatists, pacifists, or escapists. He defended the artist's right to remain independent from the state even in the apocalyptic circumstances of World War II. In the very fact of the individual's firm refusal to submit to coercion he saw genuine heroism, not different from that shown by soldiers on the battlefield: "Only that person who stands rock-wise, with his feet rooted in his faith in Man, will survive storms and disturbances. The young artists, in retaining their independence of thought and action are, therefore, already performing the task which it is their lot to fulfill: through their silence, because of their self-reliance, they are laying those foundations of heroism which will enable others to follow and to realize themselves as individuals and citizens."[45]

The critic went on to draw a comparison between Great Britain and Soviet Russia, where the war situation was much more dramatic and where relationships between the state and the arts had been established even during peacetime. These differences notwithstanding, Schimanski claimed that his position held equally true even for Soviet literature. He illustrated his point in a discussion of Russia's three greatest twentieth-century poets—Mayakovsky, Esenin, and Pasternak. Whereas the suicides of Esenin and Mayakovsky were caused by their inability to face problems, "only Pasternak survived all storms and mastered all events. He is the real hero of the struggle between individualism and collectivism, romanticism and realism, morality and technique, art and propaganda." Having quoted Pasternak's "Reply to the Party Resolution on Literature" (1925), Schimanski contrasted him to those Soviet writers who, like Sholokhov, became front-line correspondents and at best produced good journalism, not works of art. The fact that Pasternak did the Shakespeare translations was not only a proof of his unwillingness to become a "propaganda hack" but was also an act of high cultural value and moral and political virtue: "Sholokhov's present writing is . . . national, limited in scope and purpose; Pasternak's work in uniting culturally two great nations is international, further-reaching, and longer-lasting."[46]

Schimanski's essay, obviously a response to the recent publication of Pasternak's note "Concerning Shakespeare," caused much distress in the highest Soviet literary echelons, especially among those officials who were trying to rehabilitate Pasternak. The juxtaposition of Sholokhov and Pasternak, and the preference given to the latter, clearly appalled the bureaucrats in the Writers' Union. The public criticisms leveled by its general secretary, Alexander Fadeev, in 1943 against Pasternak's immersion in translations during the war were almost certainly aimed at repudiating Schimanski's essay. Similar considerations stood behind the decision not to award the poet the Stalin Prize that year. On the other hand, the same type of thinking induced the authorities finally to agree to dispatch Pasternak to the front. Inasmuch as all the earlier rejections had been an indication of mistrust toward the poet, the new decision to allow such a trip was clearly a sign of positive change in the official attitude.

Pasternak joined a brigade of prominent Soviet authors sent to the Briansk front in August 1943. The trip was organized by Nikolai Talensky, the newly appointed editor-in-chief of the army newspaper *Krasnaia zvezda* (Red Star). The group included the prose writers Vsevolod Ivanov and Konstantin Fedin, who were his close friends, the poets Konstantin Simonov and Pavel Antokolsky, a patriarch of Soviet literature, the eighty-year-old Alexander Serafimovich, and the widow of Nikolai Ostrovsky, whose two novels had laid the foundations for the official Soviet mythology of heroism. The trip was organized after the victory of the Red Army at Stalingrad, when a decisive shift in the character of the war became clear and every day brought more evidence of the superiority of Soviet military power. The writers' brigade visited the Third Army, which had just liberated Orel and continued to advance. At the head of this army stood General A. V. Gorbatov, one of the nation's most respected commanding officers.[47]

The writers left on August 28 and spent two weeks at the front. The goal of the trip was to gather reminiscences from participants in the battle for Orel and to publish them in book form. Even before the trip, Pasternak had written the poem "Speshnye stroki" (Hurried Lines), devoted to this event. For the first time in his life he found himself in an army at war. Together with his companions, he experienced all the fascination of life at the front: he was in the trenches along the frontlines, slept in tents pitched in the forest, participated in meetings, talked with generals and enlisted men, read his new poems to the wounded in hospitals, and met with inhabitants of towns that had been occupied by the Germans for many months. He saw the shattered homes, the burned villages, and the endless destruction in places that had given Russia its best writers: Zhukovsky and Delvig, Tolstoy and Turgenev, Leskov and Bunin. Pasternak's presence at the front eliminated many of the prejudices that had arisen about him. Everyone was surprised by his simplicity and accessibility, the absence of any haughtiness or snobbishness. General Gorbatov would later recall: "In 1943, we were visited in the Third Army by a group of writers which included Boris Leonidovich Pasternak. We liked him because of his open disposition, and his lively and sympathetic attitude toward people." [48] Pasternak's fearlessness at the frontlines impressed everyone. The soldiers wondered: "Is this really Pasternak?" One of the officers showed the poet a book that had never left his side throughout the war, *My Sister, Life,* and the author inscribed it: "It is impossible to live without courage." [49]

Pasternak felt just as happy with the army as he had during the first months of his stay in Chistopol. According to Konstantin Simonov, "He nobly rejoiced in everything that was pure and courageous in people, as a man might rejoice in the long-awaited confirmation of his most cherished hopes." [50] He devoted two pieces of reporting to his impressions of the journey. But the *Red Star* was clearly not pleased with his sketches: they were not included in the book by the writers who had gone to the front with Pasternak. Only one of Pasternak's two accounts was published at that time; it appeared in the newspaper *Trud* (Labor) in November and was cut in half by the censors. Among the sections removed, the most important was his thoughts on Hitler's Germany. This was the poet's only public statement on fascism, and it reveals the essence of his political views during the war years.

The characterization of German fascism here was given in logical juxtaposition to an assessment of the historical role of revolutionary Russia. Ten years earlier, when he first learned of Hitler's coming to power, Pasternak drew a similar parallel in a letter to his parents in Berlin:

> And, however strange it may seem to you, one and the same thing depresses me in both our own state of affairs, and yours. It is that this movement is not Christian, but nationalistic; that is, it runs the same danger of degenerating into the bestiality of facts. It has the same alienation from the age-old, gracious tradition that breathes with transformations and anticipations, rather than the cold statements of blind insanity. These movements are on a par, one is

evoked by the other, and it is all the sadder for this reason. They are the left and right wings of a single, materialistic night.[51]

Now, in the sketch devoted to his excursion in the army, the poet avoids such a direct identification of the two wartime adversaries. Yet the historical destinies of Russia and Germany are once again closely interwoven:

> What is striking in Hitlerism is Germany's loss of her political superiority. Her dignity has been sacrificed in order to play a secondary role. The country has been forcibly reduced to nothing more than a reactionary footnote to Russian history. If revolutionary Russia ever had need of a crooked mirror which would distort her features into a grimace of hatred or ignorance, then here it is: Germany was destined to produce it.[52]

The underlying idea behind this comparison is that there had been a kind of organic link between the Russian revolution and developments in Germany leading to the rise of fascism. However flattering for socialist Russia this comparison could have appeared, the author's very suggestion of such close kinship could only be disturbingly suspicious to Soviet editors, and they removed it from the original text. Even more dangerous, from the official viewpoint, was Pasternak's further explanation of the difference between the two forces. Whereas the Russian revolution was likened to the nature of genius—the drive for innovation, striving for independence, creative boldness and originality—its fascist counterpart was likened to an envious and dull mediocrity who starts with "preaching or lecturing" and ends with bloodshed. The deep Aesopian subtext of this passage becomes obvious when one realizes that Pasternak had spoken in exactly the same terms about the "inconceivable power" of dull, "completely cowed nonentities" and about their vicious attacks against Soviet artists in March 1936, during the campaign against formalism which, in hindsight, can be seen as a prelude to the gory years of the Great Terror.[53]

Both of Pasternak's frontline sketches—his first and only attempts at newspaper reporting—make a strange impression on today's reader: their dry and matter-of-fact narrative manner is unlike Pasternak's usual style, even in his later prose, and the details seem far removed from the interests of art. But an understanding of the subtext, in which Pasternak's conventional glorification of the revolution merges with a discussion of fascism, allows us to detect in these sketches his later, even more ambivalent conception of Russia's historical path in *Doctor Zhivago*. At the same time, in 1943 Pasternak still clung to the belief that the heroic exploits of the people, the feeling of emancipation evoked by the war, and the victories of the Soviet army were a guarantee of the regime's imminent turn away from its Hitlerian "crooked mirror."

These optimistic illusions were behind the narrative poem "Zarevo" (Nightglow), which he set out to write after his army excursion. The poem describes an officer's return home to civilian life. The main theme was supposed to be the transformation of a formerly submissive and miserable character into a genuinely courageous man—all under the influence of the bravery displayed in combat. The words he speaks to himself, "become victorious *while you are alive,*" may perhaps be read as a challenge by the author to himself. His encounters with the soldiers and generals near Orel had proved to him that the walls between him and the reading public were fictitious, and that in the popular milieu he and his poetry found a no less generous response than in the circles of the "Hamletic" intelligentsia in the capital.

But Pasternak was unable to realize this poetic conception. He finished only the introduction to the poem and its first section. The author hoped that it would be published widely in the press, and the introduction was indeed printed in *Pravda* on October 15, 1943. This alone was an unprecedented victory for the poet. Pasternak had never belonged to the circle of Soviet writers who piqued the interest and support of the main Soviet organ. *Pravda* had never before published his poetry, and it was only with reluctance that it even mentioned his name. Under the extraordinary conditions of wartime, impossible became possible. A year earlier a similar blockade had been broken by Anna Akhmatova, whose name had seemed just as inconceivable on the pages of this party paper as the name of Boris Pasternak: in February 1942 her poem "Muzhestvo" (Courage) appeared in *Pravda*. After his trip to the front, Pasternak consciously set out to "sneak into the newspapers," and "Nightglow" evidently served this purpose. His collaboration with *Pravda* was limited only to the introduction, however. When in November Pasternak delivered the next portion of the poem to the paper, it was rejected outright. The poet in turn flatly refused the editorial board's proposal to do a translation for *Pravda* of the epic poem "Childhood of the Leader" by the Georgian poet Georgy Leonidze, which was awarded the Stalin Prize in 1941.[54] The authorities' negative appraisal of the poem "Nightglow" was so strong[55] that it was not only impossible to publish it in the official newspaper, but in the literary journal *Znamia* (Banner) as well. The author had no choice but to stop working on the poem.[56] Thus all attempts by Pasternak to react publicly to the war had failed. On November 12, 1943, he wrote to his cousin: "I just can't go on fighting the tone that dominates the press. Nothing is working out; I shall probably give up and go back to Shakespeare." [57]

Pasternak began to translate *Othello*. Unlike *Hamlet, Romeo and Juliet,* and *Antony and Cleopatra,* which he had previously translated, this work was prompted not by purely artistic considerations. The poet had to begin life all over again from the beginning. In the summer of 1943 Pasternak moved his family back from Chistopol to Moscow. Their city apartment had been destroyed, and the Peredelkino dacha was also uninhabitable. The family was forced to stay with various friends and acquaintances until things were more or less restored to normal. If any of his Shakespeare translations had been staged, life would have been materially secure for a few more years. But after the death of Nemirovich-Danchenko, no hope remained at the Moscow Art Theater, and Pasternak had to settle down to work on *Othello,* a play he never much liked. Although monetary considerations had begun to outweigh purely literary ones, Shakespeare was still a better task than the ever-threatening directives to translate national minority poets. On the other hand, Pasternak could not be sure that he would be allowed to work on Shakespeare in the future, for, after Schimanski's article in *Life and Letters Today*, Fadeev had expressed his displeasure by hinting at Pasternak's unpatriotic immersion in translations during the war.

Nor was it easy for Pasternak to write lyrical poetry after the trauma of "Nightglow." It might seem that the chain of military victories by the Red Army, and the concomitant growth of optimism throughout the land, would have inspired Pasternak. But this did not happen. Almost all the lyrical poems in which the poet reacted to the events of the last years of the war struck his contemporaries as labored, dry, and stereotyped. They could have been written by anyone but Pasternak. Even literary critics very favorably disposed toward Pasternak (such as Sergei Spassky and Anatoly Tarasenkov) were puzzled and embarrassed by these verses. Pasternak's poetic genius could be felt only in those poems that strayed from official themes.

The contrast between the new and the old Pasternak was accentuated by the appearance in 1945 of two books of verse—*Zemnoi prostor* (Earthly Expanse), which contained only the lyrical poems of recent years, and a small volume of selected poems.[58] In addition to the revolutionary poems "1905" and "Lieutenant Schmidt," the latter book reprinted a number of his earlier lyrics for the first time in ten years. It omitted the longer poems in which the author expressed ambivalent feelings toward the October Revolution, "Lofty Malady" and *Spektorsky;* also absent, however, were the lyrical poems of the 1930s, which marked Pasternak's warmest relations with the socialist state. Thus it gave an incomplete picture of the poet. But the very appearance of such a book of selected work bordered on the miraculous and can only be explained by the liberal atmosphere of the last months of the war. This reflected the belief of the broadest circles of Soviet society that there would be no return to the old after such a bloody war, and that the dismal intellectual pressure and terror of the thirties was a thing of the past. The Soviet people expected that the impending victory over Nazi Germany would result in the liberation of all those who continued to languish in Soviet prisons and camps.

This intoxication with freedom, or rather with the harbingers of freedom, seized even Pasternak. Not since 1922 had his work appeared so often in the press. Not since the 1930s had he been surrounded by such warmth on the part of unofficial and semiofficial sections of society. Beginning in the fall of 1943, he repeatedly came into direct contact with an audience: with unprecedented frequency he began to take part in evening gatherings in Moscow, organized for the widest variety of reasons. There he read his new poems and translations. It seems that during these three years (1943–1946) he appeared on stage more frequently than in the previous ten. This reflected the sharp and deliberate change in his status. In his speech in Minsk in 1936, the poet had spoken against those of his colleagues who accused him of being a recluse and who insisted that he tour the country to read his verse aloud. Earlier he resented success that could be achieved too easily, merely by appearing on a stage; such success he felt was demeaning for poetry. Now Pasternak sought every opportunity to meet an audience; this was for him a kind of follow-up to his experiences at the front. Individual recitals for poets were extremely rare in 1944–45, and Pasternak usually had to perform together with colleagues. Among them were people who were quite foreign to him from both a literary and a moral standpoint—Anatoly Sofronov, Alexander Zharov, Alexei Surkov—but this did not prevent him from taking part in the recitals. His contemporaries say that Pasternak's name was always the biggest draw on posters announcing these events, and his admirers would fill the hall regardless of whoever else was included in the program.

The poet's unexpectedly wide popularity compensated for a sharp deterioration in his relations with officials in the literary establishment. In 1944–46 the chairman of the board of the Writers' Union was Nikolai Tikhonov, one of the most prominent poets to have made their debut after the revolution. In the 1920s he was heavily influenced by Pasternak's poetry and was essentially considered his disciple and follower. Until the end of the 1930s the two were united not only by similar literary tastes and social positions but by close personal friendship. It was at Pasternak's suggestion that Tikhonov became involved in the work on Georgian translations on the eve of the First Writers' Congress. But the years of terror and Tikhonov's official career in the Writers' Union sent the former friends in different directions, and under Tikhonov, Pasternak's relations with the bureaucracy became more strained than they had ever been before. There is no sense in blaming Tikhonov for this situation: as head of the Writers' Union he was no worse—and perhaps, on the contrary, was more liberal and tolerant—than the old RAPP leader, Fadeev.[59] The problem was simply that Pasternak expected a greater readiness to sacrifice privileges for the sake of principles, greater independence from the authorities and more courage, than Tikhonov could muster.

But Pasternak's independent line was expressed even more clearly outside the literary realm. During the last months of the war, he began corresponding with prisoners in the camps and with exiles. The poet did not know all of his correspondents personally, but he considered it his moral duty to comfort them in their misfortune. Whereas in the prerevolutionary times such conduct was the norm for writers, during the Stalinist epoch it acquired overtones of criminal activity. Pasternak's behavior was guided by a belief in the inevitability of radical changes for the better in society and in the state. Isaiah Berlin, who met with him in the fall of 1945, tells of the poet's mood at that time: "The dark nightmare of betrayals, purges, massacres of the innocent, followed by an appalling war, seemed to him a necessary prelude to some inevitable, unheard-of victory of the spirit."[60] Not only anticipating but outstripping these changes in society, Pasternak announced at the end of 1945: "Suddenly I am wonderfully free. Everything around me is wonderfully my own."[61] It never occurred to him that after the war millions of new prisoners would fill the Gulag Archipelago.

The need for closer contact with his readers and the sharp changes in his literary style compelled him to turn to literary criticism. He had never before written articles with the intensity he displayed in the mid-1940s. Various periodicals carried in rapid succession his essays and notes on translations of English poetry, on the Czechoslovak poet Ondra Lysohorsky, on Chopin and Verlaine. In 1946 he wrote two articles on Georgian poetry and a major article on Shakespeare, and he planned essays on Blok, Briusov, and Mayakovsky. The scope of these themes is remarkable. But it is noteworthy that (with the exception of memoir notes on Alexander Afinogenov, who died in 1941 soon after Pasternak left for Chistopol) not a single article of this period deals with Soviet literature; it is as if it did not exist. Yet Pasternak's outwardly objective literary criticism conceals a unique *ars poetica,* which would be fully developed only later, in *Doctor Zhivago.* Ten years later, in his second autobiography, Pasternak would stun all his readers with the astonishing statement: "I don't like my style prior to 1940." In the middle of the 1940s Pasternak had still not written anything that could allow him to be unreservedly proud of his new style or condescending toward his previous poetics—not the prose begun in 1936 or "Nightglow" or his abandoned drama, or his wartime verses. Therefore the new program was prepared, as it were, in advance, for the future.

The feeling of freedom allowed Pasternak to return to Georgian translations. He had abandoned them after 1937 (just when Izgoev's article had urged him to concentrate on this work). In their public statements during the mid-1940s, Georgian writers often complained that the previous interest in their national culture had disappeared and that only second-rate and ungifted writers were engaged in translating their verse. In 1944 the head of the Georgian Writers' Union became Simon Chikovani, a close friend of Titsian Tabidze and Paolo Yashvili, whom Pasternak valued highly as a poet and as a human being. He persuaded Pasternak to change his stance and once again to begin translating from the Georgian.[62] But Georgian literature was no longer a focus of attention in liberal circles in the capital, as it was in the time of Gorky and Bukharin; it was no longer the case that a privileged status could be imparted to it or to Pasternak's participation. During the years of the terror, Georgian literature suffered just as much as other spheres of Soviet culture, and its best poets vanished in 1937.[63]

As he now turned to Georgian poetry, Pasternak blatantly avoided all "permitted" authors of the Soviet period, limiting himself to prerevolutionary classics. The only exception was Simon Chikovani. Several of his poems translated by Pasternak at this time acquired a subtext just as intimate, autobiographical, and specifically Pasternakian as the rendition of *Hamlet*. On the whole, Pasternak's new contact with Georgian culture was confined to his translations from Nikolo Baratashvili, a remarkable poet of the early nineteenth century. In the course of forty days during the fall of 1945, Pasternak translated virtually the entire body of his works. At the invitation of the Georgian Writers' Union, he arrived in Tbilisi in October for celebrations marking the hundredth anniversary of the death of this founder of modern Georgian poetry. The honors bestowed on Pasternak here by his old friends contrasted sharply with his strained relations with the authorities in the capital. This was Pasternak's first visit to Georgia since 1933. Every day he met with Nina Tabidze, and despite the high status he enjoyed within the framework of the official celebrations, he used each occasion to demonstrate publicly his friendship with the wife of an "enemy of the people." The two weeks spent in Tbilisi were so inspiring that, when he returned home, he wondered if he should not settle there forever. They reminded him of the happy days of his first two trips to Georgia, and of how significant his friendship with the Georgians had been in his rapprochement with the Soviet state. He concluded his article devoted to Georgian poetry a few months later with these words: "The years of my acquaintance with Georgian lyrical poetry form a special, brilliant, and unforgettable page in my life. The memories of the stimuli and impulses that prompted these translations, as well as the details of the surroundings in which they were produced, have merged into a whole world that is distant and precious." [64] Later he would say that it was here in Tbilisi in 1945 that he found the resolve to write a novel about the fate of his generation. [65]

These plans acquired a special significance when Pasternak once again experienced the sensation of life's brevity, a feeling interwoven with the reflections about immortality that had haunted the poet from the beginning of his career. The deaths of two family members descended upon him in the spring of 1945: on April 29 Zinaida Nikolaevna's older son Adrian died at the age of twenty from tuberculous meningitis (he was buried in the garden at Peredelkino), and a month later the poet's father died in Oxford. Leonid Osipovich's death made Boris once again sense how "unconsummated" his own life had been in comparison with his father's artistic accomplishments. He approached this death not simply from the standpoint of a family tragedy, but from a much broader artistic and historical context, contrasting the modern epoch with the one in which his father had worked and lived.

Another impetus for the poet became his growing stature abroad, primarily in England. Translations of Pasternak's poems had appeared sporadically in western journals since the end of the 1920s. Even then he had been called the best modern Russian poet in articles by Dmitry Mirsky and George Reavey. Stefan Schimanski's article "The Duty of the Younger Writer" during the war marked a decisively new stage in the reception of Pasternak's poetry in the west. Previous interest in him had developed predominantly in circles of left-wing intellectuals, largely prompted by their sympathies for the Soviet Union and communism. They saw Pasternak's works as irrefutable proof of the flourishing of art under socialism. Schimanski's article introduced Pasternak in an altogether different light and evaluated him on a much broader plane—as an example of the poet's resistance to government coercion. But Pasternak was even more moved by the fact that Schimanski's article in *Life and Letters Today* was by no means the only expression of England's interest in his poetry. One of his poems had been included in the anthology *A Book of Russian Verse,* edited by Cecil Maurice Bowra in 1943, and a major article by J. M. Cohen entitled "The Poetry of Boris Pasternak" had appeared in the journal *Horizon* in June 1944. The feeling was that a circle of the poet's admirers had formed, the center of which was Stefan Schimanski.

Pasternak became familiar with Schimanski's article in the fall of 1943, when he returned from the front. He evidently received it from George Reavey, his old admirer and first translator into English.[66] From 1942 to 1945 Reavey was a member of the British embassy staff in the Soviet Union, and he directed *Britansky soiuznik* (British Ally), the paper published in Russian by the embassy for Soviet readers. Pasternak's sympathies for Schimanski and his circle increased when he learned that the group advanced the philosophy of "personalism," that Herbert Read and Steven Spender were close to it, and that the first volume of its new journal, *Transformation,* featured his *Liuvers' Childhood* in Robert Payne's translation.[67] When they met in 1945, the poet questioned Isaiah Berlin about this group of English intellectuals; he undoubtedly also talked with Reavey about *Transformation* (Reavey was himself to participate in its fourth issue: it was there that he published his survey of current Soviet literature after his return from Russia).

In more developed form, the main points of Schimanski's article were reiterated in a book of translations of Pasternak's prose, which was published with his introduction in the middle of 1945 by Lindsay Drummond in London. But this more detailed analysis of the poet's works and place in the history of Russian literature is accompanied by a new conclusion: throughout his essay Schimanski advances the idea of Pasternak's special intellectual kinship with Pushkin. This parallel acquires additional meaning if we keep in mind that all the great classics of Russian literature—Gogol and Dostoevsky, Tolstoy and Turgenev, not to mention any of the writers of the twentieth century—pale in significance to Pushkin in the Russian cultural consciousness. He is considered the progenitor of all modern Russian culture, much like Shakespeare in England. Schimanski himself was a native of Russia (born in Moscow). Quoting Dostoevsky's famous speech delivered on the unveiling of Pushkin's monument in 1880, Schimanski said: "In this spirit of all-embracing humanitarianism Pasternak stands as a direct, though not immediate, descendant of Russia's greatest poet."[68] He based his characterization of Pasternak mainly on the poet's early books, since the publications after *Second Birth* were known to him mostly by hearsay. A few of the assertions in his piece contradicted Pasternak's views (particularly on the question of romanticism), but on the whole it turned out to be strikingly close to Pasternak's thoughts during the 1940s.

This English book contained translations of *Safe Conduct* and the prose works from *Aerial Ways* of 1925. It counterbalanced, therefore, the image of Pasternak that had become established in Soviet literary criticism in the late 1940s. Not only his autobiography, which had been banned by the censors in 1933, but all his remaining prose works had been essentially forgotten in the Soviet Union. Their connection with Pasternak's lyrical poetry could no longer be felt, and very few of his poetic works were considered to have passed the test of time. Even for the author himself, these translated texts seemed to belong to an entirely different historical epoch, and the interest shown by western readers was completely unexpected. But another aspect of the London edition—a persistent emphasis on the link between Boris Pasternak's style and his father's art—undoubtedly touched him very deeply. This idea was underscored not only by the reproductions of Leonid Pasternak's works contained in the book, but by Schimanski's introduction. Schimanski had met the elderly artist in Oxford in 1943 and showed him the article in the February issue of *Life and Letters Today*. Schimanski evidently discussed his plan to publish a book of Boris' prose with the poet's father and sisters. In the Soviet Union the notion of a deep intellectual affinity between the poet and his father was never mentioned because of the artist's emigrant status, on the one hand, and Boris' ambiguous situation within official Soviet literature, on the other. Even the physical appearance of the London edition, with its reproductions of his father's works and family photographs, must have reminded Pasternak of how alien he had become in his own country. It is no wonder that he was particularly fond of this book.[69] He received a copy soon after the death of Leonid Osipovich, and everything in the introduction that mentioned the conversations of its editor with the artist about "Borya" impressed the poet as a kind of paternal testament. Among other things, Stefan Schimanski noted there: "he told me: 'I always said to him: Be honest in your art—and your enemies will be powerless against you.'"[70]

11

Zhivago and the Poet

The words of his father would resound many times in Boris Pasternak's consciousness when the air darkened around Soviet culture once again in August 1946. The poet likened these events to a powerful earthquake. On August 14 the Central Committee of the Communist Party passed a decree concerning two Leningrad literary journals, *Star* and *Leningrad*. Then the committee secretary in charge of questions of ideology, Andrei Zhdanov, delivered two speeches in which he elaborated on this pronouncement. The speeches were coarse and contained unprecedentedly abusive characterizations of Anna Akhmatova and Mikhail Zoshchenko.[1] They heralded the period of repression that later became known as Zhdanovism. New decrees followed that applied to film and theater, and they continued to appear right up to the resolutions about Shostakovich, Prokofiev, and other Soviet composers in February 1948. All these developments coincided with a sharp turn in the state's foreign policy. The cold war, which had taken shape at the beginning of 1946 and had grown ever more intense, led to the Soviet Union's isolation from the west. The Central Committee resolutions and Zhdanov's speeches denounced the so-called groveling before western ("bourgeois") culture, be it past or contemporary. Soviet patriotism now became patently xenophobic. The campaign against Akhmatova and Zoshchenko alienated many western intellectuals from the Soviet Union, including those representatives of the Russian emigration who had believed that after the world war Stalin's rule would become more humane.

The very linking of the names of Akhmatova and Zoshchenko was grotesque: except for the fact that they both lived in Leningrad, the two writers had nothing in common. But Stalin always loved wild amalgams: Zamiatin and Pilniak, formalism and naturalism, Bukhă-rin and fascist espionage. The Soviet leadership was of course disturbed and even enraged that in 1944, after her return from evacuation in Tashkent, Akhmatova was elected to the board of the Leningrad section of the Writers' Union, one of the highest positions in the social hierarchy. Her fame in the mid-1940s reached unprecedented proportions for the Soviet epoch. After 1940 books of her verse appeared in rapid succession. In 1943 a collection was published in Tashkent.[2] In 1945, in the same *Ogonek* series that brought out Pasternak's translations of Baratashvili, another of her books appeared; although it was a slender volume, it was printed in a press run of 100,000, astronomical for lyrical poetry. In 1946 a major collection of her selected verse was scheduled to be printed. It was already at the publishers when the "earthquake" struck, and it was never put on sale. At the beginning of 1946, Akhmatova read at several public gatherings in Moscow and Leningrad. The astounding success of these recitals was seen by the Kremlin authorities as an odious form of political demonstration. At one of them, on April 3, 1946, at the Hall of Columns in the House of the Soviets (the most prestigious place for a public meeting), during a visit to Moscow by a delegation of Leningrad writers, Akhmatova and Pasternak appeared side by side: Akhmatova concluded the first part of the performance devoted to the Leningrad guests, and Pasternak opened the second part, devoted to Moscow poets. They were both greeted by a standing ovation and were thus contrasted to the other participants.[3] It was on this occasion that Pasternak first read his poem "Pamiati Mariny Tsvetaevoi" (To the Memory of Marina Tsvetaeva), which had been written in 1943 but was never allowed to be printed during Pasternak's lifetime. Later several of Akhmatova's contemporaries suggested that it was her sensational success during these appearances that brought down Stalin's wrath and led to her being targeted as a victim when policy changed. Akhmatova herself was convinced that the misfortunes were provoked by her meeting with Isaiah Berlin, who was then working at the British embassy.[4]

As always during the Stalinist period, the campaign swept down like an avalanche, and at one meeting after another, speakers declared their unwavering support for the resolutions of the Central Committee. At a session of the presidium of the board of the Writers' Union on September 4, Akhmatova and Zoshchenko were stripped of their membership in the union. This meant an immediate printing ban on all their works, old or new. It also condemned them to hunger; food rationing was still in effect, and those who were not government employees, or did not have an equivalent status, had no right to ration cards. The same session announced the dismissal of Nikolai Tikhonov from his post as head of the Writers' Union and the appointment once again of Alexander Fadeev.[5]

The new events differed in essential ways from the previous campaigns. In the first place, neither in 1929 (the cases of Pilniak and Zamiatin) nor in 1936 (the attacks against formalism) did the Central Committee openly express its stance in questions of cultural life; it entrusted the fulfillment of its directives to "public organizations" or to the press. Thus a certain distance between the party leadership and the immediate instigator of the campaigns was always preserved. But this time, through its direct administrative intervention, the state showed its contempt even for the limited prerogatives—including political control—held by the Writers' Union. Henceforth all intellectual activities were unceremoniously declared to be under the immediate jurisdiction of state bodies. In addition, whereas the earlier campaigns were limited in time and usually lasted only a few weeks or months, the new purges in Soviet culture proved to be prolonged, lasting in essence until Stalin's death.

Pasternak's name was not mentioned in the official party directives in August. But he had good reason to believe that this was purely accidental, and he anticipated that in one way or another the shifting currents of literary policy would touch him as well. At first the only direct consequence of Zhdanov's speeches for the poet was the fact that his article on translations of Shakespeare, which had already been accepted for publication by *Star*, was rejected by the new editorial board.[6] Pasternak remained secluded during these days at Peredelkino, devoting himself fully to writing. But his refusal to attend meetings was in itself interpreted as an act of defiance, angering the literary functionaries. Apparently it was then that he was removed from the board of the Writers' Union, a prestigious post to which he had been elected at the First Writers' Congress in 1934 and which guaranteed a few modest perquisites. From the beginning of September, Pasternak's name began to be mentioned in the press in increasingly sinister contexts. On September 17 Fadeev declared in his official report to the All-Moscow Writers' Conference that Pasternak's works, much like Akhmatova's, displayed traits of "ideological neutrality and a lack of political awareness." [7] Simultaneous attacks were made on critics and journals that had been too indulgent toward Pasternak's poetry. A few months later, his translations of Shakespeare and Baratashvili were criticized for their ideological deficiencies. These criticisms echoed Fadeev's old claim that Pasternak's retreat into translation was symptomatic of the poet's oppositionist tendencies.

All of these accusations could have been interpreted as a signal that Pasternak would be deprived of translations, the means of existence that had sustained him during the most difficult periods of his life. Needless to say, all other literary commissions would be out of the question as well. But disarray in the upper echelons of the Writer's Union, and sympathies for Pasternak harbored by several powerful literary officials, led to a curious situation. Just when the possibility of the publication of Pasternak's translations was in doubt, it turned out that it might be possible to reprint his earlier poems. In one of his letters from this time, Pasternak states that he had never been a gambler but that life itself was placing him in that position. To mark the thirtieth anniversary of the October Revolution, the Moscow publishing house Sovetsky Pisatel was ordered to publish a series of exemplary works of Soviet literature. Pasternak's request that a collection of his poetry, *Izbrannoe* (Selected Poems), be included in this so-called Golden series was unexpectedly honored at a session of the board of the Writers' Union, and in February 1947 a contract was signed with the author.[8] The collection was indeed printed, but it remained at the publisher's for a long time and was finally banned in April 1948. Almost the entire press run of 25,000 copies was destroyed.

The campaign against Pasternak intensified. At a meeting in early March 1947, Fadeev once again referred to him as a poet who was "enshrined in individualism and purely formalist tricks." [9] It was soon to become clear that these words were a veiled warning of a full-fledged attack. On March 21 the newspaper *Kultura i zhizn* (Culture and Life), the organ of the Central Committee designed to harass the Soviet intelligentsia, ran an editorial by Alexei Surkov, "On the Poetry of B. Pasternak." The editorial was relatively mild compared with the majority of similar material in the Soviet press. But the very fact of its appearance seemed to be irrefutable proof of the poet's disfavor. It provoked a panic among Pasternak's friends. In order to calm them somewhat, the poet called them and jokingly said: "Have you seen what a public whipping I've been given? But it doesn't matter: I feel none the worse." [10] But he himself believed that the matter might end with his arrest. Recalling his cousin Alexander Freidenberg, who had disappeared in 1937, Pasternak wrote: "Of course I am prepared for anything. Why should it have happened to Sasha and everyone and not to me?" [11] He declined any attempts to defuse the situation. Clearly forestalling rumors about his possible repentance, on April 9 he wrote to his cousin Olga: "I still have written no complaints or entered into explanations with anyone. So far as I can tell I am still breathing." [12] This remark certainly alluded to Zoshchenko's personal appeal to Stalin (which, by the way, went unanswered). [13]

At the very height of these political storms, a new love entered the poet's life (he was now fifty-six). In October 1946 at the editorial offices of *New World,* he met a thirty-four-year-old employee named Olga Ivinskaia. Soon rumors of their romance were circulating widely throughout Moscow literary circles. On April 5 their affair started in earnest. [14] This situation was reminiscent of the "feast in the time of plague" that Pasternak had lived through in 1930–31. On December 22, 1946, he wrote to Nina Tabidze: "But why, why do I feel so well in this world, Ninochka? I am ready to weep—it is so startling and inexplicable." [15] In many respects Pasternak's wife and Olga Ivinskaia were exact opposites. Zinaida Nikolaevna was not much interested in her husband's literary concerns. In Olga the poet found not only a fervent admirer of his works, but a woman with literary ambitions: she herself wrote poetry. In education and cultural background she was altogether a product of Soviet system. For Pasternak she was a woman "from a different world." Her youth had been spent in the thirties, when the Soviet state had assumed its distinctly Stalinist features. Sometimes the very things in Soviet life that seemed to Pasternak so wild and repulsive were, for Olga's generation, the essence of Russia rather than peculiarities of the Stalinist epoch. Her great charm was combined with an inextinguishable joie de vivre, which never betrayed her even during the most trying times.

Just as during the period of *Second Birth,* Pasternak's new feelings placed him in an excruciating moral dilemma. Despite very strong vacillations, he never abandoned his family—Zinaida and their son Leonid. His everyday life was split between two households. In many ways the circle of his friends and acquaintances was divided along similar lines. Olga Ivinskaia visited the dacha in Peredelkino for the first time only after the poet's death. But all of his love lyrics and many lines from his translations of Petöfi and Goethe's *Faust* mirror the vicissitudes of his relationship with her. None of his previous love affairs could compare in length or the intensity of its expression in his work with this, the last romance of his life.

The attacks on Pasternak assumed new dimensions in the summer of 1947. At this time the Soviet propaganda machine concentrated on attacking the English and American media. Articles appeared one after another, denouncing western radio broadcasts intended for Soviet listeners, the newspaper *British Ally* (which was soon shut down), Oxford University, and Gleb Struve's book about Soviet literature published in London in 1947. It was in this context that Fadeev mentioned in his report of June 1947 to the Eleventh Plenum of the board of the Writers' Union Stefan Schimanski's old article in *Life and Letters Today* from 1943, in which Pasternak was set above the rest of Soviet literature. After a brief summary of its contents, Fadeev turned with a warning to "our representatives of the formalist-aesthete's school": "Beware of those who cling to you!" [16] It is notable that Fadeev cited Schimanski's article from a wartime journal but failed to mention a word about its expanded version in the collection of Pasternak's prose published in 1945. Such reticence testifies to the fact that the publication of this book abroad, and the estimation of Pasternak there as the best Russian poet since Pushkin, greatly embarrassed the literary authorities. Incidentally, in the winter of 1947 in London, in the same publishing house (and at Schimanski's initiative) another book by Pasternak was issued. This was his *Selected Poems* in J. M. Cohen's translation, which contained texts from his major poetry books of the twenties and the thirties. No other living Soviet poet was honored with the almost simultaneous publication abroad of two of his books. Neither of these publications was ever directly referred to in the Soviet press.

This "international" factor might explain the caution that Soviet authorities showed toward Pasternak, as well as their unwillingness to allow the printing of any of his new, original works. In April and May 1947 Pasternak, who had recently feared that he would be deprived of the means of earning a livelihood, was inundated with commissions for translations of world masterpieces—Goethe, Shakespeare, Petöfi. Such translations, published in enormous press runs, guaranteed the material well-being of their translators for several years ahead. Evidently the literary authorities reasoned that the more Pasternak was burdened with such commissions, the less time would remain for his own work, and the more rapidly his foreign admirers would forget about his original creations. By relegating Pasternak to the sphere of translation, the establishment took care that the poet's name would be inconspicuous and that his individual characteristics as a writer would not emerge. This is why, for example, the collection of lyrics by various authors translated by Pasternak, which was accepted by the publishers and even set in type, was banned at the last minute and destroyed in 1948, just as had happened with his *Selected Poems* in the Golden series.[17] The authorities remembered all too well the furor and excitement that had been caused in 1940 among readers when Pasternak's *Selected Translations* had appeared. For the same reason, not a single positive reference (even in passing) was made to Pasternak—even about his work as a translator—in any Soviet journal or newspaper from this time right up to Stalin's death. This is also why the officials always tried to prevent any direct contact between the poet and a major audience. Pasternak's last public recital of poetry (during Stalin's lifetime) was his participation in early February 1948 at a meeting called "For Peace and Democracy."[18]

One might well conclude that what the Soviet leaders always accused Pasternak of, that is, secluding himself in an ivory tower, was actually forced upon him by the government itself. But no matter how depressing the situation was, it did guarantee the poet a kind of immunity. Of course this immunity was never absolute: the translations especially dear to Pasternak—*Faust,* Shakespeare—were subjected to no less severe ideological control and spiteful faultfinding on the part of dull-witted censors and critics than were original works by Soviet authors. But the poet's main work, in which he intended to tell, in the purest and most complete form, the story of his generation, became possible in part because of the position to which he was consigned during the Zhdanov period. The first four chapters of *Doctor Zhivago* were completed by the summer of 1948. A contract to publish the novel was concluded in 1947 with the editor of *New World,* Konstantin Simonov. But after the banning of Pasternak's two books that had already been printed, there was no hope of its publication in the near future. As soon as the manuscript was typed in October 1948, the author began to circulate it widely among friends and acquaintances, not hesitating to send it to those who were in exile and therefore under police surveillance.

Toward the beginning of 1949, the literary and social climate in the country deteriorated even further. New critical attacks were addressed even against influential Soviet writers with irreproachable reputations: Tvardovsky, Simonov, and Fadeev. But the main thrust was directed against the influence of foreign bourgeois culture and "rootless cosmopolitans," and the struggle had begun to take on openly antisemitic overtones. In the official report read by the poet Mikhail Lukonin at the Writers' Union, Pasternak's name was mentioned in this sinister context. Lukonin's words left no doubt that the authorities had been particularly irritated by the recent publication of Pasternak's books in England. Noting with pleasure that Pasternak "had never been known to our people," Lukonin added: "Pasternak valued and appreciated only his recognition from foreign degenerates. He has always been selected by our enemies to be counterposed to us. He has spent his entire life in our poetry as a swine beneath an oak tree." [19] Once again wave after wave of arrests swept the land. In 1949 Pasternak learned about the rearrest of two people who had already gone through the horrors of the Ezhov purge and who had spent several years in the camps: Akhmatova's son, Lev Gumilyov, and Tsvetaeva's daughter, Ariadna Efron.

In the late autumn of 1949 the secret police arrested Olga Ivinskaia. [20] The investigation lasted for more than six months. According to Ivinskaia, the omnipotent state security minister, Viktor Abakumov (who was himself arrested in 1951 and shot in 1954), attended one of the interrogations. Many questions concerned Pasternak and her ties with him. "I can't believe that a Russian woman like you could ever really be in love with this old Jew—there must be some ulterior motive here!", the investigator told her. [21] He also declared that Pasternak was an English spy and that she was planning to flee abroad with him. The fact that the poet's parents lived in Oxford, that two of his books had appeared in England, that he himself had visited London on his return trip from Paris in July 1935, and finally that he had met several times in Peredelkino and Moscow with members of the British embassy—all served as undeniable proof of this story. The investigator was also curious about Pasternak's new novel. Although the first part had already been circulating rather widely, they were seeking from Ivinskaia information about the chapters in progress.

In prison Ivinskaia was apparently not subjected to the harsh physical tortures and beatings so common during the investigation period. Perhaps this can be explained by the fact that the reason for her arrest may not have been political. Some memoirists claim that her arrest was connected with an investigation into embezzlement at the editorial offices of the journal *Ogonek*.[22] Ivinskaia herself claimed that her closeness to Pasternak saved her from all the inhuman techniques at the disposal of the investigators. She was charged with anti-Soviet political activities and was given (without trial) a relatively mild punishment: five years in the camps, which she herself called in her memoirs "an act of mercy rather than a punishment."[23] As for Pasternak, he later believed that Ivinskaia's fortitude during the investigation saved him from arrest.

But there was another factor determining the line of the authorities in the "Pasternak affair." Besides his two London books, and the reissue in the United States (in 1949) of the British edition of the early prose works, Pasternak was nominated by a group of English intellectuals for the Nobel Prize. Rumors about this nomination reached Moscow by the fall of 1947, and Pasternak himself immediately learned of them.[24] Prior to World War II, no Soviet author had ever been considered for such an honor. At the beginning of the twenties, when Gorky lived outside Russia, he had been a candidate for the Nobel Prize, but it had finally been awarded to his rival, the émigré writer Ivan Bunin.[25] In the mid-forties, Swedish left-wing writers began to propose Mikhail Sholokhov, Stalin's favorite, for the Nobel Prize, and in 1946 he became an official candidate. Unable to conceal its (somewhat premature) pride, the *Literary Gazette* published a jubilant note about his nomination.[26] The fact that Boris Pasternak also began to figure on the list of those nominated for the world's most prestigious literary prize created a complicated situation. It should have (given the increasingly apparent antipathy toward him on the part of the Soviet authorities) led to ominous repressions. But the Soviet officials wanted to avoid making Pasternak a martyr in the west (as had been done with the German antifascist writer Karl von Ossietzky, who had been awarded the Nobel Peace Prize in 1936 while imprisoned in one of Hitler's concentration camps). In addition, they did not want to spoil the chances of their official favorite, Sholokhov. Indirect sanctions against Pasternak—striking a person close to him—seemed to be a much more effective means of paralyzing his literary creativity and erasing him from the memory of his readers.

The news of Ivinskaia's arrest was particularly shocking for Pasternak because he had been expecting his own arrest for over six months,[27] and because he and Olga had broken off their relations since the summer. But if the authorities had hoped her arrest would silence Pasternak, they were mistaken. Plagued about the fate of Ivin-

skaia in prison, completely uncertain about how these events would
reflect on his own situation and the life of his family, Pasternak returned to his work with redoubled energy. In the wake of Olga's arrest, he wrote the poems on Gospel themes, "Durnye dni" (Evil
Days), "Magdalina" (Magdalene), and "Gefsimansky sad" (The Garden of Gethsemane) and, proceeded, after a long interval, to write the
second part of *Doctor Zhivago*. The words of one of its heroes, Evgraf—"And remember: you must never, under any circumstances, despair. To hope and to act, these are our duties in misfortune. To do
nothing and to despair is to neglect our duty" [28]—reflect the moods
of the author himself during these gloomy days.

Just as the writing of the first part of the novel alternated with his
work on translating the first part of Goethe's *Faust,* the continuation
of *Doctor Zhivago* coincided with the translation of the second part
of *Faust*. In Pasternak's poetic biography, *Faust* played just as fundamental a role as *Hamlet*. In both cases Pasternak embarked on his
translation after constantly rereading the original over several decades. In both cases the translation was mysteriously intertwined with
his own life and thoughts. In January 1950 he wrote to Elena Orlovskaia (who was in internal exile in Central Asia): "I translated the
first part of *Faust* so quickly and so easily because at that time everything in my life was happening just as in *Faust;* I translated it with
the 'blood of my heart' and greatly feared for this new blood lest the
last scene be repeated . . . This happened in the autumn. That is what
torments and depresses me." Therefore in *Faust,* just as in *Hamlet,*
we find phrases and words that strikingly point to Pasternak's self-
consciousness during this period. But he bluntly rejected any view of
the translation that would make of it a secretly coded autobiographical testimony. "This is nevertheless a conscientious translation, and
not an excuse for self-expression," he said. "But we hardly are able
to realize how deeply *Faust* has penetrated into our [Russian] consciousness, how it exerts such an influence to this day and how many
writers draw upon it in their works." [29] From the very beginning of
this work in 1948, Pasternak was astounded at how easily *Faust*
yielded to transposition into Russian verse. It was almost as if Russian
prosody had been created specially for this task.

    Pasternak's debut in literature had coincided with the tumultuous
rise of a Goethe cult in Russia. All the leading figures of Russian symbolism—Balmont, Merezhkovsky, Viacheslav Ivanov, Blok, Briusov,

Biely—not only paid their due to Goethe but saw him as their direct predecessor (to a greater degree than, for example, Shakespeare). Only Pushkin and Dante shared with him the role of progenitor of modernism.[30] He had occupied an especially important place in the aesthetic discussions of the Musagetes circle. Thus from his earliest days Pasternak was exposed to Goethe's influence. Reminiscences from Goethe surface in Pasternak's early lyrics. But with the exception of his not very successful attempt to translate *Geheimnisse* in 1921 and the unrealized idea of collaboration with Tsvetaeva in translating *Faust* in 1924–25 (that is, when he also contemplated translating *Hamlet*), Pasternak did not turn to translations of Goethe until the end of the forties. It is worth noting that he conceived of both his unfinished play from the wartime period and the novel he began in 1946 as attempts to create a "Russian Faust."

Among the complete translations of *Faust* in the Russian language were the works of such major poets as Afanasy Fet and Valery Briusov. Nevertheless, during the thirties and forties, it was often said that the time was ripe for a new interpretation of Goethe's masterpiece, based on the new Soviet world view. It was precisely this that the authorities wanted from Pasternak. In Soviet literature there was no one else with the skill and cultural background to undertake such an immense job: Goethe's work combined lyrical and dramatic elements with philosophical and religious meditations. When the first part of *Faust* in Pasternak's translation appeared in 1950, it immediately became clear that a chasm separated the poet from his literary surroundings. In a review printed in *New World* in August 1950, Tamara Motylyova concluded that "the task of creating the so eagerly desired Soviet translation of *Faust* remains unfulfilled." Although the reviewer acknowledged Pasternak's painstaking efforts, she accused him of tendentiousness in his interpretation of the original and of allowing his reading to cut across the Soviet conception of Goethe's oeuvre. According to her, Pasternak neglected the materialist, "progressive" side of Goethe's outlook, and exaggerated the mystical elements of the original. The new book was declared to be an attempt to sneak into Soviet literature the reactionary conception of "l'art pour l'art."

It cannot be said that Motylyova's claims were totally unfounded. As we already know, the main principle for Pasternak as a translator was not scholarly scrupulousness with regard to the texts. Instead he created a kind of dialogue that entailed the freedom of the translator to interpret them. He believed that it was precisely the magical and incantatory power of the word that had prompted Goethe to create *Faust*. He was also fascinated by Goethe's motif of transformations. In 1956 Pasternak wrote: "*Faust* is a magician who invokes fates, elemental forces, and spirits of past and future by means of Lyric." [31] These qualities of the original text merged in his mind with the events of his own life. Whereas the entire Margarethe story acquired strong resonance for him as a result of Ivinskaia's arrest, the completion of the second part proceeded in expectation of her release from prison. In June and July of 1953 he reworked a considerable portion of the text in galley proofs. He wrote: "Such absorption in what I have been doing and in what is happening to me, I have experienced only once before: during the period of *My Sister, Life*. This has been a recurrence of the same creative bliss." [32] An analogous conception of the magical power of art and the poetic text lay at the foundation of Pasternak's work on *Doctor Zhivago*.

The novel was written over a span of ten years: from summer 1946 to December 1955. No other work absorbed so much of Pasternak's time and effort, not even *Liuvers' Childhood,* which he had dreamed of continuing during the twenties and thirties. During this decade Pasternak experienced flights of inspiration and sharp declines, a new and powerful love affair, the loss of friends and acquaintances, humiliating disgrace, and the daily threat of arrest. The very determination to write a novel, after innumerable fruitless attempts in the past, came as a result of the profound crisis evoked by the war and the subsequent crushing of his illusions about Russia's renewal. It was prompted by the need to correct his image in the west and to justify the interest shown there toward him as an artist: neither the translations of his early verse nor the old prose met this goal. Later, in a series of interviews given at the end of the fifties, he stressed precisely this point: his feeling of responsibility to the western reader. Although in *Doctor Zhivago* he borrowed certain situations and the names of some characters and places from his earlier, unfinished works ("Patrick's Notes" and the play written during the war), the protagonist, with his strange name and unusual character, the majority of the secondary heroes, and the underlying general outlook emerged only toward the end of the 1940s. The conception of the novel was influenced, in particular, by the ideas of the English "personalists," which united the young literary followers of Herbert Read. This was the same circle in which Pasternak's fervent admirer, Stefan Schimanski, played a prominent role. Cut off from the cultural life of the west during the thirties, Pasternak perhaps exaggerated the significance of this group and its influence on postwar European philosophy. But in the four issues of *Transformation* published by this circle, he found a surprising correspondence with the ideas that were occupying him now. He was attracted by the assertions of the contributors that their "philosophy is the Philosophy of Living," by their emphasis on the freedom of man and their consistent critique of fascism and communism, by their call for "the politics of the unpolitical," whose source they saw in the Sermon on the Mount,[33] and most of all by their emphasis on the special role of Christianity in the contemporary epoch. These ideas came out in articles by Read, Schimanski, Paul Bloomfield, and Nikolai Berdiaev.[34] All was in accord with Boris Pasternak's new train of thought in the late 1940s and obviously influenced his conception of Christianity.

Its first symptoms appear in Pasternak's works no earlier than the second half of 1946. This is evident from the fact that the preliminary version of the poem "Gamlet" (Hamlet), written in February 1946, consisted of only two stanzas, did not yet involve the parallel between Hamlet and Jesus Christ, and contained no allusion to the Gospel of Mark (14:36). The parallel appears only in the subsequent version, which was composed at the end of 1946 and was twice the size of the former. The new version had a more profound sense of the poet's loneliness, sacrifice, and special mission in life. The poem "Hamlet," in this new version, was later placed by Pasternak at the beginning of the cycle of "poems of Doctor Zhivago" which forms the last chapter of the novel. A third of these poems are devoted to the passion of Christ. Pasternak was reviving a poetic tradition that had been extremely popular before the revolution, but had disappeared without a trace during the Soviet period. In the winter of 1946–47 he wrote the first two poems on Gospel motifs: "Rozhdestvenskaia zvezda" (The Christmas Star) and "Chudo" (Miracle). From this time on, Pasternak attended services frequently (especially offices for the dead) in Russian Orthodox churches in Moscow and Peredelkino. He also read liturgical texts and copied out excerpts from them. The theme of immortality, an old obsession, came to be colored now with New Testament associations.

What can explain Pasternak's sudden turn toward religion? At the beginning of the forties, the role of the Russian Orthodox Church in the Soviet Union changed dramatically. This shift occurred after two decades of harsh persecution and attempts to eradicate religion. Thousands of churches were closed throughout the country, and clergymen were shot or sent to prisons and camps. The change in the status of the church in Soviet Russia was decisively affected by the war with Germany. In wide regions occupied by Nazi troops, the German administration, for tactical reasons, adopted a tolerant attitude, and many churches that had been closed by the Bolsheviks were opened again, attracting crowds of believers. In the apocalyptic conditions of the war, the religious feelings of the Russian people resurfaced not only in the occupied territories but also in the regions under Soviet control. At the same time, the rapprochement with the western democratic states made the Soviet government more vulnerable to accusations of persecuting religion,[35] and the authorities made concessions that would have been inconceivable before. These aimed at creating the impression of harmony between the state, the church, and the people. Official propaganda appropriated two traditional theses of Russian orthodoxy: the eternal hatred of the German nation for the Slavic peoples and the messianic role to be played by Moscow and Russia. The revolutionary messianism of the Bolsheviks now acquired transparently nationalistic and even religious overtones.

Starting in 1943, what was then called the "religious spring" began in the Soviet Union. On September 4 Stalin gave an audience in the Kremlin to three metropolitans of the Russian Orthodox Church, and on September 8 bells were rung to announce the election of the Patriarch of All Russia.[36] Contemporary observers noted with surprise that, despite the long period of unprecedentedly cruel atheistic rule, and despite the mass repressions of believers and the destruction of churches, religious feelings were still deeply rooted in the people. Pasternak's optimistic hopes and presentiments that, after the war, Soviet life would become more humane stemmed partly from these observations. His feelings were manifested themselves in his poem "Ozhivshaia freska" (The Enlivened Fresco, 1944), which was called "Voskresenie" (Resurrection) in the rough drafts and mentioned St. George's battle with the dragon.[37] Pasternak was by no means the only one to conceive of the struggle between the Red Army and the Nazis in terms of this Christian legend: it became a popular motif in Soviet literature during the war. In 1945 the head of the Writers' Union, Nikolai Tikhonov, showed his distress over this by saying in an official report: "There is one more strange thing in our literature, something which calls for special attention. Religious symbolism appears in prose and in poetry in the most unexpected ways. God with a capital letter, saints and apostles, prayers and requiems have come to life in the most inappropriate way. Religious symbolism appears in the works of writers who would not have even given it the slightest attention prior to the war." [38]

But the decisive reason for Pasternak's about-face with regard to the Russian church came from postwar developments, in the second half of 1946. The totalitarian essence of the Soviet state, which became increasingly obvious during the vilification of Zoshchenko and Akhmatova, also affected the status of the church. Although formally all the institutions reestablished in 1943 continued to exist after the war, a quiet, behind-the-scenes closing of churches began throughout the country. This was accomplished without atheistic propaganda campaigns. Nationalist overtones in the doctrine of the "Soviet people" were given greater emphasis, but Christian trappings were no longer needed.

When, back in the late thirties, the notion of the people began to drive the doctrine of class struggle from official propaganda, Pasternak's initial reaction was positive: evidence of this appears in his remarks about the Stalin constitution for *Izvestia,* and in one of his poems of the period, which contains a few panegyric lines about the people. [39] But the Ezhov terror and the fact that Hitler's Germany, no less than Stalin's state, rested upon the concept of the people compelled the poet to reconsider his attitude. Both tyrants, Stalin and Hitler, with equal cynicism used the concept of the people to justify their bloodiest crimes. So the concept of the people as the ultimate moral authority soon lost its significance for Pasternak and indeed lost any positive meaning whatsoever. The poet now stressed another concept, that of the individual and "genius." Genius represented for him the quintessence of human nature, common to all people. The genius differed from the common man only in one respect, in his freedom and independence.

In 1951, when Simon Chikovani began to come under sharp attack and was eventually removed from the leadership of the Georgian Writers' Union, Pasternak wrote to him: "The Gospel dictum to offer the left cheek in addition to the right is not a holy miracle or the epitome of heroic conduct, but the only practical escape from the situation when outward appearance passes judgment on reality." [40] The meaning of the Gospels was never confined for Pasternak to nonresistance to evil; on the contrary, an interpretation of Christ as an active fighter, triumphant and judging his time, prevails in Zhivago's poems.[41] But what is striking in the words the poet directed to his Georgian friend is the firm conviction that the truths of the Scriptures have a meaning that is not abstract, allegorical, or literary, but an immediate and literal prescription for living.

The facts of Pasternak's life force us to conclude that the only *practical* escape from the situation that had been developing since 1946 was Christianity. The decision the poet made was conscious and free but, then again, he had no real alternative. In his sharp turn to the Gospels and to the rituals of the Orthodox church we can see Pasternak's eternal proclivity to opposition or, to put it better, to legal opposition. Yet here legality for him was less important than opposition; it is no accident that Pasternak drew close to the church precisely when the regime's unfavorable attitude toward it was becoming more and more pronounced.

Very early on, in the beginning of the thirties, Pasternak sensed an internal kinship between two historical phenomena, communism and fascism, which many of his contemporaries perceived to be antithetical. He saw the basis of this kinship in the analogous attitude of both regimes to religion: their contempt for its age-old moral principles. Following Tolstoy, he might have repeated that "man's cruelty to man in our epoch results from the absence of religion." According to Alexander Gladkov, in February 1942, before the onset of the religious spring, Pasternak called Stalin "a giant of the pre-Christian era of human history." [42] The conception of Christianity elaborated in *Doctor Zhivago* developed in response to political events in the Soviet Union. The sudden "rehabilitation" of the church in the USSR during the war years aroused the hope that there would be no return to the cruelty of the past. But the clearer it became after the war that the Stalinist government was returning to its old ways, the more important it became for Pasternak to break personally from the ethical norms being imposed. The moral values cherished by the church formed in this sense the sole alternative to the oppressive political atmosphere. In these circumstances, the poet found Christianity's universal nature, its transcendence of government and politics, particularly attractive. The differences between Eastern Orthodoxy and Catholicism were irrelevant to him, as were the various shades or sects inside the Russian religious movement. Such details were of no interest at all in the broad historical doctrine expounded in *Doctor Zhivago*.

The degree of Pasternak's closeness to the Russian Orthodox Church should not be exaggerated. Although he loved to attend church services, the poet was never baptized.[43] He was fully aware of how nondogmatic and noncanonical his religious perceptions were. His attitude was colored by memories of the free religious and philosophical discussions during the years of his literary debut. This is why, at the end of the forties, he once again turned his thoughts to Dmitry Samarin—a model of the undogmatic and unofficial treatment of religious and clerical questions in youthful circles during the first two decades of the twentieth century. Now these circles, and not the literary and artistic groups such as Musagetes and Centrifuge, seemed to Pasternak to have been the most important feature of Russian culture in the prerevolutionary epoch, and its ultimate historical justification. He borrowed the names of his heroes in *Doctor Zhivago* from precisely these quarters of Moscow's intelligentsia of that time (Sventitsky, Komarovsky, Gordon). The poet's deliberately unorthodox stance in questions of Christian religion can be seen primarily in the fact that the most important statements on this theme in the novel were assigned to two heroes—the defrocked priest, Vedeniapin, and the Jew, Mikhail Gordon, whose relationship to the church was, in one way or another, problematic.

Having made Gordon one of the main spokesman for a discussion of Christianity, the author linked this theme to another: Jewry and antisemitism in Russia. Gordon expresses Pasternak's inner thoughts no less than Vedeniapin, and in the opening chapters he bears distinctly autobiographical traits. It is he who makes the declaration about the need to renounce national identity and ethnic exclusiveness, to become assimilated into universal Christianity. Pasternak made this coincide with the scene containing a cossack's mockery of a Jewish elder in the front-line zone. There is no doubt that this episode in the novel was related not only to events in World War I but obliquely— in the purely Pasternakian way—to more recent developments never directly mentioned in *Doctor Zhivago;* the Holocaust, on the one hand, and to the wave of antisemitism in the Soviet Union, which spread immediately after the war (particularly in the territories liberated from the Nazis) and which received unspoken encouragement from the authorities.[44]

As we have seen, the Jewish question had begun to worry the poet at the end of the 1920s, when he confided in a letter to Gorky his feelings of alienation from Soviet society. This confession was not a response to any display of antisemitism toward Pasternak personally, but rather a reaction to the predominance of Jews in the state and party apparatus during the early postrevolutionary years. From now on, the Jewish question inevitably surfaced in indissoluble connection with his reflections on the revolution. Thus the main hero of *A Tale* in 1929 (and of Pasternak's verse novel written in the twenties), Spektorsky, is declared to be half-Jewish. This remark is introduced as a reaction to an antisemitic comment by the heroine, Anna Arild, with whom he falls in love. The same contrast appears in embryonic form in the fragments of the novel written in the late 1930s. There, on the one hand, is the image of the ignorant porter who, in accordance with widespread antisemitic views, proclaims the revolutionary ferment as a conspiracy between Jews and Freemasons, and on the other hand there is the passing remark that Patrick is the grandson of a cantonist. Although it was by no means necessary to be a Jew in order to become a cantonist, nevertheless in this genealogy there is more similarity to be found with Spektorsky than with Zhivago.[45]

It was only in *Doctor Zhivago* that Pasternak spoke out directly on the Jewish question. Highly characteristic is the context in which Pasternak mentions this theme in a letter written to his cousin in October 1946: "For the time being I call the novel *Boys and Girls*. In it I will square accounts with Judaism, with all forms of nationalism (including that which assumes the guise of internationalism), with all shades of anti-Christianity and its assumption that there are certain peoples surviving the fall of the Roman Empire from whose undeveloped national essence a new civilization could be evolved."[46] These words leave no doubt that his statements about Jewry were a reaction to political events: the phrase in parentheses about internationalism is a sarcastic allusion to the Soviet regime, which after Zhdanov's speeches had taken the road of unrestrained xenophobia and isolationism, condemning as "cosmopolitanism" any sign of admiration for western culture. In these days the Russian émigré philosopher Nikolai Berdiaev expressed his concern about the dangers of the nationalism, adding that this threat was "a betrayal of Russian universalism and of the Russian mission in the world."[47]

Pasternak's statements on Jewry in *Doctor Zhivago* aroused stormy debates in the west after the novel's publication. Predictably, sharp indignation was provoked in Israel—in a state whose founders came from essentially the same circles of Russian intellectuals to which Pasternak belonged. In the eyes of many of his opponents and even some of his admirers, his call for assimilation into Christianity and for the renunciation of ethnic identity seemed to indicate political and moral capitulation. From 1949 to 1953, when Pasternak was still working on his novel, the anti-Jewish policies of the Soviet state began to take on extreme forms. The liquidation of Jewish schools, newspapers, and theaters, the murder of the director Solomon Mikhoels, the disbanding of the Jewish Anti-Fascist Committee, the arrest of almost all writers who wrote in the Yiddish language, the unprecedented antisemitic and anti-Zionist campaign in the press, and finally, the "Doctors' Plot,"[48] which was to have been followed by pogroms and mass deportations of Soviet Jews to Siberia—all these facts cast a suspicious light on the solutions advanced by the heroes of *Doctor Zhivago* and on the intentions of its author. But an examination of the chronology of the novel's composition will render such reproaches meaningless: the first volume of the novel, which contains most of the passages about Jews and Christianity, was completed by the summer of 1948, before the xenophobic campaign had acquired its brazenly antisemitic connotations and when, in the sphere of international politics, it appeared that the idea of a Zionist state enjoyed Soviet support. Thus the proposed solutions in *Doctor Zhivago* in many respects ran counter to the official political line. What should be surprising, then, is not the poet's response to Soviet antisemitism in 1949–1953, but the fact that even these events could not force him to rewrite his novel.

No matter how paradoxical it may seem, the reason behind this obstinacy can be found in the character of the campaign by the Soviet regime against the Jews: its foundations were based on Stalin's conviction that the Jews were not a nationality (or people). The author of *Doctor Zhivago* responded not by proving the direct opposite, but by denying the validity and the metaphysical justification for the concept of nationality (*Volkstum*). This undermined the very ground on which Soviet doctrine rested, the "Soviet people." Here we can see a fundamental feature of Pasternak's position that had surfaced many times before: the area in which his point of view coincides with the official line is commingled with the area of uncompromising opposition to it. But the strongest pronouncement against the rise of spontaneous antisemitism is made by Gordon, as he addresses the Jews: "You are the first and best Christians in the world." These words take on a particularly personal meaning in view of the fact that Pasternak himself had just turned to Christianity.[49] It is clear that in the situation of Soviet Russia at the end of the forties and the beginning of the fifties, Pasternak considered the Gospel commandments to be just as much the only practical escape for the Russian Jews as they were for the poet himself. If assimilation was inevitable, then assimilation to Christianity was obviously better than assimilation to Soviet communism.

But the full complexity of Pasternak's novel might slip from view if we give too much credence to these declarations. No matter how close they might be to what the poet was thinking in 1946–1953, they lose the appearance of finality inasmuch as they are expressed in a novel. The arguments of the heroes on the Jewish question are played with "polyphonically" and are tested in the narrative by the episodes that immediately precede or follow them. Thus Gordon's words, when set against the episode where the cossack scoffs at the Jewish elder, lose the element of unconditional conviction that they may have for Gordon himself. In a similar way, the illusion of absolute truth in Lara's tirades about Jews is shattered insofar as they are followed by an internal monologue by the antisemite Galuzina which sheds light on a different aspect of the same question. It is notable that Zhivago himself—the hero who comes closest to the author[50]—never voices his own views on this theme; he only listens to the comments made to him and never answers them. There are no authorial solutions, however authoritative those suggested by Pasternak's protagonists seem to be.

There is still another noteworthy point. In themselves, apart from their content, the arguments of Pasternak's heroes about the Gospels, Christianity, and the Jews touch on themes that were taboo in Soviet literature of the period. The author's intellectual audacity is demonstrated by the very fact that he deals with forbidden topics. Even more unacceptable was the fact that these theoretical debates were consistently introduced by the author in an ideologically ambiguous and pluralistic context. *Doctor Zhivago* is not a philosophical treatise or a political pamphlet. It is a work of art, and as with all genuine works of art there are no final truths in it; the various points of view and theoretical systems are part of the formal composition. Yet in no other work after *Safe Conduct* did Pasternak include so many intimate thoughts and ideas as in this novel. They took unexpected twists and turns for the author himself. For this reason Pasternak obstinately refused to answer questions about his philosophical positions: "my philosophy itself, as a whole, is in general rather an *inclination* than a conviction."[51] As an artist he could not help knowing the veracity of contradictory statements and the incomplete truth of each of them taken separately. Even the Christian theme, which was particularly dear to the author, is not presented directly, but through the prism of various characters. Perhaps his Christian philosophy is therefore best of all expressed not in the prose narrative but in the twenty-five poems comprising the last chapter. Lyrical poetry is by its essence far more monologic than the novel. Even in these poems on the Christian theme, however, one feels that Pasternak avoids a straightforward expression of his own point of view. It is no accident that their authorship is ascribed to the protagonist Yury Zhivago. In their basic artistic qualities, they differ sharply from the rest of Pasternak's lyrical poetry: the trace of "naive and archaic" elements reveals a tendency toward stylization and "masking," quite uncharacteristic of Pasternak. They evoke memories of medieval icons or of Dutch painting of the fifteenth and sixteenth centuries. Such an obliteration of the self in texts that so powerfully express the innermost thoughts of their author originated from the lessons Pasternak gleaned from Pushkin and Chekhov. He followed these writers in his renunciation of general theories and in his persistent questioning of established truths and concepts.

Pasternak had shown a similar degree of ambiguity of authorial statement only in *Safe Conduct*. The connection between that early book and *Doctor Zhivago* is much stronger than it might seem (especially since, in style, they appear to be diametrically opposed). For instance, the ambivalent interpretation of the revolution in the novel, with its tragically unresolved contradictions, is undoubtedly rooted in Pasternak's works of the twenties, particularly in *Safe Conduct*. Pasternak's two main works are also united by the sensation of the magic and safeguarding function of art as a whole, and of the given work in progress. It is surely deliberate that the death of his hero in the novel was timed to coincide with the publication of the first part of *Safe Conduct*, in August 1929. In essence, the novel is in many respects a replay, in the new language of the forties, of the problems raised in the writing of *Safe Conduct*. In this context we must note the author's choice of profession for his hero. By making him a physician, Pasternak echoes the theme of "disease" that permeated his earlier works, as in his poem "Lofty Malady." It originated in his feeling of the relationship between medicine and literature and from a conception of the curative function of art.[52] But a second, poetic, hypostasis of Zhivago was also inseparably linked to the author's thoughts during the period of *Safe Conduct:* Pasternak was seriously weighing the possibility of abandoning literature. Therefore the protagonist of *Spektorsky* and *A Tale* was portrayed as being on the borderline between writing professionally and not belonging to the ranks of professional authors. *Doctor Zhivago* was composed during the years when its author had been excluded from literature, and, as he confessed to one of his friends, he had lost interest in whether this had been done justly or not.[53] During the course of the novel, the hero has virtually no contact with other writers, and although he is dominated by literary interests and leaves remarkable lyrical masterpieces after his death, he displays rare indifference to the concerns of his fellow literati. Yet his mystical ties with the fate of literature in Russia are expressed not only in his ruminations about art and in his posthumous notebook filled with poetry, but in another, seemingly insignificant detail: his last living quarters in Moscow, found for him by Evgraf. The room in which Zhivago spends the last months of his life and in which his coffin is placed after his death is located in a house on Kamergersky Lane, a small street in the center of Moscow, closely associated with the history of the Trubetskoy and Samarin families.[54] This street is the site of the Moscow Art Theater, which Pasternak visited every other day (after Meyerhold's disappearance) to attend the rehearsals of his *Hamlet*. Across from the theater an apartment building was erected in 1930, inhabited by many of Pasternak's fellow writers, friends, and acquaintances (including Aseev). Mayakovsky was supposed to move there as well, before his suicide. The death of Zhivago is thus symbolically intertwined with the theme of the death of literature in Soviet Russia and with the literary biography of Pasternak himself. It is also remarkable that the death of this character resembles suicide to a certain extent.[55] This theme once again establishes a link to *Safe Conduct,* which introduces the idea of the indistinguishability of death and suicide in the life of the poet.

The deeply autobiographical nature of *Doctor Zhivago* is also shown by the fact that the protagonist dies of a heart attack on his way to a new place of work, the Botkin Hospital. One can see in this detail a deliberately inexact reflection of real events in Pasternak's life. The author endows his hero with the same illness he suffered in the fall of 1952. Through the efforts of his friends (Vsevolod Ivanov, Konstantin Fedin), he was sent to the Kremlin Section of the same Botkin Hospital that Zhivago fails to reach. Pasternak spent approximately three months there and was sent home for recuperation in the middle of January. During this illness Pasternak felt that he was on the verge of dying and was prepared to accept it. He told Anna Akhmatova, who visited him in the hospital in December, why he no longer feared death.[56] His mood in those days is reflected in a number of letters and in the poem, "V bolnitse" (In the Hospital), which deals with the themes of death overcome, the happiness of existence, and thankfulness to God for making the author an artist. In the episode of Zhivago's death, the autobiographical nature of the novel has a dual character: the author has not only placed his hero perilously close to himself, but he tries to free himself from the predetermined fate of his hero.

This episode underscores yet another aspect of the relationship between Pasternak's life and his works. The Swedish scholar Per Arne Bodin stresses the difference between the character of Zhivago as he is shown in his everyday life and his character as depicted in the poems of the last chapter. In them Yury Andreevich becomes more active than he was in life, grows in strength, and, as it were, is raised from the dead. A similar relationship between outward passivity in daily life versus the inner activity of creative self-expression is deeply characteristic of the novel's author, Boris Pasternak, throughout his life. Naturally the notion of literary creativity was joined in his mind with the notion of the miraculous transformation of life by means of the word's magical power. It is precisely this conception that unites his work on the novel and his work on *Faust*.[57]

After he left the hospital, Pasternak spent two months with his wife in a sanatorium in Bolshevo. This was the same sanitorium in which he had suffered an acute moral and psychological crisis in the summer of 1935. On March 3, 1953, two days before the announcement of Stalin's death, he contrasted the two situations in a letter to his friend Valentin Asmus. In 1935 the publishers had been eager to print anything he wrote, and he was at the zenith of the Soviet literary hierarchy; despite all this, he had been in torment. He did not understand what was happening to him, and he vainly looked for answers to the doubts plaguing him. This time he was suffering from a life-threatening disorder. He had been in disfavor for many years and was writing a novel that nobody needed and that had no chance of publication. Yet he was experiencing a feeling of freedom and independence, which inspired a creative outburst and filled him with courage and energy.[58]

In the sanatorium Pasternak learned of Stalin's death. Changes in the life of the country became noticeable almost immediately. On April 4 the newspapers ran an announcement about the suspension of the investigation into the Doctors' Plot, which in January 1953 had heralded a grotesque period in Soviet history. This statement, accompanied by a public acknowledgment of "violations of socialist legality," served as a signal that the new leadership was about to embark on anti-Stalinist policies. A few days earlier, on March 27, the first amnesty for prisoners had been declared. Ivinskaia came under the aegis of this decree. Although Pasternak felt that, after three and a half years of separation, his relationship with Olga could not be resumed, he anxiously awaited her release from prison. Throughout 1953 he hoped for Titsian Tabidze's return; rumors about his liberation became especially persistent in December. During these days Pasternak wrote to his cousin his joy that "the daily and indiscriminate disappearance of names and people has stopped, the fate of the survivors has improved, and some have returned."[59]

In the spring of 1954 the general relaxation in literary life revealed itself in Pasternak's changed status. The blockade around him was lifted. Public recitals became possible once again. In April at the Writers' Union a discussion of the translation of *Faust* was held, and Pasternak's work was hailed by those in attendance. The *Banner* printed a selection of ten of his poems, the first appearance in print by Pasternak the poet for ten years (since the publication in 1945 of *Earthly Expanse*). The poet was particularly pleased by the title given to this selection in the journal, "Poems from the novel *Doctor Zhivago*": this was the first public announcement of Pasternak's new work.[60] In a short preamble, the author gave a brief description of the novel as a whole and of its protagonist. Several of the poems chosen had already been written by the fall of 1946 and the majority in the fall of 1953, although "Svidanie" (Meeting) had been written in November–December 1949 in response to Ivinskaia's arrest. Their "simplicity" displayed something that had not been seen in Pasternak's poems from the war period: a new intimacy and sincerity. Olga Freidenberg, who knew the poet's literary career very well, was astounded by the paradox that, despite his new poetics and an absolutely different style, the latest poems resembled the poet's "youthful beginnings," *A Twin in the Clouds*.[61]

In the spring of 1954 Pasternak's *Hamlet* was performed for the first time. The production was staged at Leningrad's Pushkin Theater by the film director Grigory Kozintsev, an old admirer of Pasternak's lyrical poetry. Kozintsev (who was Ilya Ehrenburg's brother-in-law) was one of the last representatives of avant-garde traditions in Soviet theater. The sets were created by another famous avant-gardist, Natan Altman, and the music was written by Dmitry Shostakovich. The play was therefore one of the strongest manifestations of the thaw under way in Soviet life. The director consciously attempted to play up the work's openly antityrannical connotations. Instead of the final scene with Fortinbras, he decided to end the play with Shakespeare's 74th sonnet—"But be contented: when that fell arrest"—and he commissioned the poet to make a special translation for the occasion. Although the performance fulfilled one of Pasternak's cherished dreams, he was unable to travel to Leningrad because he was swamped with work on his novel. News about the play came to him from stories told by Moscow acquaintances who attended the premiere and in a letter from Olga Freidenberg. Pasternak was also asked to rework his translation of *Faust* for a theatrical production by the Moscow director Nikolai Okhlopkov, but his project never materialized.[62]

Despite the new thaw, Pasternak was skeptical about the readiness of the authorities to embark on far-reaching reforms. He was struck by the disproportion between "the gigantic changes which have taken place around the globe and in our life during this period" and, on the other hand, "the stupid attempts of our leaders to pretend that nothing special has changed."[63] His skepticism was partially based on the circumstances of literary life. The first harbingers of freethinking by writers and literary critics—the bold articles in *New World,* the first part of the Ehrenburg's novella *Thaw,* the attempt by Tvardovsky to print his satirical poem "Tyorkin in the Other World"—encountered sharp reprimands from conservative literary figures who still enjoyed the support of high party officials. Beginning in May, articles began to appear attacking "liberal" ideological deviations in Soviet literature. Among the publications *Pravda* condemned were Pasternak's poems from *Doctor Zhivago.* Although these criticisms were relatively mild compared with the Zhdanov period, the serious nature of the new offensive by conservatives could be seen in the fact that the chief editors of the journals *New World* and *October* were dismissed.

These measures were preventive in nature: the Second Congress of the Writers' Union was drawing near, the "precongress discussion" had begun in the literary press, and fears arose that the oppositional instincts of the intelligentsia would get out of control if the major instigators were not called to order. These fears proved to be exaggerated: among the writers who led the Writers' Union, the conservatives decisively outweighed the liberals. But for both literary camps, Pasternak (and, equally, Akhmatova and Zoshchenko) appeared to be historical anachronism. He belonged to the past, and his recently published poems seemed completely unrelated to the concerns of the day. Contrasting them to Pasternak's earlier revolutionary poems included in *1905*, Konstantin Simonov (who had once again become editor of *New World* after the dismissal of Tvardovsky) wrote: "The author, unfortunately, has shown no advance in his understanding of people and the times, and he has expressed neither belief in these people nor belief in his epoch." [64] At the congress, which was held at the end of December, Pasternak's name was mentioned even less frequently than in the precongress articles. The official report given by Alexei Surkov, who had replaced Fadeev in 1953 as head of the Writers' Union, made no reference to Pasternak. In the supplementary report on Soviet poetry given by Samed Vurgun, his name was grudgingly uttered only within the context of a disapproving remark made by Gorky in 1927. Only in the supplementary report on translations, and in the speech by the Georgian poet Leonidze, were there sympathetic, albeit cursory, references to Pasternak's translations from Shevchenko and from Georgian poetry (even his work on Shakespeare and Goethe received no mention). Although Pasternak was listed among those elected as delegates to the congress, there is no evidence that he actually appeared at any of its sessions. Thus the indifference of the Writers' Union and the poet was mutual. This is striking when we compare this congress with the first of twenty years before; there Pasternak had been accorded one of the top places in Soviet literature. But the contrast is even more striking in light of the fact that, precisely in the fall of 1954, on the eve of the Second Congress, Moscow and Leningrad were alive with rumors that Pasternak was about to receive the Nobel Prize. Although the rumors were premature—the prize went to Hemingway that year—the notion that Pasternak was among the leading candidates demonstrated the enormous distance between the poet's place at home and the reputation he had gained in the west.

12

The Nobel Scandal

Pasternak finished writing his novel under conditions of acute conflict with Soviet officialdom. A rough draft of part two of the novel was ready by the spring of 1955, but during the rewriting it underwent substantial revisions. In the winter of 1955–56 a typescript of the final text was presented to the *Banner* (in which the poetry from *Doctor Zhivago* had appeared earlier) and *New World* (with which Pasternak had signed a contract in 1947, later to be annulled). This was a trial move: from the very beginning Pasternak did not believe that his new work would prove acceptable to the Soviet press. But the new wave of liberalization, which arose "from below" on the eve of the Twentieth Party Congress and which, as it then seemed, had met with encouragement from the upper echelons, created a new sociocultural climate with unprecedented and unpredictable opportunities. What had seemed unthinkable two or three years ago now appeared possible. In the spring of 1955 negotiations began for the publication of a collection of Pasternak's selected verse, and in the beginning of 1956 an agreement for this book was concluded with the State Literary Publishing House (Goslitizdat). There were rumors about the preparation of collections by poets whose names were unutterable during Zhdanovism—Nikolai Gumilyov and Marina Tsvetaeva. The most striking manifestation of the new liberal tendencies was the miscellany *Literaturnaia Moskva* (Literary Moscow), the first volume of which was scheduled to coincide with the opening of the Twentieth Congress. The initiative for this literary miscellany came from a group of writers who rejected the bureaucratic structure of the Writers' Union and called for the weakening of party pressure upon literature.

Pasternak initially treated this new undertaking of liberal writers not only with skepticism but even with disdain. Although he agreed to contribute to the first issue his "Notes on Translating Shakespeare's Tragedies" (which had previously appeared only in English translation in 1946), he was relieved by the news that the editors of *Literary Moscow* had turned down some of his poems. And he refused to take part in the journal's second issue. The cautious appeals of writers for greater literary freedom and their attempt to secure sympathy for these efforts from party leaders seemed to him halfhearted and cowardly. He found them far more demeaning for literature than silence under conditions of the most severe intellectual repression. Pasternak's refusal to support this, the most radical literary organ of the time, sprang from the same uncompromising position that had made him withhold his signature from a letter of fellow travelers to the Central Committee with a request for protection from RAPP attacks in 1924. He now tied the actual changes in the country's life not to decisions or alterations in the politics of the party leadership, but rather to the ability of the intelligentsia to ignore the leadership's recommendations or instructions. A real improvement, he stated, would be a literary undertaking, addressed not to the party's but to the "non-party's congress." [1]

The history of the publication of *Doctor Zhivago* is illuminated in detail in the memoirs of Olga Ivinskaia, which were written in 1972 and appeared in the west in 1978. After her return from the labor camps, her relationship with Pasternak spread to include the poet's daily business interests. Ivinskaia became, to all intents and purposes, his literary agent, and he authorized her to carry on negotiations with publishing houses and journals—something he had previously done himself. Thus her testimony concerning Pasternak's final years might have been of special value. Regrettably, however, her book does not justify our hopes. Mostly it is a simple compilation or retelling of other published and unpublished sources. Even when Ivinskaia describes events in which she was a direct participant, her information is not always reliable and is sometimes muddled. She often distorts the chronology, contradicting incontrovertibly established facts and occasionally even contradicting herself. This book also clearly shows how insurmountable was the gap dividing the poet from his closest companion during these years. Although considerations for Ivinskaia and her children (as well as for the members of his own family) played a significant role in the poet's conduct, he made many crucial decisions on his own, refusing to submit to the arguments of close friends and relatives and not letting them in on his most important secrets.

In 1954, looking back on the "dreadful years" spent under Stalin, Pasternak had written to his cousin, "You cannot imagine the liberties I allowed myself: My future was shaped in precisely the way I myself shaped it." [2] One of these liberties was his submission of the manuscript of *Doctor Zhivago* for publication abroad. Seemingly accidental events far from his literary cares led to this fateful event. In March 1956 the Italian Communist Party dispatched a young journalist, Sergio d'Angelo, to work in the Soviet Union. This happened immediately after the Twentieth Party Congress, when enormous changes were occurring in Soviet society under the influence of Khrushchev's secret speech against Stalin and when the Western European Communists were gaining a new importance. His membership in the Communist Party and his job as a journalist allowed d'Angelo to plunge into the cultural life of the Soviet capital immediately. Besides his official appointment, he also had a private commission from a Milan publisher—the communist Giangiacomo Feltrinelli—to find new works of Soviet literature that would be of interest to the western reader.

In the beginning of May, foreign-language broadcasts originating in Moscow announced the completion by Boris Pasternak of a novel devoted to the revolutionary epoch in Russia. This short bulletin reflected the fact of the manuscript's submission to Soviet journals and Goslitizdat. D'Angelo rushed to see Pasternak at Peredelkino and, having introduced himself, proposed to issue an Italian translation of the novel at the Feltrinelli publishing house. This proposition caught the author off guard, but after some hesitation he brought the manuscript from his study and gave it to the journalist, saying with a laugh, "You are hereby invited to watch me face the firing squad." [3] He was fully aware of the risk connected with this move: after the scandal over Pilniak and Zamiatin in 1929, no Soviet writer could even contemplate direct contact with foreign publishers without the approval of authorized Soviet officials.

Nonetheless, the poet decided to accept the challenge. His decision stemmed from two considerations. First, the proposition came from a communist. The discussion was not about a Russian edition but only about a translation under the auspices of a communist publishing house, which would take upon itself the dissemination of the work in other European countries. In 1956 the concept of "Eurocommunism" with its negative connotations (a certain degree of political and ideological independence from the Kremlin) had not yet taken shape. In the Soviet Union, the Stalinist notion of the monolithic unity of all communist parties was still valid. Second, were the novel to be accepted by a Soviet press—and Pasternak had little hope this would happen—the appearance of an Italian translation would do no harm. If, on the other hand, not a single editor dared to take up the publication, then the appearance of the work in a communist publishing house would put an extra trump in the author's hand. Several days after the meeting with Pasternak, d'Angelo met with Feltrinelli in Berlin and handed the manuscript over to him.

Pasternak's action frightened both Ivinskaia and his wife Zinaida Nikolaevna. But he did not wish to go back on his decision. On May 27, in his talk with the Italian Slavicist, Professor Ettore Lo Gatto, he declared that he was prepared for any sacrifices to have this novel, which had cost him ten years of work, published abroad.[4] From the very beginning the author made no attempts to conceal his action from the Soviet literary bureaucracy. Ivinskaia told Vadim Kozhevnikov, the editor of the *Banner,* of the manuscript's submission abroad. The news created anxiety verging on panic in official circles. The story became known in the upper echelons, and, through Ivinskaia, they expressed their deep displeasure to the author. But the stronger the pressure on Pasternak became, the more important western publication seemed to him. On August 17, in a letter to another Italian Slavicist and translator of his poetry, A. M. Ripellino, Pasternak repudiated the arguments of his western well-wishers as to the necessity for caution and clearly let it be known that these considerations had no meaning for him.[5]

In the spring and summer months of 1956, the liberalizing trend brought unexpected successes each day. The position and reputation of Pasternak began to change dramatically. The manuscript of *Doctor Zhivago* was under consideration by two journals and Goslitizdat, and no one could predict whether the limits of the liberalization would expand to allow the novel's publication. The director of Goslitizdat, A. K. Kotov, had always been favorably disposed to Pasternak and had tried to help him materially during the bleakest days of Zhdanovism. At this publishing house, preparations for a retrospective edition of his verse were already in full swing. Such publications of authors once ostracized created a new cultural atmosphere and a sense of freedom. These republications in the later 1950s formed a sharp contrast to the depressingly mediocre literary work produced in the 1930s and 1940s, which were touted as the highest achievements of socialist realism. Pasternak's poems, which for many years appeared doomed to oblivion, seemed to regain importance in the revised panorama of past Soviet culture. But for the author himself, the earlier work had lost so much significance in comparison with his new novel that he had mixed feelings toward Goslitizdat's collection. It was only with great reluctance that he yielded to the requests of the editor to include in it old poems that had been famous in the 1920s. From the point of view of the new poetic style developed during his years of work on *Doctor Zhivago,* the early lyrics seemed to him anachronistic, merely formal exercises. He mercilessly left out or altered even the best of his poems for the new publication, including some from *My Sister, Life.* At the same time, submersion in his own poetic past produced a new lyrical mood in Pasternak, and in the course of a few months he wrote almost twenty new poems. They appeared subsequently in his last book of verse *Kogda razguliaetsia* (When the Skies Clear).[6]

The publishing house even offered the poet the opportunity to preface the book with an extensive autobiographical essay. This was unheard-of generosity: not long before Pasternak had been denied the possibility of accompanying the publication of his translations with short introductions or commentaries. Finished in the spring of 1956, this autobiographical sketch appeared in a Georgian translation in the Tbilisi journal *Mnatobi* (edited by Chikovani), at the end of that year.[7] In Georgia liberalization in cultural life progressed at a faster pace than in the capital, and the boldness and initiative of the Georgian intelligentsia provided a stimulus for the Moscow liberals. A similar gap existed between Polish writers, who enjoyed much more freedom, and their colleagues in the Soviet Union (where conservative groups clearly prevailed). Outside these specific historical circumstances, it is impossible to understand Pasternak's poem "Trava i kamni" (Grass and Stones). It is a panegyric to two countries, Poland and Georgia. Their appearance in the same context springs from their special role at that time: Georgia inside the Soviet Union and Poland inside the socialist camp served as models of freethinking and independence.

Of the Moscow journals, Pasternak maintained the closest ties with *New World.* In July, translations of Titsian Tabidze appeared there under his name (although they were actually done with Ivinskaia or even by her alone); and in October the poem "Khleb" (Bread). In an article in the September issue, the literary critic Sarra Shtut called for a sweeping reevaluation of former dogmatic schemas of the history of Soviet literature and appraised with particular warmth Pasternak's place within it. In its courage, this essay surpassed all that was said of Pasternak in the Soviet press from 1936 to his death. Now under the leadership of Simonov, as in 1954 under Tvardovsky, *New World* was once again at the head of a growing liberal movement. It shared this role with *Literary Moscow.* Sensation-provoking publications came one after the other in the journal. Semen Kirsanov's satirical poem "Seven Days of a Week" and Vladimir Dudintsev's novel *Not by Bread Alone* created special commotion. One might have expected that, if Pasternak's novel appeared at all in the Soviet Union, the most appropriate place would be in the pages of this journal.[8]

In comparison to all other manifestations of the liberal mood, however, Pasternak's novel was strange: it seemed to be written in a completely different language. In the other works of "literary protest" in the thaw years—by Ehrenburg, Tvardovsky, Dudintsev—many dark sides of Soviet life (in particular, the imprisonment of innocent people on trumped-up charges) were exposed no less boldly than in *Doctor Zhivago.* But Pasternak's novel posed a more fundamental challenge. It called into question the theoretical basis for the existence of a socialist state—the doctrines of Marxism—and advanced an alternative set of values. The Russian revolution was not condemned; on the contrary, in several places the author's praise of its elemental force is reminiscent of the old conception of the Scythians. But Pasternak treated it as a historical phenomenon that belonged to a distant past, long outlived. The novel was devoted to the revolution and the civil war—but as the first readers noticed, the author showed in telescopic form that the main features of Stalin's time flowed inevitably from the very nature of the Bolshevik Party and Soviet power. This conclusion was especially heretical and subversive: Stalin's indictment at the Twentieth Party Congress had been accompanied by protestations that the cult of personality was an alien phenomenon, having nothing in common with the essence of the Soviet order and socialism in general. It was an accidental historical aberration that could never happen again. Another radical departure from the Soviet literary canon involved the novel's protagonist. Yury Zhivago was a passive, unheroic hero, anemic in the "battle for ideals" and immersed in a private world. Even the novel's artistic qualities were unusual—elusiveness, no statement of ultimate truths or prescriptions. All this brought the makers of literary politics to a dead end. A potential Soviet publisher of the novel quickly realized that even the elimination of all ideologically offensive passages[9] would not save the novel from official damnation.

Meanwhile the party leadership was becoming increasingly worried about the stirrings caused by the exposure of Stalin's crimes. As early as in April 1956 an article appeared in *Pravda* attacking those who strove, under the guise of criticizing the cult of personality, to question the infallibility of the party and the legitimacy of its power. The authorities were especially troubled by the calls for liberalization from intellectuals in Poland, Hungary, and Yugoslavia and by the support they received from the writers' unions in those countries. In August it was announced that the 1946 ideological decrees of the Central Committee were still valid.

One must view in this context the decision of the editorial board of *New World* to reject Pasternak's novel. In September 1956 the manuscript was returned to the author together with a long letter containing an analysis of the novel and reasons for its rejection. The editor-in-chief, Konstantin Simonov, drafted the letter, but the other members of the editorial board who signed it—Boris Agapov, Alexander Krivitsky, Boris Lavrenyov, and Konstantin Fedin—took part in the composition of this document. The appearance of Fedin's signature was a painful blow to Pasternak. Since the 1930s they had been close friends. They were next-door neighbors in Peredelkino and lived in the same building in Moscow. The novel was written, as it were, right before Fedin's eyes and had been known to him from the earliest stages. Fedin was one of those who was well aware of how much inner, deeply nurtured truth Pasternak had put into his work. In education and cultural outlook, he stood closer to Pasternak than to the great mass of Soviet writers and, among the signatories, he alone was capable of speaking in Pasternak's language. In the 1920s and 1930s he had been a favorite of Gorky's and belonged to the liberal camp. From the first years of the revolution, Pasternak had admired Fedin's prose, and he set him higher than any of the other "Serapion Brothers" and higher than Alexei Tolstoy, Babel, and Sholokhov. Partly in order to avert attacks on Fedin, Pasternak had become involved in the debates about formalism in March 1936. The war years brought them even closer. In light of all this, Pasternak could not perceive Fedin's support of *New World*'s decision as anything but a betrayal.

Fedin not only signed the letter, but in his own hand wrote a long passage, distinguished by its special refinement and incisiveness, discussing the poetry by Zhivago and comparing Pasternak's hero to Christ.[10] Though deeply injured, Pasternak tried not to disclose his pain, and his break with Fedin occurred only later, during the Nobel scandal.

Vsevolod Ivanov, another close friend of the poet and his neighbor in Peredelkino and Moscow, took a diametrically opposed position toward the novel. When, in the summer of 1956, the idea of an independent and cooperative publishing house for writers took shape (similar to those that had briefly existed during the NEP) Ivanov became obsessed with the idea of bringing out Pasternak's novel. These plans did not materialize, and Ivanov (who, unlike Fedin, had always avoided a bureaucratic career) could offer little help to his friend. But he and his family (especially his son Viacheslav, a fine scholar and linguist who had grown up under the influence of Pasternak[11]) were able to comfort the poet during the difficult days ahead.

In many ways, New World's refusal to publish Doctor Zhivago at this point was easy to explain. But in another way it backfired: it strengthened the author's conviction that the publication of his novel was impossible in the Soviet Union, even in abridged form, and that he had acted correctly when he let the manuscript go abroad. Such a pessimistic evaluation was disadvantageous for the authorities insofar as it deprived them of the freedom to maneuver. It is not known to what degree the writers of the rejection letter considered the fact that the manuscript had been sent to Italy. The senseless and potentially counterproductive nature of their move is so obvious that Olga Ivinskaia even came to believe that the rejection letter was written not in September 1956 but much later, after the appearance of the Italian publication of the novel and intentionally antedated.[12] But other sources unambiguously confirm that New World's refusal was announced exactly in the middle of September 1956, and that Fedin's full support of the journal's position was already known to Pasternak by then.[13] Apparently, after the verdict, a meeting took place between Ivinskaia and a high-ranking Central Committee official, Dmitry Polikarpov, during which he called the director of Goslitizdat and gave the order to sign a contract to publish the novel (the manuscript had been there for several months). The publication of Doctor Zhivago was promised in the course of a year, a pace unheard of under Soviet publishing conditions. For the book's preparation, Anatoly Starostin, an employee at Goslitizdat who was an ardent admirer of Pasternak, was named editor.

These decisions meant that, in his fight for the book's publication in the Soviet Union, Pasternak had gained the first victory, despite the rejection by *New World* (and also, evidently, by the *Banner*). During a meeting on January 3, 1957, with Anna Akhmatova in Peredelkino, Pasternak confirmed that the novel would soon be released by Goslitizdat.[14] The poet, whose name had been scarcely mentioned in the official Soviet press for many years, unexpectedly found himself on equal footing with the Soviet administration. None of the other Soviet literary figures who had been out of favor could boast of a similar achievement. The positive interference by the authorities in the fate of his novel resulted from the fact that Ivinskaia's negotiations with d'Angelo to halt the Italian publication had brought no results. Feltrinelli agreed to delay the book's release, but rejected the proposition to align his activities with the interests of Moscow officials and with the constantly changing political situation in the Soviet Union. He flatly refused to return for editing the manuscript he held, since work had already begun on the translation.

Meanwhile, after the uprisings in Poland and Hungary of October and November, the liberal hopes in Soviet society were dashed. The leadership perceived a direct link between these political actions and the expression of ideological independence (or as Khrushchev called it "revisionism") in intellectual circles, in the first place in the writers' unions of Hungary and Poland. It was necessary to avert at all costs similar developments in the Soviet Union, and the conservative powers were authorized to assume the offensive. The main organs of the writers' opposition—*New World* and *Literary Moscow*—came under fierce bombardment, and the release of a third issue of the literary miscellany was forbidden. From March 1957 on, liberals accused of ideological mistakes were forced to repent publicly at a series of writers' meetings.[15] In July 1957 Khrushchev's main rivals in the Politburo were removed, and his personal power reached its zenith. That summer an extract from his speeches made to meetings of the artistic intelligentsia was published as a guiding party directive. Since the time of Zhdanov, no Soviet leader had articulated his views in matters of literature and art. This was the first time that Khrushchev had spoken on these themes, and the publication of his speeches left no doubt that it was the conservative and not the liberal camp which enjoyed his full support in the question of cultural politics.[16]

The idea of a Soviet publication of *Doctor Zhivago* seemed much less feasible than before. On the other hand, Pasternak's status had also changed. His name became known in wider circles abroad. Besides Feltrinelli, other European publishing houses expressed strong interest in the novel. Starting in the spring of 1957, references to Pasternak and his poetry began to appear more frequently in western journals. These publications also printed works that had not been allowed in the Soviet Union. Completely disregarding the patent displeasure of the officials in relation to the unauthorized submission of his novel to foreigners, Pasternak did not confine his "illegal activities" to *Zhivago* and continued impertinently to send his unpublished works abroad. An uncontrollable escalation of Pasternak's fame occurred in western circles, and this was enhanced by rumors that translations of his novel were being prepared in several languages.

Two events in particular enraged Soviet officials. The first was the publication of excerpts from *Zhivago* in the first issue of the Polish quarterly *Opinie* (Opinions) at the end of the summer of 1957. This new journal was, as the editors announced, dedicated expressly to the propagation of fraternal Soviet culture. Yet the selection of works in the journal must have seemed very odd to the literary bureaucracy. Instead of touting Surkov and Simonov, the journal printed Tsvetaeva (whose recent posthumous publication in *Literary Moscow* was one of the grounds for persecuting the literary miscellany) and Osip Mandelshtam (who was still forbidden in the Soviet Union). On September 26 Moscow's *Literary Gazette* contained an extremely cutting review of this issue of the Polish journal. The article never mentioned what had especially annoyed the Soviet authorities—that is, the appearance of excerpts from *Zhivago* (the first printed appearance of the prose part of the novel).[17] Pasternak quickly learned of the authorities' real reaction. In August he told Nina Tabidze of the "new wave of fury" this publication had occasioned and of Ivinskaya's new summons from the Central Committee.[18] The fury of the officials is explained by the fact that the Polish publication served to create a kind of alibi for Pasternak if the novel appeared in the west; it would show that interest existed not only in hostile capitalistic but also in friendly socialist countries. This alone may explain why *Opinions* was charged with subversive ideological activities and, at the insistence of the Soviet officials, was immediately closed down.

The second event that occasioned the rage of the authorities was the appearance of the poems on New Testament themes from *Zhi-*

vago, under the title "Poems from Russia," in the Russian émigré journal *Grani* (Facets, Munich) in the middle of 1957. Although neither the author nor the source of these poems was indicated, it was not difficult to identify them. Any uncontrolled foreign publications of Soviet authors caused irritation in Moscow, but placing poems in the émigré press, especially in such an uncompromisingly anti-Soviet journal as *Facets,* was considered to border on treason. This particular publication looked especially defiant because it consisted of poems based on gospel themes. The Old and New Testament were almost forbidden admittance to the USSR and were even confiscated from tourists at customs. From the point of view of official ideology, religion was considered an anachronism. It should be noted that in the sphere of church politics, Khrushchev displayed even greater intolerance than Stalin in the postwar years. Whether the publication in *Facets* was done with or without the author's permission, the Soviet authorities could only see it as a slap in the face.

Thus, beginning in August 1957, rude administrative pressure on the poet and direct intimidation replaced gentle persuasions, admonishments, and seeming searches for a compromise. The date approached (September 1) when, according to the agreement with Feltrinelli, the Italian edition of the novel was to appear. Soviet officials demanded that Pasternak send a telegram to Feltrinelli to halt the book's release, on the pretext that he had to make alterations in the text. It was clear to all that this was a sham. Feltrinelli understood, since he had just rejected the proposals of two Italian communists to abandon the project and since he knew of the author's urgent desire to see his offspring in print. The Soviet authorities understood it as well: for them, not only a revised novel but even the collection of Pasternak's verse, which had been already typeset, were inappropriate in this new situation. It goes without saying that it was well understood by the poet himself, who had already in the spring of 1957 said that negotiations had turned into a "mutual bluffing game" in which each side tried to outwit the other.[19]

Pasternak submitted to the Soviet ultimatum only when d'Angelo convinced him that no telegram could hinder the book's release: things had gone too far, and translation rights had already been sold to other western publishers. And when he sent the telegram to Feltrinelli, the poet sent him a parallel confidential letter that countermanded the order in the telegram.[20] In September a delegation of

American and West European journalists, including Miriam Berlin, came to Moscow. On the way to Russia she called upon Pasternak's sisters in Oxford. Since work on an English translation of *Doctor Zhivago* had already begun, they asked her to meet with their brother and make sure that he was still interested in the publication. Pasternak left not the smallest doubt. Miriam Berlin reports: "Without question," he replied with great conviction. "It does not matter what might happen to me. My life is finished. This book is my last word to the civilized world." A cable would be sent with his signature, asking that publication be stopped. It was to be ignored. "I must send it," he said, "but, please, tell them to pay no attention."[21]

Pasternak's dispatch of the telegram to Milan allowed him to gain some time. But the Soviet administration quickly guessed that the move would yield no results. So the head of the Writers' Union, Alexei Surkov, decided to join a delegation of Soviet poets, which was setting out for Italy, and to exert pressure on the publisher in person. His negotiations with Feltrinelli were unsuccessful. At a press conference on October 19 Surkov expressed bewilderment at the notice in the Italian press about the impending appearance of *Zhivago*. He announced that the Soviet edition had been halted. Surkov claimed that, after receiving a detailed and well-reasoned letter from a group of his Soviet colleagues with explanations for their disapproval, Pasternak "appeared to accept some of these criticisms and said he would revise the text." Thus, according to Surkov, the Italian publication of *Zhivago* went against the explicit will of the author and was a blatant violation of his rights.[22] In his statement in Italy, Surkov constructed a parallel between the publication of *Zhivago* abroad and the scandal around Pilniak's *Mahogany* in 1929. This was taken as a threat to organize an analogous social lynching of Pasternak and even to arrest him.

One must marvel at the smugness and crude power displayed by the representatives of Soviet authority in this affair, and at the extent to which they proved unable to grasp the mentality of the western world. Nothing promoted the swift growth of interest in *Doctor Zhivago* more than these clumsy attempts to prevent its publication. The novel became an international sensation even before its release. Its first printing of 6000 was sold out on the first day, November 22. Prospective publications in other European languages promised to become similar bestsellers. The release of the Italian translation was accompanied by a deluge of articles and notices in the European and

American press, where a central place was given to the ban of the novel in the Soviet Union and to the attempts of Soviet diplomats to stop its publication abroad. No work of Russian literature had received such publicity since the time of the revolution. The very passages that had embarrassed and frightened the Soviet censors most of all, and that Pasternak was ready to remove, were now widely quoted in the world press. Any mention of Pasternak's name in Moscow instantaneously spread to the pages of western newspapers and often acquired fantastic interpretations.

On November 27 in Moscow, a large meeting of writers and artists took place devoted to Khrushchev's pronouncement in matters of culture. In his official address, Surkov came down hard on the recent efforts of revisionists to rehabilitate such figures of postrevolutionary art as Vsevolod Meyerhold, Mikhail Bulgakov, Boris Pilniak, and Isaak Babel. In this context he spoke of "the attempts to canonize the works of B. Pasternak" and of the recent apologetic evaluation of Marina Tsvetaeva, which Ehrenburg gave in his article in *Literary Moscow*. Surkov's address was reported in the *Literary Gazette* on November 28 and reappeared in *Pravda* in the form of an article on December 1. In any event, Surkov's words had no direct relationship to the novel that had just been released in Italy: the real goal of his address was to criticize all aspects of the 1956 thaw (in whose ranks Pasternak was not the most typical figure). But western correspondents singled out the words concerning Pasternak, tied them to the ill-fated attempts to prevent the publication of *Zhivago,* and interpreted them as revenge for the novel's release abroad. This episode showed how damaging the Pasternak incident could be to the normal functioning of the Soviet ideological apparatus.

Having finally understood that administrative pressure and public protest were only counterproductive, the Soviet literary leaders decided to play a waiting game and not to react in the press to the release of *Zhivago.* The Soviet newspapers did not utter a word about the novel's appearance in Italy, about its stunning success with Italian readers, or about other publications planned in the west. Silence was regarded as the most rational means of solving the Pasternak problem. The publication of the edition of his poetry at Goslitizdat was frozen (and indeed was never published). After the appearance of a poem in the *Literary Gazette* on October 19 (the same day on which Surkov held his press conference in Italy), not a single Moscow or Leningrad periodical dared to publish Pasternak's lyrics. Any such appearance in the press would entail unfavorable international publicity and would be perceived as a political demonstration.[23]

The poet himself proposed another way out of the situation. He said that if Goslitizdat would publish *Doctor Zhivago* now—even in an abridged and altered version—the sensation in the western press would immediately die down. He referred to prerevolutionary precedent, when Tolstoy's *Resurrection* appeared in two versions, complete in the west and in abridged form in tsarist Russia.[24] But this sensible decision proved unacceptable to the Soviet authorities. First, the mechanical removal of the characters' tirades against the revolution, on Christianity, Jewry, Marxism, and so forth, would never transform the remaining text into a genuinely Soviet work of art or its hero into an embodiment of the favored clichés of Soviet literature. The editors of *New World* had noted this already in September 1956. Second, an abridged publication would give documentary confirmation of the existence of censorship in the USSR—something the Soviet authorities preferred not to admit, always trying to convince the world of the unanimous loyalty of the people and the freedom they enjoyed. The very fact of the belated release of a Soviet publication would create a dangerous precedent: henceforth any author could resort to western assistance in order to exert pressure on the Soviet censor.

In the search for a judicious way out of the situation, Pasternak was moved not only by general principles, such as securing a writer's freedom of expression. He was disturbed by all the stir in the western newspapers. It seemed to him that the political sensation would overshadow the significance of his novel as an artistic work and that the unending repetition of the same quotations taken out of context would turn his poetic text into an ideological pamphlet. The poet, who had always refused to take part in Soviet propaganda activities, did not want to be drawn into anti-Soviet political propaganda.

In 1922 Marina Tsvetaeva wrote of the peculiar nature of Pasternak's popularity, calling it "subterranean fame": this was an ecstatic cult of a selected few. Now in the spring of 1958 his fame "came out from underground." The poet who had been subjected to decades of silence in his native country suddenly became a celebrity abroad. The political scandals that preceded the novel's appearance were not the only reason for this energetic interest in Pasternak. Many features of the author's frame of mind struck his western audience precisely because these were the very qualities systematically eradicated from the Soviet intelligentsia during the Stalin years. In the first place, they could sense the organic, indissoluble tie with European culture, the rejection of a "superiority complex", as André Gide put it, in relation to the west, which developed in the 1930s in the Soviet Union and took on especially appalling forms in the course of campaign against cosmopolitanism at the end of the 1940s. For the foreign correspondents who visited him, Pasternak seemed a relic from the past. His solid background in philosophy, his study in Marburg, the refusal to consider Marxism the only acceptable world view, the lack of the usual clichés of official Soviet culture, a faithfulness to the principles of humanism and the absence of class biases, a lively and free relationship to religion and the Bible—all this was out of keeping with stereotypical portraits of the Soviet intellectual.

Precisely these fundamental differences between Pasternak and his milieu—even more than the oppositional aphorisms in the novel and the dramatic circumstances of its publication—compelled the western press to begin speaking of Pasternak as the most likely candidate for the Nobel Prize in the spring of 1958. In and of itself, this possibility poisoned the mood of the leaders of the Writers' Union.[25] But it also doomed the authorities to inactivity after the appearance of *Doctor Zhivago*. This looked strange against the background of their previously feverish attempts to prevent publication, but it was the result of painstaking calculations. Any punitive measure taken against Pasternak could be harmful in light of the supposition that in the following year Pasternak might share the Nobel Prize in literature with Sholokhov. In accordance with these rumors, Minister of Foreign Affairs Andrei Gromyko was even approached about the Soviet government's attitude toward this idea.[26] It goes without saying that the prospect did not delight Soviet leaders. For them, these two writers were poles apart. Sholokhov had always been Stalin's favorite, and in the middle of the 1950s, under Khrushchev, his status as the premier Soviet author became even more apparent despite the fact that no new literary works had appeared for years. This is partially explained by his personal intimacy with Khrushchev (their wives were sisters). With the goal of improving his chances for the prize, Sholokhov was even sent on a trip through Scandinavia.

By the middle of October, however, the notion was widespread that Pasternak alone would be the Nobel Prize laureate. Max Frankel, the Moscow correspondent of the *New York Times,* visited Pasternak on the evening of October 22 and discussed these rumors. Pasternak confirmed that he had heard them and said that, if he won the prize, "this will mean a new role, a new heavy responsibility. And all my life it has been this way for me." He also tried to avert political speculations by stressing that his relative anonymity in his own country had nothing to do with political oppression. He told Frankel: "I am not a victim of any injustice. I have not been singled out for special treatment. Under the circumstances nothing else could have been done." [27] A similar awareness of political repercussions led the Swedish academy to mention Pasternak's early work along with the recently published novel, when it voted him the prize. In its cablegram dated October 23, 1958, Boris Pasternak was cited "for his important achievement both in contemporary lyrical poetry and in the field of the great Russian epic tradition."

The immediate Soviet public reaction seemed restrained at first. Soviet Minister of Culture Nikolai Mikhailov said that he considered Pasternak's novel weak and mediocre, but praised him as a poet and translator. To him, the Swedish academy's decision seemed not altogether justified in view of the fact that the best of Pasternak's poems were written and published so long ago. [28] Mikhailov added that he could not predict whether Pasternak would be able to travel to Sweden to accept the prize. He said it depended entirely on the professional organization to which Pasternak belonged, the Writers' Union.

On October 24 Pasternak was visited by his long-time friend and neighbor Konstantin Fedin, who was then the head of the Moscow section of the Writers' Union. Fedin warned him about unavoidable political complications and urged him to refuse the prize. This was evidently done at the direct request of Polikarpov. After a long and difficult conversation, Pasternak decided to reject his advice. [29] He sent the following cable of acceptance to the Swedish academy: "Immensely thankful, touched, proud, astonished, abashed." The cable did not mention whether the poet would come to Stockholm. But Andreas Oesterling, the academy's permanent secretary, said that the very fact that "Pasternak had been permitted to send such a message encouraged hope that he would also be permitted to come here." [30]

Although rumors of the possible award to Pasternak had been circulating since the spring, the decision of the Swedish academy took the clumsy Soviet propaganda machine by surprise. Its leaders obviously could not believe until the end that from the four finalists—Ezra Pound, Alberto Moravia, Mikhail Sholokhov, and Boris Pasternak—the lot had fallen to the last. Awarding the prize to Pasternak turned the entire Soviet scale of cultural values upside down. It was impossible to explain to the broad public how an author who had not had a single book appear in print, other than translations, for thirteen years could be assessed in the west as one of the greatest writers of the century. And it was impossible to explain why his novel, which was unknown in the Soviet Union, could have instantaneously become one of the most popular Russian books in the west. Even the very fact of the leak of an unpublished manuscript abroad was incomprehensible to the Soviet people: since the majority of them were afraid even of corresponding with close relatives who lived in emigration, the illegal sending of an entire novel destroyed the belief in the impenetrability of the Soviet border.

Therefore, on October 24, when the entire world press was reporting Boris Pasternak's award, the Soviet media uttered not a word.[31] Ultimately, after Pasternak declined Fedin's request, a decision was made to proclaim that the award of the prize to him, as well as his publication in the west of *Doctor Zhivago*, was an act of anti-Soviet political provocation. An editorial in the *Literary Gazette* of October 25 promoted such an interpretation. It was published together with the long letter that the editors of *New World* had sent Pasternak in September 1956. The next stage of the campaign was an extraordinarily brazen and insulting article about Pasternak printed in the October 26 issue of *Pravda*. Its author, David Zaslavsky, was a notorious figure: in their time, both Lenin and Trotsky wrote about him with contempt for his complete unscrupulousness. Precisely because of that, the especially dirty propagandistic tasks of Stalin's time were entrusted to him. The fact that on this occasion *Pravda* turned to him already gave the article an especially sinister nuance. The very decision of this newspaper to engage in the campaign was significant. It became clear that the authorities did not wish to limit the affair to writers' circles and were ready to conduct the attacks on a national scale.[32] The tense and threatening atmosphere of ostracism surrounding Pasternak and his relatives was created not only by attacks in the Soviet press but also by choreographed expressions of popular indignation, threats of mob violence, the shouts of hooligans on the streets, and so forth. Western newspapers reported that since October 27 Pasternak's home in Peredelkino had been surrounded by a police detail and that it was possible to visit him only with a permit.

An expanded meeting of the presidium of the board of the Writers' Union was set for Monday, October 27. This was to be Pasternak's trial. The poet was sent a notice, but he refused to appear at the meeting. Not afraid of confrontation, however, he sent a letter in which he repudiated in advance the charges brought against him and rejected any future decisions of this gathering. Among those who attended the meeting, along with the hard-liners who had always disliked the poet, were writers who had acquired a liberal reputation in the post-Stalin years—Vera Panova, Stepan Shchipachyov, Galina Nikolaeva, and Nikolai Chukovsky (the son of Kornei Chukovsky, who had been one of the few people to rush to Pasternak on October 23 to congratulate him on the prize).

Although the speeches at this meeting were never published, it is well known that the Pasternak question evoked no dissent from those in attendance. He was expelled from the Writers' Union by unanimous vote. Since the Ezhov terror of the late 1930s, a measure of such severity had been taken with Akhmatova and Zoshchenko in 1946. Expulsion from the Writers' Union could mean the loss of essential perquisites for any Soviet man of letters. Technically Pasternak not only lost the right to his house in Peredelkino and his apartment in Moscow, but he was also deprived of all chance of literary earnings: he remembered well what it had cost him in 1948 to secure permission for Akhmatova to work on translations. The decision to expel Pasternak from the writers' organization created a storm of indignation around the world: it was impossible for people in the west to comprehend not only why the most prestigious literary award in the world had triggered anger in the poet's homeland, but also why his fellow writers were at the head of his persecution. If, for many in the west, the decision to expel Pasternak from the Writer's Union came as a shock, the poet himself had long been having premonitions. He had predicted such punishment well before the Nobel scandal—in the summer of 1958, soon after *Doctor Zhivago*'s appearance in the west.[33]

This is why the step he took immediately after the publication on October 28 of the resolution of the Writers' Union seems so puzzling even now. On Wednesday, October 29, he sent the Swedish academy the following telegram:

> In view of the meaning given to this honor in the community to which I belong, I should abstain from the undeserved prize that has been awarded to me. Do not meet my voluntary refusal with ill will.[34]

It would seem that Pasternak's refusal of the prize signified capitulation and attested to the impulsiveness and inconsistency of his behavior. It would also seem that the Soviet administration should have celebrated: this refusal was what Fedin had tried to get from Pasternak several days earlier. But Soviet officials perceived this deed not as a concession but as a new blow. And they were right. As one contemporary remembers about this telegram, "Its inconsistency with Pasternak's first cablegram was only illusory. Taking into consideration society's evaluation does not necessarily mean agreeing with it." [35] On October 31, in his opening remarks at a meeting of Moscow writers, Sergei Smirnov said of Pasternak's second telegram, "This is an even dirtier provocation that carries treachery still further." [36]

Pasternak's action, like his behavior in general, has a complex, polysemantic character. During the years of his life in Soviet society, he saw many wild witch hunts against artists who had displeased the authorities. He well remembered the campaigns against Pilniak and Zamiatin in 1929, against formalism and naturalism in 1936, and against Akhmatova and Zoshchenko in 1946. In the last two cases he himself had become (although peripherally) a target of persecution. In all these situations, the campaign begun against certain individual scapegoats escalated into a more fundamental purge in the area of the arts and in society as a whole. Unlike the victims of the previous campaigns, this time "Pasternak had deliberately brought the avalanche upon himself by calculated activity spread over more than ten years." [37] Knowing full well the mechanism of Soviet social lynching, he could assume that the persecution would not be limited to the first articles in the press and his formal expulsion from the Writers' Union. Pasternak's second telegram spoiled the plans of the campaign's organizers and interfered with the natural course of its escalation. Making the search for additional culprits superfluous, it introduced an element of bizarre surprise into the campaign.

Pasternak's refusal of the prize also solved the question of his trip to Stockholm. The Soviet authorities could breathe a sigh of relief: the second round of this political show no longer threatened them. If, on October 23, the Soviet minister of culture had laid upon the Writers' Union the decision of whether the Nobel laureate would or would not go to the celebration ceremony, and if the leadership of the union in expelling Pasternak had declined the responsibility, then Pasternak had now removed the burden of the decision from the state authorities.

But Pasternak's action had a broader significance as well. His readiness to sacrifice the highest literary award, his ability to sweep aside the flattering marks of distinction, were quite in character. At a meeting on October 31, the poet Lev Oshanin mentioned with indignation the blasphemous indifference with which Pasternak had treated the award to him, along with a large group of writers, of the medal "For Valorous Labor in the Great Patriotic War" in 1946.[38] He only reluctantly agreed to appear at the award ceremony, after proposing to send his son instead. What Oshanin was not capable of understanding was that not only the award of the Soviet government, but any official award, had a limited value for Pasternak. It seemed incommensurable with his relentless search for truth, indissolubly tied, in his mind, to the poet's vocation. No matter how flattering the fact that he was the first Slavic poet to receive the highest literary distinction, he was glad to receive it primarily as a sign of his victory in a long and unequal fight with the state for the right to free expression, and not as an honorary title of personal merit. Pasternak was absolutely sincere when he stated in the first telegram that he was "abashed" and in the second that the award was "undeserved." Here modesty is blended with a feeling of deep personal pride. In response to official attempts to attribute political bias to the decision of the Swedish academy and base motives to Pasternak himself, he was trying to show that this award was unnecessary to him as a poet and that poetry and art were worth more than any regalia.

Pasternak's refusal of the Nobel Prize was therefore not a manifestation of a momentary weakness but rather a thought-out reaction to developing events. It was also a deliberate move in a chess game, which brought along with it additional complications for the authorities. Only three Nobel laureates before him had declined the award—Adolf Butenandt, Richard Kuhn, and Gerhard Domagk. These refusals were made in 1939 in Nazi Germany at the behest of Hitler's government. Despite the poet's emphasis on the voluntary nature of his decision, the hostile reaction of the Soviet press created a kind of historical parallel between his action and the other cases. The Soviet government was still more embarrassed by the Nobel committee's announcement on October 27 that the Nobel Prize in physics would be awarded to three Soviet scientists—Pavel Cherenkov, Igor Tamm, and Ilya Frank. This was only the second time in history that Soviet science had received such an honor (the first time was in 1956), and the significance of the event was clouded by the Pasternak scandal.

The anger of the Soviet authorities toward Pasternak was expressed in full measure in attacks against him in the official address of the head of the All-Union Komsomol, Vladimir Semichastny. This address was made before an audience of thousands at a celebratory meeting at the Palace of Sports devoted to the fortieth anniversary of the Communist Youth League. The speaker likened Pasternak to "a pig that fouls its own sty" and suggested that he leave the Soviet Union and "breathe capitalist air." Semichastny, who had only in 1958 assumed his high position, was known to be Khrushchev's protégé, and Khrushchev sat with other members of the Politburo on the platform from which Semichastny spoke. Thus it was possible to suppose that his words indicated the official position of the Soviet upper echelons that had not yet been directly expressed; his speech suggested that the leadership did not intend to remain in the wings. Therefore, the threat of forced exile for this "internal émigré" was extremely weighty. Of course Pasternak had considered the possibility of being forbidden to return home if he went to Stockholm, and this was one of the reasons that led him to refuse the prize. But before Semichastny's speech the threat had not been spoken aloud. At that time, exile abroad seemed an extreme measure; Soviet society was not yet accustomed to it. The single instance within memory when this form of punishment had been used was the exile in 1929 of Trotsky, who had been proclaimed the sworn enemy of the Soviet people; his subsequent fate abroad left little illusion as to the advantages of such a journey. Regardless of how real the prospect of exile was in light of Semichastny's words, his speech with its unprecedentedly vitriolic tone removed any hopes for a natural resolution of the conflict. The fact that Semichastny's speech was delivered on the very day that Pasternak declined the Nobel Prize lent particular poignancy to the new twist of events.

Since 1923, when the poet returned from Berlin to Moscow, he had more than once asked himself whether he had acted correctly when he chose life in Soviet Russia and did not remain in the west with his parents. The sculptor Zoia Maslenikova asked him about this ten days before Nobel Prize announcement. Pasternak answered her, "Oh, that's a difficult question. But everything would have been much more trivial. A person should live the life of his country. He should live in intense, natural life, and then his works will contain internal naturalness—and if a person is cut off from his native environment, then new creative juices will not come to him. You see, émigré literature has not created anything of significance."[39] Having been isolated from the western world for decades by the iron curtain, Pasternak was mistaken in his belief that émigré literature had created nothing of significance—its achievements were not only remarkable in themselves, but in essence they saved the honor of Russian literature when, during the bleak years of Stalin's regime, talent had been suppressed or eradicated from Soviet culture. But these words help to explain not only why emigration seemed an unacceptable option for the poet, but also how he perceived all his work and conduct under the Soviet regime. To survive the horror of the purges, the privations of the war, the hopes fostered by victory, and the stifling atmosphere of Zhdanovism, to live every day under the threat of arrest and still to believe in the possibility of better times, and finally, in spite of all the attempts to force him into silence, to place all his experiences in compositions meant for the world—in comparison to this mission of the poet, life in a foreign country indeed seemed "much more trivial."

The prospect of banishment placed Pasternak in a tortuous moral dilemma in yet another respect. If his relatives were permitted to accompany him, whom would he count as members of his family— Zinaida Nikolaevna and their son Leonid or Olga Ivinskaia? Both women would still have personal family ties in Russia, particularly their children, a break with whom would be excruciatingly painful. Could he at the age of sixty-eight, and burdened by ever more frequent illnesses, sacrifice the home that had served as a shelter for him during all the storms of twenty years, to exchange it for the dubious, bitter glory of world wandering? And would not those people close to him in his native land become hostages, forcing the poet to weigh his every step so as not to inflict harm on them? Pasternak discussed the question of leaving the country with both Zinaida and Ivinskaia. Zinaida did not want to go, but considered that it was better for her husband to leave Russia and find, at long last, a tranquil haven.[40] Pasternak answered that he would leave only if everyone could leave together. Nor did Olga have a burning desire to move to the west. Pasternak wrote a letter to the Soviet government in which he requested permission for her and her children to go with him. But he tore the letter to shreds: it placed him in the humiliating position of a petitioner, and there was little chance that his request would be honored anyway. Semichastny's nasty speech excluded the possibility that the government would carry on polite negotiations with this "traitor of the homeland."

I believe that, at just this moment, Pasternak proposed to Olga that they commit a double suicide. Speaking of this in her memoirs, Ivinskaia dates the conversation on October 28. But it seems more plau-

sible that it did not take place before Pasternak sent the second telegram to the Swedish academy or before Semichastny's speech of
October 29. That is, he proposed the option either that same evening
or on October 30. Although Olga categorically refused Pasternak's
plan, she could not be assured that Pasternak would not carry it out
alone. Without warning him, she set out to see Fedin. She went to
him not only because she knew of their long friendship, but also because it was Fedin who had tried to persuade Pasternak to refuse the
prize. Despite the fact that the poet had informed the academy of his
refusal, the campaign continued to spread. Besides Semichastny's
speech, this was signaled by the fact that a general meeting of Moscow writers was set for October 31 (an announcement was printed in
the *Literary Gazette* on October 30), and it was no secret that the
single point on the agenda was Pasternak. The worst possible punishment within the jurisdiction of the literary authorities—expulsion
from the Writers' Union—had *already* been announced at the October 27 meeting. In this case, what was the purpose of a "mass" meeting of writers? Since Fedin was the head of the Moscow city organization, to tell him that Pasternak was considering suicide might
subdue the ardor of the poet's ill-wishers.

As soon as Ivinskaia told him, Fedin immediately in her presence
called Polikarpov, the same high official who had insisted that Pasternak refuse the prize. This call and Ivinskaia's meeting with Polikarpov
scheduled for the following day showed that the authorities were seriously worried by the threat of the poet's suicide. On the other hand,
it became clear to them that the threat of exile had made a sufficiently
strong impression. They saw in Olga a person through whom it was
possible to influence the poet and reach some kind of compromise.

Meanwhile, the wheels kept spinning. At the meeting of Moscow
writers at noon on October 31, the majority of those in attendance
supported with delight the idea set forth by Semichastny. In their
unanimous resolution, the participants, almost eight hundred strong,
turned to the government with a request to "deprive the traitor B.
Pasternak of Soviet citizenship" and proposed that he be deported
abroad. The prospect that the Soviet leadership would ignore this
"fair and unanimous voice" seemed improbable. Historical precedent
left some hope, however. In December 1930 millions of Soviet people
had demanded the death penalty for members of the so-called Industrial Party, with similar and even more impressive unanimity.
Strangely enough, the government then turned out to be much more

merciful than the masses and softened the lot of the condemned. In this instance, the request of the writers' organization had not yet become the voice of the entire Soviet people. This is evident if we compare the resolution with other materials on the Pasternak affair published with it on the same page of the *Gazette* on November 1. No matter how irate and abusive the letters of rank-and-file Soviet workers were, not one of them (except a letter from students of the Literary Institute closely associated with the Writers' Union) mentioned the desirability of the poet's exile. (This is not hard to understand: for the average Soviet citizen, who would never even dream of a tourist trip abroad, exile would seem to be more of a blessing than a punishment.)

Among those who attended the October 31 meeting alongside the vociferous enemies of Pasternak (such as Alexander Bezymensky, Viktor Pertsov, and Anatoly Sofronov) were writers of a liberal bent (Sergei Smirnov, Leonid Martynov, Boris Slutsky). There was the literary critic Kornely Zelinsky, who had been a friend of the poet in the 1930s and in 1957 was drawn into the attempts to "edit" *Doctor Zhivago* to make it acceptable for publication in the Soviet Union. In the new situation, these facts seemed a disgraceful blot on his political reputation, and his speech was especially malicious. He attacked not only Pasternak but also a young linguist who was a close friend of the poet, Viacheslav Ivanov. One of the consequences of Zelinsky's speech was that Ivanov was fired from his post at Moscow University. Among those who signed up for the debate was Vladimir Dudintsev, whose *Not by Bread Alone,* printed in 1956, had been taken as one of the brightest manifestations of the post-Stalin thaw and had called forth vicious attacks in the Soviet Union. Owing to lack of time and the large number of speakers, however, he did not take the floor.

Among the pejorative characteristics attributed to Pasternak, the epithet "cosmopolitan" commanded special attention. This word entered the abusive vocabulary of Soviet journalism in the second half of the 1940s and, with distinctly antisemitic overtones, was firmly associated with the Zhdanov era in the history of Soviet culture. The introduction of this term into the resolution on Pasternak reflected a conscious effort on the part of the organizers to create an impression of the natural continuity of the new campaign with those of Stalin's time. It revealed the expectations of the conservative camp that the Pasternak affair would lead to a consolidation of their influence.

The meeting's resolution was published in the *Literary Gazette* the next morning,[41] and rumors of the nature of the speeches and the decision spread through Moscow even before that.[42] Apparently, when the rumors reached Ivinskaia and Pasternak, he agreed to send a letter to Khrushchev, who received it at 6 P.M. on October 31.[43] There are no references to the Moscow gathering in the letter, and it is possible that Pasternak hurried to send it in the hope of beating the expected unanimous decision of his colleagues. He refers only to Semichastny's speech delivered at the meeting in Khrushchev's presence.

The text of the short letter (published in *Pravda* on November 1) was not written by Pasternak. It was composed (on the basis of advice she had received from the authorities) by Ivinskaia, her daughter Irina Emelianova, Ariadna Efron, and Viacheslav Ivanov. During the composition of the letter, Olga Ivinskaia was inclined to compromise with the authorities, while Irina and Ivanov took a more uncompromising position. Only one phrase belonged to the poet himself: "I am tied to Russia by birth, by life, and by work. I cannot imagine my fate separated from and outside Russia."[44] The letter to Khrushchev mentioned Pasternak's rejection of the Nobel Prize. (The Soviet public learned about it for the first time from this text.) Saying that leaving his native land would "be equivalent to death," Pasternak asked that the "extreme measure" of exile not be taken. This was an echo of the threat of suicide that, as he knew, had proven effective in Ivinskaia's dealings with Polikarpov and Fedin. Although it mentioned in passing possible "mistakes and errors" (which Pasternak, by nature, was always ready not just to admit but also to accept), the letter contained no reference to guilt and he did not apologize for anything. On the contrary, it ended with a phrase that was hardly appropriate in the context, coming from a man who had just been expelled from the Writers' Union: "With my hand on my heart, I can say that I have done something for Soviet literature and I can still be useful to it."[45]

This was not exactly what Soviet leaders would have like to hear from Pasternak. Of course his letter allowed them to demonstrate their magnanimity by not implementing the threat implied in Semichastny's speech. But they were obviously disappointed by the poet's refusal to admit his guilt publicly and to denounce having written the novel and publishing it in the west. This is why Pasternak's letter was accompanied by a statement from TASS (the government press agency) of a somewhat grotesque character. There was no mention of Pasternak's plea not to be banished. Instead it said that "Pasternak had not so far applied to any Soviet body with a request for a visa to leave for abroad, and from the side of these State bodies there has not been, nor will there be, any refusal to give him a visa." The aim of the TASS statement was twofold. It was meant to rebuke western propaganda claims that Pasternak had become a prisoner of the state and had been coerced into rejecting the Nobel Prize and giving up his plans to go abroad. And it was designed to show both the poet and Soviet readers alike that the conflict was by no means over.

Still the publication of the letter to Khrushchev and the TASS commentary helped to ease the situation. On November 1 (this was the same day that *Pravda* published both documents while the *Gazette* carried the resolution of the writers' meeting and numerous letters of condemnation from Soviet citizens), Ivinskaia and Pasternak were summoned to the Central Committee for a conversation with Polikarpov. He told them straightforwardly what the TASS statement did not say—that in response to the poet's letter to Khrushchev, he was to be permitted to stay in the Soviet Union. Though Polikarpov proved incapable (as Ivinskaia testifies) of finding an appropriate tone in which to address Pasternak, it was clear that the Kremlin had decided to adopt a more conciliatory line. The promise was also given not to expel him and his family from the dacha in Peredelkino or the apartment in Moscow. He was once again allowed to be commissioned by publishing houses to make translations from western languages. He even obtained the privilege of writing freely to correspondents in the west. In exchange, Polikarpov asked Ivinskaia to prepare Pasternak for the need of compiling a longer and more detailed public statement, which could serve as an elaboration of the terse letter addressed to Khrushchev. One should remember that the letter to Khrushchev had been Pasternak's only comment to appear in the Soviet press after the scandal erupted.

The new statement, which was printed in *Pravda* on November 6 under Pasternak's signature, was the product of cooperation between Ivinskaia and Polikarpov—the original letter written by Pasternak had turned out to be totally unacceptable. Officials deleted some of Pasternak's phrases and paragraphs and reorganized and rewrote others. Yet the general content of the printed version did not essentially contradict the poet's own position and intentions. It expanded what he regarded as his only "mistake or error" (mentioned in the letter to Khrushchev): the cablegram accepting the Nobel Prize. Pasternak claimed that this had stemmed from his strong belief that the award was an acknowledgment of his literary achievements and from his inability to see any political reason behind it. He had grounds to assume this, continued the letter in *Pravda,* because his name had already been put forward as a candidate for the prize in 1954, before *Zhivago*. Pasternak dissociated himself from the "critical appraisal" of his work which had given rise to false interpretations of his views on the Russian revolution. It seems clear that by this critical appraisal he meant not so much commentaries in the western press as the critique in the Soviet newspapers (including the letter from *New World*).

Thus the letter to *Pravda,* while seeming to demonstrate Pasternak's readiness to seek a compromise, became in fact a vehicle (the only one available at the moment) of countering lies and accusations. Moreover, it demonstrated that, despite all the vicious attacks, the poet still adhered to the principle of intellectual independence. There was no repentance whatsoever concerning the novel or its publication abroad, although Pasternak did express regret that he was given no opportunity to correct the text. This last remark, like all the others, should be understood as directed not only to publishers in the west but also to the Soviet authorities who rejected the novel out of hand without trying to find a compromise with its author. He gave no indication about the nature of such corrections. After the fierce campaign against him in 1929, Boris Pilniak had drastically rewritten his novella *Mahogany* and published it in the Soviet Union under a new title. But Pasternak gave no sign that he would follow suit.

One cannot, then, call this statement in *Pravda* a capitulation to the state. Of course it was a concession—but a concession more to Olga Ivinskaia than to Polikarpov. Pasternak did agree to sign and publish what in essence he had neither composed nor edited. But Polikarpov made a much greater concession, in my view; as one of the coauthors of the statement, he was forced to preserve the essential elements of Pasternak's arguments. Later, when comparing the Pasternak affair to Solzhenitsyn's behavior after his Nobel Prize, Ivinskaia spoke of her role in composing the letters to Khrushchev and *Pravda* with shame, and she took all the blame for Pasternak's deeds.[46] Her opinion, her interpretation of events, and her misgivings played a crucial role in Pasternak's choice of a line of action. If it were not for his concern for her and his family, the poet might have conducted himself differently. But there is no basis for seeing in these statements any cowardice, hypocrisy, or moral lapse. One cannot judge his behavior in this situation according to the criteria adopted by the Soviet dissidents of the following decade, who by the way were inspired by Pasternak's example. Political outspokenness is not necessarily an indication of an artist's internal strength or honesty. After all, the pose of unbent, stalwart hero was always alien to Pasternak: the story of a poet has "to be assembled from inessentials that would bear witness to the concessions he made to pity and coercion."[47] He never really regretted the appearance in November 1958 of the letters signed by him. He considered them the kind of "inessentials" that are unavoidable in a poet's life.

13

Last Years

After Pasternak's second letter appeared in *Pravda*, the press campaign against him died down. But events of the next few weeks demonstrated that the established equilibrium was unstable and that there was still strong antipathy toward the poet. From the accounts of foreign correspondents about their meetings with Pasternak, it is possible to trace the change in his moods and also the shifts in the pressure he faced. At first he voiced no complaints about the recent storm. On the contrary, he said that such political imbroglios are inevitable and expressed the hope that the campaign against him would promote Russia's political evolution in the long run. (The future proved the poet correct in this prognosis). He repeated that *Doctor Zhivago* was the principal work of his life but suggested that his western audience now pay attention to his new collection of apolitical lyric poems, written in the last few years and being prepared for publication abroad.[1] At the same time, the poet reaffirmed that the recent scandal had not shaken his resolution to choose his own literary fate and not to leave it in the hands of the Soviet authorities.

Despite the halt in the concentrated campaign against Pasternak, attacks against him continued to appear in the Soviet press. The statement of Sergei Smirnov, who had presided over the meeting of October 31, was published in the journal *Agitator.* Several speeches delivered at the congress of the Writers' Union of the Russian Federation in December 1958 also contained sharply hostile remarks. In one respect, these statements had an even greater significance than those of the campaign of October, since they were more spontaneous than ritualized. At the same time, there was stronger behind-the-scenes pressure of literary bureaucrats on Pasternak. This forced him to become more aggressive. In an interview given at the beginning of January to the British correspondent Alan Moray Williams, he announced, "The writer is the Faust of modern society, the only surviving individualist in a mass age. To his orthodox contemporaries he seems a semi-madman. The Union of Soviet Writers would like me to go on my knees to them—but they will never make me." [2] This interview was published on January 19 in the London *News Chronicle* and was immediately broadcast by western radio stations in Russian for Soviet listeners. Max Hayward justly remarks that this interview undid all of Polikarpov's efforts to present Pasternak as a "penitent." [3] It led to a new summons for Ivinskaya to appear before Central Committee officials and a strong reprimand to the poet, accompanied by a demand to end contacts with western correspondents. On January 27 he wrote to one of his acquaintances in Belgium, "You will never imagine the ignominious treatment to which with short intervals I am subjected. You can not imagine to what extent my means of correspondence are difficult and limited. And I have to remain silent about it." [4]

On the other hand, it was precisely in these weeks that the western repercussions of his November letters to Khrushchev and *Pravda* began to reach him. The poet could discover for himself how his motives had been misinterpreted by European intellectuals and the bewilderment that his actions evoked among his supporters. In defense of Pasternak, Manya Harari (who with Max Hayward translated *Doctor Zhivago* into English) wrote:

> No one can believe that Pasternak is acting freely, but the shocking phrases in the letters may well achieve the intended result of alienating the respect and sympathy of many people in England, including even some who are ready to believe that the pressure on him may be extreme. Nor is this disappointment merely a frustrated demand for vicarious heroism: it comes from a real and deep need, felt always and particularly in our time, not only for heroism but for heroic figures—a need to admire and to be assured that no pressure is finally irresistible to the human spirit. [5]

In November Jules Romains printed two articles in the Parisian newspaper *Aurore* which censured Pasternak for the letters published in the Soviet press. He thought that Pasternak could and should have preserved a proud silence in response to the persecution of the totalitarian state. In the middle of December, in a speech to alumni of Petersburg University in Paris, the renowned ballet master Serge Lifar announced, "Pasternak should have drunk the cup to the dregs. I condemn him for his penitential letter." [6] Regardless of the fact that western journals and newspapers were strictly forbidden in the Soviet Union, Pasternak managed to follow the controversy in the west closely: his correspondents in Europe and friends in the Soviet Union gathered journals and clippings for him.

Under the influence of these conflicting attacks, Pasternak wrote the poem "Nobelevskaia premia" (The Nobel Prize), which was first published in a London newspaper and turned out to be the most widely known of all his lyrical works. Its first stanza directly expressed the hopelessness of his situation:

I am lost like a beast in an enclosure.
Somewhere are people, freedom and light.
Behind me is the noise of pursuit,
And there is no way out.[7]

A similar tangle of insoluble contradictions also arose in the poet's personal life. The enormous strain through which he lived during the days of the Nobel scandal lay heavy on the shoulders of those closest to him, primarily Zinaida Nikolaevna and Olga Ivinskaia. Now that the storm seemed a thing of the past, the crisis in his relations with the two women became acute. He was on the verge of breaking with his family and starting a new life with Ivinskaia. Everything had been prepared—even a place to live in Tarusa—when Pasternak suddenly realized again that he did not have the strength to overturn all that had been forged over so many years. The poet's refusal to leave his family strained his relationship with Ivinskaia to the limit.

Ivinskaia claims in her memoirs that Pasternak's disagreement with her served as the impetus for "The Nobel Prize" and that the poem is exclusively private and was not intended for publication. Her interpretation is occasioned by a natural desire to exaggerate the degree of her influence on the writer. But "The Nobel Prize" has a wider meaning and, in its original version, accurately reflects the thorny situation of the poet vis à-vis both his Soviet environment and the western world. The passing of the poem to the English journalist Anthony Brown, a correspondent for the *Daily Mail*, was not a spontaneous act, as Ivinskaia claims. Pasternak was obviously seeking opportunities to inform the west of his true situation and did this at his own risk, not waiting for advice from Ivinskaia or anyone else. Moreover, he now had even firmer grounds than in May 1956 (when he gave his novel to Sergio d'Angelo) to present Ivinskaia with a fait accompli— to a significant degree his conciliatory line of action during the Nobel scandal was carried out by him as a concession to her. The poem "The Nobel Prize" belonged to an entirely different and alternative line in the poet's conduct.

In giving "The Nobel Prize," along with three other recent poems, to Anthony Brown, Pasternak wanted them to be sent to his friend in Paris, Jacqueline de Proyart, and ultimately to be published in the west. This was not the first time that Pasternak conveyed similar instructions for his friends abroad through a third (and sometimes accidental) party. But what he could not have imagined was that one of these poems would be printed in a newspaper and would immediately cause an international sensation. It is not difficult to understand the reasons for this now: "The Nobel Prize" was the poet's first confessional document attesting to the dimensions of the pressure exerted on him, and his western audience was thirsty to receive as much information as possible directly from Pasternak. But the fact that "The Nobel Prize" received so much publicity, usually not accorded to lyrics, deeply troubled the author. In a conversation with a correspondent from United Press International at Peredelkino, he expressed his anger in no uncertain terms. The journalist reports that Zinaida Nikolaevna said to her husband: "How many times have I told you not to trust journalists? They are only exploiting you for personal gain. If this continues, I will leave you." [8]

This episode further complicated the poet's relations with the authorities. Apparently, despairing of their attempts to control his actions through Olga Ivinskaia's mediation, they decided on an unprecedentedly rude and humiliating intimidation. A police car came to the dacha, and he was brought to Moscow to the public prosecutor's office at the Supreme Court building. He was informed that his actions qualified as "betrayal of the Motherland" in the criminal code. [9] Such crimes are considered extremely serious and can entail capital punishment. The clerk who was present at the interrogation stroked the poet's hand and urged him to stay calm: "Don't worry—nothing is going to happen to you." After a four-hour interrogation about his contacts with foreigners, Pasternak was released and taken home. But the investigation lasted for several more months. Such a turn of events placed not only Pasternak but also Ivinskaia in a dangerous position—she more than anyone else was involved in his literary affairs. Through her, the authorities gave Pasternak the order to leave Moscow quickly, before the upcoming visit of British Prime Minister Harold Macmillan to the Soviet Union. In the government's view, England had spawned the cult of the poet, which in the end led to the Nobel scandal. The writer's sisters lived there. The English parliament had discussed the Pasternak affair after the publication of "The Nobel Prize" in the *Daily Mail*. It was difficult to imagine that no foreign journalist accompanying Macmillan would try to see Pasternak in order to find out what had prompted him to publish "The Nobel Prize" in the west. It was even more difficult to predict how the obstinate poet would react.

Pasternak answered the order to leave Moscow with a firm refusal; Ivinskaia had to go to Leningrad without him. This led to a new falling out which was reflected in two stanzas added to "The Nobel Prize." In the new version of the poem, the tie between the campaign unleashed against the poet and the vicissitudes of his personal life became more apparent than in the initial text.

At the same time, Pasternak accepted an invitation to visit Georgia, sent to him and Zinaida by Nina Tabidze. They flew to Tbilisi on February 19, two days before Macmillan's arrival. This was Pasternak's first departure from Moscow for many years: the last time he had left—also for Georgia—was in the fall of 1945, not long before beginning work on *Doctor Zhivago*. The new trip was filled with nostalgia and appeared as a kind of reversed parallel to the past: it was here in the autumn of 1931 that Pasternak had spent the happiest days of his married life with Zinaida; here he had experienced his "second birth" with full force. Now a legal inquiry hung over his head, the results of which were impossible to predict, and it was unclear how his recent disagreement with Ivinskaia would turn out. Every day he went to the post office, sending one letter after another to Olga in Leningrad, but there was no reply. These experiences poisoned the joy of meetings with friends, Georgian writers and artists, who admired him and were not afraid to organize a warm reception for the disgraced poet. Pasternak could not dream of similar treatment in the capital.

The trip to Georgia lasted a little over three weeks. Part of his former misapprehension was dispelled as soon as Ivinskaia returned from Leningrad: their disagreement ended happily. But the investigation continued; as one of the police measures accompanying it, a blockade was imposed between the poet and the outside world. After February not a single letter from abroad reached him. This was a cruel blow not only because it obstructed the normal course of his publishing affairs—for want of avenues to express his views in art, Pasternak voiced his innermost thoughts in his letters to correspondents, regardless of whether they were his intellectual equals. These contacts allowed him to feel that the isolation to which he was doomed in Russia was surmountable. The strain grew unbearable when, in April, Ivinskaia also received a summons to the ongoing investigation. As it turned out, she was summoned merely to be informed about the decision to end the inquiry. In exchange for the poet's promise to stop seeing foreigners, the postal blockade was lifted and epistolary contact with the outside world was restored.

The authorities' conciliatory gesture was evidently a result of a new wave of liberalization in literary life, which had been initiated on the eve of the Third Congress of the Writers' Union in May 1959. One of the signs of this liberal turn was the disappearance, in the discussion that preceded the congress and in official addresses and debates at the congress, of references to Pasternak and to the Nobel scandal. This was amazing not only in view of the campaign that had been unleashed in the Soviet press in October 1958, but also with respect to the writers' congress of the Russian Federation in December. Without specific instructions from above, it would have been impossible to achieve such a disciplined response and such unanimity. But the most unequivocal signal of the new course was Khrushchev's own speech at the congress, which was patently moderate. It advised more tolerant treatment for intellectuals who strayed from the official party line. He called on writers to stop castigating one another and claimed that the battle against revisionists was over. The new task was "to help those Comrades in their transition from mistaken views to the correct principled positions." Khrushchev spoke specifically of the Dudintsev case, but one could assume by analogy that his principle of reeducating writers could be applied to Pasternak as well. In conjunction with reports of the Third Congress, the western press carried the news that the way was clear for Pasternak's return to the Writers' Union, if he would submit "a letter requesting readmission and expressing regret for the disturbance raised last fall." [10]

These rumors multiplied when, after the congress, Konstantin Fedin replaced Alexei Surkov as head of the Writers' Union. It was said that the authorities' irritation at the inappropriate actions of the literary bureaucrats during the Nobel uproar had brought about the shift. The rumors that were also circulating of Khrushchev's beneficial intervention in the Pasternak affair—a stormy outburst against Surkov, for providing him with misleading information on *Doctor Zhivago*—surfaced later, in florid detail, in the memoirs of the literary critic and dissident Arkady Belinkov.[11] The western press even claimed that *Zhivago* would be published in the Soviet Union in a year or two.[12] One imagines that all these rumors were carefully orchestrated by government circles in Moscow and had more to do with Soviet foreign policy than anything else. They were connected with the detente in the relations between the great powers which followed Macmillan's visit to the Soviet Union and preceded Khrushchev's trip to the United States in the autumn of 1959. Of course the Soviet leaders could help feeling a justified displeasure with the manner in which the campaign against Pasternak had been conducted in October 1958. Khrushchev's memoirs, in which he admits that his administration committed serious blunders in the Pasternak affair, are a belated reflection of this embarrassment. Yet it would be a mistake to attribute the Nobel campaign exclusively to Surkov's personal envy of Pasternak or his hard-liner instincts. As head of the Writers' Union, Surkov simply tried to demonstrate his administrative zeal; it was not he but higher powers who determined literary politics. The realignment of the literary bureaucracy in the spring of 1959 was strictly cosmetic, and Surkov preserved real power in the Writers' Union even after the largely ceremonial post of first secretary had passed to Fedin. A radical change in the attitude of the authorities toward Pasternak did not take place. As is known all too well, the prose text of *Doctor Zhivago* would not appear in the poet's native land for another thirty years. Pasternak himself considered it necessary to refute the rumors of official lenience. In August 1959 he wrote to Steven Spender: "My situation is worse, more unbearable and endangered than I can say or you [can] think of." [13]

Nonetheless, several minor changes in Pasternak's official status did become perceptible in May. His name once again appeared on the posters of the Moscow theaters in which his versions of Shakespeare and Schiller were being performed. In Moscow literary circles, there was talk of renewed negotiations for the publication of his collected poems, the galley proofs of which had been held since the autumn of 1957. Some attempts had also been made to broach Pasternak about his readiness to return to the Writers' Union.[14] As the condition for his readmission, it was proposed to the poet that he write a new novel about the achievements of socialism in the Soviet Union. But all this proved unsuccessful. Pasternak flatly refused to take any steps to return to the Writers' Union.

As for a new novel, Pasternak had in fact thought of another large prose work. But it would not have pleased the authorities. According to the testimony of Zoia Maslenikova, it would have been a detective novel describing how an emigrant illegally returns to Soviet Russia with high patriotic motives. A story based on an emigrant's infiltration into Soviet territory would certainly have been unacceptable, since it would shatter the myth of sealed Soviet borders so firmly rooted in the consciousness of the people. But it would have been even more inconceivable to see elevated, patriotic motives in such a criminal action. It is not known in precisely which period of Soviet history the author planned to set his novel. Similar journeys by emigrants over the Soviet border (in many instances organized and controlled by the Soviet secret police) were known to have taken place only in the 1920s. The trips of Boris Savinkov and Vladimir Shulgin, who stood at opposite political poles in prerevolutionary Russia,[15] gained the most publicity of these excursions. But more likely the prototype of Pasternak's planned novel was neither of these men, but Prince Pavel Dolgorukov. A prominent figure in the Constitutional Democratic Party, he was acquainted in the prerevolutionary years with Leo Tolstoy and belonged to exactly those circles of the liberal Moscow intelligentsia that make up the background of *Doctor Zhivago*. During his years in emigration, he illegally crossed the border of Soviet Russia twice. His first attempt, in 1924, ended in failure and he was deported by frontier guards. In June 1926, at the age of sixty, he completed the difficult and extremely risky journey across the border. He spent a month and a half at large in Soviet Russia but was eventually identified and arrested on the way from Kharkov to Moscow. After eleven months in prison, he was shot in June 1927, together with eighteen other Russian aristocrats.[16]

The idea for this novel did not only represent Pasternak's desire for an exciting plot. With the exception of the short period 1945–46, when the victory of the Red Army over Hitler led to the rapid growth of pro-Soviet sentiments in émigré circles, over the course of three decades—since 1929—there had been almost no contact between the emigration and Soviet society. Russian life in the diaspora, which was rich in diverse trends of political thought, philosophy, and art, was wholly unknown in the Soviet Union. To the Soviet people, the emigration seemed to belong to another planet. Conversely, since the 1930s, interest in what was happening in Stalin's Russia dwindled in the émigré press. For émigrés, the last vestiges of the prerevolutionary era in Soviet literature were Boris Pasternak and Anna Akhmatova, both out of favor.

The publication of *Doctor Zhivago* in 1957 and the award of the Nobel Prize to Pasternak were greeted ecstatically by most Russian émigrés.[17] Pasternak's novel, his autobiography of 1956, and new poems that seemed to show a deliberate rupture with modernist aesthetics elicited enthusiastic response even from such émigré literati as Wladimir Weidlé and Yury Terapiano, who in the 1920s had spoken about him with skepticism or dislike. Pasternak was one of the first writers in the Soviet Union who scorned the official ban on contacts with émigré literary figures. Among his correspondents in the west were old acquaintances from Moscow and Berlin whom he had not seen since 1923—Boris Zaitsev, a prominent émigré writer, and Fyodor Stepun, a philosopher who was Pasternak's mentor in Musagetes.

The admiration of the émigré audience for Pasternak's work found expression in a three-volume edition of his work edited by Gleb Struve of the University of California[18] and Boris Filippov. Although the publication appeared in 1961, work on it had begun in the autumn of 1958. Struve and Filippov were considered "nonpersons" in the Soviet Union, and the very interest of such people in a Soviet writer was highly compromising. In this case things were even worse: Pasternak not only supported the idea of a Russian-language edition abroad, but also agreed that it would be carried out by those particular scholars.[19] At the request of the author, they used as the base of the texts to be included the smuggled galleys of the unpublished Moscow edition of 1957, in which many early verses had undergone significant revisions. But the editors also carried out formidable independent research and discovered a wealth of forgotten publications of Pasternak in rare literary miscellanies and journals. Until the 1980s, this splendid publication remained the most complete and reliable source of information about the poet. Another expression of the cult of Pasternak that arose in emigration was the first volume of the literary miscellany *Aerial Ways* (1960), whose name was taken from his novella of 1924 and symbolically alluded to the inability of state borders to halt the intense contact between the halves of Russian culture. This volume, which consisted of poetry and essays, constituted a kind of festschrift to the poet.

This explains why, when thinking over a novel about contemporary Russia, Pasternak proposed to construct it around a patriotically disposed émigré. But at the same time he also cherished a distant historical theme. His trip to Georgia in February 1959, and the "archeological" impressions he brought back from it, strengthened his desire to write a novel whose action would lie in the third century, the period of the Christianization of Georgia. Its main theme would have been that of the organic unity of pagan pantheism and Christianity,[20] an idea already lurking in *Safe Conduct*. But the historical novel about Georgia, just like the novel about an émigré, never went beyond the planning stage. Frequent ailments during his last years sharply reduced the poet's productivity. He forbade himself to write if he did not feel well: such indispositions might have an adverse effect on the content and quality of the work in progress.

Beginning in the summer of 1959, Pasternak turned to the genre in which he felt least confident, prose drama. He set about writing one with some anxiety: he did not wish it to be in any way inferior to *Doctor Zhivago*. Regardless of the experience he had accumulated in drama by that time as a translator (from Swinburne to Shakespeare and Schiller) and of his efforts to write a play during the war years, he felt himself to be a novice in this area. Work on the new play, entitled *Slepaia krasavitsa* (The Blind Beauty), progressed slowly and with difficulty, and in April 1960 only two scenes of the prologue and two scenes of act one were ready in rough draft. This constituted only a fraction of his ambitious project for a "historical chronicle" that would have encompassed a sixty-year period of Russian history in the nineteenth century, on the basis of life on a single manorial estate. As if foreseeing that this project would remain unrealized, the author confided its contents in detail several months before his death to the writer and artist Olga Carlisle.[21] The authenticity of her detailed account of the conversation was confirmed when the surviving fragments of the play were first published seven years later.

Pasternak's panorama would have treated the decades before liberation of the serfs in 1861, during the period of crisis in the institution of serfdom, and the vast changes in Russian life after the reform. Two motifs connect this dramatic project with *Doctor Zhivago*. First, the theme of the human versus the social would have been sounded powerfully. The characters of this play—whether landowners or serfs—possessed features of striking physical similarity. Both groups resembled the founding father of the estate, whose bust was gathering dust on a shelf. Here, in an unexpected twist, the poet repeats his favorite idea concerning the universal kinship of all things in the universe. Second, just as *Doctor Zhivago* is a novel about the novel, so *The Blind Beauty* was to be a play about the theater. The central heroes were not just peasants, but peasant actors. "The historical chronicle," therefore, echoed the poet's eternal theme—the nature of an artist's freedom. Its central event—the emancipation of 1861—had something in common with the atmosphere of portentous change expressed in the concluding passages of *Doctor Zhivago*. The new project turned out to be an attempt "to play with fate" just as the creation of the novel had been. In a letter to Jacqueline de Proyart, he defined his new work as a painful effort to "leap forward, get away from the ground, from the present, to seize a small part of that obscure and magic thing called destiny, the future." [22]

Pasternak's illness cut work on the play short. He felt sick after Easter Day of 1960, immediately following his first and only meeting with his great admirer in Germany, the poet Renate Schweitzer, with whom he had been corresponding for two years. His last months were darkened by an increased tension and confusion in his personal life. Since the summer and autumn of 1959, one quarrel with old friends followed another. His friendships with Boris Livanov, Genrikh Neuhaus, and Valentin Asmus were on the verge of breaking, and his relationship with Anna Akhmatova (whom he no longer saw) and Nina Tabidze (who in the conflict between Olga Ivinskaia and Zinaida Nikolaevna took the side of the latter) became strained. The poet's desire to break sharply with the past found expression in his intention to destroy the draft manuscripts of his early literary works—prose, poems, and translations of Rilke—which he had preserved throughout his life. [23] From April 23 to May 5, Pasternak was still able to write and sent Ivinskaia notes about the state of his health. But during the night of May 7–8 he had a massive heart attack (a previous one, less severe, took place several days before and went undetected). Three days later the doctors diagnosed for the first time cancer of the left lung, which had spread to his stomach; but even before their diagnosis Pasternak had guessed that he was fatally ill. In his last days he was conscious and said that he "wanted to die," that he "heard the breathing of another world." On the morning of May 30 he bid his relatives farewell, and during the night of May 30–31 he died in his sleep.

There were no reports in the Soviet press about the death of the poet. Only *Literatura i zhizn* (Literature and Life) and the *Literary Gazette* placed the Literary Fund's one-sentence official notice about the death of one of its members, in which even the phrase "with regret" (standard in such formulas) was absent. The date and place of the funeral were printed nowhere, and the authorities took pains to prevent the gathering of a crowd at the cemetery. Appearance at the funeral in Peredelkino was regarded as a demonstration of political disloyalty,[24] and the secretary of the Writer's Union, Voronkov, wrote down the names of those who attended. Still, close to two thousand people gathered at the cemetery. Western correspondents noted that there was no religious service at the grave. The unusually short ceremony consisted of a graveside speech by Valentin Asmus, a short comment by an admirer in working clothes whom no one knew, and a reading of Pasternak's poetry. The fear in official circles that the poet's death would lead to a disruption of public order created a strained atmosphere at the burial, evoking parallels with Pushkin's funeral in 1837.

The events of the ensuing days strengthened the parallel. Just as the post-mortem sorting out of Pushkin's manuscripts had been carried out under the unremitting eye of a gendarme, so the authorities hurried to take Pasternak's literary legacy into their own hands after his death. Immediately after the burial, KGB agents confiscated the manuscripts of *The Blind Beauty* from Ivinskaia. In August and September 1960 she and her daughter Irina were arrested, and after several months of investigation they were sentenced to eight and three years imprisonment, respectively, in a labor camp. The threat of arrest and imprisonment, which constantly hovered over the poet in the last two decades of his life and was so characteristic of the atmosphere described in *Doctor Zhivago*, did indeed materialize for the people close to him. Although Ivinskaia and her daughter were charged with illegal possession of foreign currency, it is clear that their alleged transgression was only a pretext. The real reason was the resolution of the Soviet authorities to place the posthumous publication of Pasternak's works under their complete control. Moreover, they tried to play upon the old frictions between Ivinskaia and the members of Pasternak's family.

The author himself, who was distinguished in his financial affairs by an extraordinary indifference and naiveté, left unclear and contradictory instructions about his literary rights both within Russia and abroad.[25] His illegal (from the viewpoint of Soviet law) contacts with foreign publishing houses further complicated the issue. A month and a half before his death, he signed a document giving Ivinskaia power of attorney in his literary and financial affairs. She had every reason to suppose that she alone was authorized to decide all matters connected with the posthumous publication of the poet's works. Apparently the secret police found out about Ivinskaia's intention to smuggle out to Feltrinelli the manuscripts of Pasternak's unpublished works[26] and decided to intervene. It is worth noting that precisely at this time the KGB undertook another action in order to gain full control of a literary creation: in February 1961 they confiscated all copies of the manuscript of Vasily Grossman's novel *Life and Fate,* including rough drafts and even the typewriter ribbons, either in the author's possession or elsewhere. Ivinskaia's anonymity in the west allowed the authorities to assume that her arrest would pass unnoticed. In the numerous interviews with Pasternak and articles about him that had been printed abroad since 1957, his first and second wives and sons from both marriages were often mentioned, but Ivinskaia and her role in his life became known only after the first news of her arrest reached the west toward the end of 1960. It called forth a new tempest of indignation in the world press.

Paradoxically, the new ordeals that came to Ivinskaia after the poet's death somehow paved the way for his posthumous literary rehabilitation. After she and her daughter had been tried, the ban on publishing Pasternak in the Soviet Union was lifted, and in October 1961 a collection of his poetry was released. One of the reasons for the hasty publication of the book was clearly the desire to counter the campaign in the west in defense of Ivinskaia, and to demonstrate a concern for the poet's widow, who proved to be in difficult material straits after his death. The publication was timed to coincide with the Twenty-Second Party Congress and served as a harbinger of liberal changes. The new collection did not take into account the author's wishes as expressed in the unpublished proofs of 1957.[27] In 1962 preparation of a more complete collection of Pasternak's poems began in the prestigious series *Biblioteka poeta* (The Poet's Library), which appeared only in 1965 with Andrei Siniavsky's introductory article.[28] This was a brief period when, after Khrushchev had been overthrown, censorship was somewhat weakened and the liberal camp of the Soviet intelligentsia was able to achieve a number of successes.[29]

But this by no means led to the rehabilitation of *Doctor Zhivago* in the Soviet Union. The situation of the novel became ever more problematic: liberal admirers of the poet avoided mentioning it so as not to irritate the authorities and to receive permission to publish and reprint as many of Pasternak's texts as possible; the conservative circles continued to dream of erasing from the cultural memory any work that did not conform to their standards. In the 1960s not only disseminating *Doctor Zhivago* underground but even reading it were considered criminal offenses, and a number of people paid for their curiosity with several years in prison.[30]

Only the sweeping changes in the cultural climate of the country under Mikhail Gorbachev brought about a full rehabilitation of the novel and its author, along with reevaluations of a great number of previously forbidden texts of Soviet and émigré literature. The first signal of this new trend was an article by Dmitry Likhachev, one of the most prominent figures in the new system, which was published on January 1, 1987, in the *Literary Gazette*. He mentioned his recent memorandum on *Doctor Zhivago,* which called for a revised official evaluation. Soon the Writers' Union announced that it had repealed its resolution of October 27, 1958 (to expel Pasternak from the union) and approved the impending publication of the novel in the Soviet Union. In the torrent of literary works that have flooded the Soviet presses after decades of prohibition, and also against the background of massive de-Stalinization, Pasternak's novel has lost the pungency of political sensation imparted by the circumstances of its appearance in the west and by the Nobel controversy. Its publication in *New World* at the beginning of 1988 was accompanied by appeals to canonize Pasternak, in accord with the habitual ways of Soviet society. Yet, whatever scale the official cult of the poet will take as a result of all this, and no matter how consonant the various slogans of *perestroika* may seem with many of his pronouncements and convictions, Pasternak's works and fate serve as a constant reminder of the eternally nonconformist essence of art.

Notes

Index

Notes

1. Origins

1. The translation is by Christopher Barnes, from Boris Pasternak, *The Voice of Prose*, ed. Barnes (Edinburgh: Polygon, 1986), I, 57.
2. *Pisateli. Avtobiografii i portrety sovremennykh russkikh prozaikov*, ed. V. Lidin (Moscow: "Sovremennye problemy" N. A. Stoliar, 1926), p. 227.
3. In 1953 Akhmatova expressed her admiration for Pasternak's language: "Boris Leonidovich speaks marvelously, with a purely Muscovite tongue. I have never heard better language." Lydia Chukovskaia, *Zapiski ob Anne Akhmatovoi* (Paris: YMCA Press, 1980), II, 27.
4. Although in the nineteenth century the cosmopolitan character of this port city on the banks of the Black Sea yielded ever more to Russification, many of the exotic features of Odessa's inhabitants survived up to the revolution. This is evident in many leading writers who emerged during the early Soviet years: Isaak Babel, Yury Olesha, Ilf and Petrov, Eduard Bagritsky, and Valentin Kataev.
5. Boris' cousin of the same age, the Soviet classicist Olga Freidenberg, was annoyed by the "Odessa" and "Jewish" roots of their family.
6. See V. A. Yakovlev, "Koe-chto ob inoplemennikakh v istorii g. Odessy," *Iz proshlogo Odessy. Sbornik statei*, ed. L. M. de Ribas (Odessa: Izdanie G. G. Marazli, 1894), pp. 382–383.
7. *The Memoirs of Leonid Pasternak*, trans. Jennifer Bradshaw (London: Quartet Books, 1982), p. 89.
8. Leonid Pasternak, *Zapisi raznykh let* (Moscow: Sovetskii khudozhnik, 1975), p. 101.
9. It was only in 1907 that Rozalia resumed sporadic concert activity.
10. Leonid Pasternak, *Zapisi raznykh let*, pp. 106–107 (entry dated 1943), p. 101 (entry dated 1941).
11. See Sergei Shcherbatov, *Khudozhnik v ushedshei Rossii* (New York: Izdatel'stvo imeni Chekhova, 1955), p. 30.

12. Works of the impressionists were shown in Moscow in 1891 at the French Art and Industry Exhibit.

13. Ilya Ehrenburg spoke about the "chaotic impressionism" of Pasternak's poetry in a review of Osip Mandelshtam's book *Tristia* in *Novaia russkaia kniga* (Berlin), 2 (1922), 19.

14. Published in *Den' poezii. 1981* (Moscow: Sovetskii pisatel', 1981), pp. 160–161. Cf. Z. Maslenikova, "Portret poeta," *Literaturnaia Gruziia*, 10–11 (1978), 271.

15. A detailed comparison of the aesthetic views of Boris Pasternak and his father was presented by Daša Di Simplicio at the Pasternak Symposium in Jerusalem, May 1984.

16. Marina Tsvetaeva, *Neizdannye pis'ma*, ed. G. Struve and N. Struve (Paris: YMCA Press, 1972), pp. 251–252; *Novyi mir*, 4 (1969), 202.

17. *The Correspondence of Boris and Olga Freidenberg, 1910–1934*, ed. Elliott Mossman, trans. Mossman and Margaret Wettlin (New York: Harcourt Brace Jovanovich, 1982), pp. 192–193.

18. *A Vanished Present: The Memoirs of Alexander Pasternak*, trans. Ann Pasternak Slater (New York: Harcourt Brace Jovanovich, 1984), p. 16.

19. Boris Pasternak, *Vozdushnye puti: Proza raznykh let* (Moscow: Sovetskii pisatel', 1982), pp. 416–417; *An Essay in Autobiography*, trans. Manya Harari (London: Collins and Harvill Press, 1959), pp. 34–37.

20. Lydia Chukovskaia, *Zapiski ob Anne Akhmatovoi*, II, 5 (entry of June 13, 1952).

21. Christopher Barnes, "Biography, Autobiography and 'Sister Life': Some Problems in Chronicling Pasternak's Earlier Years," *Irish Slavonic Studies*, 4 (1983), 51.

22. "During a pianissimo passage, this door opened and our nyanya, without batting an eyelid, walked slowly and with an air of importance across the whole room, empty teacup in hand. 'Squeak! squeak!' went the floorboards. 'Shsh! Nyanya! Quiet!'—but she paid no heed and at a leisurely pace proceeded diagonally across the room into the kitchen as if nothing had happened." *Memoirs of Leonid Pasternak*, p. 138.

23. Alexander Pasternak, *A Vanished Present*, p. 66.

24. Boris Pasternak, *Vozdushnye puti*, pp. 422–423; *Essay in Autobiography*, p. 45.

25. *Memoirs of Leonid Pasternak*, p. 68.

26. A pastel rough draft of the painting was kept for many years in the Pasternaks' Moscow apartment, but was lost during World War II.

27. *Voprosy literatury*, 9 (1972), 144.

28. In contrast to western Christianity, in the Russian Orthodox Church this holiday has special significance.

29. It is noteworthy that the first events described in *Doctor Zhivago* are once again concerned with 1903.

30. This story, never finished, was published posthumously. The full text of the extant manuscript appeared in *Slavica Hierosolymitana. Slavic Studies of the Hebrew University*, 1 (Jerusalem, 1977). The exact date of its composition is

unknown; the poet's son Evgeny suggests that his father worked on it during the winter of 1916–17.

31. Z. Maslenikova, "Portret poeta," *Literaturnaia Gruziia*, 3 (1979), 142 (entry of September 14, 1959).

32. L. O. Pasternak, *Zapisi raznykh let*, pp. 80–82; cf. *Memoirs of Leonid Pasternak*, pp. 68–69. Pasternak took the painting *Congratulations* with him when he left for Germany, and it now resides with the Oxford collection of the artist's family. Many years later, Igor Grabar praised the painting highly in his obituary article, "Pamiati Leonida Pasternaka," which was published in the Moscow newspaper *Sovetskoe iskusstvo*, July 13, 1945.

33. *Memoirs of Leonid Pasternak*, pp. 33–34, 58.

34. Abram Efros, an art critic who was extremely hostile to Leonid Pasternak, speaks about this in his "Zametki ob iskusstve," published in *Novyi put'* (Moscow), 8 (February 26, 1917), 36–37.

35. Maxim Gorky was one of those who had particularly strong pro-Jewish sentiments. Leonid Pasternak met him and painted his portrait in 1906 in Berlin.

36. The portrait of Bialik that Pasternak painted at this time was reproduced in the Moscow journal *Evreiskaia zhizn'*, 14–15 (April 3, 1916).

37. An expanded version of this article was included with an article by the eminent German art critic, Max Osborn, in an album about Leonid Pasternak published in 1924 in Berlin by the publisher Sztybel. A German translation of Bialik's article was included in his *Essays*, trans. Viktor Kellner (Berlin: Jüdische Verlag, 1925), pp. 191–214.

38. Gershon Svet, "Pamiati L. Pasternaka. K stoletiiu so dnia rozhdeniia," *Vestnik Izrailia*, 30–31 (March–April 1962), 40.

39. L. S. Fleishman, "K publikatsii pis'ma L. O. Pasternaka k Bialiku," *Slavica Hierosolymitana. Slavic Studies of the Hebrew University*, 1 (Jerusalem, 1977), 309–310. Bialik and Pasternak met again in Germany at the end of the 1920s.

40. L. O. Pasternak, *Zapisi raznykh let*, p. 108. Parallel with the jubilee exhibition of Pasternak, which was organized in Berlin in connection with his seventieth birthday and was a great success, Sztybel printed a large album about him (with the article by Max Osborn). Almost the entire press run of the book was burned at the printer's after the Nazis came to power. The Tolstoy scholar, V. F. Bulgakov, who was living in emigration in Prague, later indicated that the book was burned by order of the Nazi authorities. See Valentin Bulgakov, "Leonid Osipovich Pasternak (1862–1945)," *Vstrechi s khudozhnikami* (Leningrad: Khudozhnik RSFSR, 1969), pp. 50–51. This evidence conforms to hints in Leonid's memoirs (*Zapisi raznykh let*, pp. 94–95).

41. See his letter to David Shor in Tel-Aviv on September 16, 1936. The letter is preserved at the Jewish University and National Library, Hebrew University, Jerusalem. A facsimile is published in Boris Gass, *Pasynki vremennykh otchizn* (Tel-Aviv, 1985).

42. "The whole world has gone out of its mind," he writes in his notes from that time. *Memoirs of Leonid Pasternak*, p. 76.

43. *Correspondence of Boris Pasternak and Olga Freidenberg*, pp. 89–90.

44. Valentin Parnac, "Les poètes russes d'aujourd'hui," *Europe, Revue mensuelle* (Paris), 40 (April 15, 1926), 501. Parnac returned to Russia in 1922 after a few years in France. He served as the prototype for Parnok in Osip Mandelshtam's *Egyptian Stamp*.

45. Gass, *Pasynki vremennykh otchizn*, pp. 56–58. "The Abravanels themselves were both certain and proud of the nobility of their origin—so proud and certain, indeed, that they claimed descent from the Davidic dynasty and settlement in Spain in pre-Roman times. Although the family's genealogical tree does not go back farther than five generations before Don Isaac's times, there is evidence that the claim received credence, at least among some leading Jews, not only in Don Isaac's day, but also four centuries earlier."—B. Netanyahu, *Don Isaac Abravanel. Statesman and Philosopher* (Philadelphia: Jewish Publication Society of America, 1972), p. 3.

46. Jacqueline de Proyart, *Pasternak* (Paris: Gallimard, 1964), p. 40.

47. *New York Times Book Review*, October 29, 1961.

48. Alfred Rammelmeyer, "Die Phillips-Universität zu Marburg in der russischen Gestesgeschichte und schönen Literatur," *Mitteilungen Universitätsbund Marburg*, 2/3 (1957), 80.

2. University Years

1. Marina Tsvetaeva, "Epos is lirika sovremennoi Rossii (Vladimir Maiakovskii i Boris Pasternak), *Izbrannaia proza v dvukh tomakh* (New York: Russica Publishers, 1979), II, 9.

2. We find an oblique reference to this state in the poet's earliest poems from 1912–13, where the imagery includes the sculptor-molder and the plaster mask covering the author.

3. Pasternak was able to hear Scriabin's Third Symphony for the first time in final form only at the beginning of 1909.

4. Engel was best known for his incidental music to the dramatic legend *Hadybbuk*, staged by the Hebrew Habimah Theater. In 1922 he emigrated to Berlin and in 1924 moved to Palestine, where he became one of the founders of Israeli musical culture.

5. See Christopher Barnes, "Pasternak as Composer and Scriabin-Disciple," *Tempo*, 121 (1977), 13–25; Barnes, "Boris Pasternak, The Musician-Poet and Composer," *Slavica Hierosolymitana. Slavic Studies of the Hebrew University*, 1 (1977), 317–335.

6. Boris Pasternak, *Sonata*, ed. N. Bogoslovsky (Moscow: Sovetskii kompozitor, 1979). All that survives from this period in the family archive are four unfinished musical plays by Boris Pasternak. See *Den' poezii. 1981* (Moscow: Sovetskii pisatel', 1981), p. 161.

7. Iu. Engel, "A. N. Skriabin. Biograficheskii ocherk," *Muzykal'nyi sovremennik* 4–5 (December–January 1916), 75.

8. Ibid., pp. 56–57.

9. Boris Schloetzer published it in the sixth volume of the series *Russkie Propi-*

lei: Materialy po istorii russkoi mysli i literatury, ed. M. Gershenzon (Moscow: Izdatel'stvo M. i S. Sabashnikovykh, 1919). For an English translation, by George Reavey, see Faubion Bowers, *Scriabin: A Biography of the Russian Composer, 1871–1915* (Tokyo and Palo Alto: Kodansha International, 1969), II, 271–276.

10. James M. Baker, *The Music of Alexander Scriabin* (New Haven: Yale University Press, 1986).

11. Leonid Sabaneev, *Vospominaniia o Skriabine* (Moscow: Muzykal'nyi sektor Gosizdta, 1925), p. 249.

12. Alisa Koonen, *Stranitsy zhizni* (Moscow: Iskusstvo, 1975), p. 123.

13. G. G. Neigauz [Neuhaus], "Zametki o Skriabine (K sorokaletiiu so dnia smerti)," *Razmyshleniia, vospominaniia, dnevniki. Izbrannye stat'i. Pis'ma k roditeliam* (Moscow: Sovetskii kompozitor, 1983), p. 207.

14. For A. A. Grushka see Alexei Faiko, *Zapiski starogo teatral'shchika* (Moscow: Iskusstvo, 1978), p. 87. From 1912 to 1915, Scriabin lived in Grushka's home in Moscow.

15. Pasternak, *Voice of Prose*, I, 36.

16. Lazar Fleishman, *Stat'i o Pasternake* (Bremen: K-Presse, 1977), pp. 8–13.

17. Lanz emigrated to the United States after the revolution and began to teach at Stanford University, where he started the Slavic Department. See Lazar Fleishman, "Sredi filosofov: Iz kommentariev k *Okhrannoi gramote* Pasternaka," *Semiosis, Semiotics and the History of Culture. In Honorem Georgii Lotman* (Ann Arbor: University of Michigan, 1984), pp. 70–71.

18. Andrei Biely, *Mezhdu dvukh revoliutsii* (Izdatel'stvo pisatelei v Leningrade, 1934), p. 304. Hermann Cohen visited Russia to give lectures—at the invitation of Jewish circles—three months before the beginning of World War I, in April–May 1914. See S. Al—in, "German Kogen (ocherk)," *Evreiskoe studenchestvo, Dvukhnedel'nyi zhurnal, posviashchennyi interesam evreiskoi molodezhi* (Moscow), 3–4 (1 May 1914), 11–29.

19. M. Kagan, "German Kogen," *Nauchnye izvestia* (Moscow), 2 (1922), 110.

20. Pasternak's university notebooks are filled with exercises in integral and differential calculus. They also contain library requests (dated January 1910) for Lorentz' books on physics, Abraham's *Theorie der Elektricität* and *Die Elektricität,* and Hoeppl's monograph *Einführung in die Maxwell'sche Theorie der Elektricität* (Leipzig, 1894).

21. Pavel Mansurov belonged to the religious and philosophical circle led by Mikhail Novoselov, which played an extraordinarily important role in the intellectual life of Moscow during those years. Members of this circle included the prominent philosophers and theologians V. A. Kozhevnikov, S. N. Bulgakov, Evgeny Trubetskoy, Pavel Florensky, and others. For information about this circle see Nikolai Berdiaev, *Sobranie sochinenii,* vol. 1, *Samopoznanie (opyt filosofskoi avtobiografii)* (Paris: YMCA Press, 1983), pp. 212–214.

22. Members of this circle also included the scholars N. S. Arseniev and the brothers Mikhail and Fyodor Petrovsky. See N. Arseniev, "Iz iunosti (Kartiny moskovskoi zhizni)," *Vozrozhdenie* (Paris), 17 (September–October 1951),

85; Arseniev, "Moskovskii universitet (1906–1910)," *Dary i vstrechi zhiznennogo puti* (Frankfurt-am-Main: Posev, 1974), pp. 67–68.

23. Dmitry Samarin, "Bogoroditsa v russkom narodnom pravoslavii," *Russkaia mysl'*, 3–6 (1918), 1–38 (2nd pagination).

24. After 1910 the nature of Russian popular Orthodox religion attracted the attention of such great philosophers as Pavel Florensky and Nikolai Berdiaev. Its "Virgin Mary" aspect was later studied in the works of émigré and western scholars (Frank, Smolitsch, Benz).

25. Mikhail Koriakov, "Zametki o poliakh romana *Doktor Zhivago*," *Mosty*, 2 (1959), 216–220.

26. Albert Deman, "Une lettre inédite de Boris Pasternak," *Revue des pays de l'est* (Brussells), 1 (1972), 7.

27. Alfred Rammelmeyer, "Die Philipps—Universität zu Marburg in der russischen Geistesgeschichte und schönen Literatur," *Mitteilungen Universitätsbund Marburg*, 2/3 (1957), 80.

28. *Personal-Verzeichnis der Königlichen Universität Marburg. Sommer-Semester 1912* (Marburg, 1912).

29. Frida Hartmann, "Biographische Notizen zu Nicolai Hartmann (1882–1950)," *Nicolai Hartmann und Heinz Heimsoeth im Briefwechsel* (Bonn: Bouvier Verlag Herbert Grundmann, 1978), pp. 317–321.

30. Elliott Mossman mistakenly claims that this seminar was taught by Paul Natorp. See *The Correspondence of Boris Pasternak and Olga Freidenberg, 1910–1954*, ed. Elliott Mossman (New York: Harcourt Brace Jovanovich, 1982), p. 33. Pasternak himself mentions Hartmann's seminar in *Safe Conduct*.

31. In *Safe Conduct* Natorp's textbook on logic is mentioned before Pasternak's stay in Marburg.

32. *Verzeichnis der Vorlesungen die im Sommerhalbjahre 1912 vom 15.April bis 15.August 1912 an der Universität Marburg gehalten werden sollen* (Marburg: Univ.-Buchdruckerei von Joh. Aug. Koch, 1911), p. 21.

33. See Pasternak's letter to Shtikh on July 22, 1912, *Voprosy literatury*, 9 (1972), 143.

34. From the poem "Byt' znamenitym nekrasivo" (It's unbecoming to be famous).

35. *Stranitsy avtobiografii V. I. Vernadskogo* (Moscow: Nauka, 1981), p. 242.

36. *Voprosy literatury*, 9 (1972), 142.

37. This was first published with a short commentary by S. G. Gellershtein in *Slavica Hierosolymitana*, 4 (1978).

38. Paul Natorp, *Allgemeine Psychologie nach kritischer Methode,* vol. 1, *Objekt und Methode der Psychologie* (Tübingen: J. C. B. Mohr [Paul Siebeck], 1912). See also Helmut Holzhey, *Cohen und Natorp,* vol. 1, *Ursprung und Einheit. Die Geschichte der "Marburger Schule" als Auseinandersetzung um die Logik des Denkens* (Basel-Stuttgart: Schwabe, 1986), p. 47; Erika A. Freiberger Sheikholeslami, "Der deutsche Einfluss im Werke von Boris Pasternak," diss., University of Pennsylvania, 1974.

39. The Russian edition of Natorp's *Über Philosophie als Grundwissenschaft der Pädagogik* appeared in 1910 in Moscow with a foreword by Shpet (by 1913

four more books by Natorop had come out in Russian translation). The question of the relationship between the views of Natorp and Husserl is examined in Iso Kern, *Husserl und Kant. Eine Untersuchung über Husserls Verhältnis zu Kant und zum Neukantianismus* (The Hague: Martinus Nijhoff, 1964), pp. 321–373.

40. Unpublished notes from the Pasternak family archive (Moscow).

3. Literary Debut

1. Vladislav Khodasevich, "Russkaia poeziia. Obzor," *Al'tsiona,* 1 (Moscow, 1914), 207.

2. See I. A. Belousov, *Literaturnaia sreda. Vospominaniia, 1880–1928* (Moscow: Nikitinskie subbotniki, 1928), p. 250.

3. In his account in *An Essay in Autobiography,* Pasternak confuses these two different stages.

4. They were published only posthumously.

5. E. V. Pasternak, "Iz rannikh prozaicheskikh opytov B. Pasternaka," *Pamiatniki kul'tury. Novye otkrytiia. Pis'mennost'. Iskusstvo. Arkheologiia. Ezhegodnik. 1976* (Moscow: Nauka, 1977), pp. 106–118; Elena Pasternak, "Iz pervykh prozaicheskikh opytov Borisa Pasternaka. Publikatsiia II," in Nils Åke Nilsson, ed., *Boris Pasternak. Essays* (Stockholm: Almquist and Wiksell International, 1976), pp. 26–66; D. Di Simplicio, "Iz rannikh prozaicheskikh opytov B. Pasternaka," *Slavica Hierosolymitana,* 4 (1979), 286–293; Anna Ljunggren, *Juvenilia B. Pasternaka: 6 fragmentov o Relikvimini* (Stockholm: Almquist and Wiksell International, 1984).

6. In a radically transformed version this character, or his namesake, appears for the last time in the first of Pasternak's published prose works, *The Apelles Mark.*

7. Pasternak, "The Quintessence," *Voice of Prose,* I, 245.

8. Ljunggren, *Juvenilia,* pp. 12–13.

9. *Pamiatniki kul'tury,* p. 113.

10. In 1910 Pasternak raved about *Niels Lyhne* by Jens Peter Jakobsen, which he read in the Russian translation by Sergei Gorodetsky in the fourth issue of *Severnye sborniki izdatel'stva "Shipovnik"* (Petersburg, 1908).

11. Pasternak, "Neskol'ko slov o novoi gruzinskoi poezii" (1946), *Voprosy literatury,* 1 (1966), 171.

12. Unpublished memoirs by Konstantin Loks.

13. In this respect Pasternak was closest of all to the poetry of Innokenty Annensky, who was not yet commonly considered either a central figure in Russian twentieth-century poetry or a notable representative of the symbolist camp.

14. Yet from the most extravagant of them, Alexander Dobroliubov, he borrowed the formula that became the title of his best book of poetry, *My Sister, Life.* This is mentioned by D. L. Plank, "Readings of *My Sister Life,*" *Russian Literature Triquarterly,* 2 (1972), 327.

15. It was precisely then that relations between Ivanov and Scriabin became particularly close.

16. Andrei Biely, *Mezhdu dvukh revoliutsii* (Izdatel'stvo pisatelei v Leningrade, 1934), p. 384.

17. It dissolved after the outbreak of the war in 1914. For information about the sculptor Krakht see *Gosudarstvennaia Tret'iakovskaia galereia, Moskva. Skul'ptura i risunki skul'ptorov kontsa XIX–nachala XX veka. Katalog.* (Moscow: Iskusstvo, 1977), p. 503.

18. The theses of the report "Symbolism and Immortality" were published in an appendix to my article in *Russian Literature,* 12 (1975), and in my book *Stat'i o Pasternake* (Bremen: K-Presse, 1977).

19. Andrei Biely, "Krititsizm i simvolizm," *Vesy,* 2 (1904), 11.

20. Viacheslav Ivanov, "Mysli o simvolizme," *Trudy i dni,* 1 (1912), 3–10.

21. "Symbolism in a wide sense is not a school in art. Symbolism is art itself."— Andrei Biely, *Arabeski* (Moscow: Musaget, 1911), p.263.

22. Andrei Biely, "Simvolizm i sovremennoe russkoe iskusstvo," *Vesy,* 10 (1910): 38–48.

23. Pasternak, *Voice of Prose,* I, 58.

24. In his unpublished memoirs Loks states that in 1912–13 Pasternak "fled" from symbolism by seeking refuge in Flaubert.

25. The fragment has been published by Christopher Barnes in *Slavica Hierosolymitana,* 1 (1977), 332.

26. Vladimir Markov, *Russian Futurism: A History* (Berkeley: University of California Press, 1968).

27. This report was published in *Trudy Vserossiiskogo s"ezda khudozhnikov . . . Dekabr' 1911–ianvar' 1912* (Petrograd, 1914), pp. 41–46.

28. Boris Pasternak, *An Essay in Autobiography,* trans. Manya Harari (London: Collins and Harvill Press, 1959), p. 66.

29. Aseev introduced Bobrov to the Siniakov family in Kharkov. Later Lily Brik would declare that futurism was born in this household. The five Siniakov daughters made friends with the leading poets and painters of the avant-garde; Mayakovsky, Khlebnikov, and Pasternak all spent time here. (In 1913 the Siniakov sisters moved to Moscow.) Khlebnikov fell in love with all five sisters in succession, Aseev married Oksana, and Pasternak had a love affair with Nadezhda in 1913–1915.

30. A. Izmailov, *Na perelome. Literaturnye razmyshleniia* (Petersburg: Teatr i iskusstvo, 1908), p. 40.

31. "Pervye opyty Borisa Pasternaka," ed. Elena Pasternak, *Trudy po znakovym sistemam,* 4 (1969), 239–281.

32. S. Durylin, "O liricheskom volnen'i. Zametka po povodu odnoi knigi," *Trudy i dni,* 1–2 (1913), 111–115. This issue was published in the spring of 1914.

33. Viacheslav Ivanov, "O sushchestve tragedii," *Trudy i dni,* 6 (November–December 1912), 1–15. The section on lyrics was singled out as an independent "excursus" when the article was reprinted in Ivanov's *Borozdy i mezhi* (Moscow: Musaget, 1916), pp. 256–258.

34. See Sergei Bobrov, "O liricheskoi teme (18 ekskursov v ee oblasti)," *Trudy i dni,* 1–2 (1913), 116–137. Pasternak's poem, with a dedication to Bobrov, appeared in *A Twin in the Clouds,* which was published in December 1913.

When he reprinted his article in the form of a separate pamphlet in 1914, Bobrov included Pasternak's entire poem. See Lazar Fleishman, "Fragmenty 'futuristicheskoi' biografii Pasternaka," *Slavica Hierosolymitana*, 4 (1979), 88–98.

4. In the Futurist Camp

1. Anthroposophy, along with other occult interests, acquired many followers in Russia after the turn of the century. See Nikolai Berdiaev, *Sobranie sochinenii, 1:Samopoznanie* (Paris: YMCA Press, 1983), pp. 217–218. Ellis quickly became disillusioned with Steinerism and expressed his changed attitude in the pamphlet *Vigilemus* (Moscow: Musaget, 1914).

2. The duel never took place thanks to the intervention of Loks and Aseev. See Lazar Fleishman, *Stat'i o Pasternake* (Bremen: K-Presse, 1977), p. 66. Later, after the revolution, cordial relations between Pasternak and the Anisimovs were renewed.

3. Vladimir Markov, *Russian Futurism: A History* (Berkeley: University of California Press, 1968). The English equivalents of the titles of Russian futurist editions are borrowed from Markov's book.

4. Abbat Fanferliush (V. Shershenevich), "Symvolicheskaia deshevka (*Lirika. Al'manakh*, Moskva, 1913)," *Vernissazh*, 1 (Moscow: Mezonin poezii, September 1913), 28–30.

5. *Priazovskii krai* (Rostov-on-Don), July 28, 1914, p. 4. See also Vadim Shershenevich's review, "Boris Pasternak. *Bliznets v tuchakh*," *Svobodnyi zhurnal*, 11 (November 1914), cols. 134–135.

6. Reinhard Lauer is mistaken when he suggests that Pasternak and Aseev also took part writing it. See his "Das poetische Programm der Centrifuga," *Text, Symbol, Weltmodell: Johannes Holthusen zum 60. Geburtstag*, ed. Johanna Renate Döring-Smirnov, Peter Rehder, and Wolf Schmid (Munich: Otto Sagner, 1984), p. 373.

7. "Wassermann Test" was reprinted in Vladimir Markov's anthology *Manifeste und Programmschriften der russischen Futuristen* (Munich: W. Fink, 1967).

8. In the spring of 1914 the first volume of Khlebnikov's *Works* had just been published.

9. For the grasshopper poem, see Velimir Khlebnikov, *The King of Time*, trans. Paul Schmidt (Cambridge: Harvard University Press, 1985), pp. 24–25.

10. Roman Jakobson, "Randbemerkungen zur Prosa des Dichters Pasternak", *Slavische Rundschau* (Prague), 7 (1935), 357–374; Jakobson, "Marginal Notes on the Prose of the Poet Pasternak," in Krystyna Pomorska and Stephen Rudy, eds., *Language in Literature* (Cambridge: Harvard University Press, 1987), pp. 301–317.

11. The title of the article ironically alluded to one of the fashionable themes of futurist imagery, syphilis. In 1906 the German biologist August von Wassermann discovered a way of diagnosing syphilis by a blood test.

12. Indeed it was absurd to expect that Zdanevich, who later became a noted artist and the author of transrational verses, would endorse Centrifuge, since

he felt that even the cubo-futurists' poetic experiments were not radical enough. He also reacted very disdainfully to Pasternak's poetry.

13. This was important because the opponents of Centrifuge tried to gloss over its innovative tendencies.

14. Valery Briusov, "God russkoi poezii (Aprel' 1913 g.–aprel' 1914 g.). Porubezhniki," *Russkaia mysl'*, 6 (June 1914), 17 (3rd pagination).

15. See his letter to Bobrov from the middle of July 1914, in Fleishman, *Stat'i o Pasternake*, pp. 71–74.

16. Its content is briefly summarized by the poet's younger sister. See Lydia Pasternak-Slater, "Introduction," in Boris Pasternak, *Poems* (London: Unwin Paperbacks, 1984), pp. 15–16. See also Christopher Barnes, "Notes on Pasternak," in *Boris Pasternak and His Times* (Berkeley: Berkeley Slavic Specialties, 1989), pp. 407–411.

17. S. A. Vengerov, "Etapy neo-romanticheskogo dvizhenia," *Russkaia literatura XX veka (1890–1910)*, vol. 1 (Moscow: Mir, 1914), pp. 22–24.

18. During the same summer of 1914, Balmont was translating Kalidasa's *Sakuntala* for Tairov.

19. This production was never realized at the Chamber Theater. In the early 1920s, Pasternak's translation was staged in other Moscow theaters.

20. D. Aminado, *Poezd na tret'em puti* (New York: Izdatel'stvo imeni Chekhova, 1954), p. 181.

21. In the fall of 1914 the still unknown Sergei Esenin was published there.

22. Vladimir Mayakovsky, *Polnoe sobranie sochinenii*, vol. 1, *1912–1917* (Moscow: Gosudarstvennoe izdatel'stvo khudozhestvennoi literatury, 1955), p. 366.

23. Many years would pass and, in a letter to Meyerhold, Pasternak offered, in completely different social and cultural circumstances, a similar thought: "It's only that sort of futurism, a futurism with a family tree, that I understand." Pasternak to Meyerhold, March 26, 1928, in V. E. Meyerhold, *Perepiska, 1896–1939* (Moscow: Iskusstvo, 1976), p. 279.

24. Translation by Angela Livingstone. See *Pasternak on Art and Creativity*, ed. Angela Livingstone (Cambridge: University Press, 1985), p. 45.

25. Recall Pasternak when he "cut across boundaries" by declaring that the meaning of rhythm in music is located in poetry.

26. *Futurist Manifestos*, ed. Umbro Apollonio (London: Thames and Hudson, 1973), p. 21. Cf. the Russian translation in *Manifesty ital'ianskogo futurizma*, trans. Vadim Shershenevich (Moscow, 1914), p. 7.

27. Vadim Shershenevich, *Zelenaia ulitsa. Stat'i i zametki ob iskusstve* (Moscow: Pleiady, 1916), p. 36. In the 1930s Pasternak used to say that in the age of high speeds, man must learn to think slowly.

28. Vasily Kamensky, *Put' entuziasta* (Moscow: Federatsiia, 1931), p. 169.

29. *Literaturnoe nasledstvo*, vol. 70, *Gor'kii i sovetskie pisateli. Neizdannaia perepiska* (Moscow: Izdatel'stvo Akademii Nauk SSSR, 1963), pp. 295–296. During the revolutionary years Pasternak translated three more pieces by Kleist for Gorky's publishing house, World Literature: the tragedy *Die Familie Schroffenstein*, the drama *Prinz Friedrich von Homburg*, and the frag-

ment "Robert Guiscard." See Heinrich von Kleist, *Sobranie sochinenii v dvukh tomakh* (Moscow-Petrograd: Vsemirnaia literatura, 1923).

30. After death throes of several months, *Sovremennik* ceased to exist.

31. In the summer of 1915 Pasternak was replaced as Walter's tutor by Alexei Losev, who had just finished the university and would later become a prominent Soviet philosopher and classical scholar. See A. F. Losev, "V poiskakh smysla," *Voprosy literatury,* 10 (1985), 215.

32. Sergei Bobrov, "Sovremennyi stikh", *Sovremennik,* 14–15 (August 1914), 236–237. Bobrov's prediction proved inaccurate.

33. Laforgue was a source of inspiration at that time for Shershenevich (who translated him), Bobrov, and Bolshakov.

34. Anna Ljunggren also perceives in *The Apelles Mark* a kaleidoscope of self-citations from the fragments of 1910–1913. See her *Juvenilia B. Pasternaka: 6 fragmentov o Relikvimini* (Stockholm: Almquist and Wiksell International, 1984), p. 81.

35. Michel Aucouturier, "The Legend of the Poet and the Image of the Actor in the Short Stories of Pasternak," *Studies in Short Fiction,* 3 (Winter 1966), 225–235; reprinted in Victor Erlich, ed., *Pasternak. A Collection of Critical Essays* (Englewood Cliffs: Prentice Hall, 1978), pp. 43–50.

36. V. Katanian, *Maiakovskii. Khronika zhizni i deiatel'nosti* (Moskva: Sovetskii pisatel', 1985), pp. 100–101.

37. The meaning of the title is revealed in the anecdote cited in the epigraph, evidently invented by Pasternak. The Greek painter Apelles was regarded, in antiquity and the Renaissance, as the model of the artist. See E. H. Gombrich, *The Heritage of Apelles: Studies in the Art of the Renaissance* (Ithaca: Cornell University Press, 1976).

38. This was how the poet's brother Alexander interpreted the style of *The Apelles Mark*. The dynamic depictions of city scenes in the novella vigorously recall the paintings of the Italian futurists and even seem to be copied directly from them.

39. Clara Hollosi, "View on Heine in Russia in the Beginning of the 20th Century," *Heine-Jahrbuch,* ed. Joseph A. Kruse (Hamburg: Hoffman und Campe, 1978), p. 176.

5. Revolutionary Years

1. For three decades, beginning in January 1924, Zbarsky was in charge of the preservation of Lenin's corpse, which lay in the mausoleum near the Kremlin wall in Moscow.

2. Pasternak, "Unpublished Letters," *Quarto* (London, May, 1980), p. 11. In 1924 Ivan Aksyonov wrote of Swinburne's influence on Pasternak in a review of the Russian translation of Coleridge's "Christabel," published in *Pechat' i revoliutsiia.*

3. Pasternak's interest in the juxtaposition of epochs and in parallel readings was reflected in his decision to translate Swinburne's sonnet "John Ford," the

only one of Swinburne's lyrical poems he translated. The translation was recently published: "Sonet Svinberna v perevode Boris Pasternaka," ed. M. A. Rashkovskaia and E. B. Rashkovsky, *Izvestiia Akademii nauk SSSR. Seriia literatury i iazyka.* 43. 6 (1984), 544–550. Pasternak never used the sonnet form in his own work. His poem "Shakespeare" (1918), however, is written in the form of a dialogue between the poet and his sonnet.

4. Johanna Renate Döring-Smirnov, "Ein karnavaleskes Spiel mit fremden Texten. Zur Interprtetation von B. Pasternaks poem *Vakchanalija*," in: *Text. Symbol. Weltmodell. Johannes Holthusen zum 60. Geburtstag* (Munich: Otto Sagner, 1984), pp. 59–80.

5. It was published posthumously, in 1965, in *Literaturnaia Rossiia.*

6. The poem had been forwarded to him by Osip Brik.

7. *Letopis'* and *Russkaia mysl'* had both rejected it.

8. R. Rajt-Kovaleva, "Vse luchshie vospominan'ia," *Trudy po risskoi i slavianskoi filologii,* 9, *Literaturovedenie* (Tartu, 1966), 283–284; Rita Wright-Kovaleva, "Mayakovsky and Pasternak: Fragments of Reminiscence," *Oxford Slavonic Papers,* 13 (1967), 128.

9. K. Loks, "Povest' ob odnom desiatiletii (1907–1917) (unpublished manuscript). Quoted in Lazar Fleishman, *Boris Pasternak v dvadtsatye gody* (Munich: Wilhelm Fink, 1981), p. 164.

10. Letter of March 7 (20), 1917. Quoted in N. Baranova-Shestova, *Zhizn' L'va Shestova. Po perepiske i vospominaniiam sovremennikov* (Paris: La Presse Libre, 1983), p. 151.

11. Boris Mirsky, "Zodiak v shtanakh," *Zhurnal zhurnalov,* 15 (1917), 4. See also I. Ehrenburg, "Bol'sheviki v poezii," in the newspaper *Ponedel'nik vlasti naroda* (Moscow), February 25 (12), 1918; Sergei Gorodetsky, "Futurizm i bol'shevizm," in the newspaper *Kavkazskoe slovo* (Tiflis), June 4, 1917.

12. Ten years later, in the 1926 poem "Lieutenant Schmidt," Pasternak emphasized the similar martyr-like characteristics of his revolutionary hero.

13. See Pasternak's statement to the Department of Literature of Narkompros, October 18, 1920. Manuscript Department, Institute of World Literature, Moscow (120, op. 1, no. 2).

14. N. N. Aseev, "Vospominaniia o Maiakovskom," *V. Maiakovskii v vospominaniiakh sovremennikov* (Moscow: Gosudarstvennoe izdatel'stvo khudozhestvennoi literatury, 1963), p. 425.

15. This period of Mayakovsky's life is meticulously scrutinized by Bengt Jangfeldt in his *Majakovskij and Futurism, 1917–1921* (Stockholm: Almquist and Wiksell, 1976).

16. Max Polianovsky, *Poet na ekrane. Maiakovskii—kinoakter* (Moscow: Sovetskii pisatel', 1958).

17. Genrikh Tasteven, *Futurizm. Na puti k novomu simvolizmu* (Moscow: Iris, 1914), p. 49.

18. In addition to three poems, including "Marburg," from *Above the Barriers,* Pasternak contributed two new poems that later appeared in *My Sister, Life.*

19. As it turned out, he did not stay in Russia long and soon returned to Paris. The son of a millionaire tea merchant, Tsetlin had begun his work with the Social Revolutionaries at an early age. His cousin was Ida Vysotskaia, to

whom Pasternak addressed some love poems and who was one of the subjects in the second part of *Safe Conduct.*

20. Evgeny Lundberg, "Pod znamenem Zodiaka. 2. O 1917 gode," *Znamia truda,* 108 (December 31, 1917), 2. It was also thanks to Lundberg that *The Apelles Mark* was published in the collection *Vremennik Znameni truda.*

21. E. P. Kamen (Sergei Bobrov), "Professionaly," *Knizhnyi ugol,* 3 (1918), 16–18.

22. Ippolit Udushiev (Ivanov-Razumnik), "Vzgliad i nechto. Otryvok," *Sovremennaia literatura. Sbornik statei* (Leningrad: Mysl', 1925), p. 172.

23. Alexander Blok, *Zapisnye knizhki, 1901–1920* (Moscow: Khudozhestvennaia literatura, 1965), p. 458.

24. The list of poetry books did not include one by Pasternak; either he had not shown his poems from 1917 to his friends, or he had not yet decided to publish them.

25. Vladimir Markov, *Russian Imagism, 1919–1924* (Giessen: Wilhelm Schmitz, 1980).

26. M. Kemshis, "Noveishaia russkaia poeziia," *Darbai ir Dienos. Literatūros skyriaus žurnalas,* 2 (Kaunas, 1931), 236–238; K. V. Driagin, *Lirika prolet-poetov epokhi voennogo kommunizma* (Viatka, 1933).

27. In 1920 Vadim Shershenevich had published his translation of the book by Duhamel and Vildrac on vers libre.

28. A translation of the first draft of "The Quintessence" is found in Boris Pasternak, *The Voice of Prose,* vol. 1 (Edinburgh: Polygon, 1986), pp. 242–247.

29. Letter from Pasternak to N. A. Tabidze, November 16, 1953, "Pis'ma gruzinskim druz'iam," *Literaturnaia Gruziia,* 2 (1980), 29.

30. This theme had pursued him constantly starting with "The Poem on the Neighbour" in 1917. He was planning to collect his articles from that period under the title "Quinta Essentia: Humanistic Articles about Man." His cycle of verses, "Theme and Variations," placed Pushkin vis-à-vis the Sphinx and the famous riddle about man.

31. These deleted segments are now included in the commentary to Soviet editions.

32. Pasternak, *Voice of Prose,* vol. 1, p. 208 (trans. Christopher Barnes).

33. Pasternak's words in *Liuvers' Childhood* echo Hillel's statement as translated by Semyon Frug. See the Russian edition of *Sefer ha-Agadah: Agada. Skazaniia, pritchi, izrecheniia Talmuda i midrashei,* Yehoshua Rawnitski and Chaim Bialik, eds. (Berlin: S. D. Saltzman, 1922), II, 66. The first edition came out in 1910.

34. Christopher Barnes, "Notes on Pasternak," in *Boris Pasternak and His Times* (Berkeley: Berkeley Slavic Specialties, 1989), pp. 398–399.

35. See my analysis of the poem "So they begin" in the Warsaw collection of articles on Pasternak (forthcoming).

36. František Kubka, *Básnící revolučního Ruska* (Prague, 1924), p. 100.

37. Mayakovsky, with whom Pasternak often met in the spring of 1919, imbued both his art and his life with demonic elements. The Demon is mentioned directly in his poem "Man," where it appears in an openly suicidal context. Mayakovsky was conscious of the veiled polemic against him in Pasternak's

"In Memory of the Demon"; in 1924 he made ironic, albeit indirect, mention of it in his own poem "Tamara and the Demon."

38. "Literaturnaia Moskva za 1918–1920 gg.," *Krasnaia Moskva. 1917–1920 gg.* (Moscow Soviet, 1920), col. 621.

39. This book is mentioned in the catalogue of the publishing house World Literature. Pasternak finished his translation in 1923, and it was published in Moscow in 1925.

40. Georgy Adamovich, "Literaturnye besedy," *Zveno* (Paris), 163 (March 14, 1926), 2.

6. Factions in the Twenties

1. N. L. Meshcheriakov, "O chastnykh izdatel'stvakh," *Pechat' i revoliutsiia,* 3 (July–August 1922), 129.

2. See Robert A. Maguire, *Red Virgin Soil: Soviet Literature in the 1920's* (Princeton: Princeton University Press, 1968).

3. Yakov Cherniak, "Boris Pasternak. *Sestra moia zhizn'*," *Pechat' i revoliutsiia,* 6 (July–August 1922), 303. Pasternak was struck by how closely this review paralleled his thoughts.

4. N. Vilmont, "Boris Pasternak. Vospominaniia i mysli," *Novyi mir,* 6 (June 1987), 179.

5. *Pravda,* March 18, 1922, p. 4.

6. Osip Mandelshtam, "Vulgata. Zametki o poezii," *Russkoe iskusstvo,* 2–3 (1923): 70.

7. Olga Petrovskaia, "Nikolai Aseev," *Vospominaniia o Nikolae Aseeve* (Moscow: Sovetskii pisatel', 1980), p. 70; N. Khardzhiev, "Novoe o Velimire Khlebnikove (K 90-letiiu so dnia rozhdeniia)," *Den' poezii, 1975* (Moscow: Sovetskii pisatel', 1975), pp. 207–208; *Russian Literature,* 9 (The Hague, 1975), 24.

8. Testimony to this is the inscription on *My Sister, Life,* given to Lunacharsky on the same day. The inscription was quoted in full in N. Trifonov, "Samoe vysshee masterstvo est' prostota," *Ogonek,* 48 (2525) (November 1975), 18–19.

9. When he returned to Russia, Pilniak discussed with Pasternak the possibility of publishing a new monthly, *Uzel,* in collaboration with the Serapion Brothers and the prominent realist prose writer of the older generation, Boris Zaitsev. See *Nakanune. Literaturnoe prilozhenie* (Berlin), 3 (May 14, 1922), 12. *Uzel* was supposed to begin publication in June 1922, but evidently the plan was never realized because Zaitsev emigrated.

10. Boris Pilniak, "Otryvki iz dnevnika," *Pisateli ob iskusstve i o sebe. Sbornik statei,* vol. 1 (Moscow-Leningrad: Krug, 1924), p. 83.

11. "Pis'mo B. Pasternaka Iu. Iurkunu," ed. N. Bogomolov, *Voprosy literatury,* 7 (July 1981), 229.

12. *Novaia russkaia kniga,* 2 (1922), 39–40.

13. Three fragments from it were published in June 1922 in the newspaper *Mos-*

kovskii ponedel'nik. Spektorsky, the main protagonist of Pasternak's works of the 1920s, appears here for the first time.

14. V. I. Lenin, *Collected Works*, vol. 33, August 1921–March 1923 (Moscow: Progress Publishers, 1966), p. 151.

15. The increased interest had already been expressed by the fact that in the spring of 1922 poems by Mayakovsky, Khlebnikov, Aseev, and Pasternak were published in the pages of *Izvestiia* (which had earlier published only the hack party poet, Demian Bedny). This fact was noted with delight in Ilya Ehrenburg's Berlin journal *Veshch'* (1922, no. 3, p. 2).

16. "Pasternak i Briusov. K istorii otnoshenii," ed. Elena Pasternak, *Russia. Rossiia*, 3 (1977), 248–249.

17. Iu. Annenkov, *Dnevnik moikh vstrech. Tsikl tragedii*, vol. 2 (New York: Inter-Language Literary Associates, 1966), p. 295. Annenkov provides a valuable detail: Trotsky was keenly interested in the art of the avant-garde and was particularly fond of Picasso.

18. Leon Trotsky, *Literature and Revolution* (Ann Arbor: University of Michigan Press, 1960), p. 150.

19. Robert C. Williams, *Culture in Exile: Russian Emigrés in Germany, 1881–1941* (Ithaca: Cornell University Press, 1972).

20. I. Levitan, "Russkie izdatel'stva v 1920-x gg. v Berline," *Kniga o russkom evreistve, 1917–1967* (New York: Soiuz russkikh evreev, 1968), p. 448.

21. Elie Ehrenbourg, "La Poésie russe et la révolution," *Signaux de France et de Belgique. Revue de littérature* (Paris), 4 (1921), 178–191; see also his articles and reviews in the Berlin journal *Novaia russkaia kniga*.

22. She soon moved to Prague, just before Pasternak arrived in Germany.

23. "This is not criticism, but a Bacchic dithyramb. And it is so clamorous and resounding, such a polyphony of tropes, that it takes one's breath away. This is a new species of ecstatic lyricism, much like the old impressionism, but with added hysterics." This was how Tsvetaeva's article was ironically characterized in a note published in the Paris newspaper *Zveno*, May 16, 1923, p. 3.

24. Lazar Fleishman, Robert Hughes, and Olga Raevsky-Hughes, *Russkii Berlin, 1921–1923* (Paris: YMCA Press, 1983).

25. Besides Pasternak, writers who were printed in *Novaia Rossiia* included Andrei Biely, Kuzmin, Khodasevich, Mandelshtam, Pilniak, Zamiatin, and Ehrenburg.

26. The letter is from February 7, 1923, published in *Novyi zhurnal*, 95 (1969), 229–230. Quoted in Gordon McVay, *Esenin: A Life* (Ann Arbor: Ardis, 1976), p. 204.

27. At the time the organization was called MAPP (Moscow Association of Proletarian Writers); later its name changed. I will adhere to the name under which it became best known, RAPP (Rossiiskaia Assotsiatsia Proletarskikh Pisatelei, Russian Association of Proletarian Writers).

28. Lev Trotsky, "Futurizm," *Pravda*, September 26, 1923, p. 2. For the English translation see Leon Trotsky, *Literature and Revolution* (Ann Arbor: University of Michigan Press, 1960), p. 160.

29. Yury Libedinsky, "O Maiakovskom," *Sovremenniki. Vospominaniia* (Moscow: Sovetskii pisatel', 1961), p. 172.
30. V. Pertsov, "Vymyshlennaia figura," *Na postu,* 1(5) (May 1924), cols. 209–224.
31. Pasternak would later speak about this in *Doctor Zhivago.* We find an interesting parallel in an account by the philosopher Nikolai Berdiaev of War Communism. He recalls that he did not feel depressed or unhappy but, on the contrary, experienced "the greatest intensity and sharpness of life, the greatest contrasts." "At one time life was half-starved, but every morsel of food seemed more delicious than in the years of plenitude." Berdiaev, *Sobranie sochinenii,* vol. 1, *Samopoznanie, opyt filosofskoi avtobiografii* (Paris: YMCA Press, 1983), p. 268.
32. Tynianov's article was not published in the journal in full.
33. These and many other translations of modern German poets made by Pasternak were included in a collection edited by Grigory Petnikov: *Molodaia Germaniia. Antologiia sovremennoi nemetskoi poezii* (Kharkov, 1926).
34. This position was spelled out in his later reply to the resolution of the Central Committee on literature in 1925. See Lazar Fleishman, *Boris Pasternak v dvadtsatye gody* (Munich: Wilhelm Fink, 1981), pp. 47–53; *Pasternak on Art and Creativity,* ed. Angela Livingstone (Cambridge: University Press, 1985), pp. 153–157.

7. Against Romanticism

1. N. Vilmont, "Boris Pasternak. Vospominaniia i mysli," *Novyi mir,* 6 (June 1987), 213–219.
2. Iu. I. Levin, "Zametki o 'Leitenante Shmidte' B. L. Pasternaka," *Boris Pasternak: Essays,* ed. Nils Åke Nilsson (Stockholm: Almquist and Wiksell International, 1976), pp. 85–161.
3. V. I. Maksakov, "Predislovie," *Leitenant P. P. Shmidt. Pis'ma, vospominaniia, dokumenty* (Moscow: Novaia Moskva, 1922), p. vi.
4. Letter from October 10, 1927, *Literaturnoe Nasledstvo,* vol. 70, *Gor'kii i sovetskie pisateli. Neizdannaia perepiska* (Moscow: Izdatel'stvo Akademii Nauk, 1963), pp. 297–298.
5. For the first time they switched to the personal pronoun "ty" instead of the more formal "vy."
6. After this publication Viacheslav Polonsky, the editor of *Novyi mir,* experienced difficulties and was forced to reprimand Pasternak. See Lazar Fleishman, *Boris Pasternak v dvadtsatye gody* (Munich: Wilhelm Fink, 1981), pp. 56–57.
7. Leonid Čertkov, *Rilke in Russland. Auf Grund neuer Materialien* (Wien: Verlag der Österreichischen Akademie der Wissenschaften, 1975), p. 28.
8. This journal was edited by Paul Valéry and Saint-John Perse, and not long before it had published French poems by Rilke himself. Hélène Iswolsky spoke with Rilke in Paris about Pasternak's lyrical poetry. See her *No Time to Grieve: An Autobiographical Journey* (Philadelphia: Winchell, 1985), p. 165.

9. Rilke called Russia his "spiritual homeland." See these valuable works about Rilke's ties to Russia: Felix Philipp Ingold, "Rilke, Russland und die 'russische Dinge,'" in F. Ph. Ingold, ed., *Zwischen den Kulturen. Festgabe für Georg Thürer zum 70. Geburtstage* (Bern und Stuttgart: P. Haupt, 1978), pp. 63–85; Konstantin Asadowski, ed. *Rilke und Russland. Briefe. Erinnerungen. Gedichte* (Frankfurt-am-Main: Insel, 1986); Patricia Pollock Brodsky, *Russia in the Works of Rainer Maria Rilke* (Detroit: Wayne State University Press, 1984).

10. Translated by Walter Arndt in Boris Pasternak, Marina Tsvetaeva and Rainer Maria Rilke, *Letters. Summer 1926* (New York: Harcourt Brace Jovanovich, 1985), pp. 53–54.

11. Simon Karlinsky, *Marina Tsvetaeva: The Woman, Her World and Her Poetry* (Cambridge: University Press, 1985), chap. 7.

12. Yury Terapiano, "Dva nachala russkoi sovremennoi poezii," *Novyi dom* (Paris), 1 (1926), 21–31; Terapiano, *Vstrechi* (New York: Izdatel'stvo imeni Chekhova, 1963), p. 84.

13. During her stay in Prague, the Social Revolutionaries formed Tsvetaeva's closest circle. She wrote in the spring of 1924 to Roman Gul: "I am friends with the S.R.'s—they are *not* stifling. I didn't intend to mix with the S.R.'s, but for some reason it just turns out that way: if you are broad-minded, and love poetry, that means you're an S.R. They still retain something of the old (1905) heroism." In the same letter she announces that she has become acquainted with Kerensky and presented him with her poems, as well as "Spring Rain" from Pasternak's *My Sister, Life* (where mention is made of Kerensky's speech in May 1917 in Moscow). According to Tsvetaeva, Kerensky was "touched and moved." See *Novyi zhurnal*, 165 (1986), 286.

14. *Literaturnoe nasledstvo*, vol. 93, *Iz istorii sovetskoi literatury 1920–1930-x godov. Novye materialy i issledovaniia* (Moscow: Nauka, 1983), p. 725.

15. *The Correspondence of Boris Pasternak and Olga Freidenberg. 1910–1954* (New York: Harcourt Brace Jovanovich, 1982), p. 95.

16. Pasternak's letter to Vladimir Pozner of May 13, 1929, *Literaturnoe nasledstvo*, vol. 93, p. 724.

17. This evaluation of Pasternak by Polonsky and his circle was most clearly expressed in Viktor Krasilnikov's article, published in the fall of 1927 in Polonsky's journal, *Pechat' i revoliutsiia*. See Krasilnikov, "Boris Pasternak," *Pechat' i revoliutsiia*, 5 (1927), 78–98; Krasilnikov, *Za i protiv. Stat'i o sovremennoi literature* (Moscow: Federatsiia, 1930), pp. 148–184. Compare Pertsov's sarcastic response to this article in Mayakovsky's journal *Novyi lef*, 7 (1927), 10–11.

18. *Literaturnoe nasledstvo*, vol. 93, pp. 684–685.

19. Viacheslav Polonsky, "Lef ili blef?", *Izvestiia*, February 27, 1927.

20. The accusations were never substantiated, and in August 1928 he returned to the journal.

21. Nikolai Aseev, "Khudozhestvennaia literatura," *Pechat' i revoliutsiia*, 7 (September–October 1922), 70–74.

22. This edition was never printed. Gorky's foreword was first published in the series *Lteraturnoe nasledstvo*, vol. 70, pp. 308–310.

23. While he was in Italy, Gorky was financially dependent to a significant degree on the Soviet government.

24. *Literaturnoe nasledstvo*, vol. 70, p. 297.

25. In a letter to Romain Rolland on January 29, 1928, Gorky named Pasternak first among the poets when he spoke of the flourishing of postrevolutionary literature in Soviet Russia. See Gorky, *Pis'ma o literature* (Moscow: Sovetskii pisatel', 1957), p. 361.

26. "Boris Pasternak v perepiske s Maksimom Gor'kim," ed. E. B. and E. V. Pasternak, *Izvestiia Akademii Nauk SSSR. Seriia literatury i iazyka*, 45.3 (1986), 278 (letter of January 7, 1928).

27. Valentin Parnach, "In the Russian World of Letters," *The Menorah Journal*, 12 (June–July 1926), 303.

28. Sofia Parnok, "B. Pasternak i drugie," *Russkii sovremennik*, 1 (1924), 310.

29. V. K., "V redaktsii *Krasnaia nov'*, *Chitatel' i pisatel'*, 24 (June 16, 1928), 4.

30. Translation by Max Hayward in Alexander Gladkov, *Meetings with Pasternak: A Memoir*, ed. Max Hayward (New York: Harcourt Brace Jovanovich, 1977), p. 40.

31. *Correspondence of Boris Pasternak and Olga Freidenberg, 1910–1954*, p. 108. See also Bertram D. Wolfe, "Dress Rehearsals for the Great Terror," *Studies in Comparative Communism*, 3 (April 1970), 1–24.

32. Edward J. Brown, *Mayakovsky: A Poet in the Revolution* (Princeton: Princeton University Press, 1973), pp. 362–363.

33. Vera T. Reck, *Boris Pil'niak: A Soviet Writer in Conflict with the State* (Montreal: McGill-Queen's University Press, 1975).

34. Just the opposite of Pasternak's novel in this regard was *Pushtorg* by Ilya Selvinsky. This work was another example of the verse-novel genre in Soviet literature of the 1920s. The characters and events were depicted with the same detail as in a traditional prose novel.

35. Olga Raevsky-Hughes, "Pasternak and Cvetaeva: History of a Friendship," *Books Abroad*, 44 (Spring 1970).

36. In actual fact it corresponds roughly to the two last (eighth and ninth) chapters of the final version.

37. "One thing already placed me on guard: the fact that the piece was untitled," recounts Nikolai Vilmont, who heard *A Tale* read by the author before it was published. Vilmont, "Boris Pasternak. Vospominaniia i mysli," *Novyi mir*, 6 (1987), 175. In George Reavey's English translation it is known under the title of "The Last Summer."

38. Pasternak, Tsvetaeva, and Rilke, *Letters*, p. 157.

39. Leon Trotsky, *Literature and Revolution* (Ann Arbor: University of Michigan Press, 1960), p. 155.

8. The Thaw of the Thirties

1. In addition, it bore the acrostic dedication to Tsvetaeva.

2. The author considered this publication "a perfect miracle."

3. Letter to I. Postupalsky of December 9, 1929. Quoted in Lazar Fleishman, *Boris Pasternak v dvadtsatye gody* (Munich: Wilhelm Fink, 1981), p. 143.

4. A. M. Toporov, "Derevnia o sovetskoi poezii," *Sibirskie ogni*, 5 (1928), 176; Toporov, *Krest'iane o pisateliakh* (Moscow-Leningrad: Gosudarstvennoe izdatel'stvo, 1930), pp. 267–268.

5. All those indicted in the cases of the Industrial and Agricultural parties were rehabilitated in the Soviet Union in the late 1980s.

6. Pasternak and Zinaida Nikolaevna occupied Pilniak's cottage during the latter's journey abroad.

7. Alexei Tolstoy's novel, which appeared at the same time, was also based on this parallel.

8. This letter was not included in the correspondence between Pasternak and Tikhonov printed in volume 93 of *Literaturnoe nasledstvo*. It is cited (with an incorrect date) in Dmitry Khrenkov, *Nikolai Tikhonov v Leningrade* (Leningrad: Lenizdat, 1984), p. 83.

9. Marina Tsvetaeva embraced this sentence in her article "Poet i vremia," *Volia Rossii*, 1–3 (1932), 22.

10. He was simultaneously editor-in-chief of *Izvestiia*.

11. Pasternak mentions the suicide attempt in a letter of June 1, 1932, in *Perepiska s Ol'goi Freidenberg*, ed. Elliott Mossman (New York: Harcourt Brace Jovanovich, 1981), p. 140; in the English edition of 1982, this passage in Pasternak's letter is translated incorrectly. See also Markoosha Fischer, *My Lives in Russia* (New York: Harper, 1944), p. 96.

12. K., "O Pasternake," *Literaturnaia gazeta*, May 29, 1932. The author of this article may have been Valery Kirpotin.

13. Robert Conquest, *The Harvest of Sorrow: Soviet Collectivization and the Terror-Famine* (Oxford: Oxford University Press, 1986).

14. "N. S. Allilueva," *Literaturnaia gazeta*, November 17, 1932, p. 1.

15. M. Koriakov, "Termometr Rossii," *Novyi zhurnal*, 55 (December 2, 1958), 140–141.

16. Anon., "Impressions of Boris Pasternak," *The New Reasoner: A Quarterly Journal of Socialist Humanism*, 4 (Spring 1980), 89.

17. Pasternak, "Unpublished Letters," *Quarto* (May 1980), 10.

18. The poem was first published posthumously thirty years later in the Russian émigré press. On the history of its appearance, see my publication of the letters from Yulian Oksman to Gleb Struve in the first volume of *Stanford Slavic Studies* (1987).

19. Anon., "Zametki o peresechenii biografij Osipa Mandel'shtama i Borisa Pasternaka," *Pamiat'. Istoricheskii sbornik* 4 (Moscow, 1979; Paris, 1981), 316.

20. Roy Medvedev, *Nikolai Bukharin: The Last Years* (New York: Norton, 1980); Nicolas Baudi, "Boukharine aux *Izvestia*," *Preuves*, 139 (September 1962), 66–69.

21. The decision to lighten the sentence of Mandelshtam by replacing jail with internal exile in Cherdyn was evidently made between May 26 and May 28.

22. The slogan of "mastery" was central to the program advanced by Gorky and his supporters on the eve of the congress. It is no accident that the term "master" was chosen by Mikhail Bulgakov for the title of his famous novel.

23. See Isaiah Berlin, "Meetings with Russian Writers in 1945 and 1956" in his *Personal Impressions* (New York: Viking, 1981), p. 181; Robert Payne, *The Three Worlds of Boris Pasternak* (London: Robert Hale, 1961), p. 123.

24. Lydia Chukovskaia, *Zapiski ob Anne Akhmatovoi* (Paris: YMCA Press, 1980), II, 351.

25. Yury Krotkov, "Pasternaki," *Grani,* 63 (1967), 62; N. Seliutsky, "Eshche odna versiia zvonka Stalina Pasternaku," *Pamiat'* 2 (1979), 441.

26. Quoted from Jean Lacouture, *André Malraux,* transl. Alan Sheridan (London: André Deutsch, 1975), pp. 223–224.

27. Max Eastman, *Artists in Uniform: A Study of Literature and Bureaucratism* (New York: Knopf, 1934), p. 73.

9. Premier Soviet Poet

1. E. Mindlin, *Neobyknovennye sobesedniki* (Moscow: Sovetskii pisatel', 1968), p. 429.

2. Pasternak, "Pis'ma k zhene," *Vestnik Russkogo Studencheskogo Khristianskogo Dvizheniia,* 106 (1972), 212–213. Compare this to the account by Kaverin: "The solemn, official tone [of the Congress] broke apart during the second half. Everyone noticed the break and picked up on it, as if they had only been waiting for the moment when the reports and greetings would end." V. Kaverin, "Zametki o pervom s″ezde pisatelei," *Novyi mir,* 7 (1984), 317.

3. Nikolai Bukharin, "Poetry, Poetics and the Problems of Poetry in the U.S.S.R.," *Problems of Soviet Literature: Reports and Speeches at the First Soviet Writers' Congress* (Westport, Conn.: Greenwood Press, 1979), pp. 185–260.

4. *Pasternak on Art and Creativity,* ed. Angela Livingstone (Cambridge: University Press, 1985), p. 172.

5. Pasternak to Titsian Tabidze, March 10, 1935, in *Literaturnaia Gruziia,* 1 (1966), 82.

6. Josephine Pasternak, "Patior," *London Magazine,* 4 (September 1964).

7. Lazar Fleishman, *Boris Pasternak v tridtsatye gody* (Jerusalem: Magnes Press, 1984), pp. 251–252. Serge was released and sent with his family to Europe in the spring of 1936, shortly before Gide's visit to the Soviet Union.

8. D. Khrenkov, *Nikolai Tikhonov v Leningrade* (Leningrad: Lenizdat, 1984), p. 105.

9. Boris Pasternak, Marina Tsvetaeva, and Rainer Maria Rilke, *Letters. Summer 1926* (San Diego: Harcourt Brace Jovanovich, 1985), p. 233.

10. Pasternak to Titsian Tabidze, September 6, 1935, in Boris Pasternak, *Letters to Georgian Friends,* trans. David Magarshak (New York: Harcourt, Brace and World, 1968), p. 62. The letter's date is given incorrectly in this edition.

11. And, in fact, after this episode Akhmatova's poetry was allowed once again to appear in the Soviet press, for the first time in twelve years.

12. Louis Fischer, *Men and Politics: An Autobiography* (New York: Duell, Sloan and Pearce, 1941), p. 231.

13. "An Interview with Boris Nicolaevsky," in Nicolaevsky, *Power and the Soviet Elite,* ed. Janet D. Zagoria (New York: Praeger, 1965), pp. 22–23.

14. Olga Ivinskaya, *A Captive of Time* (New York: Doubleday, 1978), p. 59.

15. In fact, as Erwin Šinko reports, it was not the work of Barbusse but of a German émigré journalist in Moscow, Alfred Kurella. See Šinkó, *Roman eines Romans. Moskauer Tagebuch* (Cologne: Wissenschaft und Politik, 1962), pp. 185, 269.

16. Pasternak, *An Essay in Autobiography* (London: Collins and Harvill Press, 1959), p. 103.

17. Cf. *Testimony: The Memoirs of Dmitry Shostakovich as related to and edited by Solomon Volkov* (New York: Harper and Row, 1979), p. 114.

18. *Pasternak on Art and Creativity,* ed. Angela Livingstone (Cambridge: University Press, 1985), pp. 173–178.

19. Robert Conquest, *The Pasternak Affair: Courage of Genius* (Philadelphia: Lippincott, 1962), p. 41. *Komsomol'skaia pravda* called this statement by Pasternak "monstrous."

20. Howard was president of the Scripps-Howard newspapers.

21. Pasternak and Pilniak were among those who came to see Malraux off at the train station on March 14.

22. P. A. Garvi, "Reforma sovetskoi konstitutsii," *Sotsialisticheskii vestnik* (Paris), 362–363 (April 8, 1936), 11.

23. Soon afterward an article by Titsian Tabidze was also published.

24. Pasternak, "Novoe sovershennolet'e," *Izvestiia* (June 15, 1936).

25. This echoed his statement made at the Paris congress in 1935.

26. Letter from November 14, 1936, in Marina Tsvetaeva, *Pis'ma k A. Teskovoi* (Prague: Academia, 1969), p. 145.

27. He had moved to Peredelkino and settled into a new home, anticipating that his parents would soon have to flee Germany and that they would then need his city apartment. At the same time, knowing very well how difficult it would be for Leonid Osipovich to adapt to Soviet life, Boris tried to prevent his parents from returning to the Soviet Union. He was relieved when he learned that his younger sister Lydia had married an Englishman and that the family would be moving to Oxford.

28. A. Orlov, *The Secret History of Stalin's Crimes* (New York: Random House, 1953), pp. 169–171.

29. Testimony from Bukharin's widow. See Felix Medvedev, "On khotel peredelat' zhizn', potomu chto ee liubil," *Ogonek,* 48 (1987), 30; Roy Medvedev, *Nikolai Bukharin: The Last Years* (New York: Norton, 1980), p. 138.

30. Alexander Bakhrakh, "Po pamiati, po zapisiam. Andre Zhid," *Kontinent,* 8 (1976), 364–365.

31. Hence the sinister term "enemy of the people," widely used in connection with mass repressions.

32. Fleishman, *Boris Pasternak v tridtsatye gody,* pp. 392–393.

33. Medvedev, *Bukharin,* p. 30.

34. Bukharin had still not been arrested.

35. Besides serving as a defense, this comment also functioned as a warning: it was an indirect signal to Gide that he was not to use Pasternak's name in his public statements, and Gide caught the meaning of the signal very well.

36. Pasternak's poetry was never again published in such a large volume during the remainder of his life.

10. The Trials of Hamlet

1. There is some evidence that there were not even any sessions of this tribunal: the appointed juges simply signed the papers they were given.
2. Boris Pasternak, *Letters to Georgian Friends,* trans. David Magarshak (New York: Harcourt, Brace and World, 1967), pp. 70–73.
3. *Literaturnaia Gruziia,* 1 (1966), 180.
4. Herbert Read, *Poets and Politicians* (London: Faber and Faber, 1938), p. 69.
5. The first of these fragments appeared in *Literaturnaia gazeta* on December 31, 1937, on the day that a son was born to Boris and Zinaida (he was named Leonid for his grandfather).
6. She has the same name as Zhivago's wife, Tonia Gromeko, and shares similar features.
7. B. Zingerman, "K probleme prostranstva v p'esakh Chekhova. Turgenev, Chekhov, Pasternak," *Voprosy teatra: Sbornik statei i materialov* (Moscow: Vserossiiskoe teatral'noe obshchestvo, 1981), pp. 210–247.
8. An analysis of this government decree was made in an article by the émigré poet Vladislav Khodasevich entitled "Holders of Decorations," which was published a few weeks before his death in the Paris newspaper *Vozrozhdenie* (February 17, 1939).
9. A. Gladkov, "Master rabotaet," *Vstrechi s Meierkhol'dom. Sbornik vospominanii* (Moscow: Vserossiiskoe teatral'noe obshchestvo, 1967), p. 500; see also Alexander Gladkov, "Piat' let s Meierkhol'dom," *Teatr. Vospominaniia i razmyshleniia* (Moscow: Iskusstvo, 1980), pp. 182–188.
10. L. Snezhnitsky, "Poslednii god," *Vstrechi s Meierkhol'dom. Sbornik vospominanii,* p. 565.
11. A. Fevralsky, *Zapiski rovesnika veka* (Moscow: Sovetskii pisatel', 1966), p. 300.
12. At this time the prerevolutionary translations already seemed completely anachronistic.
13. Meyerhold, who was arrested on Stalin's direct orders, perished in 1940. Recently in the Russian émigré and Soviet press there have been accounts of the tortures to which he was subjected during his interrogation. The investigator beat his legs with a rubber strap, broke his left hand, and forced him to drink the investigator's urine. Meyerhold wept, crawled on his knees, and was forced to sign all the fabricated accusations against him. See "Stalin, chelovek i simvol," *Russkaia mysl;* (Paris), May 29, 1987; Arkady Vaksberg, "Protsessy," *Literaturnaia gazeta,* May 4, 1988.
14. Pasternak's letter of February 14, 1940, in *Correspondence of Boris Pasternak and Olga Freidenberg, 1910–1954* (New York: Harcourt Brace Jovanovich, 1982), p. 183.
15. Alexander Gladkov, *Meetings with Pasternak,* trans. Max Hayward (New York: Harcourt Brace Jovanovich, 1977), p. 158; Vaksberg, "Protsessy."
16. *Molodaia gvardiia,* 5–6 (1940).
17. On April 12, 1952, Pasternak wrote to Livanov and his wife: "You entered my life and proved to be such an enriching influence! The place you occupied in it is similar to that of nature, of art, of the aggregate combination of all my past, and the remembrances of my paternal home." Cited in E. K. Liva-

nova, "Vstrechi, druz'ia, gody," *Boris Livanov. Kompozitsiia po materialam zhizni i tvorchestva. Stat'i, pis'ma, vospominaniia* (Moscow: Vserossiiskoe teatral'noe obshchestvo, 1983), p. 91.

18. In particular, he was forced to look at the art of the MKhAT in a new way by their production of Chekhov's *Three Sisters* in the spring of 1940; this performance was the crowning achievement of the late work of Nemirovich-Danchenko.

19. V. I. Nemnirovich-Danchenko, *Izbrannye pis'ma* (Moscow: Iskusstvo, 1979), II, 672.

20. V. Vilenkin, *Vospominaniia s kommentariiami* (Moscow: Iskusstvo, 1982), p. 84.

21. V. I. Nemirovich-Danchenko, *Nezavershennye rezhisserskie raboty. Boris Godunov, Gamlet* (Moscow: Vserossiiskoe teatral'noe obshchestvo, 1984), p. 170.

22. Eleanor Rowe, *Hamlet: A Window on Russia* (New York: New York University Press, 1976), p. 135; Olga Ivinskaya, *A Captive of Time,* trans. Max Hayward (New York: Doubleday, 1978), p. 303; Isaiah Berlin, "Meetings with Russian Writers in 1945 and 1956," *Personal Impressions* (New York: Viking, 1981), pp. 186–187.

23. One of the signs of this influence was the performance of Wagner's *Die Walküre* at the Bolshoi Theater.

24. *Voprosy literatury,* 9 (1969), 174–175.

25. In the diary of Vsevolod Ivanov, the Pasternaks' neighbor in Peredelkino, there is an account of how frightened Zinaida was as she grabbed her children and tried to hide in the forest. Ivanov, *Perepiska s A. M. Gor'kim. Iz dnevnikov i zapisnykh knizhek,* 2nd ed. (Moscow: Sovetskaia Rossiia, 1985), p. 316. The experiences of these days are reflected in one of Pasternak's first poems of the war period ("Strashnaia skazka"), where the fascist invasion is likened to Herod's massacre of the innocents.

26. The poem "Bobyl" reflects this isolation from his family and the anxiety for his son.

27. Pasternak's letter to his wife of September 10, 1941, *Vestnik Russkogo Studencheskogo Khristianskogo Dvizheniia,* 106 (1972), 222–223.

28. It was in the Elabuga region, in Tikhie Gory, that Pasternak had spent the last winter before the revolution of 1917.

29. Margarita Aliger, "Dom na Chkalovskoi," *Ia dumal, chuvstvoval, ia zhil. Vospominaniia o S. Ia. Marshake* (Moscow: Sovetskii pisatel', 1971), p. 227.

30. The presidium of the board, along with its general secretary Fadeev, had settled in Kazan.

31. I. V. Saburov, *S dumoi o fronte* (Kazan: Tatarskoe knizhnoe izdatel'stvo, 1984), p. 64. This same international and political context should be kept in mind regarding the publication of Pasternak's notes, "Concerning Shakespeare," in the Soviet English-language periodical *VOKS Bulletin,* 3–4 (1943), which addressed a Western audience.

32. The miscellany was never published. Only two poems appeared in the journal *Krasnaia nov'* in 1942; the remaining translations by Pasternak were discovered posthumously and published in 1973.

33. The reference to such a form of realism was a conscious act of defiance on

Pasternak's part, insofar as the only form allowed in Soviet literature was socialist realism. This statement alone underscored the author's intention to secure an independent position.

34. This is an echo of the idea familiar from "Dialogue" of 1917.

35. The play was called *Na etom svete* (In This World). The first right to produce the play was offered to Serafim Ilovaisky at the Novosibirsk theater. Gladkov, *Meetings with Pasternak*, p. 93.

36. "K perevodam shekspirovskikh dram (Iz perepiski Borisa Pasternaka)," *Masterstvo perevoda*, 6 (1970), 351.

37. "The Unpublished Letters of Boris Pasternak," trans. Elliott Mossman, *New York Times Magazine*, January 1, 1978, p. 28; Elliott Mossman and Michel Aucouturier, "Perepiska Borisa Pasternaka," *Revue des études slaves*, 53 (1981), 281.

38. A similar theme was widely used in plays created during these months by Leonov, Trenyov, and Fedin, all of whom were Pasternak's friends in Chistopol.

39. The verses in praise of Stalin and the poems dedicated to Pasternak's Tbilisi friends, Tabidze and Yashvili, who had fallen victim to the Ezhov terror in 1937, did not appear in this publication.

40. Gladkov, *Meetings with Pasternak*, p. 101.

41. K. Simonov, "Pravil'nyi put'," *Ogonek*, 34–35 (August 30, 1943), 13; reprinted in *Den' poezii, 1971* (Moscow: Sovetskii pisatel', 1971), pp. 170–171.

42. P. Antokolsky, "Boris Pasternak," *Znamia*, 9–10 (1943), 312–316; reprinted in Antokolsky, *Ispytanie vremenem. Stat'i* (Moscow: Sovetskii pisatel', 1945), pp. 99–107. Incidentally, Antokolsky was a participant in the same almanac of 1922, *Sovremennik*, which printed Pasternak's "The Quintessence."

43. Undoubtedly this characterization reflects Antokolsky's disappointment that Pasternak's work on his play (and, earlier, on his novel about the revolution) had been abandoned.

44. Gladkov, *Meetings with Pasternak*, pp. 87, 75.

45. Stefan Schimanski, "The Duty of the Younger Writer," *Life and Letters Today*, 36 (February 1943), 93.

46. Ibid., p. 95.

47. See A. V. Gorbatov, *Years off My Life*, trans. Gordon Clough and Anthony Cash (New York: Norton, 1965).

48. A. V. Gorbatov, "Kharakter priamoi, muzhestvennyi," *Vospominaniia ob A. Tvardovskom. Sbornik* (Moscow: Sovetskii pisatel', 1982), p. 335.

49. Semyon Tregub, "Voenno-polevoi Soiuz pisatelei," *Sputniki serdtsa* (Moscow: Sovetskii pisatel', 1964), pp. 201–202.

50. Konstantin Simonov, *Raznye dni voiny. Dnevnik pisatelia* (Moscow: Molodaia gvardiia, 1975), p. 300.

51. Pasternak to his parents, March 5, 1933, "Pasternak. Unpublished Letters," *Quarto* (London) May 1980, p. 10.

52. *Novyi mir*, 1 (1965), 176; Boris Pasternak, *Vozdushnye puti. Proza raznykh let* (Moscow: Sovetskii pisatel', 1982), pp. 375–376. Cf. Pasternak, "A Jour-

ney to the Army" (translated by Halina Willens), *Novy Mir: A Selection 1925–1967,* ed. Michael Glenn (London: Jonathan Cape, 1972), p. 247.

53. Pasternak's letter of October 1, 1936, *The Correspondence of Boris Pasternak and Olga Freidenberg* (New York: Harcourt Brace Jovanovich, 1982), p. 162.

54. Pasternak to Nina Tabidze, December 10, 1943, *Literaturnaia Gruziia,* 1 (1966), 89.

55. The unacceptability of the poem became obvious as soon as the author submitted the first part.

56. Alexander Gladkov and Olga Ivinskaia both said that Fadeev advised Pasternak not to continue the poem.

57. *Correspondence of Boris Pasternak and Olga Freidenberg,* p. 231.

58. Boris Pasternak, *Izbrannye stikhi i poemy* (Moscow: Goslitizdat, 1945).

59. It is not surprising that Tikhonov did not last long at this post.

60. Isaiah Berlin, "Meetings with Russian Writers in 1945 and 1956," *Personal Impressions,* p. 184.

61. *Correspondence of Boris Pasternak and Olga Freidenberg,* p. 249.

62. In turn, preparations were being made in Georgia to publish a translation of poems from Pasternak's *Zemnoi prostor.* See "Novye proizvedeniia gruzinskikh pisatelei," *Literaturnaia gazeta,* November 24, 1945.

63. When he returned to Georgian translations in the winter of 1945–46, Pasternak had still not lost hope that Titsian was alive and might reappear any day.

64. *Voprosy literatury,* (1966), 172.

65. Zoia Maslenikova, "Portret poeta," *Literaturnaia Gruziia,* 10–11 (1978), 278.

66. They became personally acquainted in 1935 in Paris, during the International Anti-Fascist Writers' Congress.

67. This was a reprint of the text that had first come out in 1941 in Singapore.

68. Stefan Schimanski, Introduction, in Boris Pasternak, *Collected Prose Works* (London: Lindsay Drummond, 1945), p. 22.

69. Ivinskaya, *A Captive of Time,* pp. 96, 398. On June 7, 1946, Schimanski wrote to Gleb Struve: "Herbert Read and I've recently had a letter from him [Pasternak] from Moscow and he seems well-satisfied with the book." Struve papers in the Hoover Institution Archives (box 6), Stanford University.

70. Schimanski, in Pasternak, *Collected Prose Works,* p. 12. Herbert Read stressed the significance of this edition in his note published in *The Listener,* March 19, 1959.

11. Zhivago and the Poet

1. An abridged version of Zhdanov's speeches was made public on August 21.

2. Pasternak wrote an enthusiastic review of this book for the newspaper *Literatura i iskusstvo,* but it was not published.

3. Vladimir Barlas, "O Pasternake," *Neva,* 8 (1987), 189.

4. Other Soviet authors also met with him, including Pasternak (who candidly discussed with his guest the period of the Ezhov terror).

5. Harold Swayze, *Political Control of Literature in the USSR, 1946–1959* (Cambridge: Harvard University Press, 1962), pp. 40–41.

6. An English translation of Pasternak's article managed to sneak through; it was printed in the September issue of the Moscow journal for foreign readers, *Soviet Literature.*

7. "Bol'shevistskaia ideinost'—osnova sovetskoi literatury. Na obshchemoskovskom sobranii pisatelei", *Literaturnaia gazeta,* September 21, 1946.

8. Fyodor Levin, "Avtografy Borisa Pasternaka," *Iz glubiny pamiati: Vospominaniia* (Moscow: Sovetskii pisatel', 1973) p. 92.

9. *Literaturnaia gazeta,* March 8, 1947.

10. Ivinskaya, *A Captive of Time,* p. 77. The word "whipping" was an ironic allusion to the report by Zhdanov, who used the word in reference to one of the critical articles in the Soviet press about Zoshchenko.

11. Letter of March 26, 1947, *Correspondence of Boris Pasternak and Olga Freidenberg,* p. 269.

12. Ibid., p. 272.

13. Zoshchenko's letter to Stalin is published in *Druzhba narodov,* 3 (1988), 173–174.

14. Ivinskaya, *A Captive of Time,* p. 19.

15. Pasternak, *Letters to Georgian Friends* (New York: Harcourt, Brace and World, 1968), p. 114.

16. "Sovetskaia literatura posle Postanovleniia TsK VKP(b) ot 14 avgusta 1946 goda o zhurnalakh *Zvezda* i *Leningrad.* Doklad general'nogo sekretaria SSP SSSR tov. A.Fadeeva," *Literaturnaia gazeta,* June 29, 1947.

17. M. O. Chudakova, "Neizvestnyi korrekturnyi ekzempliar sbornika perevodov B. L. Pasternaka," *Zapiski otdela rukopisei,* 39 (1978), 106–118.

18. Max Hayward gives a vivid account of this meeting in his introduction to Alexander Gladkov, *Meetings with Pasternak* (New York: Harcourt Brace Jovanovich, 1977), pp. 20–24.

19. Mikhail Lukonin, "Problemy sovetskoi poezii (Itogi 1948 goda)," *Zvezda,* 3 (1949), 184–185. Ten years later, the comparison of Pasternak to a pig was seized upon by a prominent party functionary, Vladimir Semichastny.

20. In her memoirs Ivinskaia places the date of her arrest on October 6, 1949 (*A Captive of Time,* p. 83).

21. Ibid., p. 101.

22. Nina Skorbina (N. Muravina), "Boris Pasternak. Vstrechi i pis'ma," *Novoe russkoe slovo* (New York, February 18, 1973); Lydia Chukovskaia, *Zapiski ob Anne Ahmatovoi,* vol. 2 (Paris: YMCA-Press, 1980), p. 552.

23. Ivinskaya, *A Captive of Time,* p. 133.

24. Gladkov, *Meetings with Pasternak,* pp. 154–155; P. Olberg, "Shvetsiia i Boris Pasternak", *Sotsialisticheskii vestnik,* 11 (1958), 211.

25. The Soviet representatives in Paris made some overtures to Bunin in the first postwar years.

26. "M. Sholokhov, kandidat na nobelevskuiu premiiu," *Literaturnaia gazeta,* October 19, 1946.

27. Skorbina, "Boris Pasternak."

28. Boris Pasternak, *Doctor Zhivago*, trans. Max Hayward and Manya Harari (New York: Pantheon, 1958), p. 499.

29. Z. Maslenikova, "Portret poeta" (entry of October 12, 1958), *Literaturnaia Gruziia*, 10–11 (1978), 293. For a meticulous comparison of Pasternak's text with the original and with other translations of Goethe's works, see Wilma Pohl, *Russische Faust. Übersetzungen* (Meisenheim-am-Glan: Anton Hain, 1962).

30. V. Zhirmunsky, *Gete v russkoi literature* (Leningrad: Khudozhestvennaia literatura, 1937); André von Gronicka, *The Russian Image of Goethe*, vols. 1, 2 (Philadelphia: University of Pennsylvania Press, 1968–1985).

31. Lew Kopelew, *Zwei Epochen deutsch-russischer Literaturbeziehungen* (Frankfurt-am-Main: S. Fischer, 1973), p. 82; Lev Kopelev, "Faustovskii mir Borisa Pasternaka," *Boris Pasternak, 1890–1960. Colloque de Cerisy-la-Salle* (Paris: Institut d'études slaves, 1979), p. 502.

32. Pasternak's letter to Valentina Zhuravlyova of September 16, 1953, in *D. N. Zhuravlyov. Zhizn', iskusstvo, vstrechi* (Moscow: Vserossiiskoe teatral'noe obshchestvo, 1985), p. 342.

33. Herbert Read, "The Politics of the Unpolitical," *Transformation*, ed. Stefan Schimanski and Henry Treece (London: Victor Gollancz, 1943), p. 17.

34. Olga Raevsky-Hughes has drawn an insightful parallel between Pasternak and Nikolai Berdiaev. See her *The Poetic World of Boris Pasternak* (Princeton: Princeton University Press, 1974), p. 104; also Guy de Mallac, *Boris Pasternak: His Life and Art* (Norman: University of Oklahoma Press, 1981), pp. 310–317.

35. For an account of the pressure exerted by President Roosevelt on the Soviet leadership to ameliorate the situation of the church in the USSR, see Henry C. Cassidy, *Moscow Dateline: 1941–1943* (Boston: Houghton Mifflin, 1943), p. 354.

36. Mark Popovsky, *Zhizn' i zhitie Voino-Iasenetskogo, arkhiepiskopa i khirurga* (Paris: YMCA Press, 1979), pp. 370–372.

37. Before Pasternak, in May 1942 the parallel was drawn between the Red Army and Saint George, on the one hand, and fascist Germany and the horrible dragon, on the other, by Ilya Ehrenburg in his pamphlet *Nenavist'* (Moscow: Voenizdat, 1942). In 1953 the same legend served as the basis for Pasternak's poem "Skazka" (Fairy Tale), where it alludes to the incarceration of Ivinskaia and her liberation after Stalin's death. Valuable comments on the significance of the theme of Saint George in *Doctor Zhivago* are contained in articles by Edmund Wilson. See his *The Bit Between My Teeth: A Literary Chronicle of 1950–1965* (New York: Farrar, Straus and Giroux, 1965).

38. Nikolai Tikhonov, *Pered novym pod"emom. Sovetskaia literatura v 1944–45 gg.* (Moscow: Izdatel'stvo *Literaturnaia gazeta*, 1945), p. 17.

39. "Vse naklonen'ia u zalogi" (All of grammar's moods and voices), first published in *Znamia*, April 1936.

40. Elliott Mossman and Michel Aucouturier, "Perepiska Boris Pasternaka," *Revue des études slaves*, 53 (1981), 289.

41. Per Arne Bodin, *Nine Poems from "Doctor Zhivago": A Study of Christian*

Motifs in Boris Pasternak's Poetry (Stockholm: Almquist and Wiksell International, 1976), pp. 6–7.

42. Gladkov, *Meetings with Pasternak,* p. 78.

43. Galina Neigauz [Neuhaus], "O Borise Pasternake", *Literaturnaia Gruziia,* 2 (1988), 207.

44. Grigory Aronson, "Evreiskii vopros v epokhu Stalina," *Kniga o russkom evreistve, 1917–1967* (New York: Soiuz russkikh evreev, 1968), pp. 145–154.

45. "Cantonist" was the name given in the nineteenth century in Russia to children who were separated from their family by the state, who underwent military training from early childhood, and who were bound to military service for the rest of their lives. Although representatives of other nationalities were also recruited, the institution of cantonism played an especially tragic role in the history of the Russian Jews, since it involved a forced conversion to Christianity and total assimilation.

46. *Correspondence of Boris Pasternak and Olga Freidenberg,* p. 255.

47. Nikolai Berdiaev, *Sobranie sochinenii,* vol. 1, *Samopoznanie, Opyt filosofskoi avtobiografii* (Paris: YMCA Press, 1981), p. 394.

48. One of those arrested in 1952 was an old friend of the Pasternak family, Boris Zbarsky, with whom the poet had spent the winter before the revolution in Prikamie (in Tikhie Gory).

49. *Doctor Zhivago,* p. 123. The best examination of Pasternak's views on Jewry is contained in the articles by the Israeli Russian journalist, Yury Margolin, published in 1958–1961 in the newapapers *Russkaia mysl'* and *Novoe russkoe slovo,* and in the essay by Dmitry Segal, "Pro Domo Sua: The Case of Boris Pasternak", *Slavica Hierosolymitana,* 1 (1977), 199–250.

50. See Neil Cornwell, *Pasternak's Novel: Perspectives on "Doctor Zhivago"* (Essays in Poetic Publications, no. 2, Keele, 1986).

51. Boris Pasternak's letter to John Harris, *Scottish Slavonic Review,* 3 (1984), 88.

52. Here again one can see the reflections of Pasternak's views on Chekhov.

53. Pasternak's unpublished letter to Elena Orlovskaia, April 21, 1952.

54. Mikhail Koriakov, "Zametki na poliakh romana *Doktor Zhivago,*" *Mosty,* 2 (1959), 216–220.

55. This is noted in Alberto Moravia, "Un adolescent aux cheveux gris," *Preuves,* 88 (June 1958), 5.

56. V. Vilenkin, "Ob Anne Andreevne Akhmatovoi," *Vospominaniia s kommentariiami* (Moscow: Iskusstvo, 1982), p. 424.

57. Czeslaw Milosz called *Doctor Zhivago* "a book of hide-and-seek with fate," in "On Pasternak Soberly," *Books Abroad,* 44 (Spring 1970), 206. Cf. Nicola Chiaromonte, "Pasternak, Nature, and History," *The Paradox of History: Stendhal, Tolstoy, Pasternak, and Others* (Philadelphia: University of Pennsylvania Press, 1985), p. 136.

58. "The Unpublished Letters of Boris Pasternak," *New York Times Magazine,* January 1, 1978, pp. 29, 32.

59. *Correspondence of Boris Pasternak and Olga Freidenberg,* p. 314.

60. Foreign observers saw this publication as one of the many stunning symp-

toms of liberal change. See Harrison E. Salisbury, *Stalin's Russia and After* (London: Macmillan, 1955), p. 272.

61. *Correspondence of Boris Pasternak and Olga Freidenberg*, p. 332.
62. Chukovskaia, *Zapiski ob Anne Akhmatovoi*, p. 51.
63. Pasternak's letter to Nina Tabidze, Octobert 15, 1954, *Literaturnaia Gruziia*, 2 (1980), 30–31.
64. K. Simonov, "Chelovek v poezii", *Literaturnaia gazetta*, November 4, 1954.

12. The Nobel Scandal

1. Lydia Chukovskaia, *Zapiski ob Anne Akhmatovoi*, vol. 2 (Paris: YMCA Press, 1980), pp. 129–130. The miscellany *Literaturnaia Moskva* also brought forth a sarcastic reaction from Akhmatova, who appraised it as an attempt to replace "the old lie" with a new one. Pasternak changed his opinion of the almanac when in the fall of 1956, it became the object of savage attacks that threatened its further publication. To its third, unpublished, issue he contributed his autobiography of 1956.
2. *The Correspondence of Boris Pasternak and Olga Freidenberg, 1910–1954* (New York: Harcourt Brace Jovanovich, 1982), p. 317.
3. Sergio d'Angelo, "Pasternak's Dollars from *Zhivago*," *Sunday Telegraph*, May 7, 1961; d'Angelo, "Der Roman des Romans," *Osteuropa*, 18 (July 1968), 490. Interesting information on Feltrinelli can be found in Luigi Barzini, "Feltrinelli," *Encounter*, July 1972, pp. 35–40.
4. Olga Ivinskaya, *A Captive of Time* (New York: Doubleday, 1978), p. 198. The date of his meeting with Lo Gatto is attested in Ettore Lo Gatto, *I miei incontri con la Russia* (Milan: Mursia, 1976), p. 125.
5. Pasternak, "Pis'ma k A.M.Ripellino," *Rossiia. Russia*, 4 (1980), 319.
6. This name reflects the new mood of the author and alludes to the new social atmosphere forming after Stalin's death.
7. It was published in Russian in the Soviet Union only ten years later.
8. The editor of *Literaturnaia Moskva*, Emmanuil Kazakevich, although a great admirer of Pasternak's lyric poetry, strongly disliked his late prose.
9. Pasternak indicated his readiness to discuss the possibility of abridgments.
10. *Novyi mir*, 11 (1958), 13–14; Robert Conquest, *The Pasternak Affair: Courage of Genius* (Philadelphia: Lippincott, 1962), pp. 158–159. Konstantin Simonov spoke of this many years later. See his "Uroki Fedina," *Vospominaniia o Konstantine Fedine* (Moscow: Sovetskii pisatel', 1981), pp. 193–195.
11. Vsevolod Ivanov said, "My son was born for you, Boris!" Andrei Voznesensky, "Mne chetyrnadtsat' let. Rifmy prozy," *Sobranie sochinenii* (Moscow: Khudozhestvennaia literatura, 1983), I, 422.
12. D'Angelo, "Der Roman des Romans," p. 491; Ivinskaya, *A Captive of Time*, p. 207. It was first published on October 26, 1958, in *Literaturnaia gazeta*.
13. Compare the entries in Chukovskaia's diary of September 14–17 (*Zapiski ob Anne Akhmatovoi*, pp. 174–175) with Pasternak's note to Ivanova in Tamara Ivanova, *Moi sovremenniki, kakimi ia ikh znala. Ocherki* (Moscow: Sovetskii pisatel', 1984), p. 426.

14. Chukovskaia, *Zapiski ob Anne Akhmatovoi*, p. 178.

15. See the introduction to Hugh McLean and Walter N. Vickery, eds., *The Year of Protest, 1956: An Anthology of Soviet Literary Materials* (New York: Vintage Books, 1961), pp. 25–26.

16. Ilya Ehrenburg, "Liudi, gody, zhizn'," *Ogonek*, 24 (June 1987), 28.

17. Conquest, *The Pasternak Affair*, p. 58.

18. "The Unpublished Letters of Boris Pasternak," *New York Times Magazine*, January 1, 1978, p. 32.

19. See Pasternak's letter to Ivinskaia of April 22, 1957, in *A Captive of Time*, p. 374.

20. D'Angelo, "Der Roman des Romans," p. 492.

21. Miriam Berlin, "A Visit to Pasternak," *American Scholar*, Summer 1983, p. 333.

22. Conquest, *The Pasternak Affair*, pp. 70–71.

23. Only in Tbilisi, far from the central authorities, did work continue on the preparation of Pasternak's collection of verse about Georgia and his translations of Georgian poets, which appeared in the spring of 1958. In the local magazines, his new lyric poems were also published in the original and in translation.

24. "Zhivym i tol'ko do kontsa," *Ogonek*, 16 (April 1987), 28; Gerd Ruge, "A Visit to Pasternak," *Encounter*, 10 (February 1958), 23.

25. Gerd Ruge, "Conversations in Moscow," *Encounter*, 11 (October 1958), 31.

26. Guy de Mallac, *Boris Pasternak: His Life and Art* (Norman: University of Oklahoma Press, 1981), p. 225.

27. See Max Frankel's dispatch in the October 25 issue of the *New York Times* (p. 19). Although Pasternak's statement did not sound particularly persuasive, it was candid and absolutely true. Pasternak reiterated there what he had told his friends many times before. The fate of some of Pasternak's fellow writers, such as Anna Akhmatova, Osip Mandelshtam, Marina Tsvetaeva, Boris Pilniak, Titsian Tabidze, and Isaak Babel, was of course incomparably more tragic than his own.

28. He had not mentioned that it was because of the cultural climate in the Soviet Union under Stalin that Pasternak's poetry could not find its way into print for so many years.

29. Yury Krotkov, "Pasternaki," *Grani*, 63 (1967), 75.

30. *New York Times*, October 26, 1958.

31. The degree to which the news on western radio about the prize was unexpected is shown by the fact that the poet Ilya Selvinsky, who was on vacation in the Crimea at the time, sent Pasternak a congratulatory telegram but that very evening realized he had committed a "political blunder" and hurried to send him a letter advising him to refuse the award. After this, he issued a condemnation of the laureate in a local paper (Ivinskaya, *A Captive of Time*, pp. 230–231). Later, before his death, Selvinsky repudiated this conduct.

32. The English translation of the article printed in *Literaturnaia gazeta* on October 25 and in *Pravda* on October 26, in Conquest, *The Pasternak Affair*, pp. 131–171.

33. See Pasternak's letter to Natalia Reznikova of July 10, 1958, in N. V. Rezni-

kova, *Ognennaia pamiat': Vospominaniia ob Aleksee Remizove* (Berkeley: Berkeley Slavic Specialties, 1980), p. 128.

34. *New York Times,* October 30, 1958.

35. Vladimir Barlas, "O Pasternake," *Neva,* 8 (1987), 192.

36. "Judgment on Pasternak: The All-Moscow Meeting of Writers, 31 October 1958, Stenographic Report," *Survey,* 60 (July 1966), 142.

37. Ronald Hingley, *Pasternak: A Biography* (London: Weidenfeld and Nicholson, 1983), p. 240.

38. The announcement that many Soviet writers were awarded this prize was published in *Literaturnaia gazeta* on January 12, 1946.

39. Z. Maslenikova, "Portret poeta," *Literaturnaia Gruziia,* 10–11 (1978), 290 (entry of October 12, 1958).

40. Yury Krotkov, "Pasternaki," *Grani,* 63 (1967), 77.

41. A stenographic report of the meeting made its way to the west after several years, published in *Survey,* July 1966.

42. A short, unofficial account of the meeting was already printed in the *New York Times* on November 1.

43. *Russkaia mysl'* (Paris), November 6, 1958.

44. The testimony of Viacheslav Ivanov, in M. Chudakova, "Neokonchennoe sochinenie Mikhaila Bulgakova," *Novyi mir,* 8 (1987), 201.

45. Conquest, *The Pasternak Affair,* p. 177; *New York Times,* November 2, 1958.

46. Ivinskaya, *A Captive of Time,* pp. 244–246.

47. *Safe Conduct,* quoted from Pasternak, *Voice of Prose,* I, 30.

13. Last Years

1. This collection, which consists of original texts with Italian translations, preceded by a translation of his 1956 autobiography, appeared in December 1958. See Boris Pasternak, *Autobiografia e nuovi versi* (Milan: Feltrinelli, 1958).

2. Quoted from Robert Conquest, *The Pasternak Affair: Courage of Genius* (Philadelphia: Lippincott, 1962), pp. 100–101.

3. See Max Hayward's notes in Ivinskaya, *A Captive of Time,* p. 404.

4. *Books Abroad,* 35 (1961), 132.

5. Manya Harari, "Pasternak," *The Twentieth Century,* 164 (December 1958), 527.

6. Nora Lidartseva, "Sergei Lifar' o russkoi kul'ture," *Russkaia mysl',* December 20, 1958.

7. *London Daily Mail,* February 11, 1959; *New York Herald Tribune,* February 14, 1959.

8. *New York Times,* February 14, 1959.

9. Renate Schweitzer, *Freundschaft mit Boris Pasternak* (Wien: Kurt Desch, 1963), p. 125.

10. "Khrushchev Bids Writers to Calm," *New York Times,* May 24, 1959.

11. *Soviet Censorship,* ed. Martin Dewhirst and Robert Farrell (Metuchen, N.J.: Scarecrow Press, 1973), p. 12; cf. "The Two Faces of Mr. K.," *Newsweek,*

May 18, 1959, p. 43; "The Rehabilitation of Pasternak," *The Nation,* May 23, 1959, p. 467; Edmund Wilsons' letter to Eugenie Lehovich of June 19, 1959, in Wilson, *Letters on Literature and Politics, 1912–1972,* ed. Elena Wilson (New York: Farrar, Straus and Giroux, 1977), p. 588; Harrison E. Salisbury, *To Moscow—and Beyond: A Reporter's Narrative* (New York: Harper, 1960), pp. 102–106.

12. "Soviet Scans *Zhivago,*" *New York Times,* August 1, 1959; Harrison E. Salilsbury, "Khrushchev Bid to Sholokhov Follows a Dispute Over Novel," *New York Times,* September 1, 1959.

13. Pasternak, "Three Letters," *Encounter,* 11 (August 1960), 4.

14. The telegram of the Writers' Union sent to Pasternak at the beginning of August 1959 was probably tied to the effort to establish a dialogue with the stubborn author. Zoia Maslenikova mentions this in passing in her diary entry of August 13, 1959. See Maslenikova, "Portret poeta," *Literaturnaia Gruziia,* 3 (1979), 138.

15. Pasternak could have even met personally with Savinkov, a well-known figure in the Social Revolutionary Party and a prose writer and poet, in the literary salon of Mikhail Tsetlin right after the revolution.

16. Pavel D. Dolgorukov, *Velikaia razrukha* (Madrid, 1964).

17. Vladimir Nabokov, who was just as skeptical of Pasternak's later work as he had been of his early poetry in the 1920s, was one of the few exceptions. So was the right-wing camp of the monarchists to whom the stance toward the revolution in *Zhivago* was unacceptable.

18. Gleb Struve was one of those who put forward Pasternak's name as a candidate for the 1958 Nobel Prize in literature.

19. For comparison, note that Anna Akhmatova and Nadezhda Mandelshtam declined to publish their works in the émigré press until the mid-1960s.

20. Andrei Voznesensky, "Mne chetyrnadtsat' let. Rifmy prozy," *Sobranie sochinenii,* vol. 1 (Moscow: Khudozhestvennaia literatura, 1983), p. 440.

21. Olga Carlisle, the granddaughter of the writer Leonid Andreev and stepgranddaughter of the Social Revolutionary Viktor Chernov, came to the Soviet Union for a short visit in January 1960. See her "Three Visits with Boris Pasternak," *Paris Review,* 24 (1960), 61–66. Cf. Elliott Mossman, "Pasternak's *Blind Beauty,*" *Russian Literature Triquarterly,* 7 (Fall 1973), 227–242.

22. Quoted in Max Hayward's foreword to Boris Pasternak, *The Blind Beauty,* trans. Hayward and Manya Harari (London: Collins and Harvill Press, 1969), pp. 6, 12.

23. Viacheslav Ivanov, "Peremeny vsegda vnutri cheloveka," *Daugava,* 5 (1987), 114.

24. Vladimir Barlas, "O Pasternake," *Neva,* 8 (1987), 194.

25. See Pasternak's letter to George Reavey of February 7, 1960, *Harvard Library Bulletin,* 15 (October 1967), 328.

26. See Ivinskaia's letter to Giangiacomo Feltrinelli of June 5, 1960, in Franz Schewe, *Pasternak privat* (Hamburg: Christians, 1974), p. 55; cf. Kornei Chukovsky's testimony as quoted in Alexander Werth's *Russia: Hopes and Fears* (London: Barrie and Rockliff, Cresset Press, 1969), pp. 332–333.

27. Gleb Struve, "O sovetskom odnotomnike Pasternaka 1961 g.," *Sbornik sta-*

tei, posviashchennykh tvorchestvu Borisa Leonidovicha Pasternaka (Munich: Institut der Erforschung der UdSSR, 1962), pp. 225–228; see also Andrei Siniavsky's review "Poeticheskii sbornik B. Pasternaka," *Novyi mir*, 3 (1962), 261–263.

28. In essence, this article was written in 1957 and was approved by the poet himself.

29. By a strange twist of fate, this book, which for the next twenty years surpassed all other Soviet publications of Pasternak in scholarly authority and completeness, immediately became unacceptable after its appearance—the author of its preface, Andrei Siniavsky, was together with Yuly Daniel arrested in September 1965, tried, and sentenced to a labor camp. All references to his work were forbidden in the Soviet press.

30. Raisa Berg, *Sukhovei. Vospominaniia genetika* (New York: Chalidze, 1983), p. 258.

Index